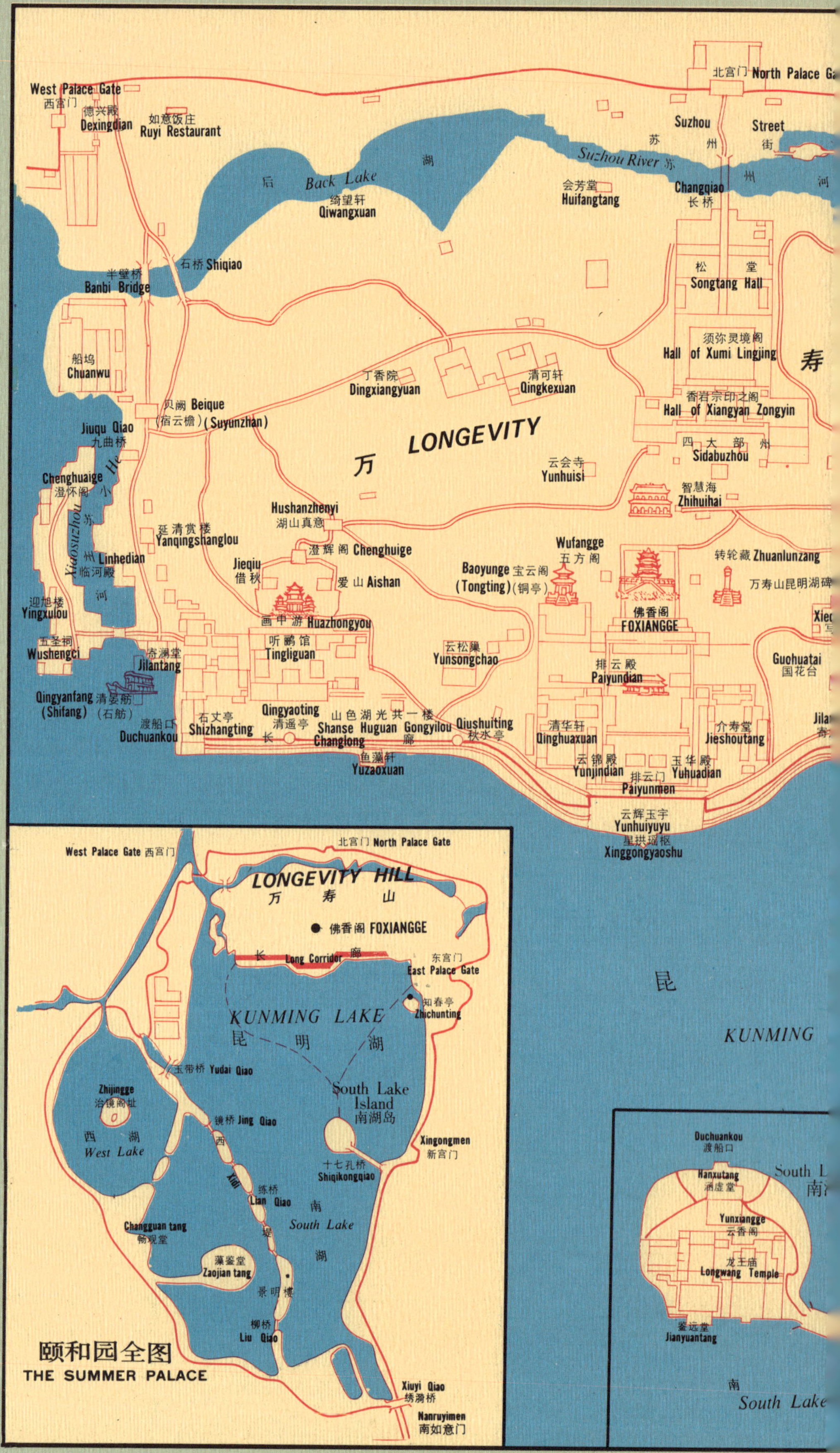
West Palace Gate 西宫门
德兴殿 Dexingdian
如意饭庄 Ruyi Restaurant
北宫门 North Palace Gate
Suzhou Street 苏州街
Suzhou River 苏州河
Changqiao 长桥
后湖 Back Lake
绮望轩 Qiwangxuan
会芳堂 Huifangtang
半壁桥 Banbi Bridge
石桥 Shiqiao
松堂 Songtang Hall
须弥灵境阁 Hall of Xumi Lingjing
船坞 Chuanwu
丁香院 Dingxiangyuan
清可轩 Qingkexuan
贝阙 Beique
(宿云檐)(Suyunzhan)
香岩宗印之阁 Hall of Xiangyan Zongyin
Jiuqu Qiao 九曲桥
万 LONGEVITY 寿
四大部洲 Sidabuzhou
云会寺 Yunhuisi
Chenghuaige 澄怀阁
Xiaosuzhou He 小苏州河
Hushanzhenyi 湖山真意
智慧海 Zhihuihai
延清赏楼 Yanqingshanglou
Wufangge 五方阁
澄辉阁 Chenghuige
转轮藏 Zhuanlunzang
Linhedian 临河殿
Jieqiu 借秋
爱山 Aishan
Baoyunge 宝云阁
(Tongting)(铜亭)
万寿山昆明湖碑
迎旭楼 Yingxulou
画中游 Huazhongyou
佛香阁 FOXIANGGE
五圣祠 Wushengci
听鹂馆 Tingliguan
云松巢 Yunsongchao
Guohuatai 国花台
寄澜堂 Jilantang
排云殿 Paiyundian
Qingyanfang 清晏舫
(Shifang)(石舫)
石丈亭 Shizhangting
Qingyaoting 清遥亭
山色湖光共一楼 Shanse Huguan Gongyilou
Qiushuiting 秋水亭
清华轩 Qinghuaxuan
介寿堂 Jieshoutang
渡船口 Duchuankou
长廊 Changlong
鱼藻轩 Yuzaoxuan
云锦殿 Yunjindian
排云门 Paiyunmen
玉华殿 Yuhuadian
云辉玉宇 Yunhuiyuyu
星拱瑶枢 Xinggongyaoshu
昆 KUNMING
West Palace Gate 西宫门
北宫门 North Palace Gate
LONGEVITY HILL 万寿山
佛香阁 FOXIANGGE
长 Long Corridor 廊
东宫门 East Palace Gate
知春亭 Zhichunting
KUNMING LAKE 昆明湖
玉带桥 Yudai Qiao
Zhijingge 治镜阁址
西湖 West Lake
镜桥 Jing Qiao
South Lake Island 南湖岛
Xingongmen 新宫门
十七孔桥 Shiqikongqiao
西堤 Xidi
练桥 Lian Qiao
南湖 South Lake
Changguan tang 畅观堂
藻鉴堂 Zaojian tang
景明楼
柳桥 Liu Qiao
颐和园全图
THE SUMMER PALACE
Xiuyi Qiao 绣漪桥
Nanruyimen 南如意门
Duchuankou 渡船口
Hanxutang 涵虚堂
Yunxiangge 云香阁
龙王庙 Longwang Temple
鉴远堂 Jianyuantang
South Lake 南

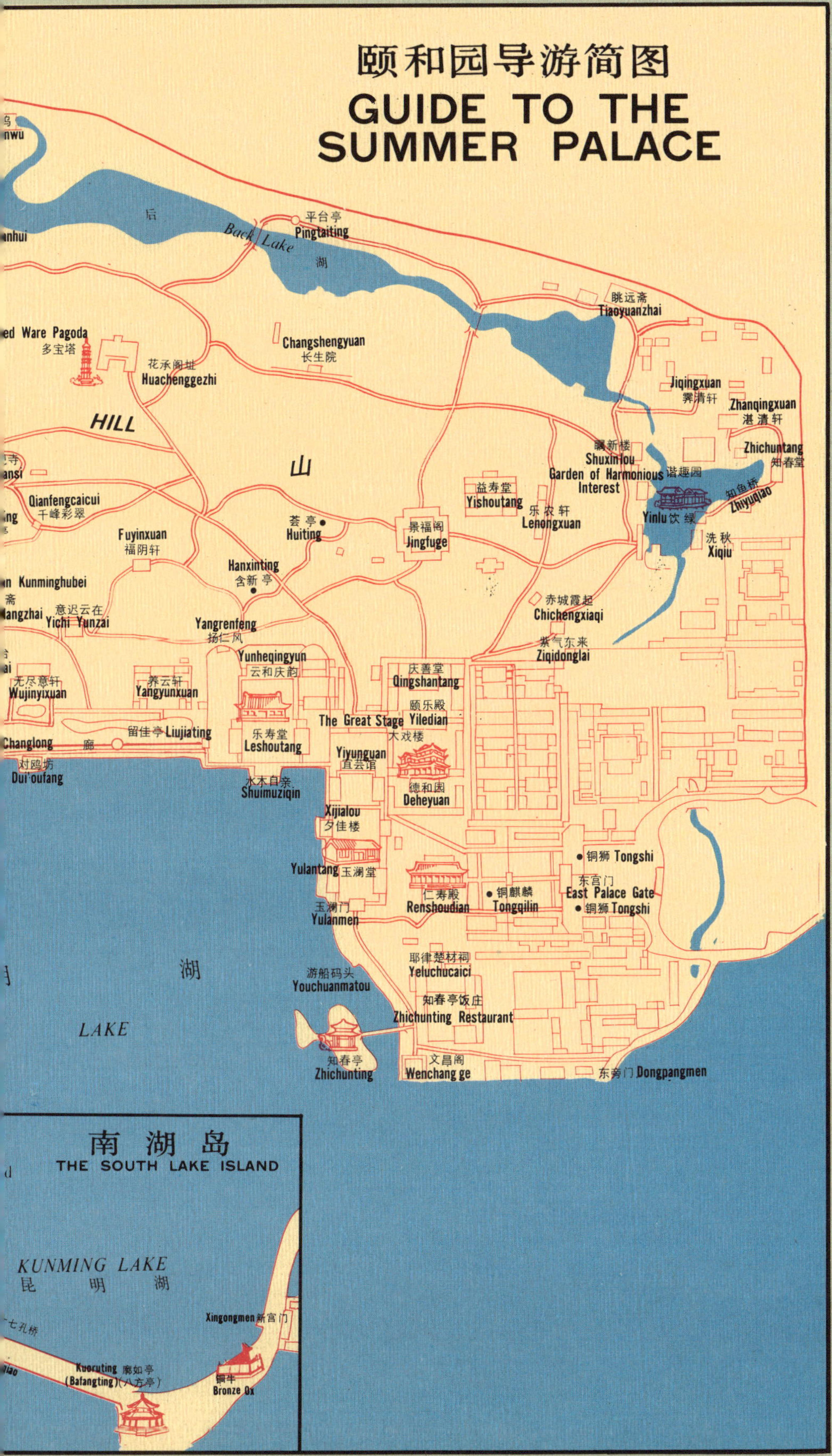

颐和园导游简图
GUIDE TO THE SUMMER PALACE
后
Back Lake
湖
平台亭 Pingtaiting
眺远斋 Tiaoyuanzhai
多宝塔
花承阁址 Huachenggezhi
Changshengyuan 长生院
HILL
山
Jiqingxuan 霁清轩
Zhanqingxuan 湛清轩
Zhichuntang 知春堂
瞩新楼 Shuxinlou
Garden of Harmonious Interest 谐趣园
益寿堂 Yishoutang
乐农轩 Lenongxuan
知鱼桥 Zhiyuqiao
Yinlu 饮绿
洗秋 Xiqiu
Qianfengcaicui 千峰彩翠
荟亭 Huiting
景福阁 Jingfuge
Fuyinxuan 福阴轩
Hanxinting 含新亭
赤城霞起 Chichengxiaqi
Kunminghubei
意迟云在 Yichi Yunzai
Yangrenfeng 扬仁风
紫气东来 Ziqidonglai
Yunheqingyun 云和庆韵
庆善堂 Qingshantang
无尽意轩 Wujinyixuan
养云轩 Yangyunxuan
颐乐殿 Yiledian
The Great Stage 大戏楼
Changlong 廊
留佳亭 Liujiating
乐寿堂 Leshoutang
Yiyunguan 宜芸馆
对鸥舫 Dui'oufang
水木自亲 Shuimuziqin
德和园 Deheyuan
Xijialou 夕佳楼
铜狮 Tongshi
东宫门 East Palace Gate
铜狮 Tongshi
Yulantang 玉澜堂
仁寿殿 Renshoudian
铜麒麟 Tongqilin
玉澜门 Yulanmen
耶律楚材祠 Yeluchucaici
湖
游船码头 Youchuanmatou
知春亭饭庄 Zhichunting Restaurant
LAKE
知春亭 Zhichunting
文昌阁 Wenchang ge
东旁门 Dongpangmen
南湖岛
THE SOUTH LAKE ISLAND
KUNMING LAKE
昆明湖
Xingongmen 新宫门
Kuoruting 廓如亭
(Bafangting) (八方亭)
铜牛 Bronze Ox

頤和園

濤

The Summer Palace

中國世界語出版社　　北京

Published by the China Esperanto Press
Beijing

Fifth Edition 1996

ISBN 7－5052－0072－0

Published by the China Esperanto Press, P.O. Box 77. Beijing, China

Distributed by China International Book Trading Corporation
35 Chegongzhuang Xilu, Beijing, China
P.O. Box 399, Beijing, China Postcode: 100044

目　　　録
CONTENTS

漫話頤和園
About the Summer Palace

宮廷區　17
Palace Area

前山前湖景區　53
The Southern Slope and Lake Area

後山後湖景區　123
The Back Hill and Back Lake Area

編後話　156
Afterword

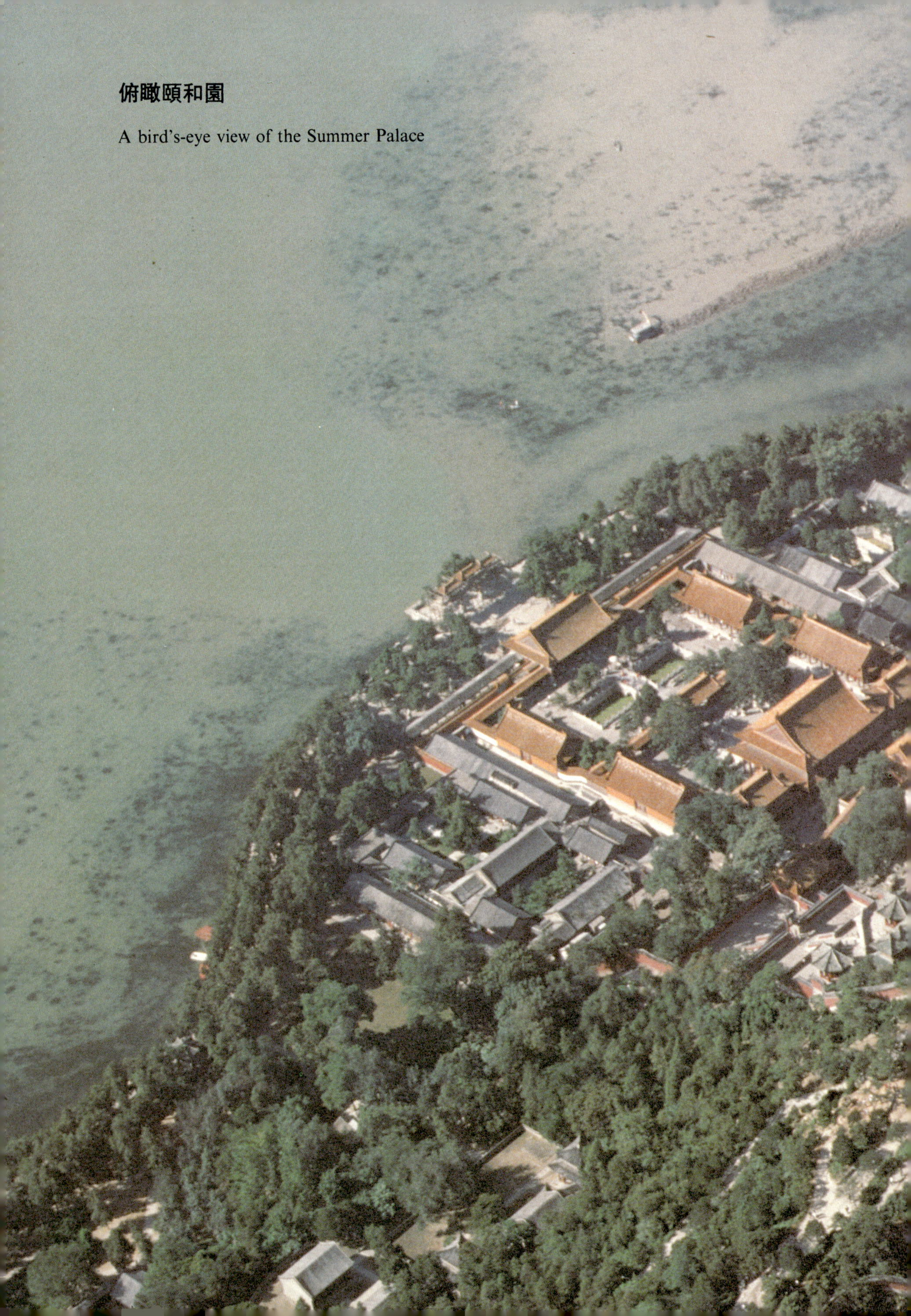

俯瞰頤和園

A bird's-eye view of the Summer Palace

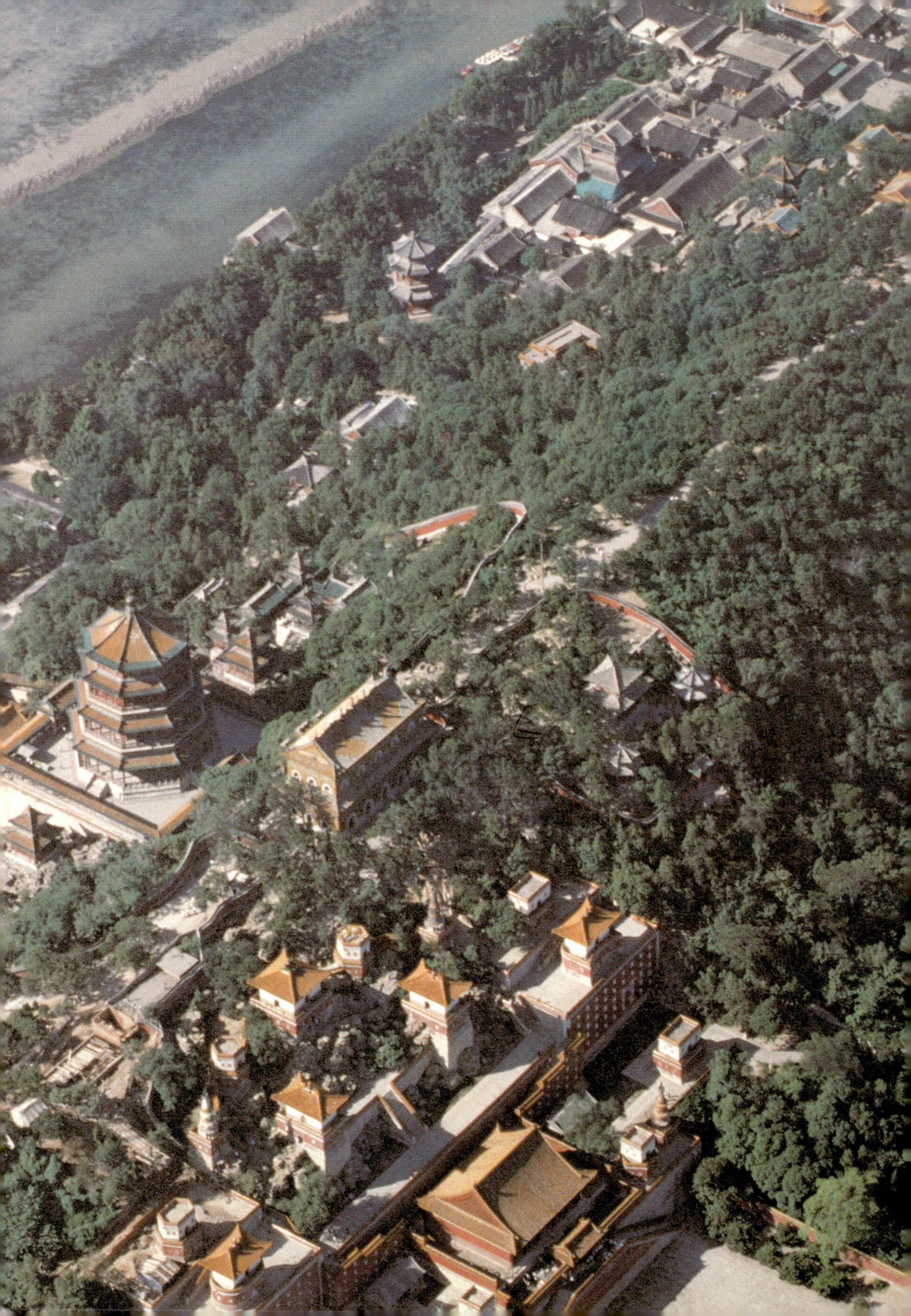

漫話頤和園

頤和園位於北京市西北郊，距市中心約十五公里。它是中國現存的保護最完整、建築規模最大的皇家園林和行宮。頤和園佔地二百九十多公頃，其中水面約二百二十公頃。內有殿堂樓閣、亭臺水榭三千餘間，是帝、后進行政治活動和遊憩的地方。其規模之大，佈局之精，建築之巧爲國內外所罕見，因而是中國園林藝術的瑰寶，有皇家園林博物館之稱。

頤和園也是中國目前保護最完整、歷史遺迹最多的皇家園林，倍受國內外觀光客的青睞。

頤和園原名清漪園，主要由萬壽山和昆明湖組成。萬壽山爲燕山支脈，初名瓮山，高不足六十米。十二世紀初，金代遷都燕京，在此始建行宮。金章宗完顏璟在位期間（公元一一九〇——一九〇八年），下令引玉泉水至瓮山脚下形成湖泊，元世祖忽必烈（公元一二六〇——一二九四年在位）大興漕運，兩次命都水監郭守敬主持疏浚拓展此湖，把挖出的土石運堆瓮山，引昌平神山和京西玉泉山的泉水以及沿途溪流於湖中，正式定名爲大泊湖，並將湖水引至元大都城內，使其成爲可以接濟漕運的大水庫。這就是昆明湖的前身。那時，京西羣山叠翠，萬木葱蘢，十里湖畔綠柳成蔭，湖面蓮花千畝，宛如一幅山高水闊的江南風景畫。

公元十六世紀至十九世紀中葉的三百多年間，是中國園林建築空前發展的時期，人們利用或者摹擬天然山水作爲造園基礎，瓮山一帶的地貌和水貌，自然成爲建造皇家苑囿的最佳環境。

就在這一時期的最初年代，明代弘治皇帝（公元一四八八——一五〇五年在位）爲給他乳母助聖夫人祈福，在瓮山建造了圓静寺。其後，喜愛山水的正德皇帝朱厚照（公元一五〇六——一五二一年在位），在湖濱建造了好山園行宮。有人把這時的大泊湖比作杭州的西湖，這裏的風景被稱爲西湖景，甚至有“泉液流珠”、“湖水鋪玉”等“西湖十景”的美名。

十八世紀中葉，正值清代（公元一六四四——一九一一年）“乾隆盛世”，皇家園林的興建進入鼎盛時期。乾隆皇帝（公元一七三六——一七九五年在位）在位的六十年間，僅在京城的西北郊由他親自主持擴建和新建的大型園林就有五座。這就是著名的“三山五園”：暢春園、圓明園、香山静宜園、玉泉山静明園、萬壽山清漪園（頤和園前身）。

公元一七五〇年，乾隆皇帝爲慶賀他生母孝聖皇太后的六十大壽，下令動工修建清漪園。人們首先將西湖向東部擴展，使其面積和深度增加一倍；拆毁明代的圓静寺，在原址上修建大報恩延壽寺。次年，乾隆皇帝把瓮山改名爲萬壽山，並依據漢武帝（公元前一四〇——前八七年在位）在京城長安開鑿昆明池操演水軍的故事，把西湖改名爲昆明湖。清漪園全部工程前後進行了十五年，至一七六四年完成，其規模與現在的頤和園大體相當。那時的京城西北郊山青水秀，風景優美，極目所見，皆爲緑樹掩映、館閣連綿的名苑勝宫。這位對於"園林之樂，不能忘懷"的皇帝，六次下江南巡幸遊覽，把他看中的園林和名勝，均命隨行的宫廷畫師摹繪下來，作爲建園的參考。造園匠師們在建造這些皇家園林時，不但繼承了中國北方傳統的造園技藝，而且大量吸取了江南園林的意趣和造園手法；既不失北方的雄渾氣概，又能體現江南園林的婉約多姿。這些皇家園林兼具南北造園藝術之長，從而形成了中國園林藝術發展史上的高峰。

第二次鴉片戰争時期，一八六〇年英法聯軍攻入北京，"三山五園"被聯軍一把火燒毁。當時正是清代第七個皇帝咸豐（公元一八五一——一八六一年在位）當政，他帶着后妃逃到熱河（今河北省承德市），次年病死於熱河行宫。咸豐皇帝的貴妃葉赫那拉氏（慈禧太后）在"垂簾聽政"的名義下，獨攬朝綱長達四十八年之久。在强鄰四逼、國勢日衰之際，她於同治年間（公元一八六二——一八七四年）幾度指使親信奏請皇帝修復清漪、圓明諸園，因王公大臣堅持異議，祇好作罷。一八七五年光緒皇帝繼位後，其父醇親王奕譞主持海軍事務衙門，爲討好慈禧太后，也希望自己的兒子是個握有實權的皇帝，借口營建海軍學堂，動用海軍經費，動工修復清漪園。此項浩大工程一直在暗中進行。直到一八八八年工程行將結束時，慈禧太后才以光緒皇帝的名義發布"上諭"，向外公開，並取"頤養冲和"之意，將清漪園改名爲頤和園。儘管如此，當時也祇恢復了萬壽山前山的建築，後山依然是殘垣斷壁，荒草萋萋。一九〇〇年，八國聯軍侵入北京，慈禧太后出逃西安，頤和園又遭浩劫，文物陳設被掠奪一空，建築物也受到嚴重破壞。一九〇二年慈禧太后回到北京，下令立即修復頤和園，次年完工。從此，她晚年的大部分時間都是在頤和園度過的，一般是春二月進園，冬十一月才回紫禁城。

頤和園是封建時代中國最後建造的一座皇家園林，也是慈禧太后長期居住的地方。她爲了在這裏接見臣僚，處理朝政，專門建造了一個宫廷區。在園林的總體規劃上，它形成宫、苑分置的特點，即宫廷區相對獨立於廣大的園林區。但宫廷區畢竟不是紫禁城，因此建築羣的所有屋頂都用樸素的青灰瓦代替華麗的琉璃瓦，庭院内栽植長青樹木，點綴着假山花壇，使其具有較多的庭園氣氛，與園林區的風格統一起來。

宫廷區的後面，是以萬壽山和昆明湖爲主體的廣大園林區。由於萬壽山山脊南北的地貌結構不同，又自然形成了園林區内的兩個不同景觀特色的景區—開朗的前山前湖景區和幽静的後山後湖景區。

前山前湖景區包括萬壽山南坡和昆明湖。萬壽山南坡衹佔全園面積的極小部分。建築師們運用了突出重點、烘雲托月的建築手法，在前山的中央部位建置了一組體量大、形象豐富的中央建築羣——排雲殿羣落和佛香閣，整個前山的建築佈局以它們爲中心而展開。這兩組建築以華麗的殿堂臺閣密密層層地把山坡覆蓋，構成一條貫穿前山上下的中軸綫，在其兩側又有對稱配置的建築羣作爲兩翼的陪襯。由於佛香閣高於其他建築物，尤其顯得氣宇軒昂，從而成爲總攬前山乃至整個景區的構圖中心。

園中的臨水長廊是前山和中軸綫横向聯絡的紐帶。它自山麓的東西兩端透迤匯結於中軸綫南端的排雲門。這一縱一横構成了前山建築佈局的綱領。其他體量較小的建築物和建築羣，則自由地、疏朗地佈置在山脚、山坡或山脊上，以此來烘托中央建築羣的濃密、端莊、華麗。整個前山重點突出，脈絡清晰，主賓分明，寓變化於嚴整，嚴整中又有變化。這既體現了帝王苑囿雍容磅礴的氣勢和仙山瓊閣的畫境，又不失園林婉約清麗的風姿。

昆明湖的迷人之處在於水。早在清漪園建園之初，人們在向西拓展水面時同時修造了西堤。它縱貫昆明湖，並以支堤將湖面劃分爲三個大小不等的水域。每個水域有一中心島嶼，三島嶼成鼎足佈局。這種“一池三山”的理水方式是中國歷代皇家園林的傳統内容。遠在公元前二三世紀，就流行着東海有蓬萊、方丈、瀛洲三座仙島的神話傳説。帝王們大都迷信神仙，希望長生不老，因而在御苑内開鑿水池，堆築三島，作爲東海三仙島的象徵。

昆明湖内最大的島嶼是南湖島，它與萬壽山隔水相望。島的北、西、南都有很好的景觀，衹有東面景色平平。於是建園匠師們在島的東岸堆築土石山，廣植花木，將東堤遮擋起來。這就是中國造園藝術中的所謂“障景”手法。島北端的涵虚堂雄居於臨湖的高臺上，正好與湖對岸的佛香閣遥相呼應，構成對景。其次，南湖島與東堤的十七孔橋相連，並通過長橋、廓如亭、文昌閣等建築物的過渡，與景區的構圖中心佛香閣在氣勢上聯貫起來。如果從湖的最南端繡漪橋北望，但見碧波蕩漾，在萬壽山遠景的前面有十七孔橋和南湖島障隔，湖景顯得格外深遠。

後山後湖景區不像前山前湖景區那樣開闊。這裏以構成山水的近觀小品爲主，遠眺爲輔，着意創造一個幽静深邃、富於山林野趣的環境。除了那組特殊的“四大部洲”寺廟建築羣外，大部分都是自成一體的小型園林，或沿山，或倚坡，或臨水，結合具體地貌而錯落設置。

所謂後湖實際上是沿萬壽山北麓開鑿的一條河道，全長約千米。由於地勢侷促，看上去頗有“兩岸夾青山，一江流碧玉”的意趣。巧妙的是，人們利用峽口、石磯把河道障隔成六個段落。六段水面的形狀各異，自然形成一串具有各種景觀特色的小湖面。遊人泛舟湖上，或沿河岸散步，大有山重水複、柳暗花明之趣。

頤和園是國家重點文物保護單位。四十多年來，政府多次撥專款修繕。五十年代初期，國家對破舊的建築進行了整修，在園内遍植花草樹木，初步改變了昔日荒蕪的景象。以後又對長廊進行了兩次維修和油飾，使它重放異彩。八十年代以來，國家再次撥巨款對後山的寺廟建築羣“四大部洲”、前山的主體建築佛香閣以及德和園大戲樓進行了全面的、大規模的整修，使這些古建築恢復了當年的風采。著名的具有江南水鄉特色的蘇州街，經過四年重建，又重現了歷史上的熱鬧情景。一九九一年，北京市政府動員十八萬人參加昆明湖的清淤工程，使成湖二百四十年來的淤泥第一次得到徹底清理。現在，碧波蕩漾的昆明湖已真正成爲一顆燦爛的明珠。

隨着旅遊業的發展，國家還投資興建了一些娱樂設施，供遊人參觀遊覽。

頤和園景點的恢復，參觀項目的增加，遊湖活動的豐富，宫廷御膳餐廳的營辦，都使這座世界名園更加富有魅力。

About the Summer Palace

THE Summer Palace is in the northwestern suburbs of Beijing, about 15 kilometres away from the centre of the city. It is the largest imperial garden in existence in China, covering an area of over 290 hectares, about 220 hectares of which are covered by a lake. It has more than 3,000 bays of buildings including halls, pavilions, towers and courtyards. A complex of audience halls, imperial living quarters and pleasure grounds, the Summer Palace represents an apex in the development of Chinese landscape gardening, in terms of scale, layout, craftsmanship and artistic elegance. It is a gem in the treasure trove of the Chinese gardening art.

The Summer Palace, originally called the Garden of Clear Ripples, is formed mainly by Longevity Hill and Kunming Lake. Longevity Hill, an offshoot of the Yanshan Mountain Range, was first called Golden Hill, about sixty metres high. At the beginning of the 12th century, after the Jin Dynasty moved their capital to Yanjing, they began to build a temporary palace here. During the reign of Emperor Zhangcong, Wan Yanjing (reigned 1190-1201), an order was issued to channel the water from the Jade Fountain Hill to what was then called Golden Water Pond at the foot of the Golden Hill. It is said that in the Yuan Dynasty (1206-1368), an old man had dug up a jar here, and the hill's name was changed Wengshan (Jar Hill). Emperor Shizu, Kublai (reigned 1260-94), developed a water transportation system and ordered Guo Shoujing, an engineer, to supervise the project of dredging the Golden Water Pond and directing the springs of Shenshan and Jade Fountain Hill into the pond. Then the name of the pond was changed to Dabo Lake, and its water was led to the city of the Great Capital. The lake became a reservoir for the canal. At that time the Western Hills were covered by green trees and the lake was surrounded by weeping willows, with lotuses growing in it. The area was developed into fertile well-tended fields much resembling the countryside south of the Yangtze River.

In the four hundred years from the 16th century to the middle of the 19th century, Chinese gardening saw an unprecedented development, people built gardens by making use of the natural beauty of mountains and rivers. Wengshan and its surrounding area naturally became the best place for the emperors to build an imperial garden.

It was during the early stage of this period that Emperor Hongzhi (reigned 1488-1505) of the Ming Dynasty built Yuanjing Temple on Wengshan Hill to pray for longevity for his wet nurse. Later, Emperor Zhengde, Zhu Houzhao, who was fond of visiting places of outstanding natural beauty, built the Haoshanyuan Imperial Residence by the lake. Wengshan Lake was then favourably compared to West Lake in scenic Hangzhou, and the scenery about Wengshan was described in terms used for West Lake scenery, such as "a fountain of pearls", "jade-surfaced lake" and so on.

In the middle of the 18th century, with the Qing Dynasty (1644-1911) entering its flourishing period, the building of imperial gardens also reached its high peak. In the sixty years Emperor Qianlong reigned, five large gardens were built or enlarged under the emperor's personal supervision in the northwestern suburbs of the capital city. They were known as the "three hills and five parks": Park of Everlasting Spring, Park of Perfection and Brightness, Park of Tranquillity and Pleasure in the Fragrance Hill, Park of Tranquillity and Brightness in the Jade Fountain Hill and Park of Clear Ripples in Longevity Hill (the predecessor of the Summer Palace).

In 1750 Emperor Qianlong, to celebrate the sixtieth birthday of his mother, Empress Xiaosheng, ordered the Garden of Clear Ripples rebuilt. The West Lake was expanded eastward, so that the size and the depth of the lake was greatly increased. Then, the Ming-Dynasty Temple of Perfection and Tranquillity was taken down and on its site was built the Temple of Gratitude for Longevity. The following year Emperor Qianlong changed Wengshan's name to Longevity Hill and the West Lake's to Kunming Lake. The whole project took 15 years and was completed in 1764. The newly-built Garden of Clear Ripples, approximately the size of the present-day Summer Palace, was a pleasure park of poetic charm, a living scroll painting of almost unrivalled beauty. In Qianlong's time, the northwestern outskirts of Beijing, abounding in streams and fountains, was the site of pleasure grounds and gardens. Pavilions and lodges were nestled in the lush green woods as far as the eye could see. Qianlong, who described himself as a true lover of gardens, made six trips south of the Yangtze in his lifetime and, wherever he saw a scenic spot or a garden that caught his fancy, he would order the court painters who accompanied him to do sketches of the place to be used as reference materials for the construction of gardens in the north. Incorporating southern ideas and skills without giving up northern traditions, these imperial gardens had both the grandeur of the north and the restraint and refinement of the south. They represented another high point in the development of Chinese landscape gardening.

However, during the Second Opium War, the Anglo-French Allied Forces invaded Beijing and reduced the Three Hills and Five Parks to ashes in 1860. Xianfeng (reigned 1851-61), the seventh emperor of the Qing Dynasty, fled with his wife and concubines to Rehe (present-day Chengde) and died there the next year. After the emperor's death, Empress Dowager Cixi came into power and thus began the period known as "the rule behind the curtain", or "power behind the throne", which lasted for 48 years. In total disregard of the welfare of the nation, she ordered the rebuilding of the Garden of Clear Ripples and other gardens several times during the reign of Emperor Tongzhi (reigned 1862-74), but her orders were not carried out because of the strong resistance of the imperial house and high officials. In 1875 Emperor Guangxu succeeded to the throne. His father, Prince Yihuan, who was in charge of the Office of the Navy, wanted to curry favour with Empress Dowager Cixi in the hopes that his son would have some real power. He used the navy's funds and began to restore the Garden of Clear Ripples under the pretext of setting up a naval academy there. The restoration was done secretly. It was not announced to the public until 1888 when the project was about to be completed. Empress Dowager Cixi made the announcement by issuing an imperial edict in the name of the emperor and changed the garden's name to the Summer Palace. Nevertheless, only the buildings on the front slope of Longevity Hill were restored; the back hill still remained a desolate scene of broken walls.

In 1900 the Eight-Power Allied Forces invaded Beijing, Empress Dowager Cixi fled to Xi'an, the Summer Palace was devastated a second time. The invaders took away everything valuable and destroyed the buildings. Upon her return to Beijing in 1902, the Empress Dowager ordered the garden rebuilt immediately. After the garden was completed the following year, she spent the greater part of the year here from February in early spring until November in winter when she returned to the Forbidden City.

The Summer Palace, based on natural scenery, was the last imperial garden built in this country and the residence of Empress Dowager Cixi. Because she had to give audience to her ministers and hold court sessions here, a special precinct was established for this purpose. The Summer Palace was thus a complex of audience halls, imperial living quarters and pleasure grounds. The audience halls occupied only a small part of the complex, the greater part being taken up by the garden. The two parts were separated from each other and yet linked up in one way or another. However, as a component part of garden architecture, they were built somewhat differently from the palatial architecture of the Forbidden City. Instead of the respendent yellow glazed tiles, the roofs were covered with plain bluish grey tiles and, in harmony with the landscape, the courtyards were embellished with evergreens, rocks and flower beds, making the place look more like a garden than an imperial court. This, while marking off the two parts of the Summer Palace, still makes the place one integrated whole.

The vast garden area beyond the audience halls includes Longevity Hill and Kunming Lake. As the hill's topographical features are different, the garden area has two distinctly different kinds of scenery: a spacious open area with a lakescape south of the hill — the Front Hill and Front Lake Area — and a quiet, subdued landscape in the north — the Back Hill and Back Lake Area.

The front hill and front lake area is formed by the southern slope of Longevity Hill and Kunming Lake. Although the southern slope is only a fraction of the whole garden, a large number of buildings are concentrated here, becoming the key part of this area. Here our landscape architects resorted to the method of giving prominence to one or several main buildings or, to use a Chinese saying, the practice of "painting clouds to set off the moon". This they did by building an impressive architectural complex at the centre of the front hill, from which the other buildings radiated. This complex is the Hall That Dispels the Clouds which consists of a succession of magnificent buildings arranged along the central axis of the hill from the top to the bottom. The two main buildings in this complex are the hall with the same name and the Tower of the Fragrance of Buddha. These buildings are flanked by other smaller complexes to the east and west. The Tower of the Fragrance of Buddha is the largest single building in the Summer Palace, the centre of the landscape.

The Long Promenade is a link to connect the front hill and the central axis. It runs east-west along the foot of the hill and is bisected by the axis at the Gate That Dispels the Clouds. It is perpendicular to the axis and together with the latter forms the centre line of the whole architectural layout in the front hill area. The smaller buildings and minor architectural groups in this area are spaced freely and sparsely, which has the effect of enhancing by contrast the solemnity, grandeur and compactness of the central complex. Such a layout, with the main buildings brought into relief, with clear-cut outlines and a marked distinction between the principal and auxiliary buildings, suggests both orderliness and variation. It manifests the grandeur of an imperial palace while retaining the elegance of a pleasure garden.

The charm of Kunming Lake lies on the vast expanse of the water. In the early days when the Garden of Clear Ripples was constructed, the lake was expanded westward and the West Dyke was built. The dyke expanded clear through the lake and branched out to break the surface and divide the lake in three, each with a small island in the centre. There are three small islands on the lake. This "one pool, three hills" pattern became a tradition in the building of all imperial gardens. It is based on a Taoist myth prevalent in the second and third centuries B. C., according to which there were three islands, called Penglai, Fangzhang and Yingzhou, inhabited by immortals on the eastern seas. Most of the Chinese emperors believed in immortals and wished for eternal life, so the pools and lakes in their gardens were built with three protruding rocks or islands in them to simulate the land of the immortals.

South Lake Island is the largest of the three islands on Kunming Lake. It faces Longevity Hill across the water, and serves as an important link in the chain of scenes in the front hill and front lake area. There are scenic views to the north, west and south of the island but not much worth seeing along the East Dyke. So a mound was piled up on the eastern shore of the island and thick groves were planted to screen off the dyke. This is the technique known as "obstructing the view".

At the northern end of the island stands the Hall of Forbearance and Humbleness on a high platform overlooking the lake and facing the Tower of the Fragrance of Buddha. South Lake Island is linked to the East Dyke by the Seventeen-

Arch Bridge, and then through the bridge, the Spacious Pavilion, the Studio of Literary Prosperity and other buildings, it is picturesquely connected to the Tower of the Fragrance of Buddha, the centre of the landscape. If one looks northward across the water from the Bridge of Embroidered Ripples at the southernmost tip of the lake, the Seventeen-Arch Bridge and the South Lake Island are interposed like a screen in front of Longevity Hill. This design increases the dimensions of the lakescape.

Compared with the front hill and front lake area, the back hill and back lake area is a narrower strip of land. It is a place mainly for enjoying the natural beauty of the woods and hills close up. Except for a specially designed group of lamaseries in the centre of the slope, the buildings here are sparsely laid out, most of them in small self-contained gardens on the slope, at the foot of the hill, or near the water as befits the topographical features.

The so-called back lake is actually a long watercourse of about 1,000 metres excavated along the northern foot of Longevity Hill. As the hillocks run parallel to the natural slope on the south bank of the lake, the scene here is of a clear stream flowing between wooded hills. A number of offshore stone structures are erected at various places to break the watercourse into six sections, each of which is in a different shape but all are of the size of small lakes with distinctive natural settings. The waterscape is enchanting whether one is boating on the lake or strolling along the shore.

The Summer Palace is an important historical site under state protection. Over the last forty years the Chinese government has frequently allocated special funds to repair it. As early as the 1950s, the state began to renovate the broken buildings and plant trees and flowers in the garden, so that its old face of desolation was preliminarily changed. Later, in successive years, two large-scale renovations and repaintings were made to the Long Promenade, which enabled this long gallery of art to shine with splendour once again. After the 1980s the state allocated a large amount of funds to rebuild the massive temples, the Four Great Regions, on the slope of Back Hill, and repair the complex of buildings, the Tower of the Fragrance of Buddha and the Great Stage in the Garden of Virtue and Harmony on the front hill. These antique buildings have been restored to their original splendour. The famous Suzhou Street typical of the riverside landscape in South China has, through four years of rebuilding, become a place of attraction as it used to be in history. In 1990 the Beijing Municipal Government organized 180,000 people to clear away the sludge from the bed of Kunming Lake; this was the first big thorough clean up in 240 years. Today, the vast Kunming Lake has become a bright pearl in northwest Beijing.

With the development of tourism, a number of facilities have been added to the Summer Palace. One finds it more convenient when he comes to visit the imperial garden.

The Summer Palace, with the restoration of more scenic spots, the increase of visiting programmes, the enrichment of activities and the establishment of a restaurant to supply imperial food, is shining with ever greater splendour.

宫廷區

這是以仁壽殿爲正殿，包括東宫門、仁壽門以及分列其兩側的配殿、内外朝房、值房共三進院落的一組嚴整的建築羣。

中國近代史上發生的一些重大事件，如變法維新運動的發端與流産，鎮壓義和團運動的敕令和詔書，諸多喪權辱國條約的醖釀和簽訂，都是在這龐大的宫廷區裏炮製、釐定和批准的。清末實際上的最高統治者慈禧太后晚年的大部分時間都是在這裏度過的。光緒皇帝在這裏斷斷續續地被囚禁了近十年。這些都給這個佔地不大的宫廷區蒙上了一層神秘的色彩。

人們在這個區域裏不僅可以看到華麗的建築，精美的裝飾，奢侈的陳設，還可以了解到許多帝、后生活的軼聞和趣事。

Palace Area

THIS group of buildings consists of the Hall of Benevolence and Longevity, the East Palace Gate, the Gate of Benevolence and Longevity, the side halls and courtyards. They are cleverly laid out and exquisitely constructed.

These buildings are closely connected with some major events in modern Chinese history. It was here that the Constitutional Reform and Modernization plan rose and fell; and it was also here that the imperial decrees and edicts were issued to suppress the Yihetuan Movement. Many treaties of national betrayal and humiliation were given birth to here. Empress Dowager, Cixi, the manipulator at the end of the Qing Dynasty, spent most of her later years here, and Emperor Guangxu was imprisoned here for nearly ten years. All this added a layer of mystery to this small palace area.

From here visitors can see the magniticent buildings, beautiful decorations and luxuriant furnishings of the palace and hear many anecdotes and stories about the emperor and empress.

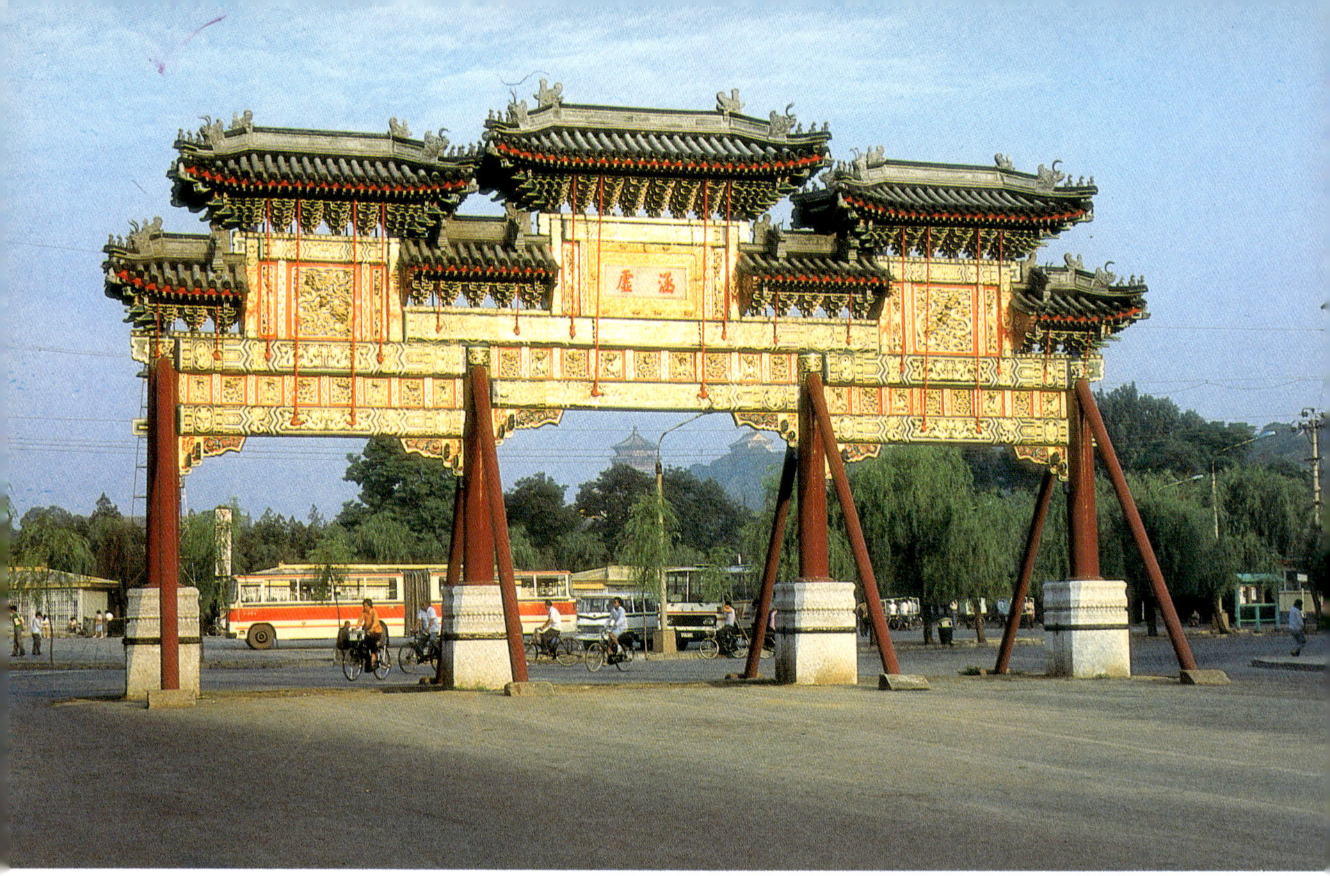

牌樓 是頤和園的第一座建築。牌樓正面題“涵虛”兩字，提示湖波浩渺；背面寫“罨秀”兩字，意指園林清幽。短短四字，把頤和園的雄渾宏闊、婉約清麗概括無餘。

The Archway. This is the first building of the Summer Palace, on the front side of which are the characters “涵虛”, which imply water, and on the back side “罨秀”, which suggest the tranquillity of the park just behind it.

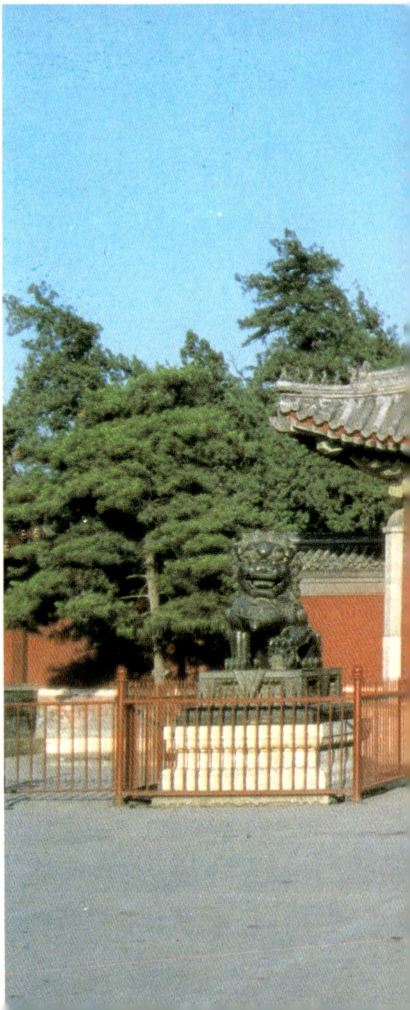

東宮門　頤和園正門。門爲三明兩暗的廡殿式建築。中間正門專供帝、后出入，稱爲“御路”；兩邊門洞供王公大臣出入；太監、兵卒從南北兩側的邊門出入。

East Palace Gate. The front entrance to the Summer Palace is a palatial building. The gate in the middle, called "The Imperial Gateway", was for the emperor and empress, the gates on either side were for princes and high officials, and the northern and southern sidedoors were for eunuchs and guards.

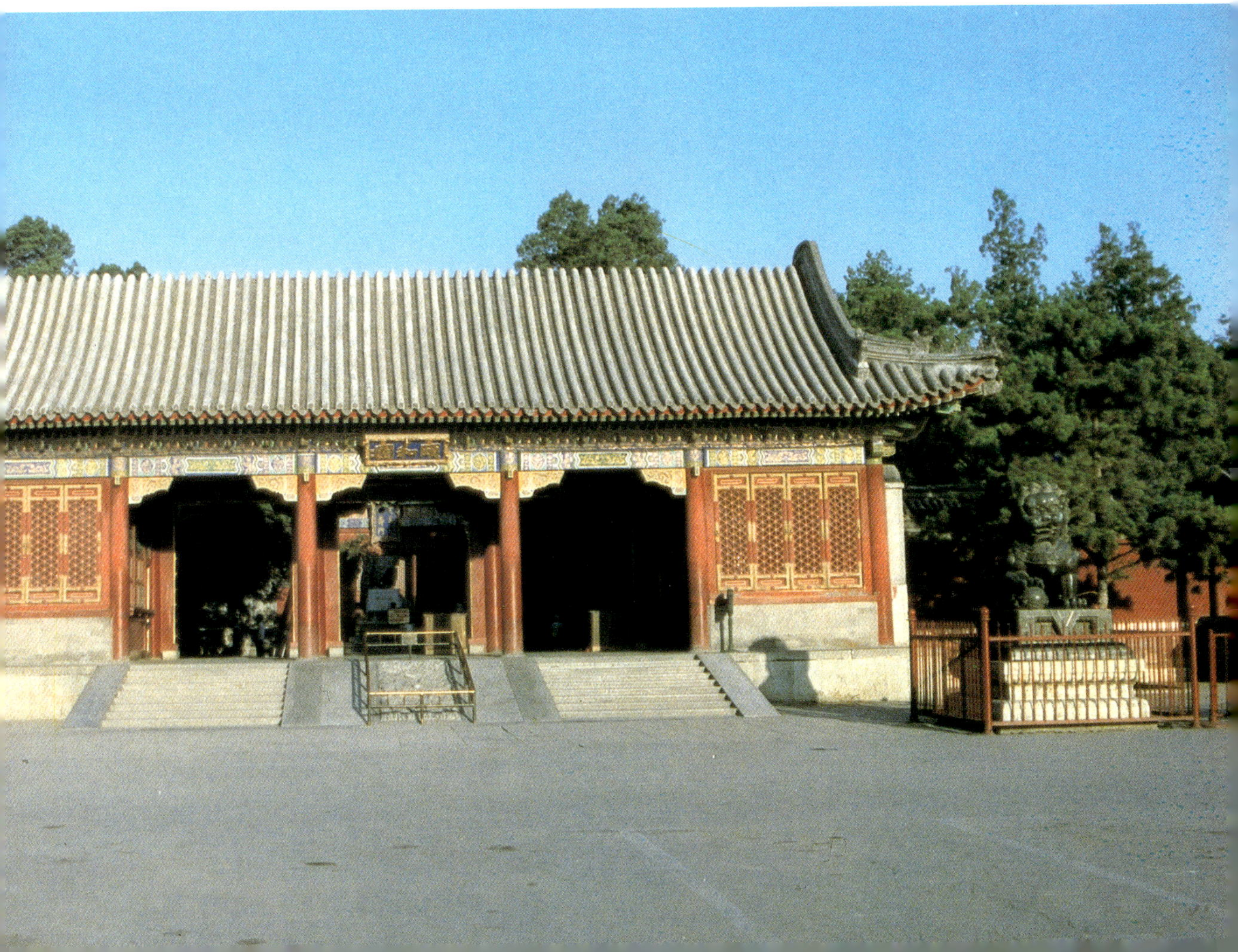

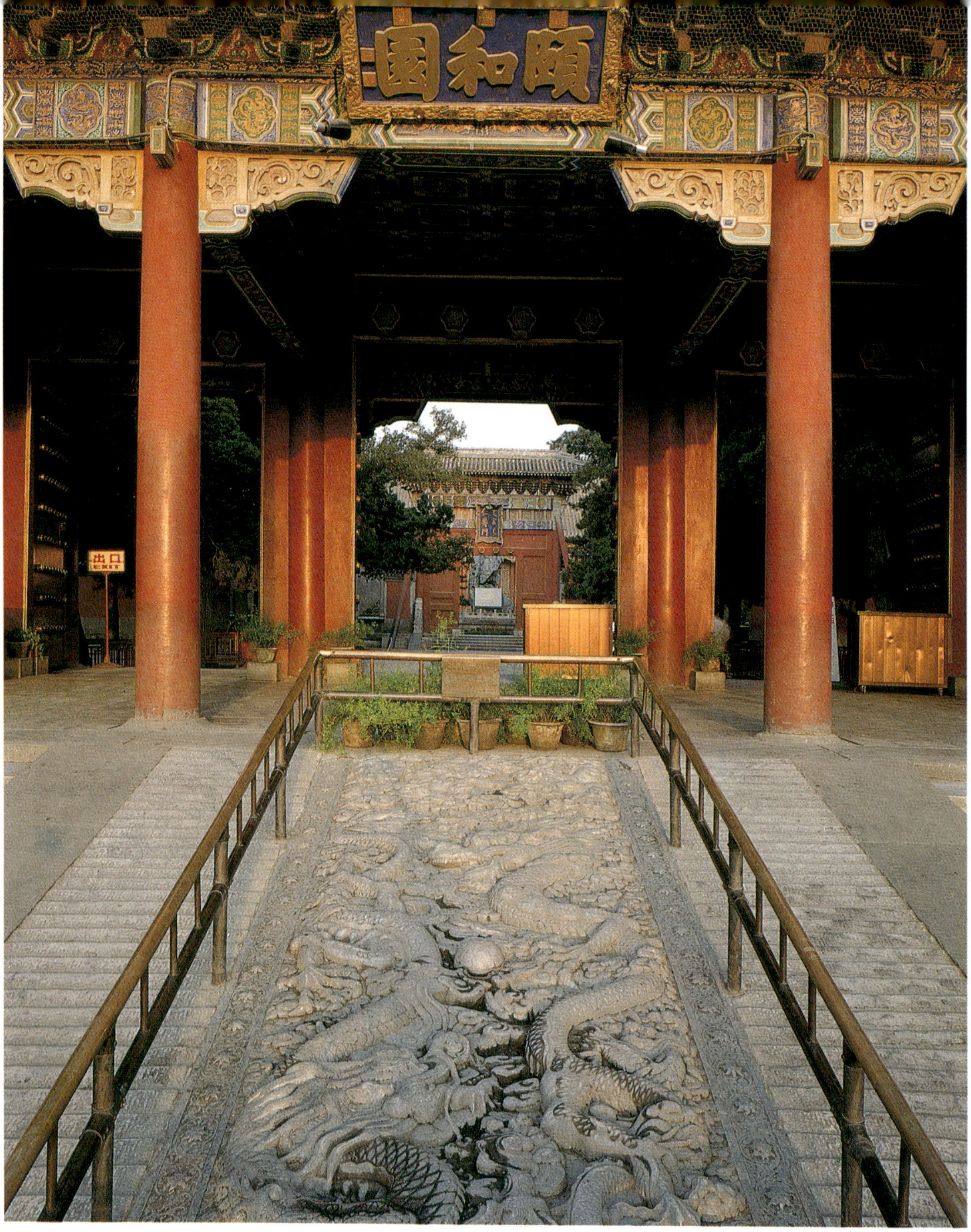

匾額和雲龍石 匾上"頤和園"三字是光緒皇帝御筆。雲龍石上有雙龍戲珠浮雕，它是皇家尊嚴的象徵，又是諭旨和敕令的標誌。

The Horizontal Inscribed Board and the Cloud-and-Dragon Stone Slab. The three Chinese characters "頤和園" (Yiheyuan) on the board are in Emperor Guangxu's handwriting. The two dragons playing with a pearl carved in relief on the stone slab symbolize the dignity of the imperial family.

銅獅 東宮門前兩側各有一隻銅獅，且分雌雄。雄獅左爪踏球，名曰"獅子滾繡球"；雌獅右爪踩幼獅，謂之"太師少師"。

Bronze lions. On either side of the East Palace Gate stand two bronze lions: a male one and a female one. The male lion has a ball under its paw, which means "the lion plays with a ball", whereas the female lion with a young lion means that "the old is always with the young".

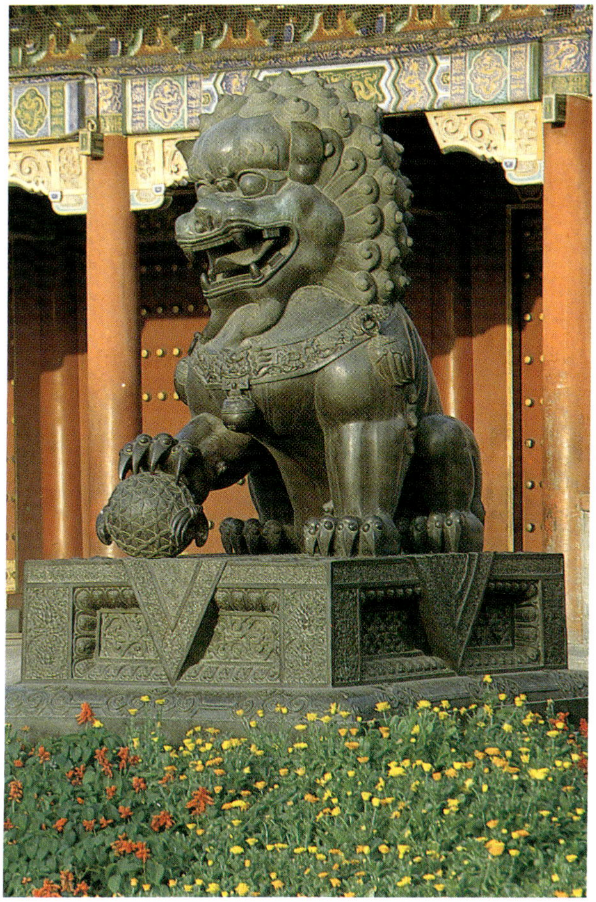

仁壽門 爲宮廷區的二重門。它巧妙地把牌樓、衙署儀門和祠廟欞星門的形式特點結合在一起，於典麗中透出莊重，是頤和園較有特色的門。

The Gate of Benevolence and Longevity. This is the second gate of the Palace Area. Its combination of different styles gives it a sense of solemn elegance.

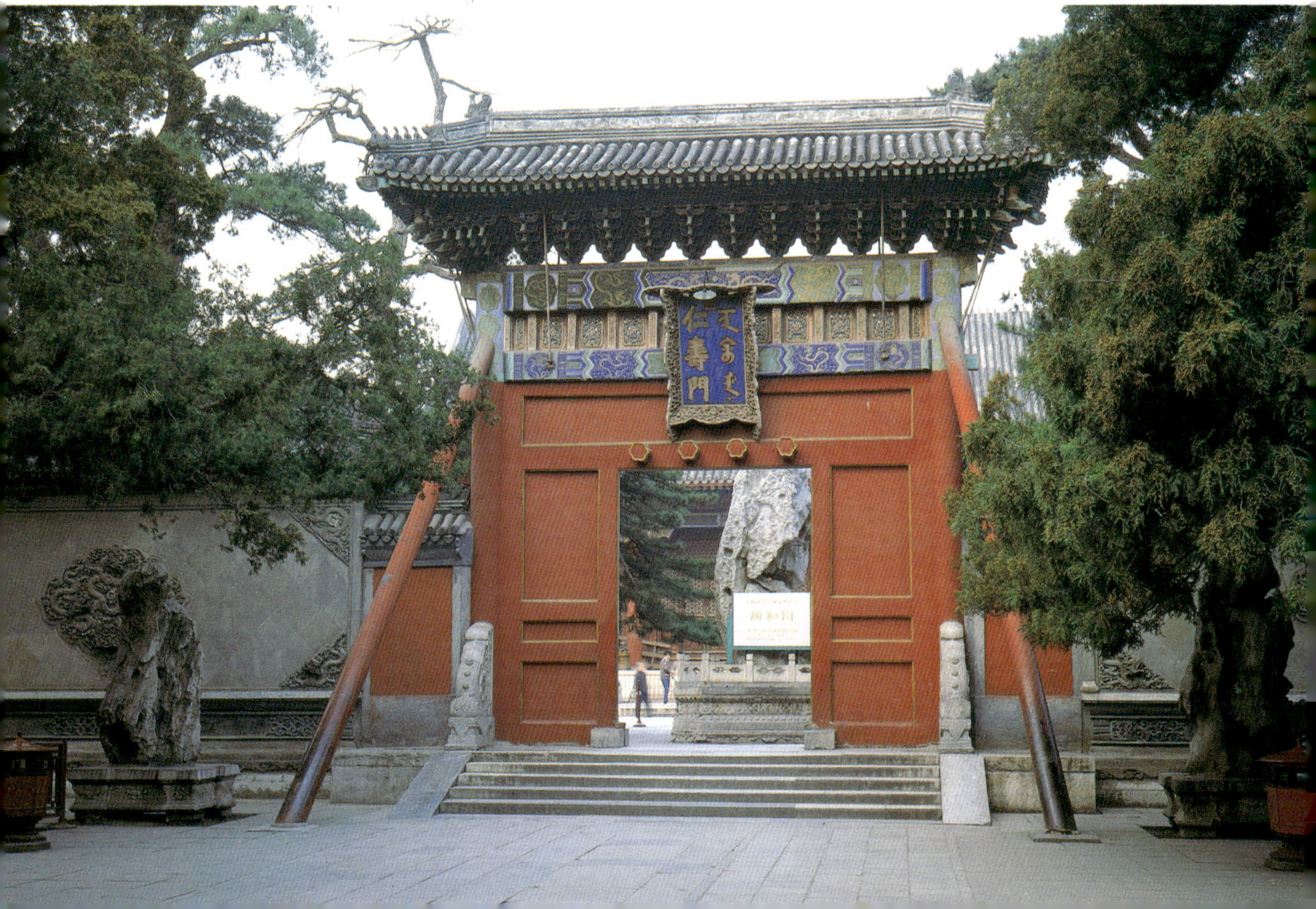

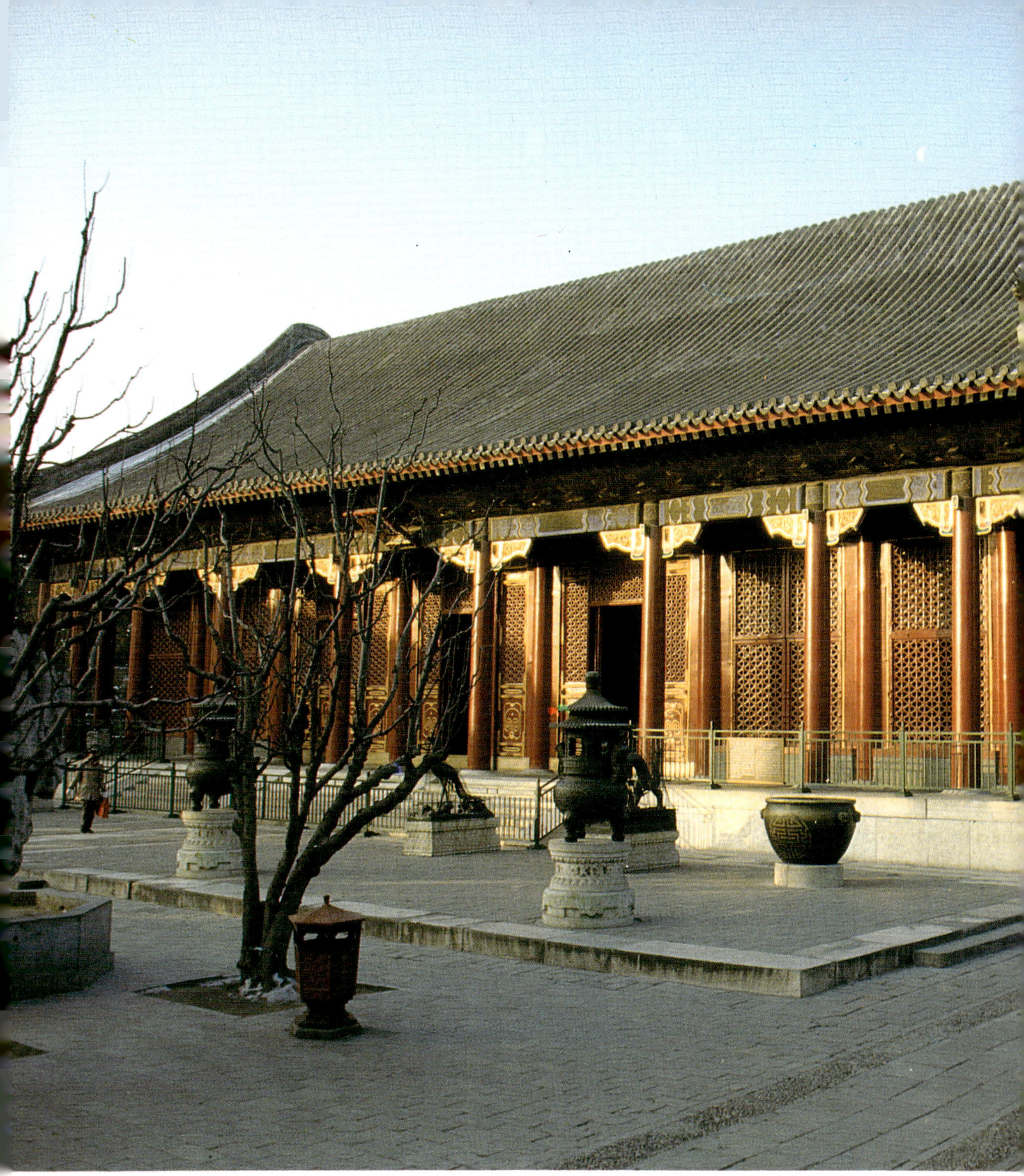

仁壽殿 原名勤政殿，意爲不忘勤理政務；光緒年間改爲今名，意爲施仁政者長壽。它是慈禧太后和光緒皇帝聽政的大殿。

The Hall of Benevolence and Longevity. Formerly called the Hall of Diligent Government, the hall was changed to its present name during the reign of Emperor Guangxu. This was where Empress Dowager Cixi and Emperor Guangxu held court and administered state affairs.

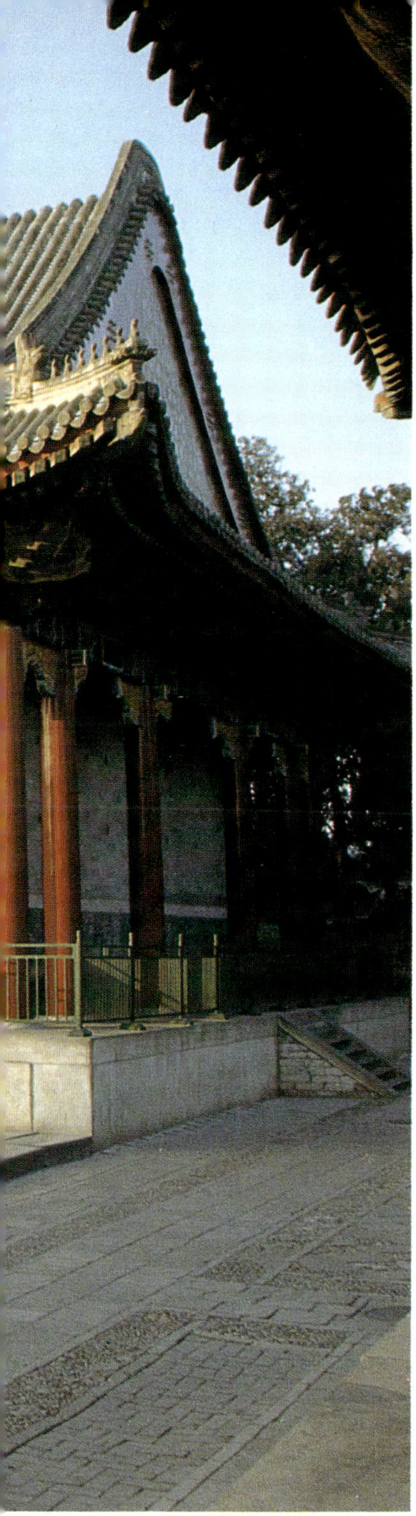

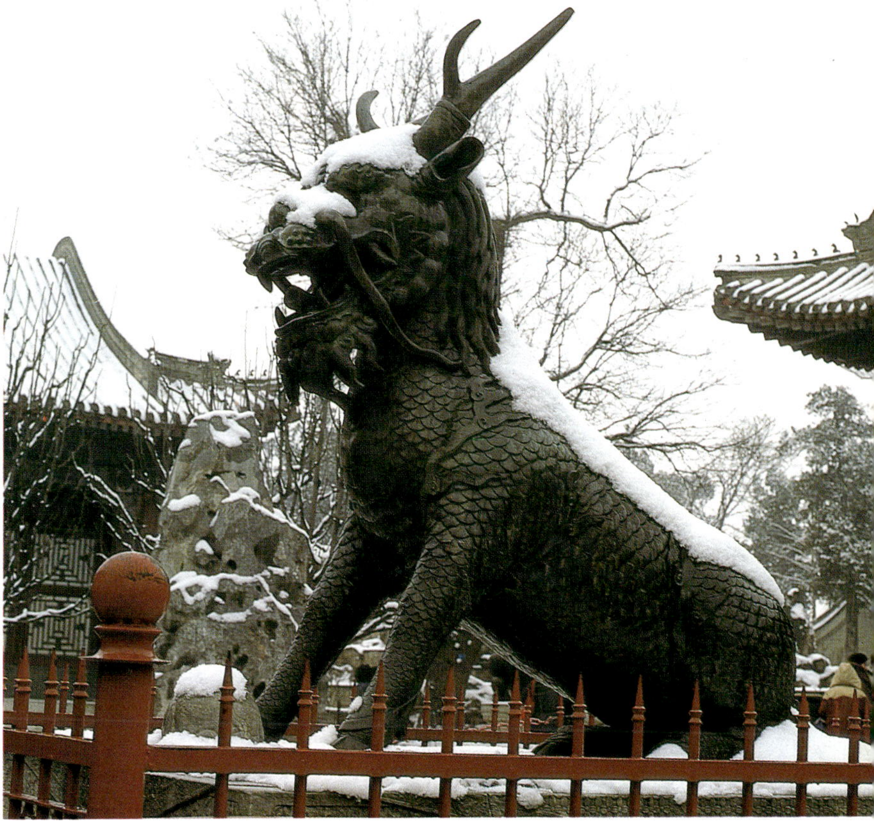

銅鑄異獸 設於殿前正中，龍頭、獅尾、鹿角、牛蹄、遍體鱗甲，造型離奇怪異，是傳說中的瑞獸麒麟。

Unusual bronze beast. Crouching on a pedestal in the centre of the courtyard, the beast has the head of a dragon, the tail of a lion, the antlers of a deer, cloven hooves, and scales all over its body. This is the fabulous *qilin* in Chinese mythology.

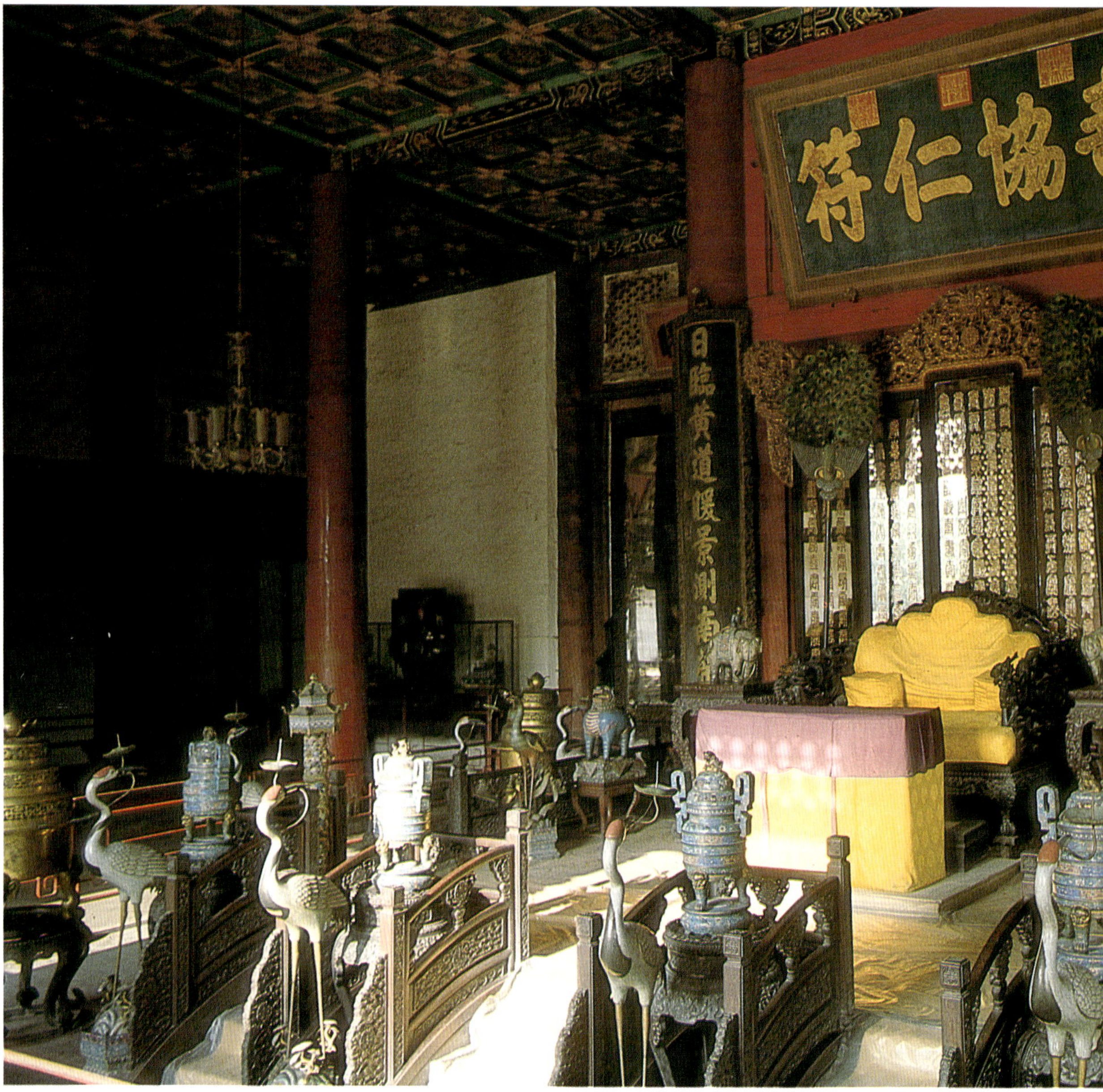

仁壽殿内景 其陳設一如當年帝后臨朝狀。正中高臺爲地平床，上設屏風、寶座、御案，兩側爲宫扇、珐琅塔、仙鶴和犼熏爐等。這裏是中國近代史上變法維新運動的策劃地之一。一八九八年，光緒皇帝曾在此殿召見改良派領袖康有爲，任命他爲總理各國事務衙門章京上行走，准其專摺奏事，從而揭開了維新變法的序幕。但好景不長，由於封建保守勢力的反對，“百日維新”終歸失敗。

Interior view of the Hall of Benevolence and Longevity. In the centre is the dais, throne and imperial table. Around it are screens, fans, crane-shaped lanterns and enameled tripods for incense and candles. This was also one of the places where the Constitutional Reform and Modernization plan was hatched. In 1898, Emperor Guangxu met Kang Youwei, leader of the reformists, and appointed him reform counsellor, declaring an institutional reform. But soon the reform was aborted.

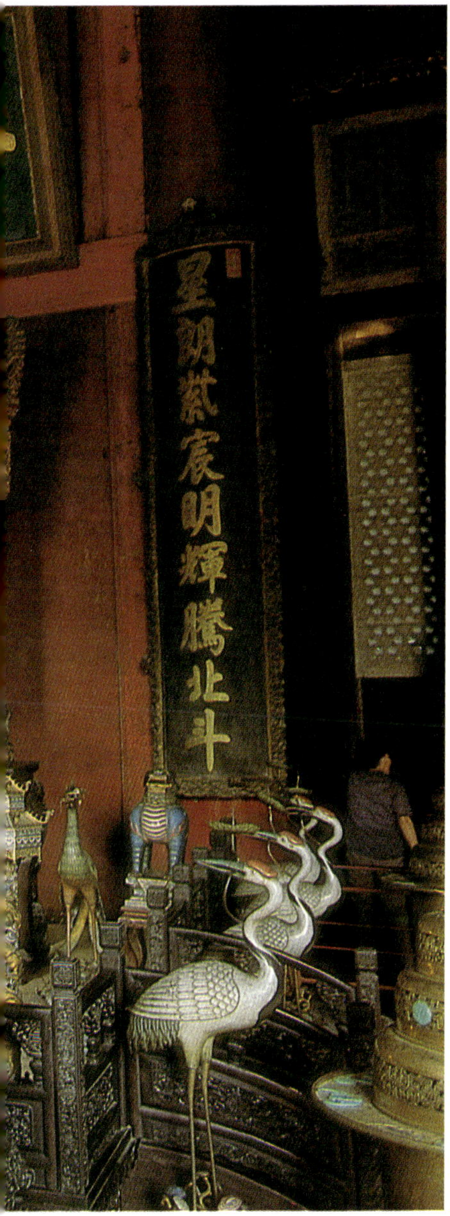

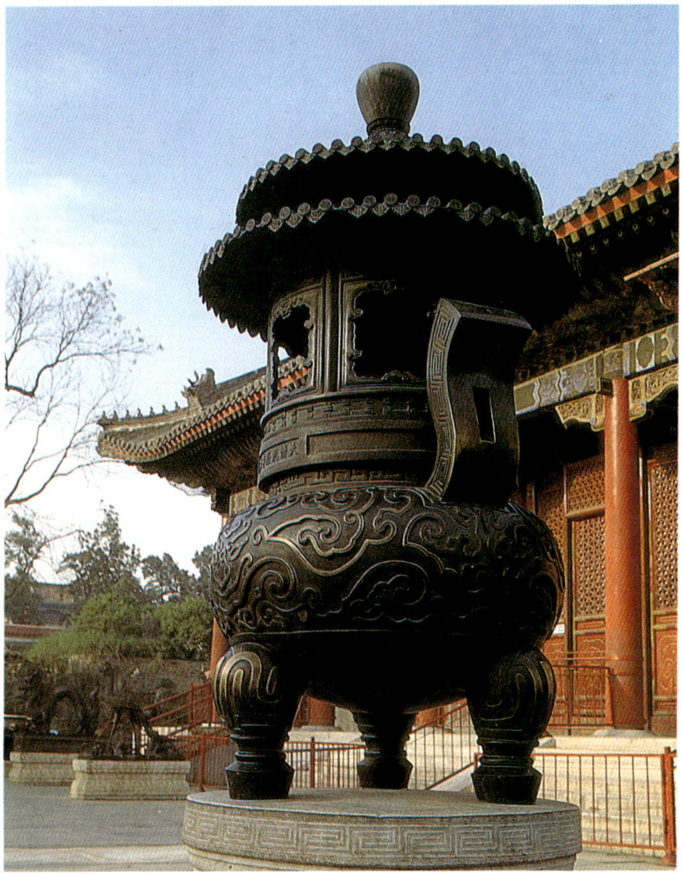

鼎式香爐 是皇家建築的特徵之一，體現皇權，象徵威嚴。每遇大朝，爐内點燃檀香和藏香，青煙繚繞，香氣襲人。

Incense burner. Typical of imperial buildings, it symbolized power and dignity. When an important ceremony was held, sandalwood and incense were burned in it, giving off wisps of fragrant smoke.

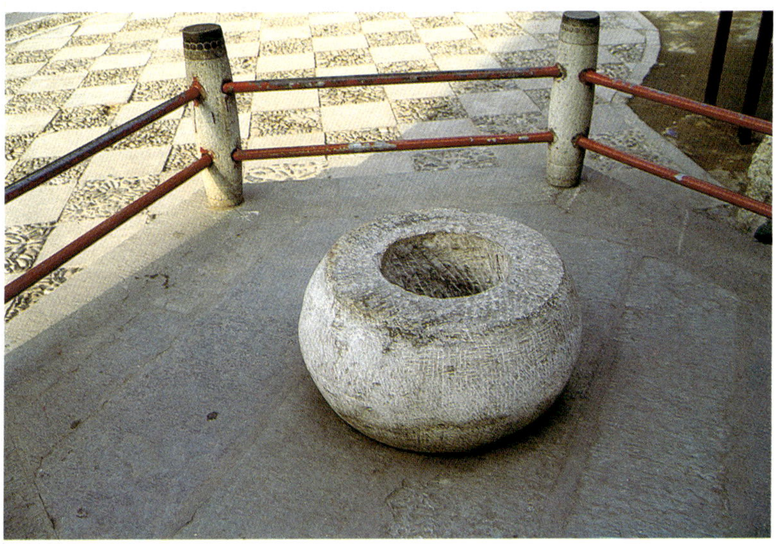

延年井 位於仁壽殿北，水味清甜。慈禧太后曾用此水服藥解暑，賜名"延年井"。

Long Life Well. Located to the north of the Hall of Benevolence and Longevity, the well had sweet water, with which Empress Dowager Cixi took medicine in the summer time. So she named it "Long Life Well".

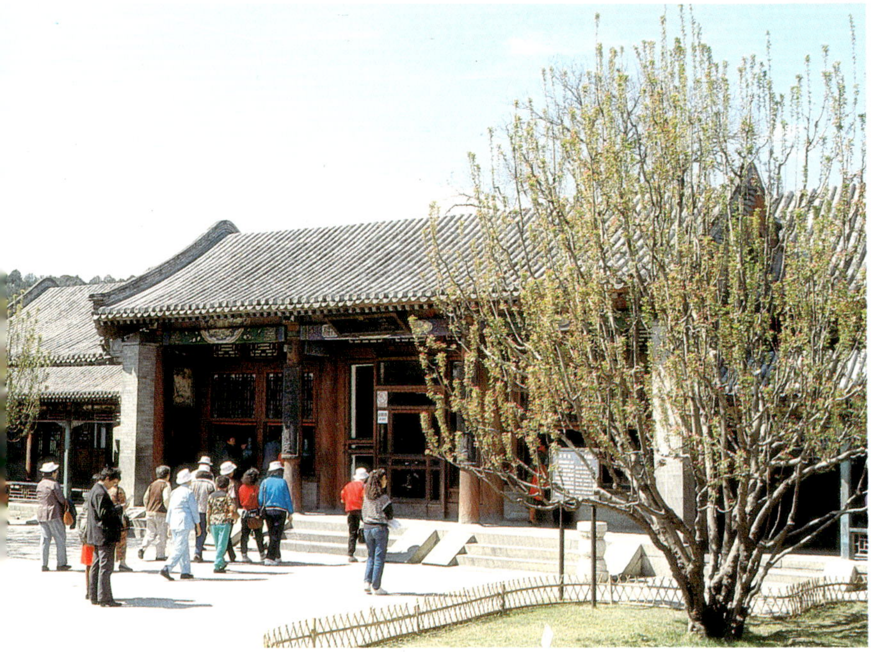

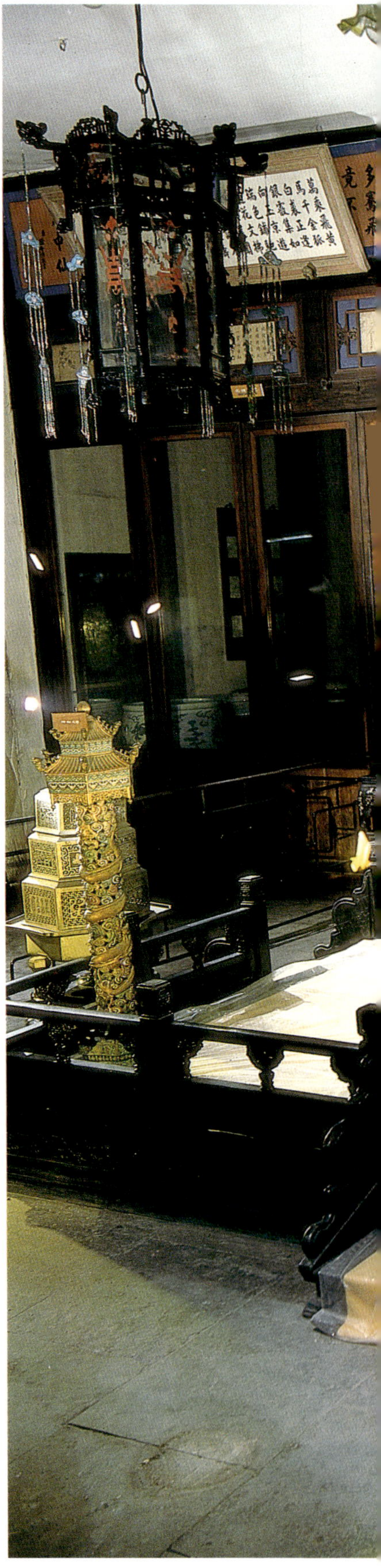

玉瀾堂 光緒皇帝的寢宮，也是他維新變法運動失敗後的囚室。這是一座臨湖而建的四合院。

Hall of Jade Billows. This was Emperor Guangxu's private living quarters and later his prison, when he was under house arrest after the failure of the 1898 constitutional reforms. This courtyard was built along the bank of the lake.

玉瀾堂正殿 其陳設與仁壽殿形制相同，但較爲簡樸。一八九八年九月十六日光緒皇帝曾在此召見握有兵權的袁世凱，令其助行新政。袁陽奉陰違，轉而告密。五天以後，慈禧太后發佈"上諭"，説皇帝有病，她要再次"訓政"。從此，她每年住園時都把光緒皇帝帶到園中，並將他囚禁於玉瀾堂。爲防光緒皇帝逃遁，玉瀾堂東、西、北三面的通道都被堵死，正南由慈禧太后的親信太監日夜監視。

The main building in the Hall of Jade Billows. The display and furnishings are as they were in Guangxu's time. On September 16, 1898, Emperor Guangxu called in Yuan Shikai, an army commander, here and instructed him to help the reformists. But Yuan Shikai quickly informed against the reformists. Five days later Cixi staged a coup and placed Emperor Guangxu, who had backed the reforms, under "palace arrest". Whenever she went to the Summer Palace, she took the Emperor with her and imprisoned him in this hall. To prevent the Emperor from escaping, a brick wall reaching to the ceiling was built lengthwise across the chamber, while specially appointed eunuchs kept a round-the-clock watch on him.

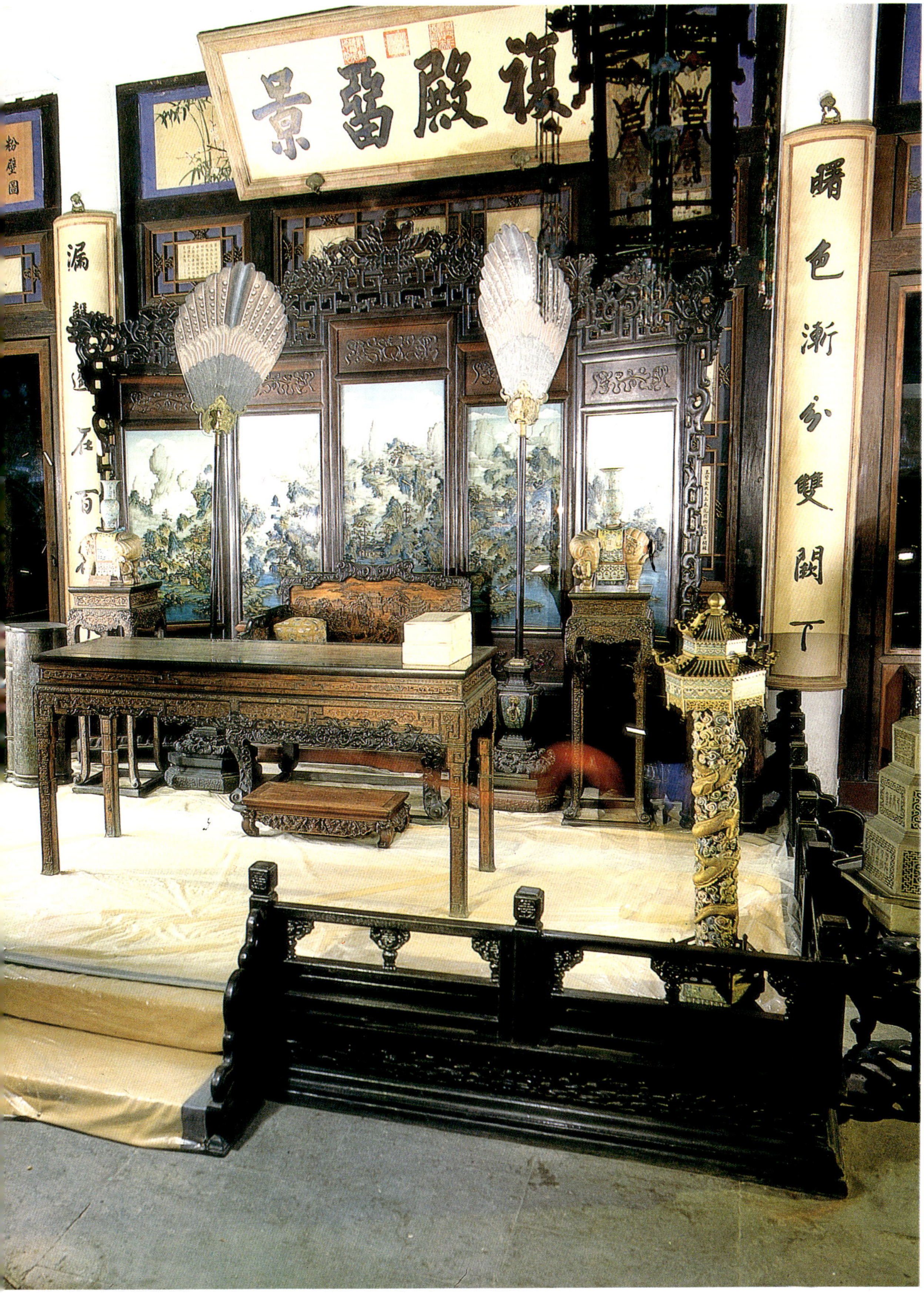
曙色漸分雙闕下

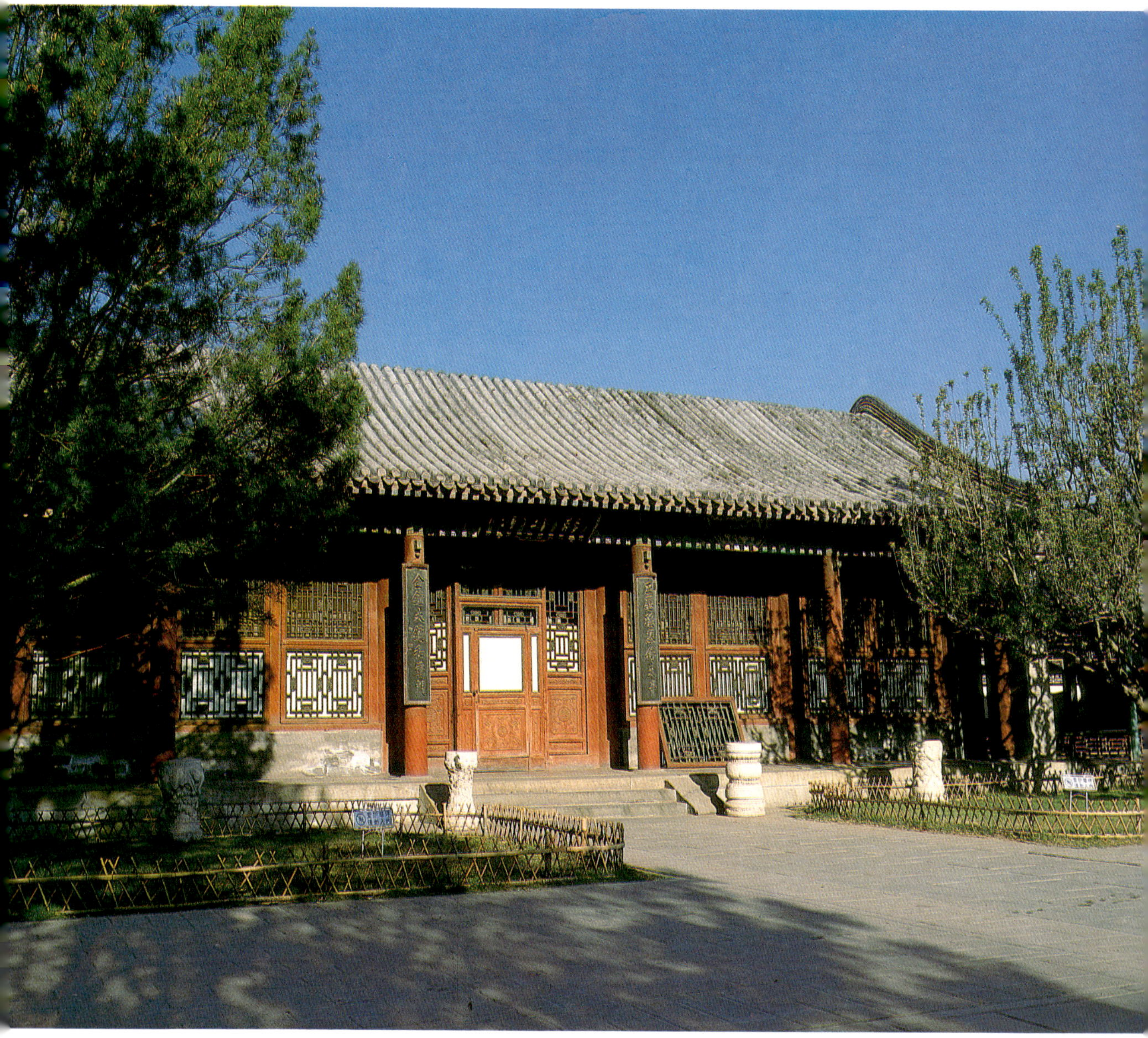

藕香榭 是玉瀾堂的西配殿，光緒皇帝的寢宫。原爲前後門的穿堂殿，出後門可到湖邊碼頭。慈禧太后“訓政”後，後門和通道都被阻隔。

Pavilion of Lotus Fragrance. This is the western side-building in the Hall of Jade Billows. It was originally a through building with front and back entrances and led to a pier on the lake. Later, it was blocked off after the Emperor was under house arrest here.

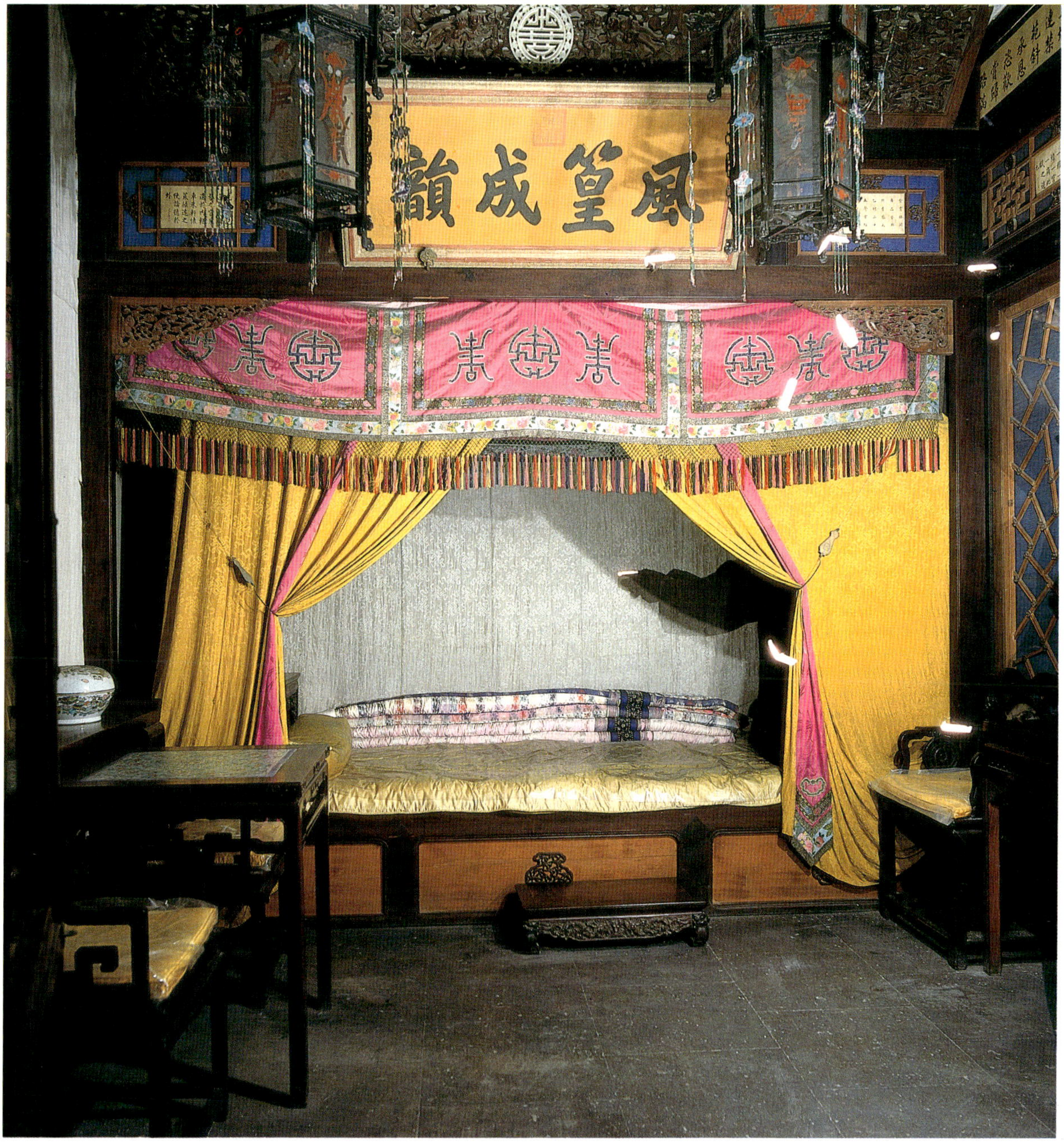

寢宮内景 炕床上的卧具爲原物，至今猶新。光緒皇帝在這幽室裏斷斷續續地被囚禁了十年，一九〇八年十一月十四日病逝，年僅三十八歲。第二天，慈禧太后也死了。

Emperor Guangxu's bedroom. They are the same bed, canopy, pillow and quilts as used by the Emperor who was imprisoned here intermittently for ten years. He died of illness on November 14, 1908 at the age of 38, and a day later Empress Dowager Cixi also breathed her last.

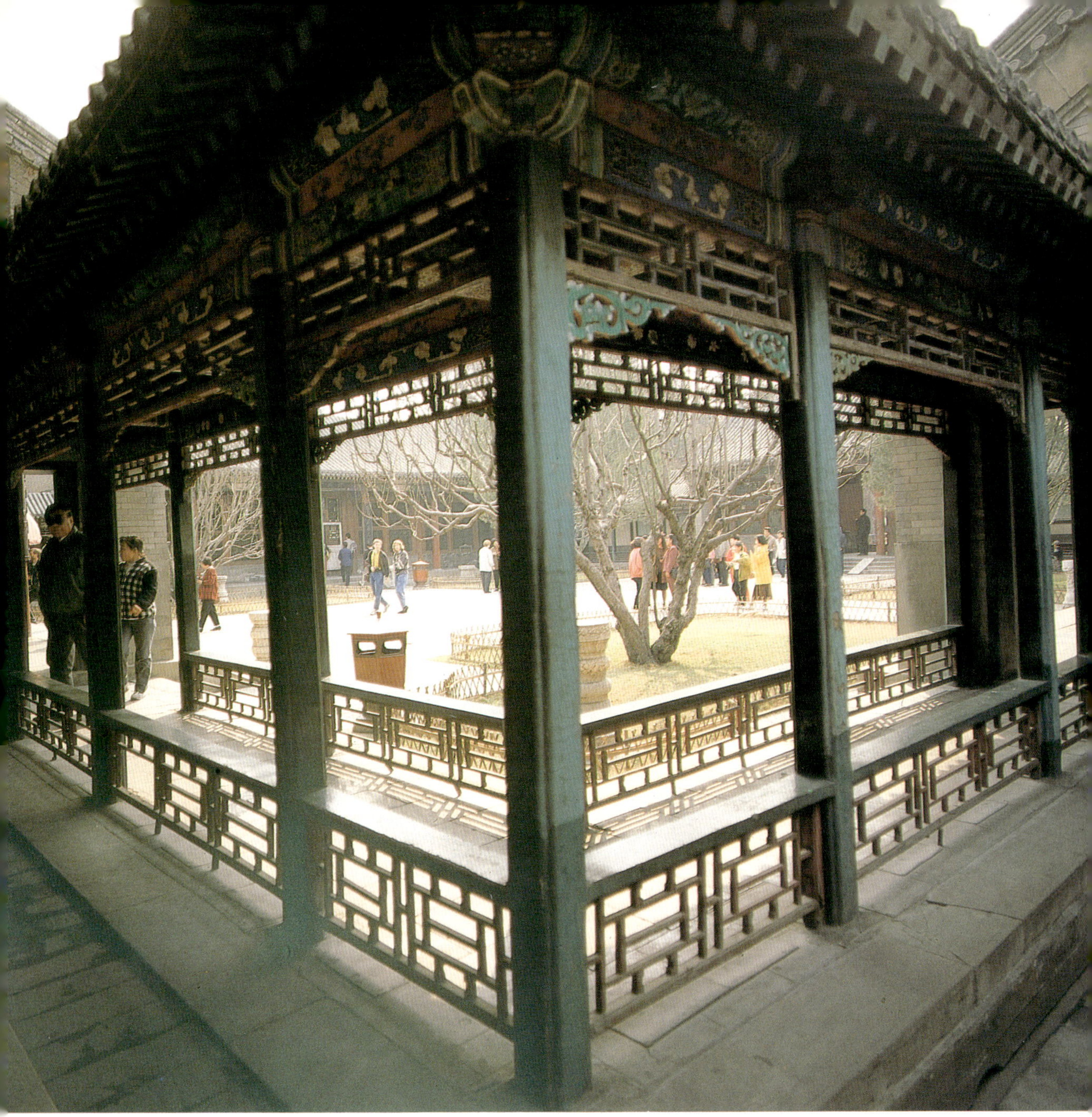

抄手遊廊　中國的園林佈景，凡重要的庭院和大型建築物之間，都在正房、兩厢及正門兩側設置廊，人們把這種廊叫作"抄手遊廊"。其作用是連接建築物和貫通走道，既可爲主體建築增輝，又可避雨雪。圖爲玉瀾堂的廊。

Chaoshou Veranda. In the art of Chinese gardening all major buildings such as courtyards, halls, towers and gates are usually connected by corridors, which people call "Chaoshou Verandas". It serves not only as a decoration for the park but also as a shelter from rain and snow. In the picture is the veranda of the Hall of Jade Billows.

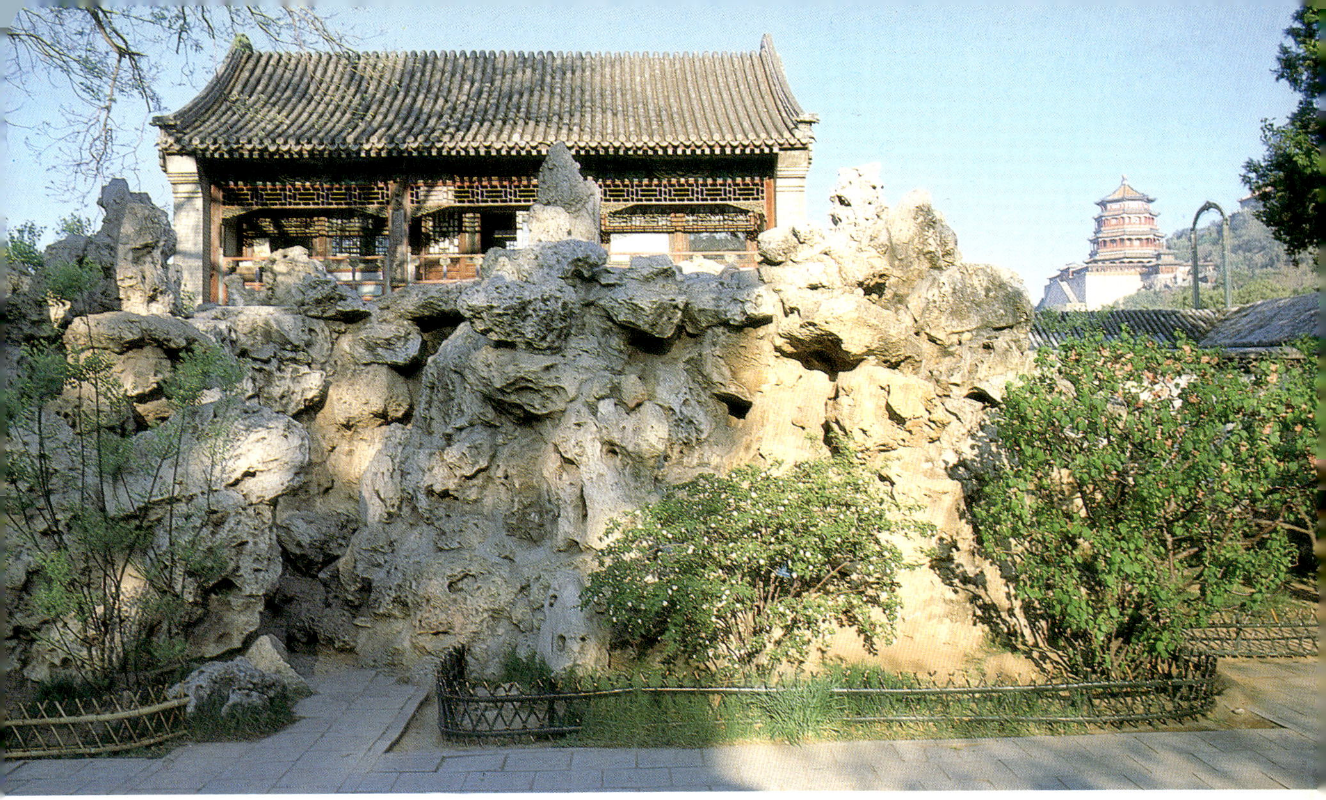

跨院 是連接玉瀾堂和宜芸館的小庭院。院西有一座臨湖的觀景建築——夕佳樓。

The courtyard. This is a small courtyard connecting the Hall of Jade Billows and the Lodge of the Propriety of Weeding. On its western side is the two-storeyed Pavilion of Beautiful Sunset.

夕佳樓 是帝、后夏天納凉和觀景的最佳處所。

Pavilion of Beautiful Sunset. On hot summer evenings the emperor and empress used to cool themselves and enjoy the scenery on this building.

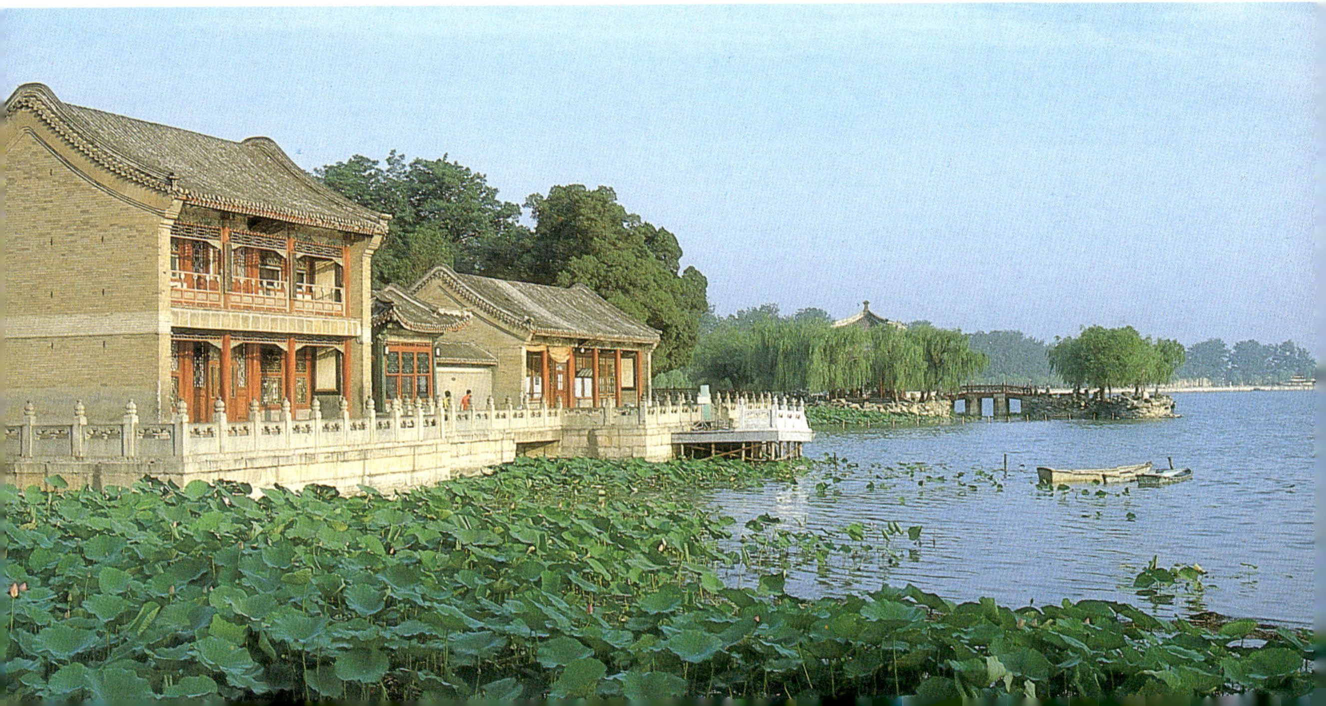

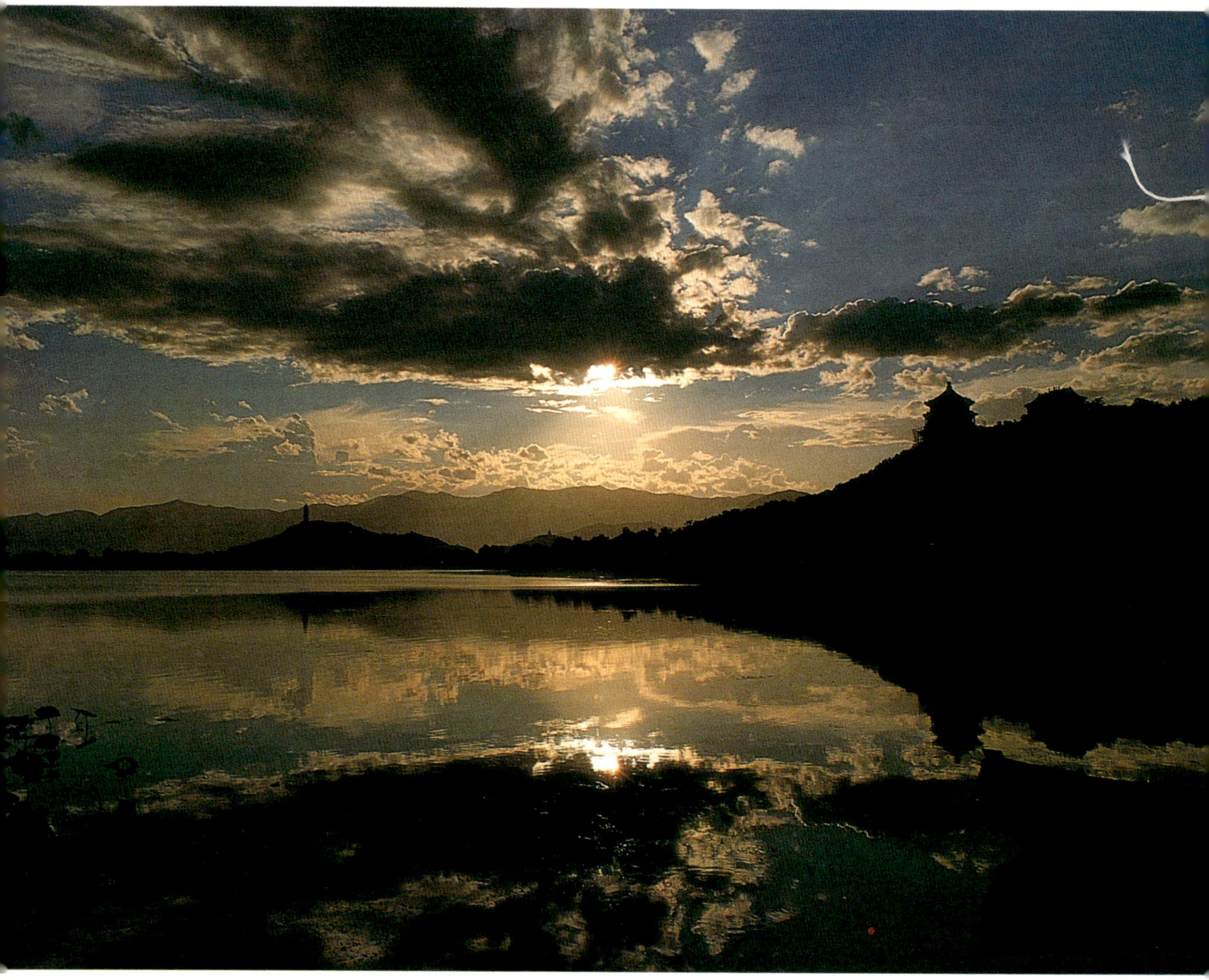

夕佳樓觀景 登上樓臺，視野開闊，遠處的西山羣峰，玉峰寶塔，近處的萬壽山樓閣，浩渺的湖面，盡收眼底。

View from the Pavilion of Beautiful Sunset. When one ascends the pavilion, the distant Western Hills, the pagoda on the Jade Hill, the tower on the Longevity Hill, and the vast Kunming Lake, all come into view.

宜蕓館 殿內爲隆裕皇后的臥室。隆裕姓葉赫那拉，是慈禧太后娘家的侄女。慈禧太后選她爲皇后，旨在控制光緒皇帝。

Lodge of the Propriety of Weeding. The main hall in this courtyard was the bedroom of Empress Longyu. Longyu was Empress Dowager Cixi's niece. Cixi made her the empress with the purpose to control the emperor.

宜蕓館垂花門樓 進入門樓又是一重院落，這是光緒皇帝的皇后隆裕的寢宮。

Gate with Hanging Flowers. Behind the gate is another courtyard, which was the bedroom of Empress Longyu, wife of Emperor Guangxu.

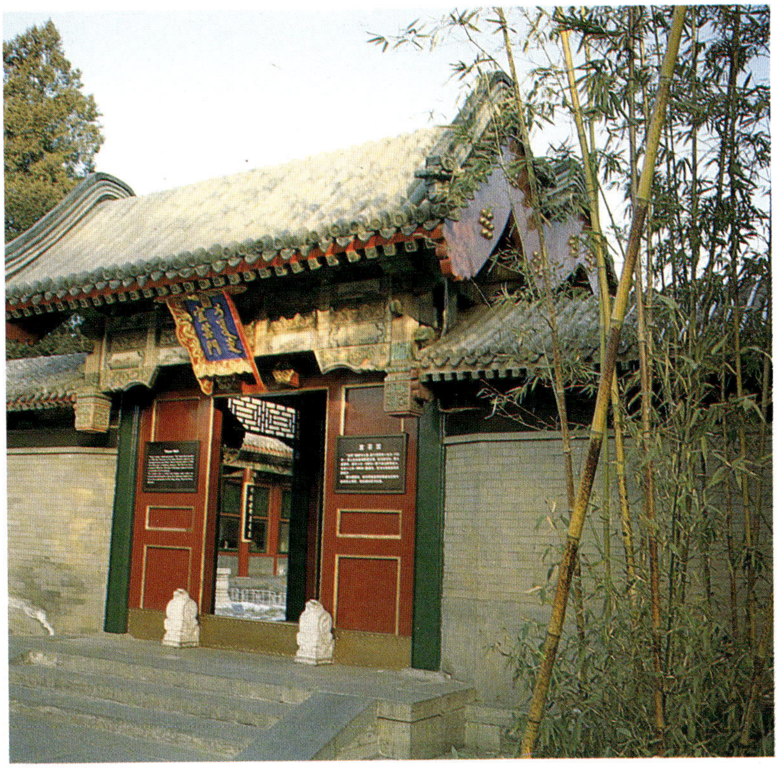

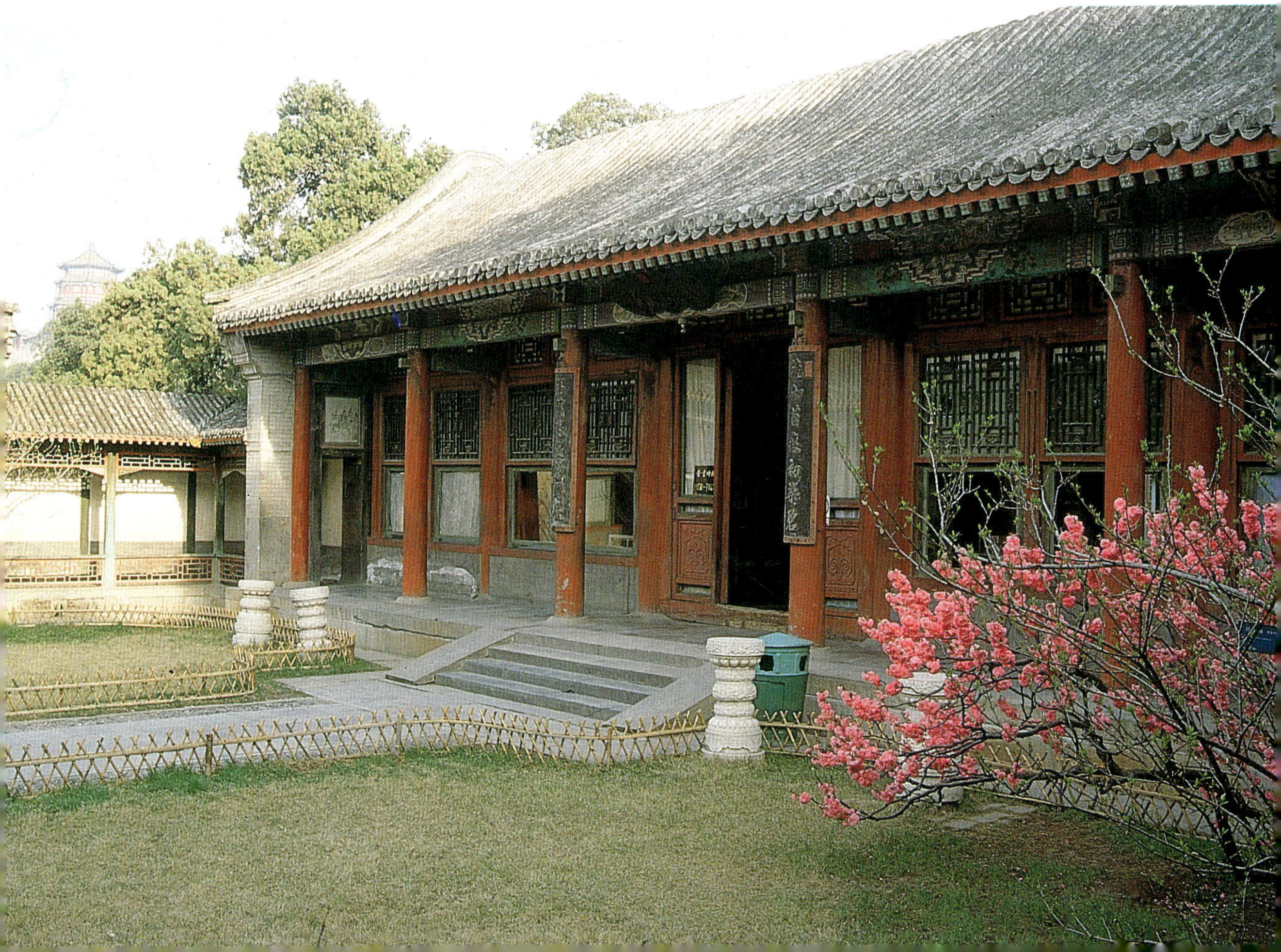

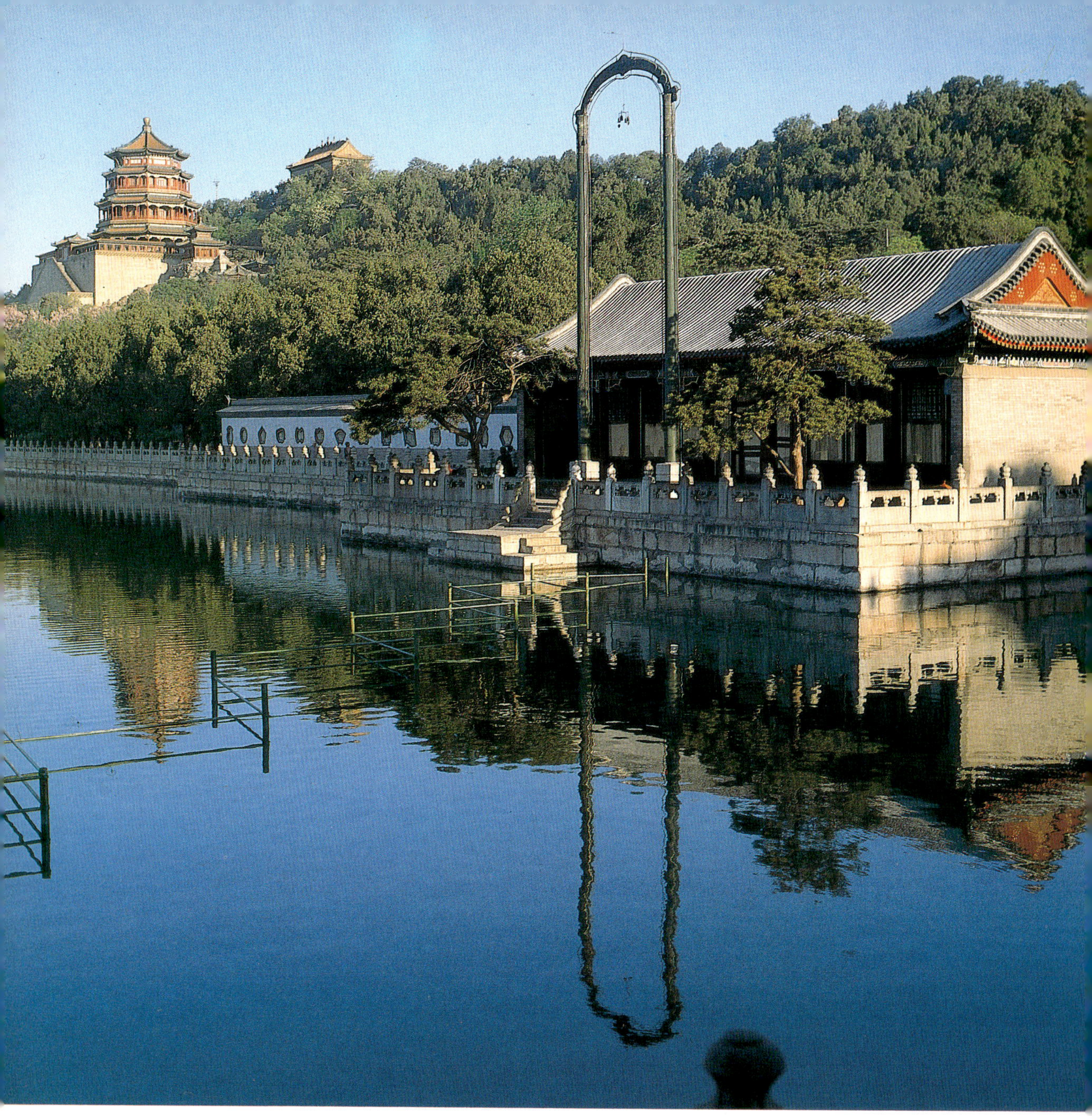

水木自親 位於昆明湖北岸，前軒臨水，爲慈禧太后的寢宮樂壽堂的正門。她由水路入園時，在這裏下船直進樂壽堂大院。

Hall of Affinity Between Wood and Water. Located on the northern bank of Kunming Lake, it is the front entrance of the Hall of Happiness in Longevity. When the Empress Dowager came to the Summer Palace by water, her boat docked here.

樂壽堂 爲一大型四合院，慈禧太后的寢宮。大殿紅柱灰頂，垂脊捲棚歇山式，造型别致，富麗堂皇。

Hall of Happiness in Longevity. This large complex was Cixi's residential quarters. With red pillars and a grey roof, this magnificent hall was built in a unique style.

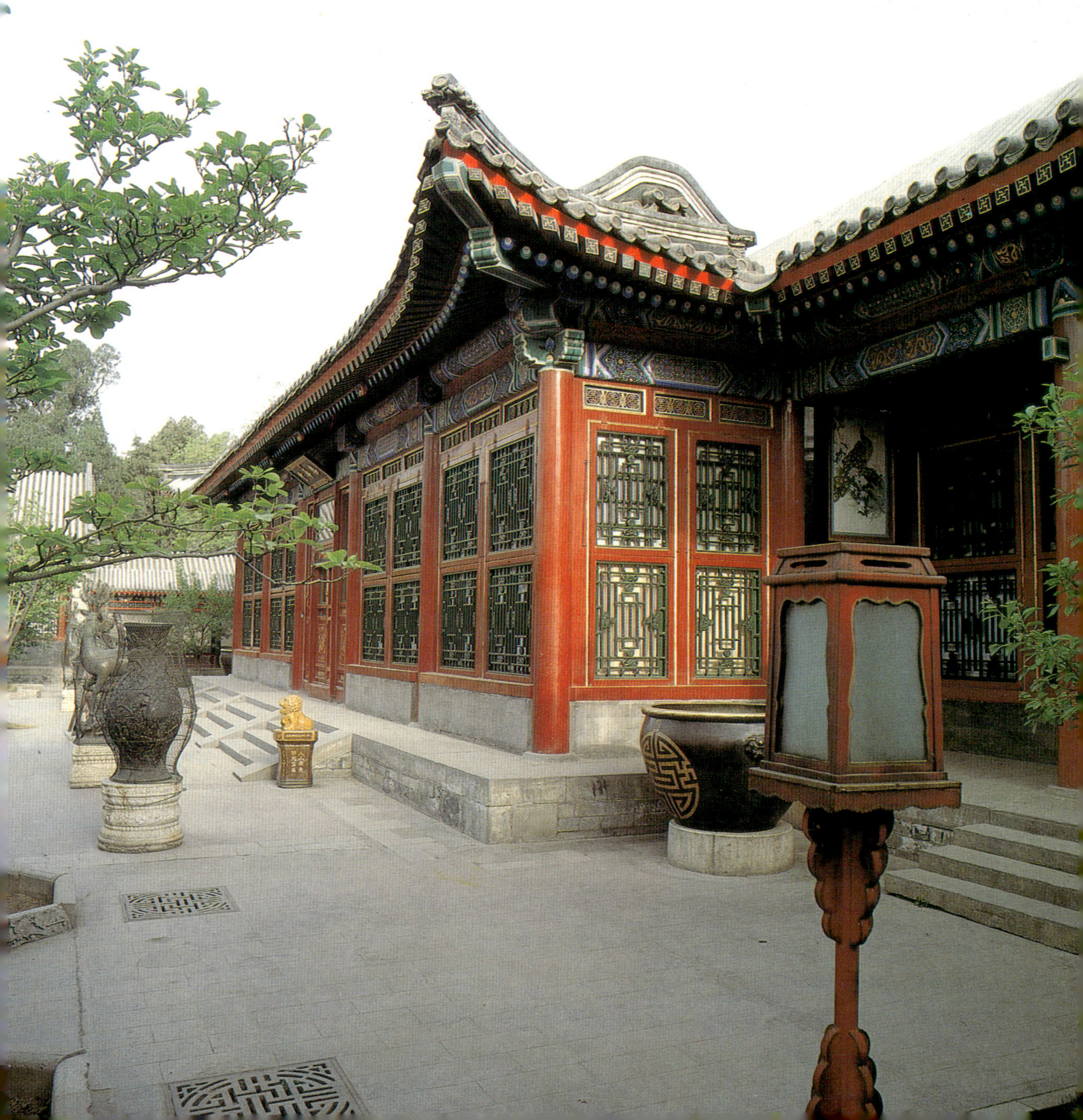

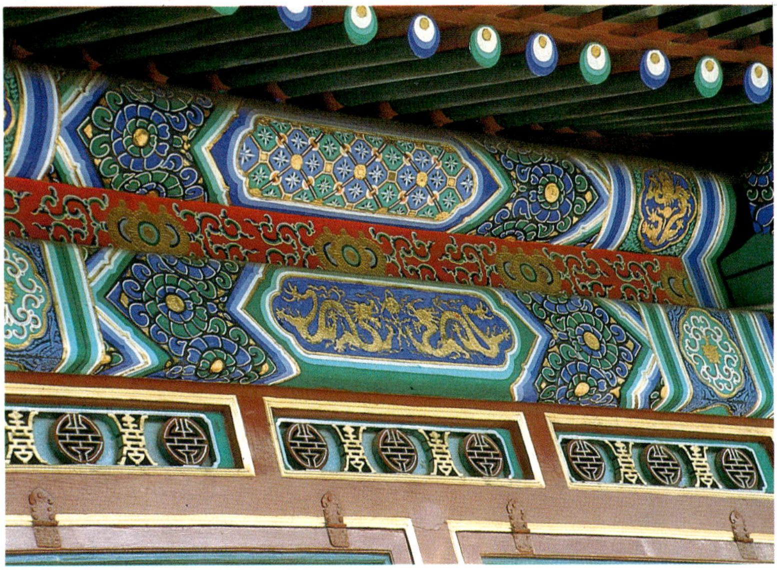

樂壽堂彩繪 這種彩畫以金、紅、青、緑相間，圖案以龍鳳爲主，被稱爲“和璽彩畫”。

Colour paintings in the Hall of Happiness in Longevity. Painted in gold, red, blue and green in the pattern of dragons and phoenixes, these paintings were known as "Hexi Colour Paintings".

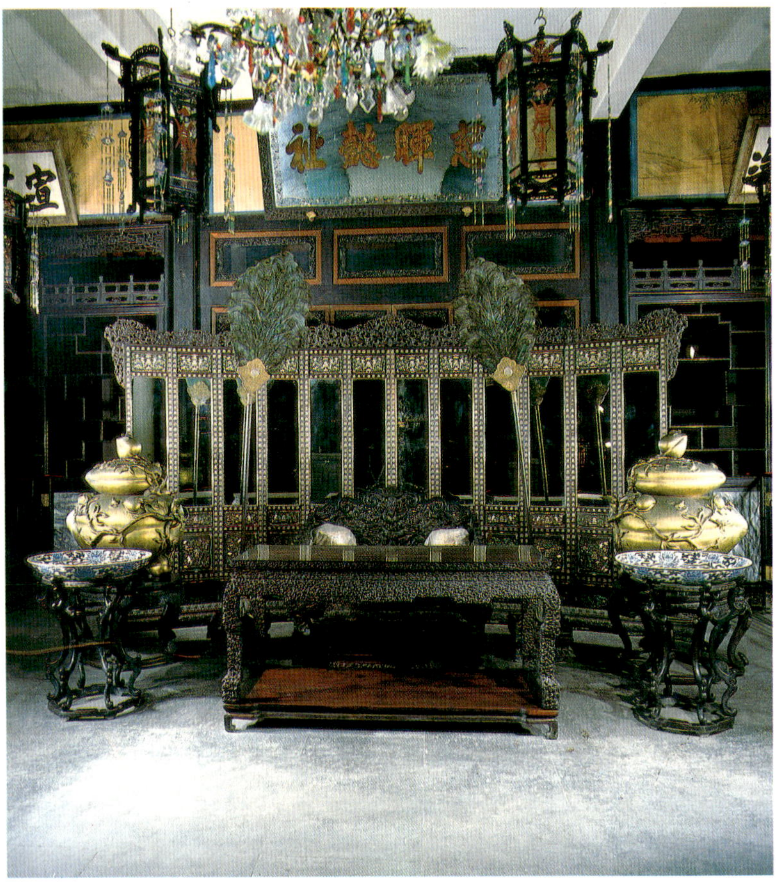

樂壽堂内景 正中爲寶座、御案、寶扇和圍屏，寶座四周擺放着四隻像大壽桃一樣的鍍金銅爐，還有兩隻青花大瓷盤。頂上懸掛的五彩玻璃燈是中國引進的最早的電燈。

Interior view of the Hall of Happiness in Longevity. In the centre is the throne and imperial desk, surrounded by ornamental fans and screens. On the four sides are gilt incense burners shaped like a peach. On either side of the throne is a large ceramic dish with blue floral designs. The chandeliers hung in the hall probably were the first electric lamps in China.

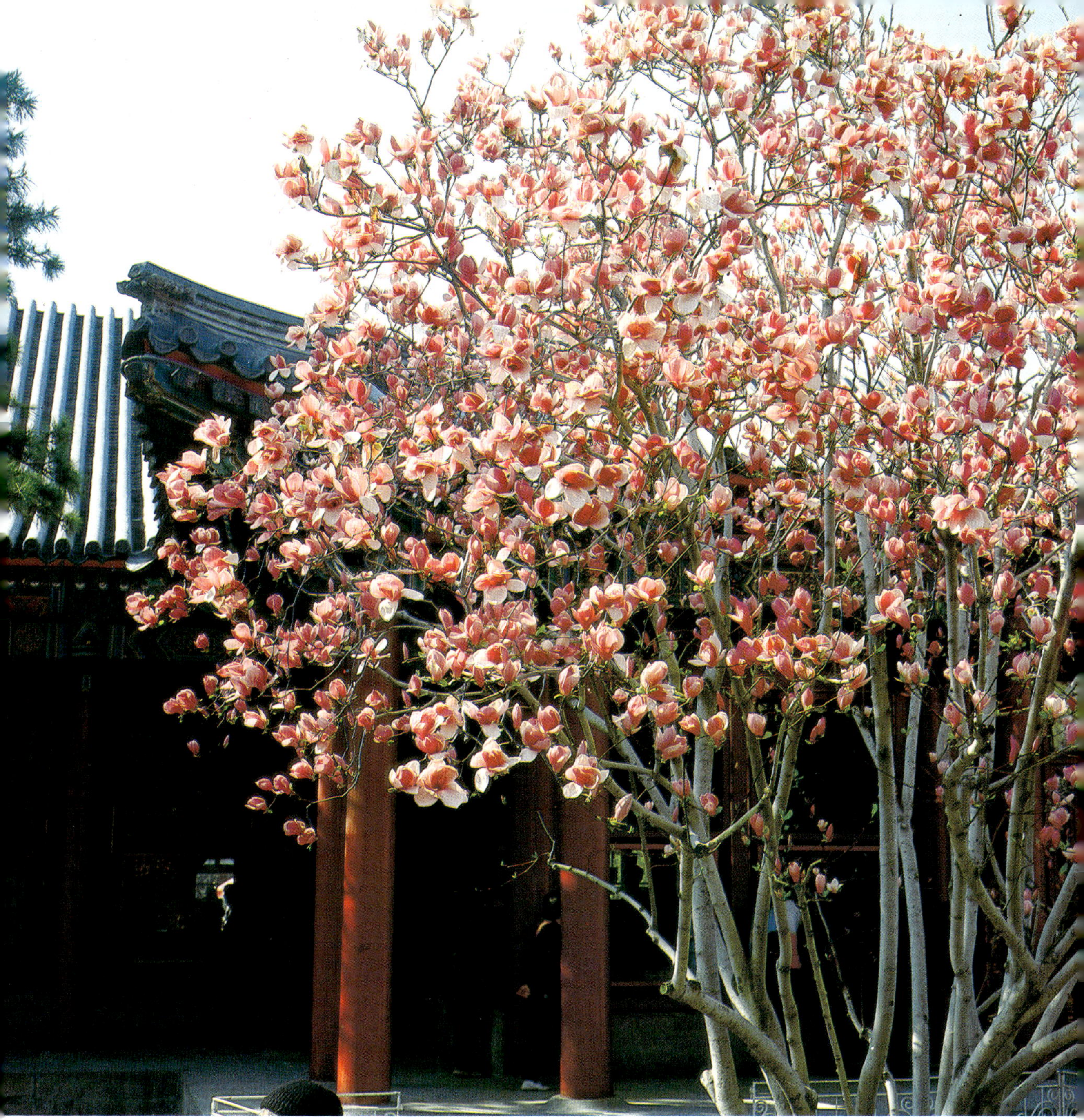

紫玉蘭　樂壽堂院内的玉蘭十分著名，有些是乾隆年間從中國南方引栽的，已有二百多年歷史。一八六〇年以前，這裏玉蘭成林，有"玉香海"的美稱。

Purple yulan. Yulan magnolia is a gorgeous flower, and the yulan behind the Hall of Happiness in Longevity is very famous. Some of the flowers were transplanted from south China during Qianlong's time 200 years ago. Before 1860 there was a forest of yulan here known as "The Sea of Yulan Fragrance".

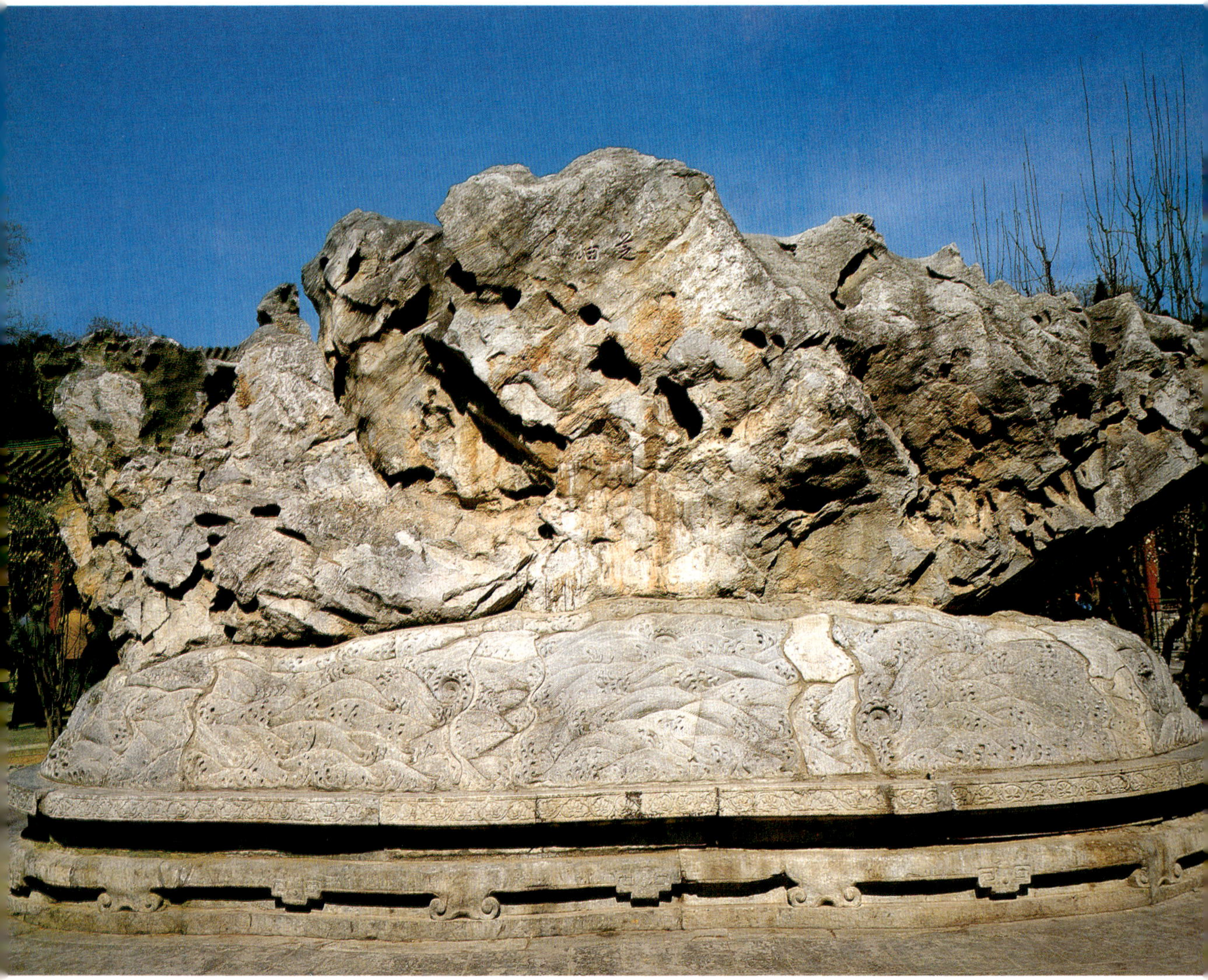

青芝岫 俗名敗家石，是明代太僕米萬鍾的遺物，後被乾隆皇帝發現，令人置於此處，取名青芝岫。巨石兩面分別刻有乾隆皇帝題寫的“玉英”、“香蓮”四字。

Blue Iris Hill. This huge boulder was abandoned by the Ming-Dynasty official Mi Wanzhong and was later found by Emperor Qianlong who ordered it brought here and gave it its name. On either side of the boulder are carved the words "Yuying" and "Xianglian" to show the emperor's fondness.

汽車 是袁世凱送給慈禧太后的禮品。這是中國引進的第一輛汽車。

Car. This car was a present given to Empress Dowager Cixi by Yuan Shikai. This was the first car in China.

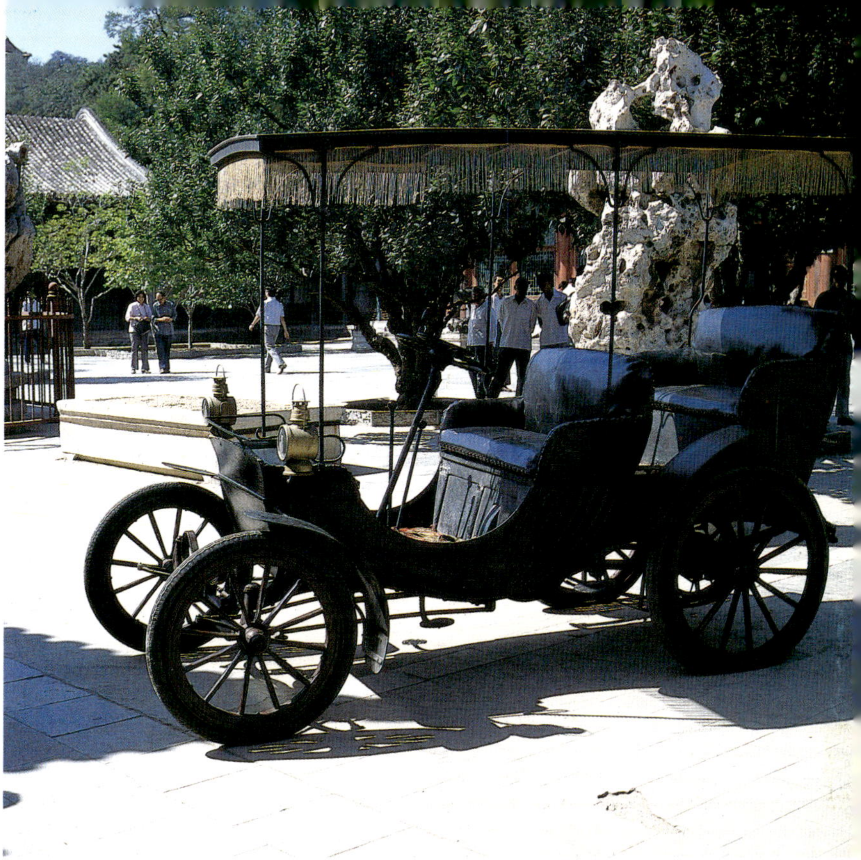

雙輪人力車 爲日本國所贈，慈禧太后專用。車把頂端鑲有銅龍，車襯和坐墊用黄軟緞製做，並以金綫繡有多種圖案。清廷規定，一品大臣乘藍轎，宫内大員乘紅、綠轎，祇有帝、后才可乘黄轎，坐黄車。

Ricksha. This ricksha was given by Japan to the Empress Dowager. On the top of the two shafts are bronze dragons, and on the cushion and lining made of silk are embroidered various designs in gold thread. It is said that the Qing court stipulated that the top officials took blue rickshas, palace officials had red or green rickshas, only the emperor and empress used yellow ones.

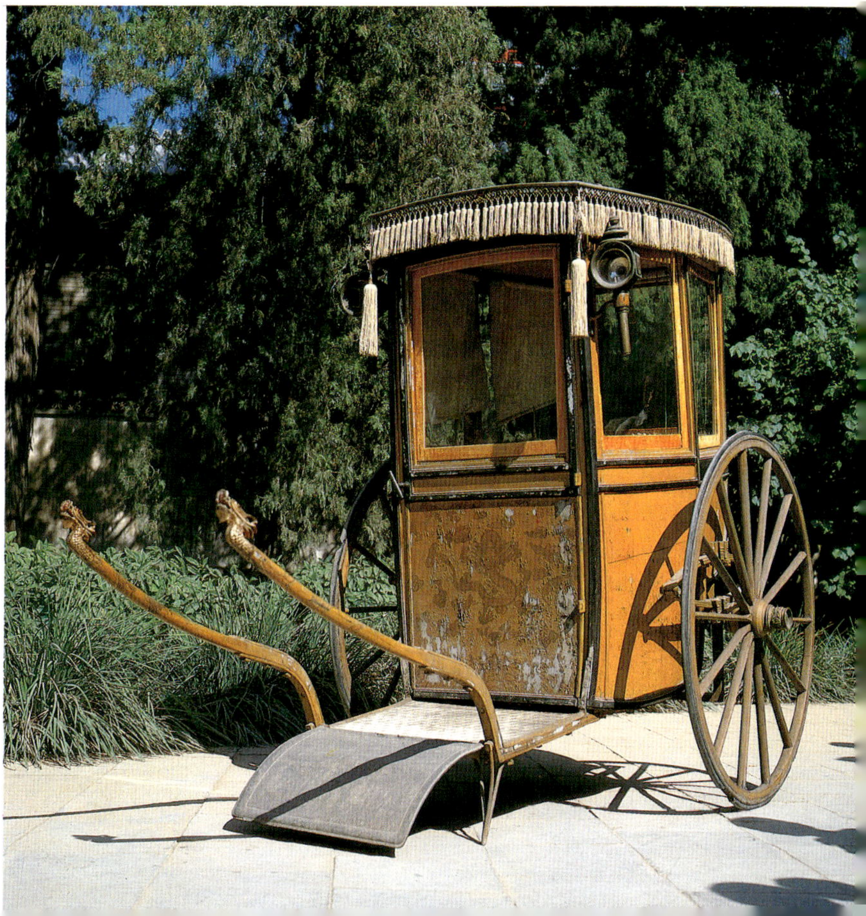

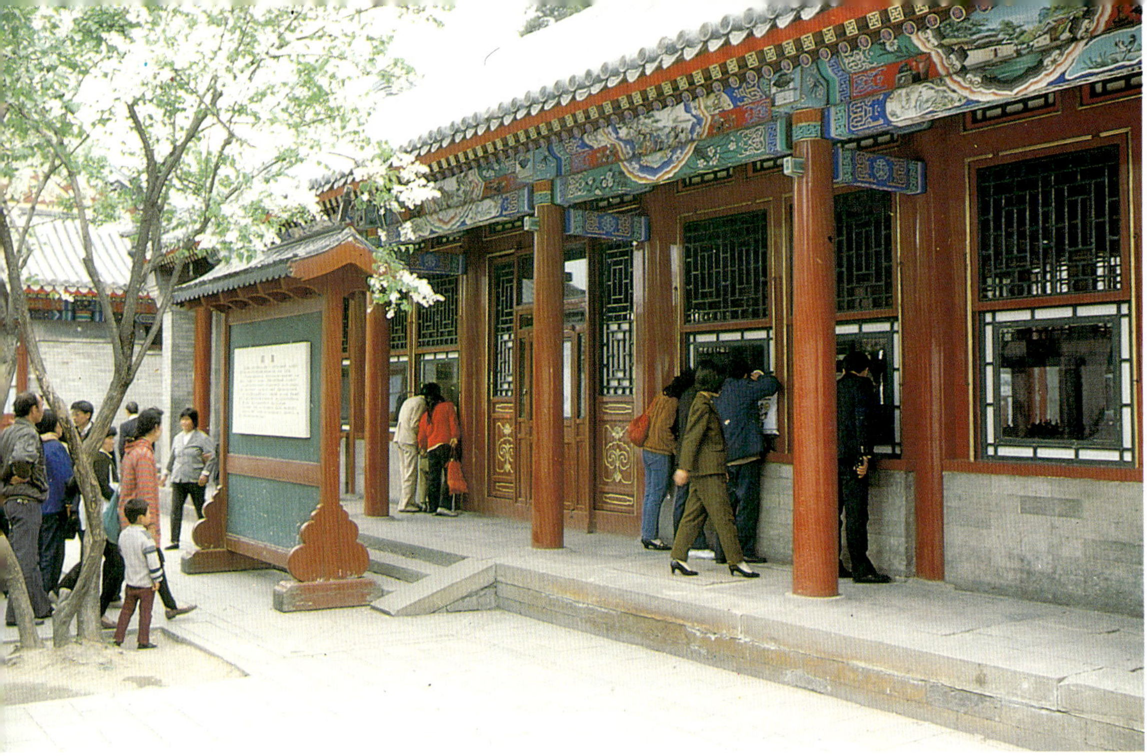

永壽齋　這裏是慈禧太后的心腹太監李蓮英的住所。此殿紅柱灰瓦，樑枋上遍繪蘇式彩畫。

Hall of Longevity. This was the living quarters of Li Lianying, the trusted eunuch of Empress Dowager Cixi. The hall has red pillars and a grey tiled roof, much the same as the Hall of Jade Billows where Emperor Guangxu lived. The only difference is the paintings on the beams.

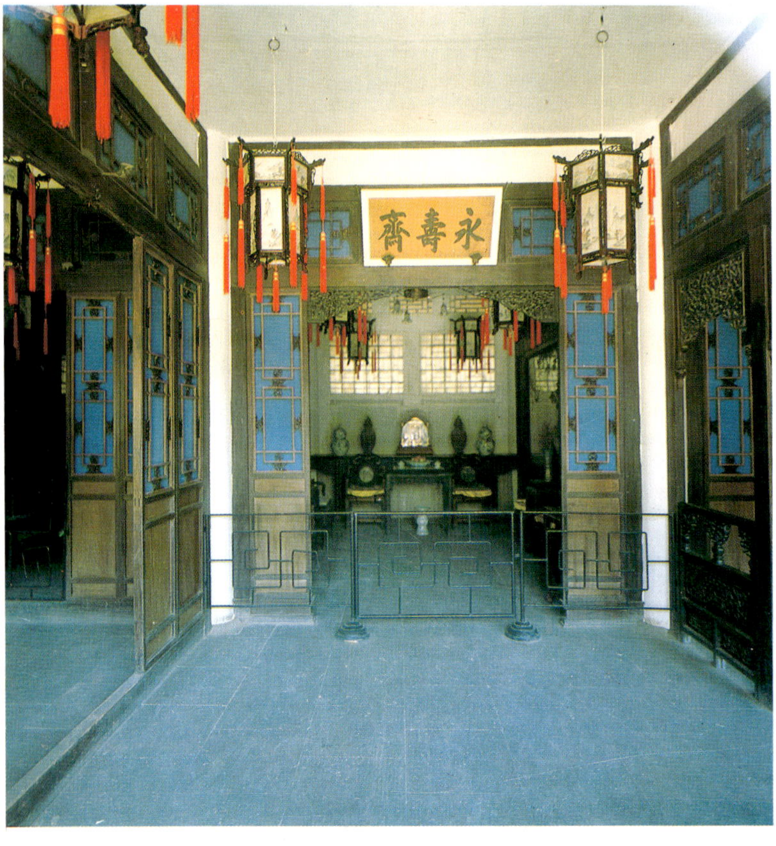

永壽齋内景　裝飾華麗，陳設考究。據資料記載，李蓮英的卧室内掛黄軟緞簾，鋪黄軟緞褥，與帝王無異。

Interior view of the Hall of Longevity. The hall was also lavishly furnished. According to records, Li Lianying's beddings were made of yellow silk, which were almost the same as the emperor's.

揚仁風　是樂壽堂西側的附屬建築。相傳晉代文學家袁宏（公元三二八——三七六年）得官上任前，朋友送他一把折扇，並說："願君多施仁政，揚仁義之風。"這座頗爲别致的小院就是根據這個故事修建的。院内最著名的建築是"扇面殿"，殿前地面用漢白玉石拼成扇骨形；凹進的扇面墻恰似漢字"風"的"几"旁。建築之巧，令人稱奇。

Wind of Virtue. This is a courtyard northwest of the Hall of Happiness in Longevity, forming an adjunct to the latter. Legend has it that in the Jin Dynasty, when the writer Yuan Hong (328-376 AD) assumed office, his friend sent him a folding fan saying: "I wish you to apply a policy of benevolence and promote the spirit of justice and virtue." Based on this story, the courtyard was later built. The most attractive building in the courtyard is the Fan Hall, before which the terrace was paved with white marble slabs radiating out like the ribs of a fan. The architecture is magnificent.

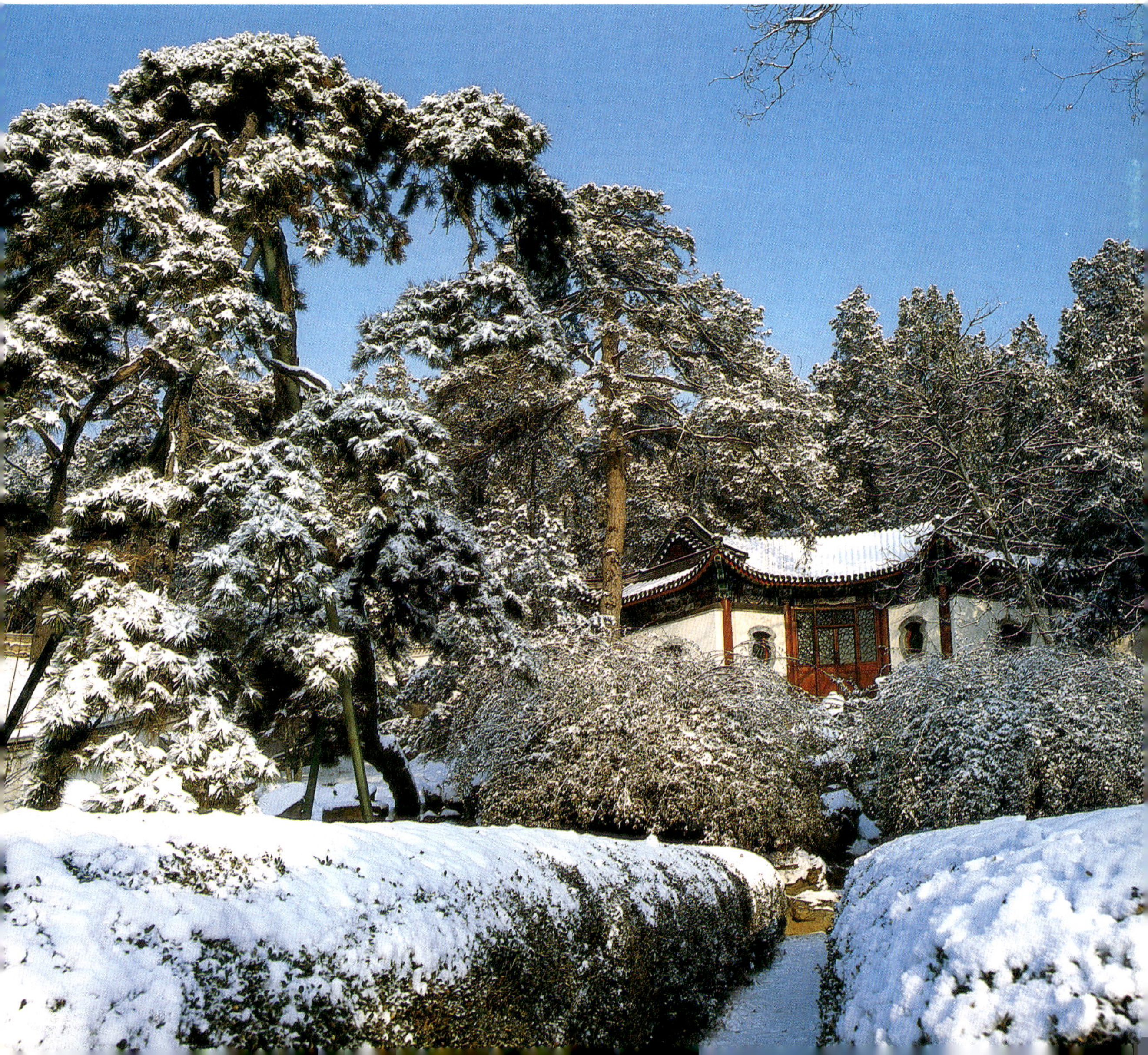

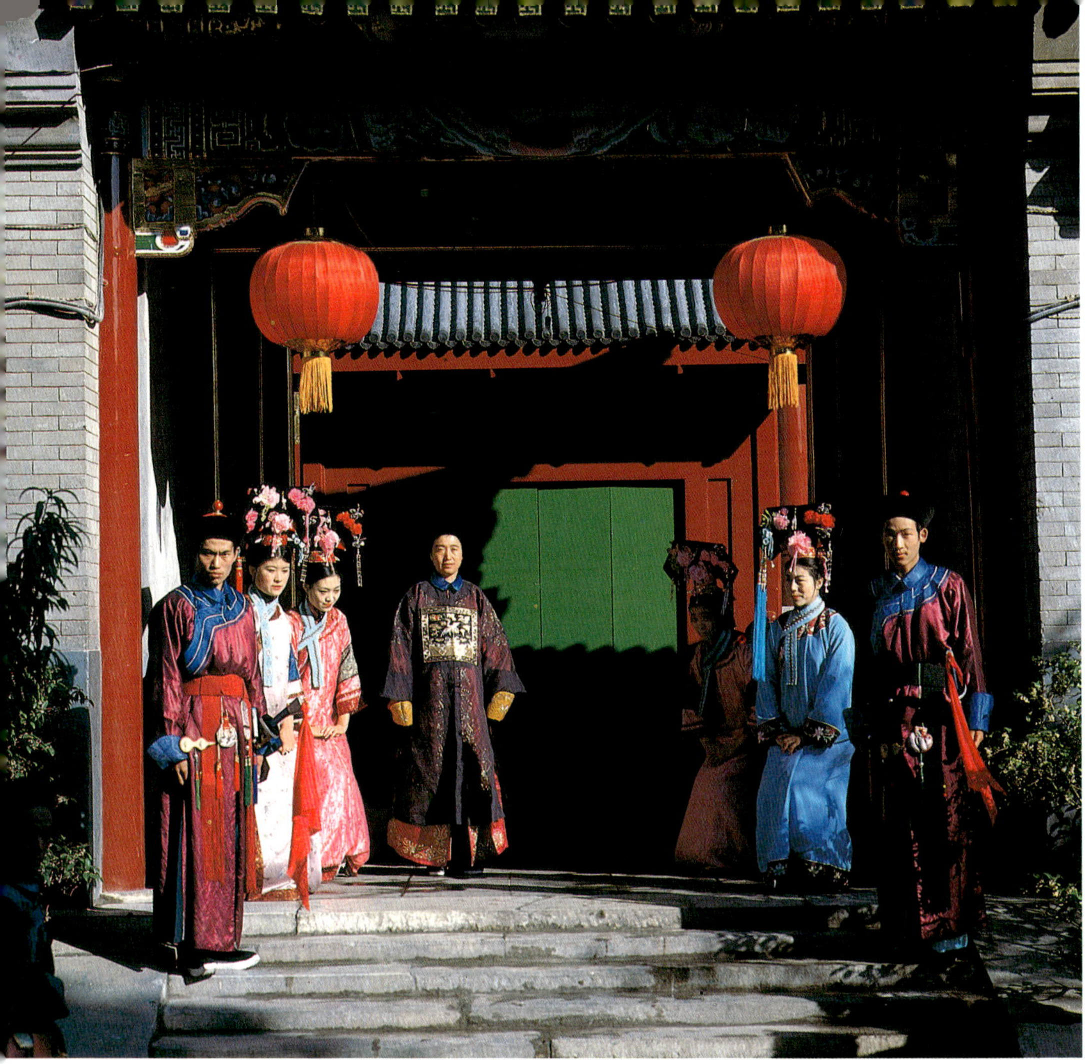

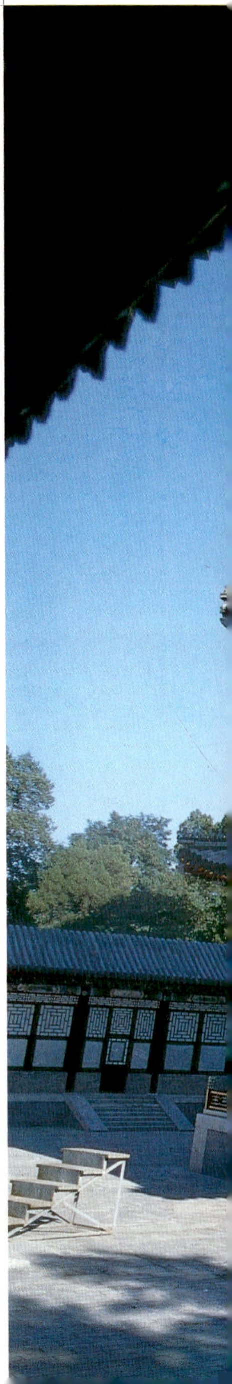

德和園　在仁壽殿西北，宜蕓館東。其主要建築爲大戲樓、頤樂殿和慶善堂。圖爲德和園大門。

Garden of Virtue and Harmony. Lying northwest of the Hall of Benevolence and Longevity and east of the Lodge of the Propriety of Weeding, the garden consists of the Great Stage, the Hall of Health and Happiness, and Qingshan Hall. In the picture is the gate of the Garden of Virtue and Harmony.

大戲樓　始建於一八九一年，一八九五年建成，它與故宮的暢音閣和河北承德避暑山莊的清音閣，同被稱爲清代三大戲樓，但以它爲最大，且建築精美，氣勢宏偉。

The Great Stage. The construction of the stage started in 1891 and was completed in 1895. This stage and the other two — the Studio of Unimpeded Sound in the Forbidden City and the Studio of Clear Sounds in the Summer Villa at Chengde in Hebei — are known as the three great stages of the Qing Dynasty. But this one is the largest of the three.

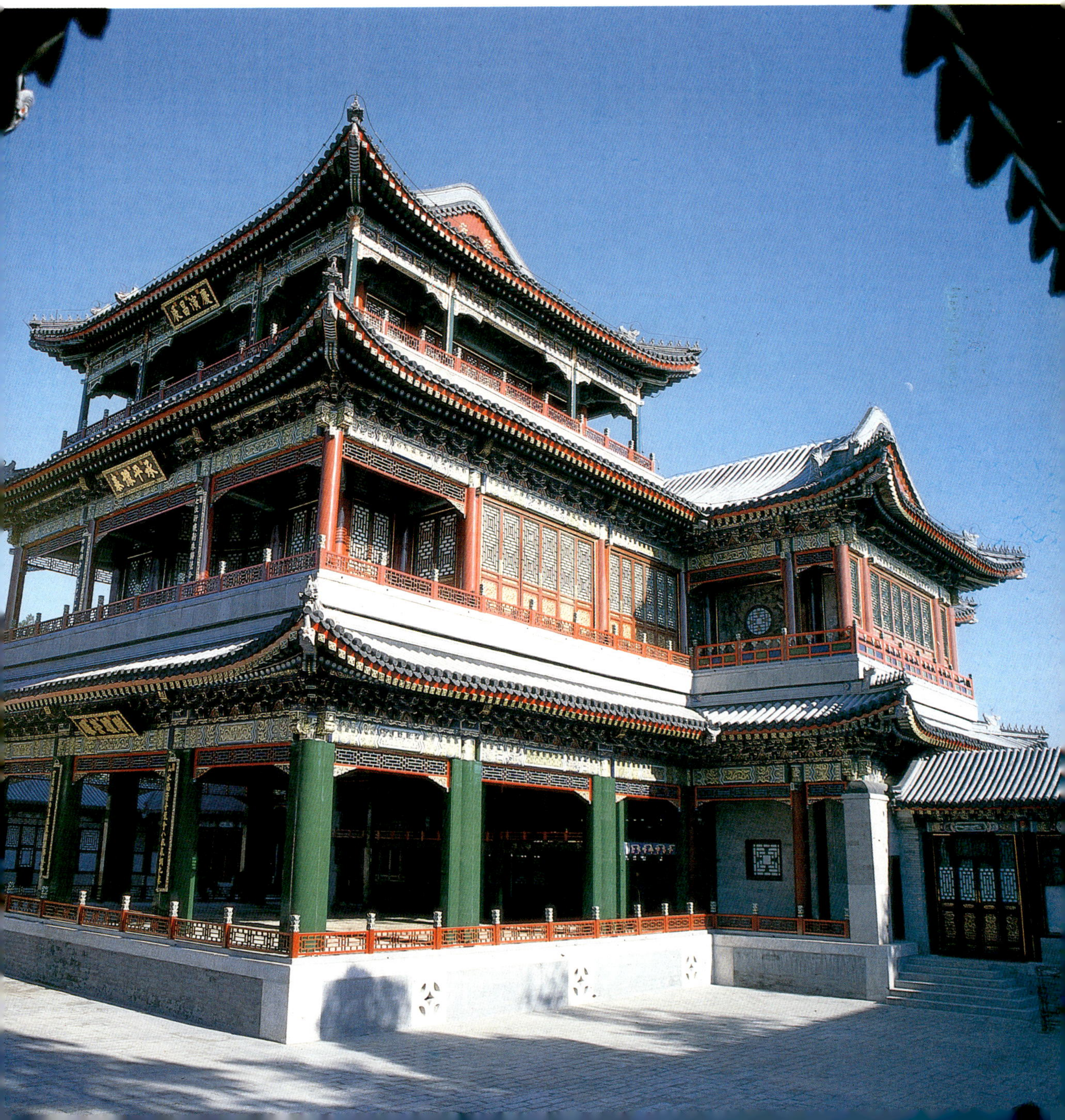

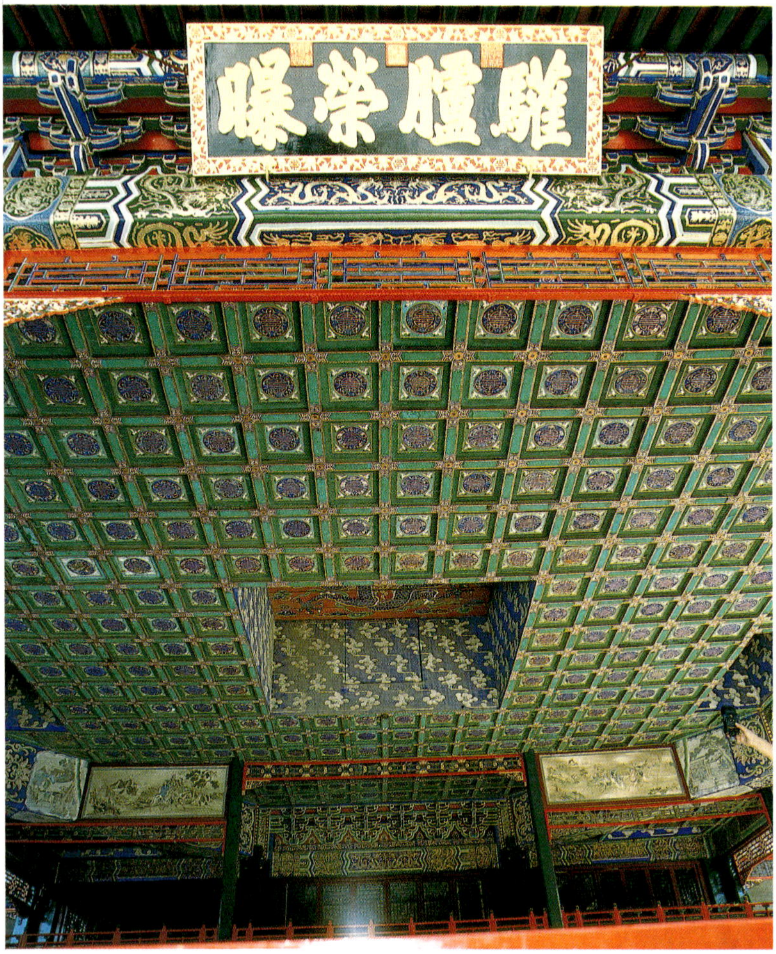

下層戲臺　大戲樓高二十一米，分上中下三層。下層戲臺寬十七米，天花板中心有天井與上層戲臺串通，二層戲臺設有絞車，可巧設機關佈景，上天入地，變幻無窮。戲臺底部還有一眼深井和五方水池，作爲表演時所需的水源。

The stage on the lowest floor. The Great Stage is a three-storeyed structure, 21 metres high and 17 metres wide on the lowest floor. There are chambers above and below it, with trapdoors for "angels" to descend from the "sky" and "devils" to rise up from the "earth". There is also a deep well and five square pools under the stage for water scenes.

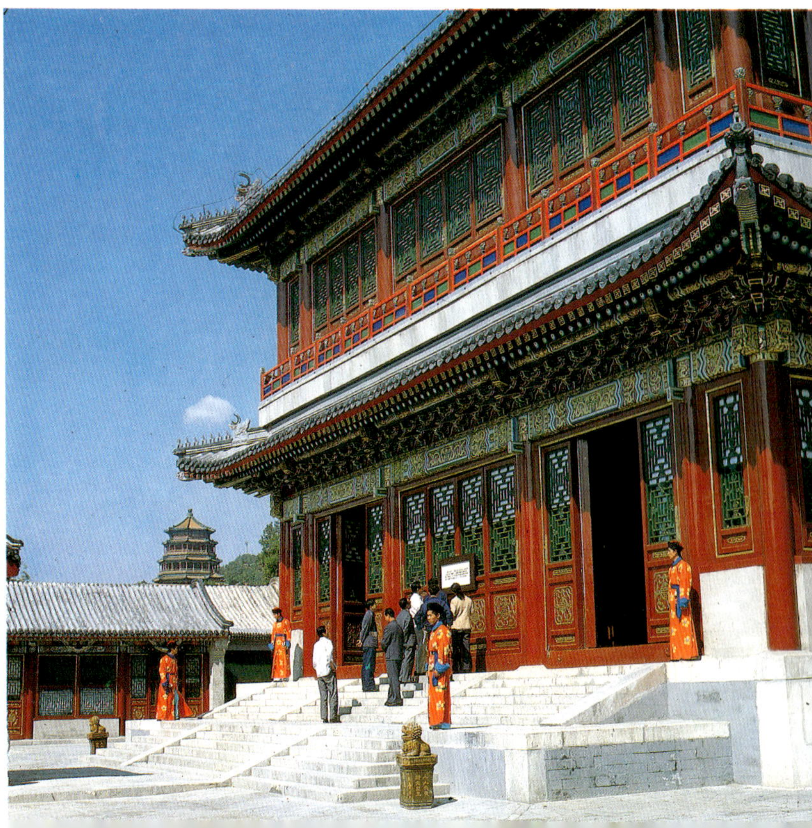

扮戲樓　與舞臺相連，由兩層裝飾華麗的殿堂構成，是演員化妝的地方。

Makeup Tower. Connected with the stage, this magnificent two-storeyed building was the place for performers to make up.

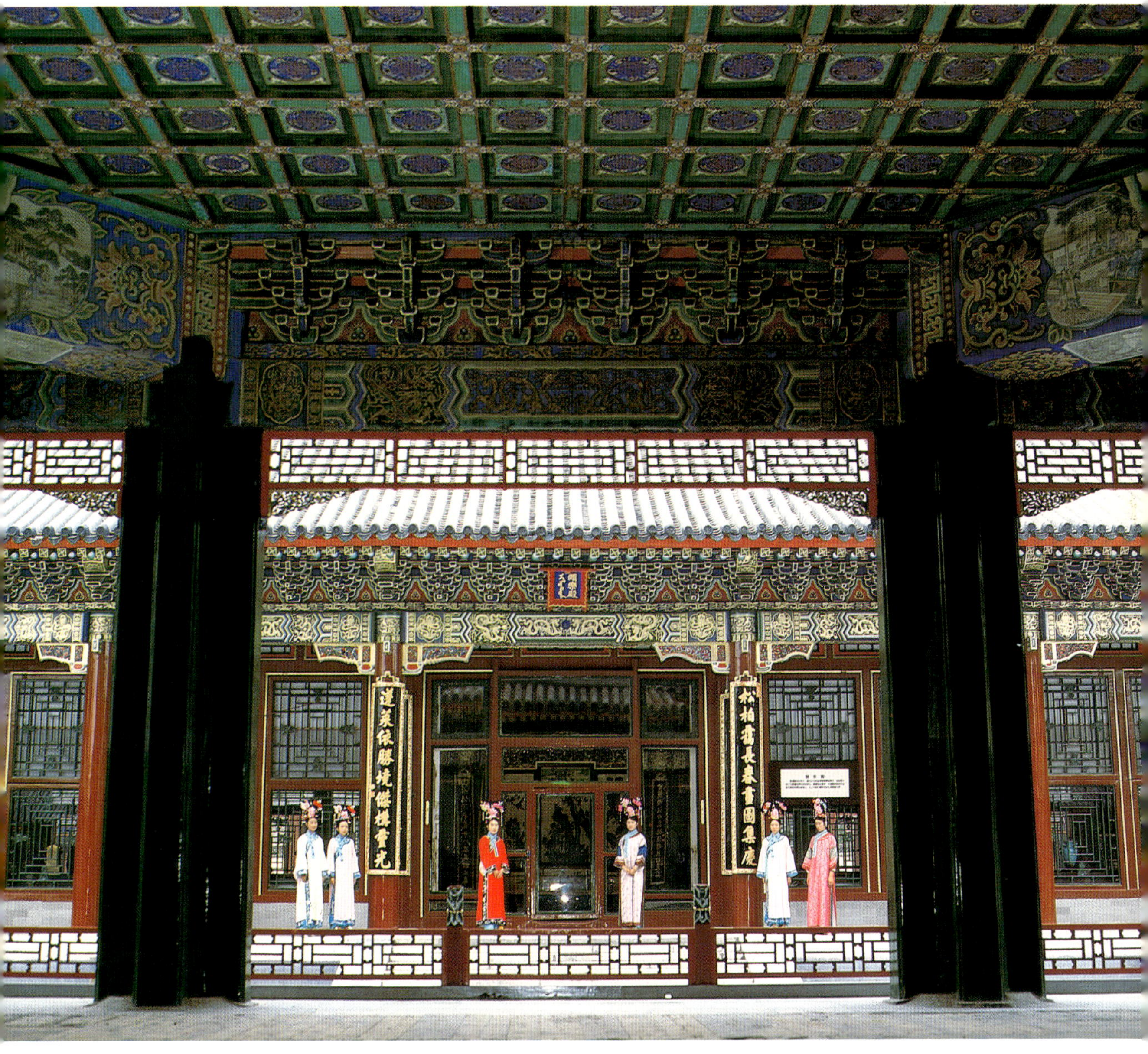

頤樂殿 該殿坐北朝南，與大戲樓剛好相對，相距不足二十米。這是一座專供慈禧太后看戲的大殿，殿内正中設有寶座。

The Hall of Health and Happiness. Facing south, this hall stands opposite to the stage in a distance of less than 20 metres. This was the place where the Empress Dowager enjoyed theatrical performances.

寶座　座後是五折屏風，寶座和屏風係用紅木製作，漆以金地，上貼浮雕的珐琅百鳥朝鳳。這是慈禧太后七十歲生日時製作的，至今璀璨如新，十分富麗。

The throne. In the centre of the hall stands this gold lacquered throne with a design of a hundred birds paying homage to the phoenix. It was specially made for Cixi's seventieth birthday. It is still new and dazzling today.

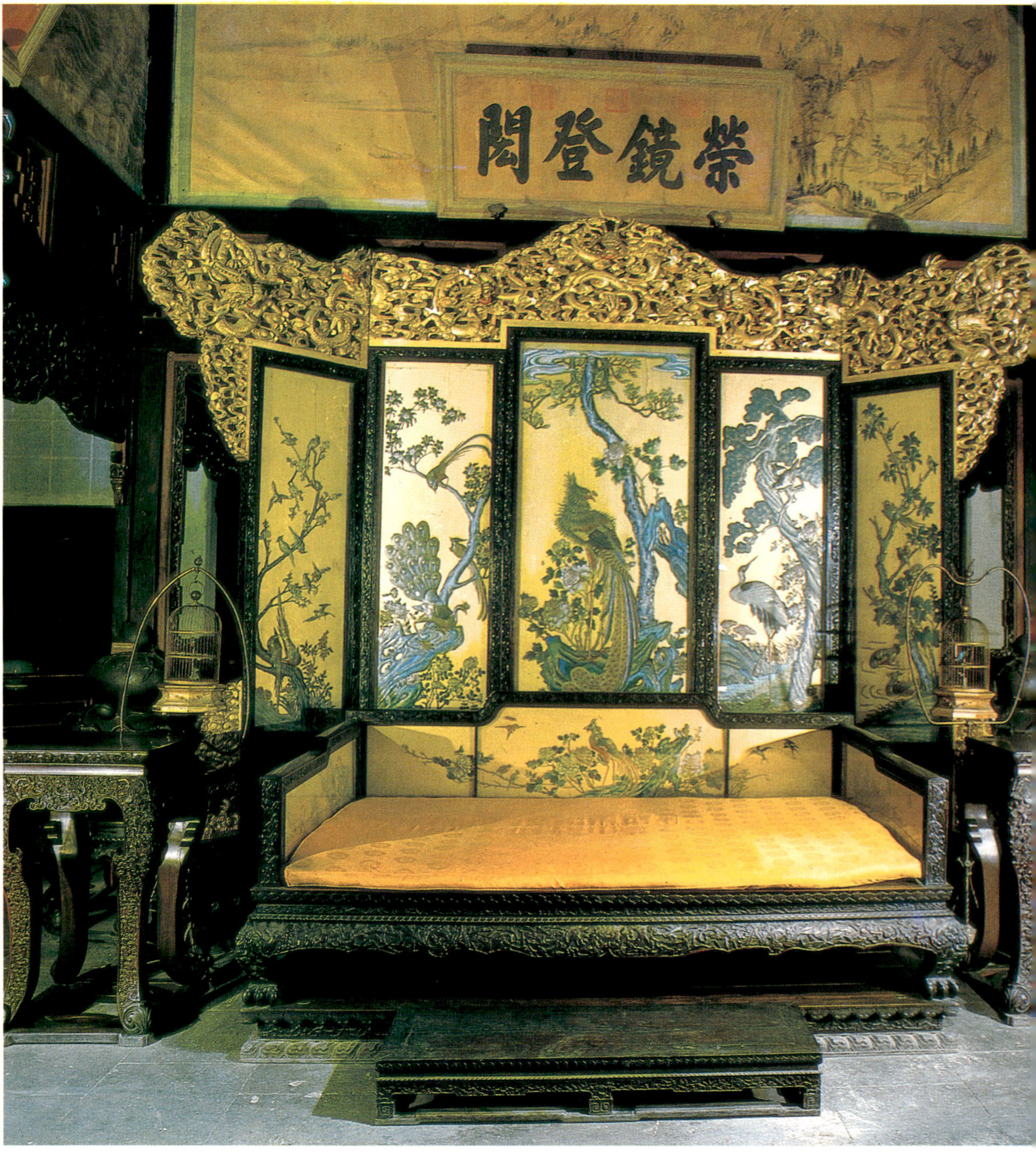

金絲鳥籠 原放置於寶座兩側。籠内小鳥由羽毛粘貼的金屬製成。開動機關，小鳥便會摇頭擺尾地鳴叫。據説，這對鳥籠是外國送給慈禧太后的禮品。

Gold-thread bird cages. These two bird cages were put on either side of the throne. The clockwork birds made of feather and metal can dip their heads and tails and sing. It was said they were a tribute paid to Cixi by a foreign country.

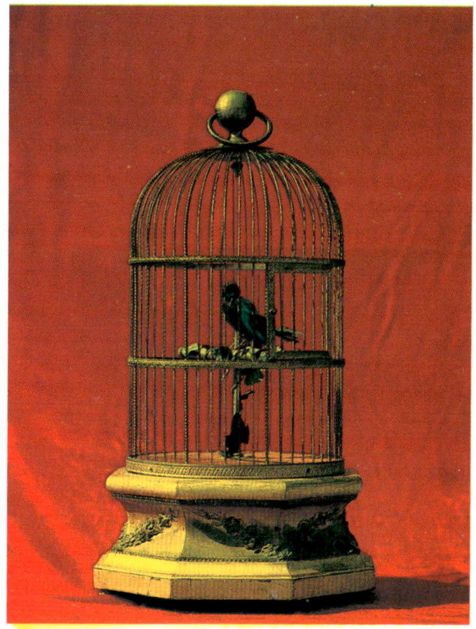

慈禧太后蠟像 據故老相傳，慈禧太后看戲並不一定坐寶座，有時坐在正殿東西兩次間的炕床上隔窗觀看（如圖）。光緒皇帝則坐在殿外廊檐下東窗臺處，而被賞看戲的王公大臣們則按事先排定的次序，分坐在頤樂殿兩側的看戲廊裏。

Waxwork of the Empress Dowager. It was said the Empress Dowager sometimes didn't sit in the throne to watch the performances but sat in bed in the wing halls to watch from the window (see the picture). Emperor Guangxu sat out on the front porch to the left of the entrance, while princes, dukes, ministers and other high officials sat along the east and west verandas on the sides.

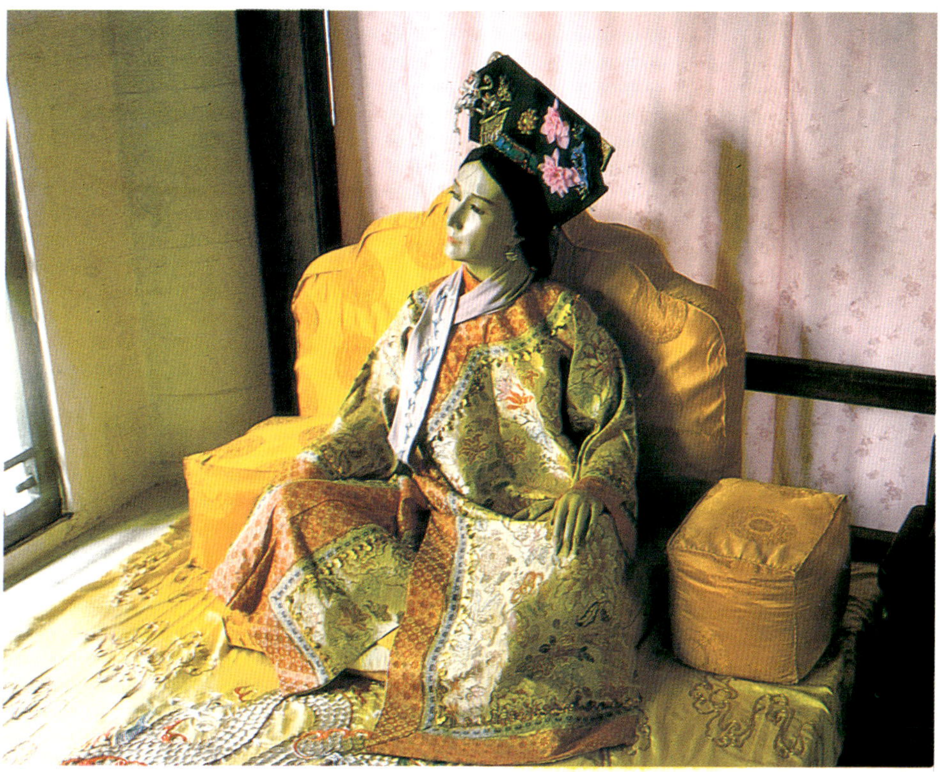

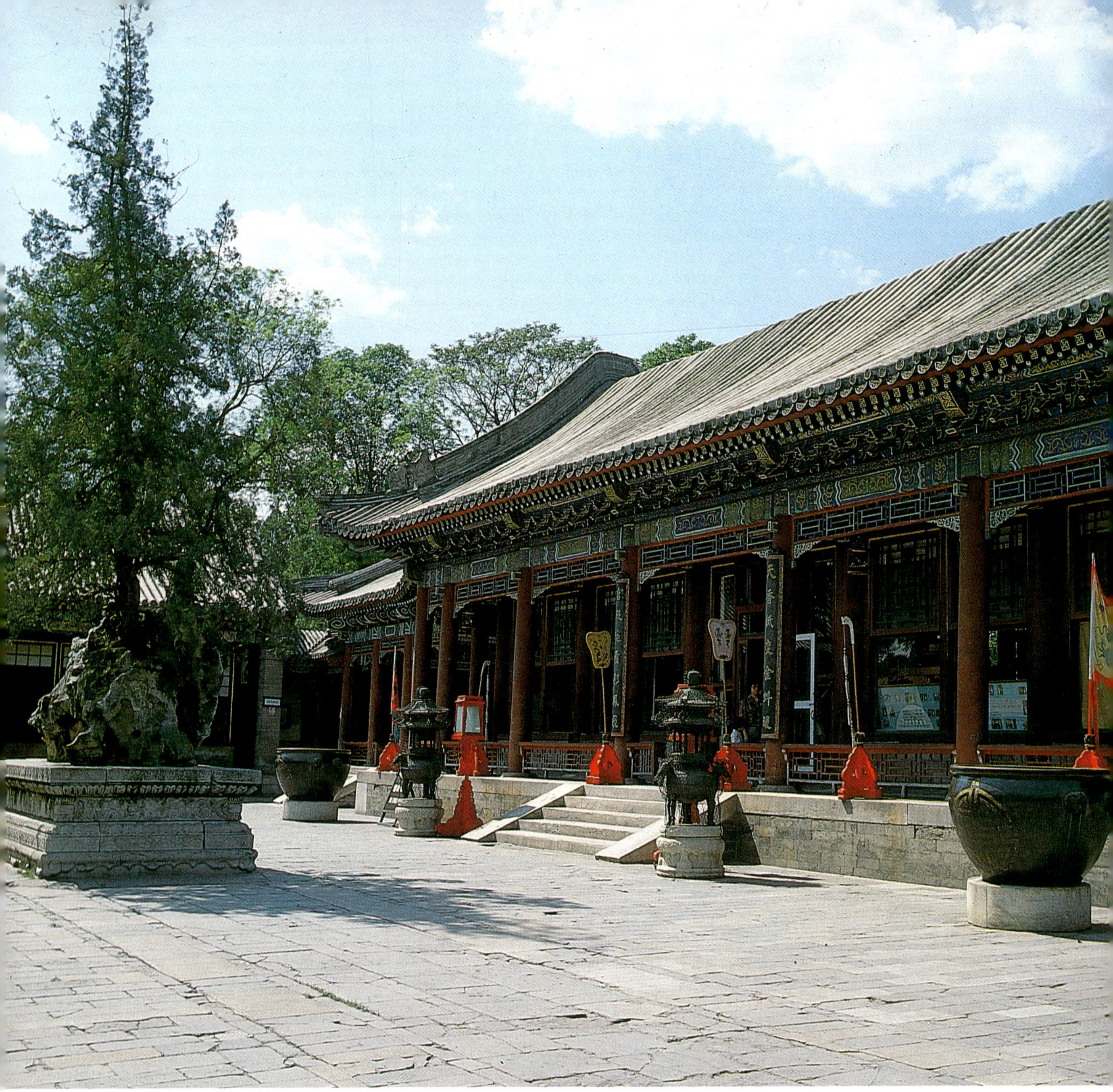

慶善堂 在頤樂殿北還有一重院落，院内面闊五間的正殿叫慶善堂。其左右各有一座配殿。慶善堂是慈禧太后看戲時臨時休息的殿堂。殿的西暖閣曾作過畫室，有一幅“傳神秋毫”的肖像最爲她喜歡，曾被送往美國展出，至今仍在美國華盛頓博物館。

Qingshan Hall. On the north of the Hall of Health and Happiness there is a compound, the main hall of which is called Qingshan Hall, the resting place of Cixi when she came to see performances. The west side-chamber was once used as a studio. There was a gorgeous portrait Cixi liked best. She ordered it sent to the United States as an entry to an art contest. Now the portrait is still housed in the Washington Museum.

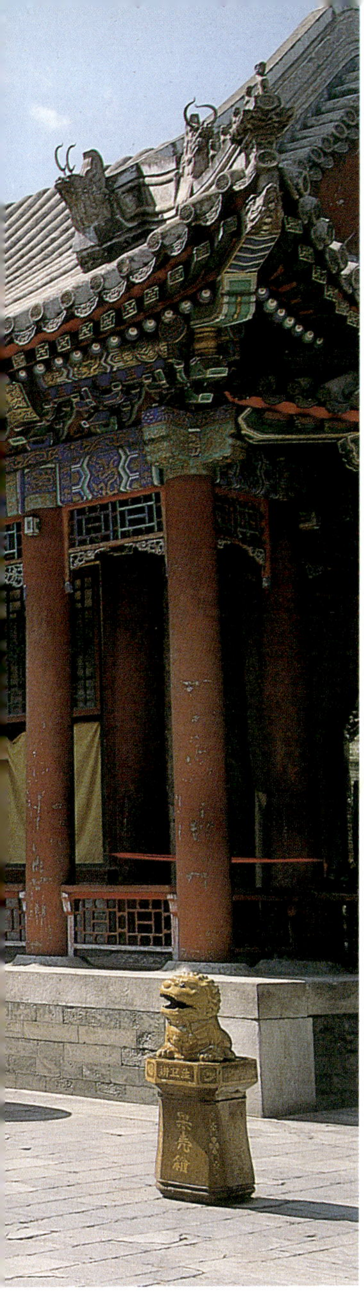

西暖閣畫室 端坐者爲慈禧太后模擬像。

The west side-chamber studio. Sitting in the chair is Empress Dowager Cixi.

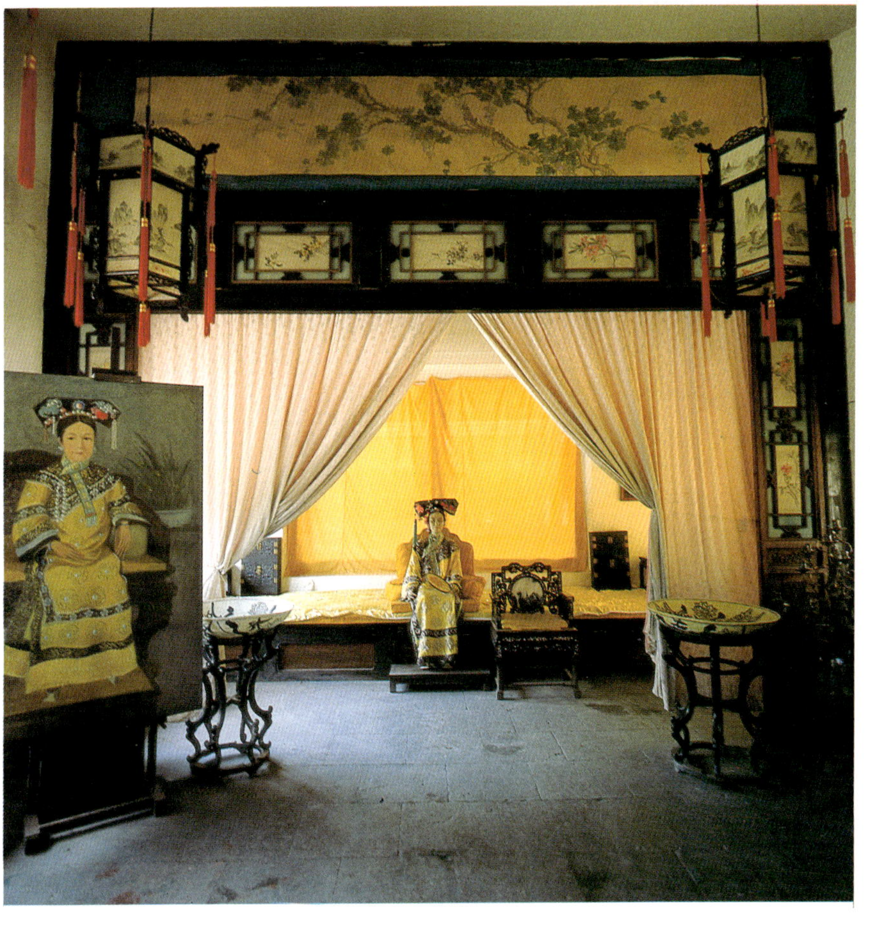

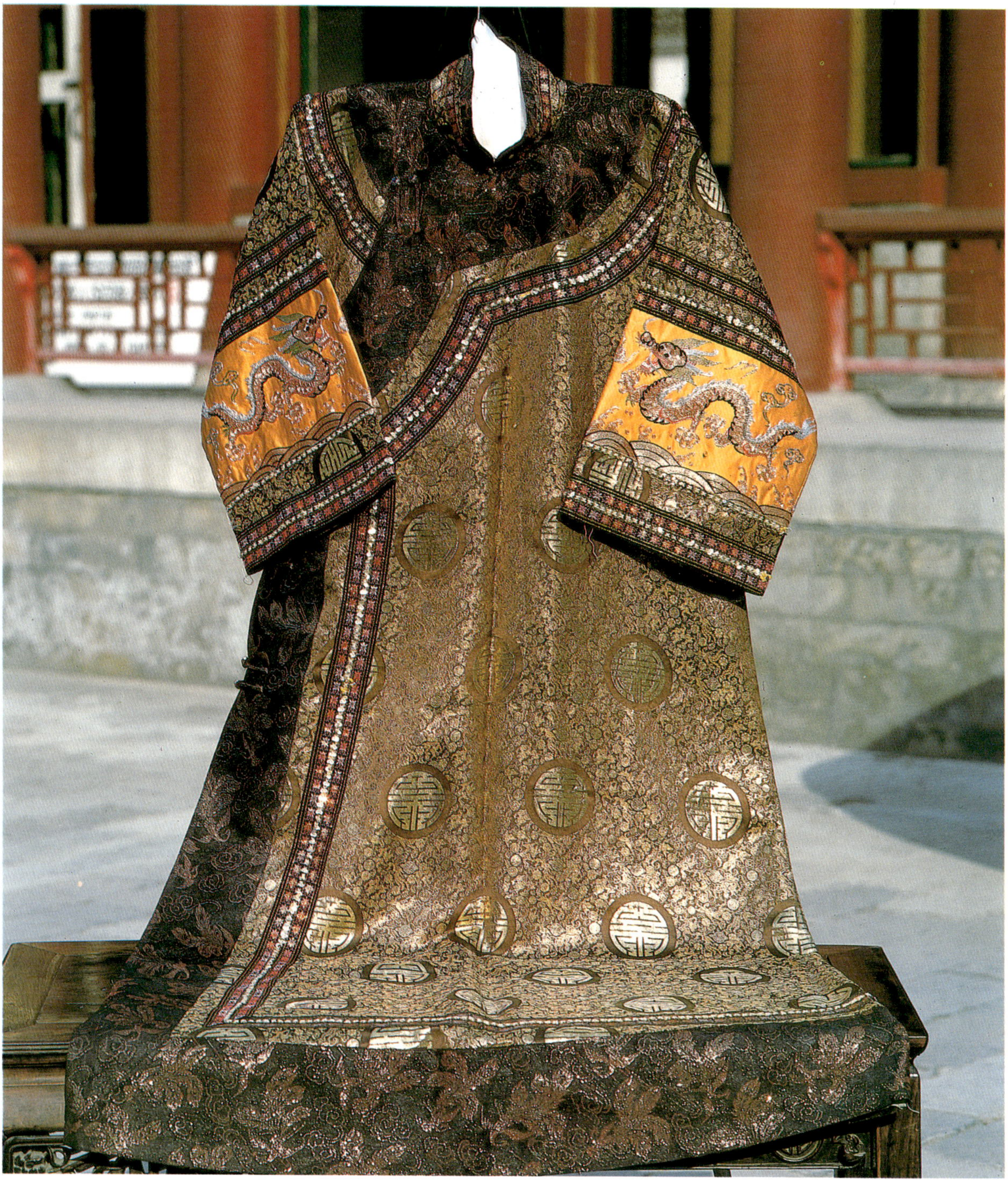

慈禧太后龍衣　用金絲綫在衣上繡滿龍、鳳、雲和壽字圖案，極爲華貴。據説，慈禧太后僅存放在頤和園的服飾和珍寶古玩竟有三千多箱，其中一幅披肩是用三千五百顆“大如黄鳥之卵”的珍珠串連編織而成的。現有部分服飾和珍寶陳列於德和園展室。

Empress Dowager Cixi's clothes. These clothes were embroidered in the pattern of dragon, phoenix and cloud in gold thread. It was said Cixi had more than 3,000 trunks of clothes, jewellery and rare curios in the Summer Palace. One of her shawls was made of 3,500 pearls, each the size of bird eggs. Some of her clothes and jewellery are displayed at the exhibition in the Garden of Virtue and Harmony.

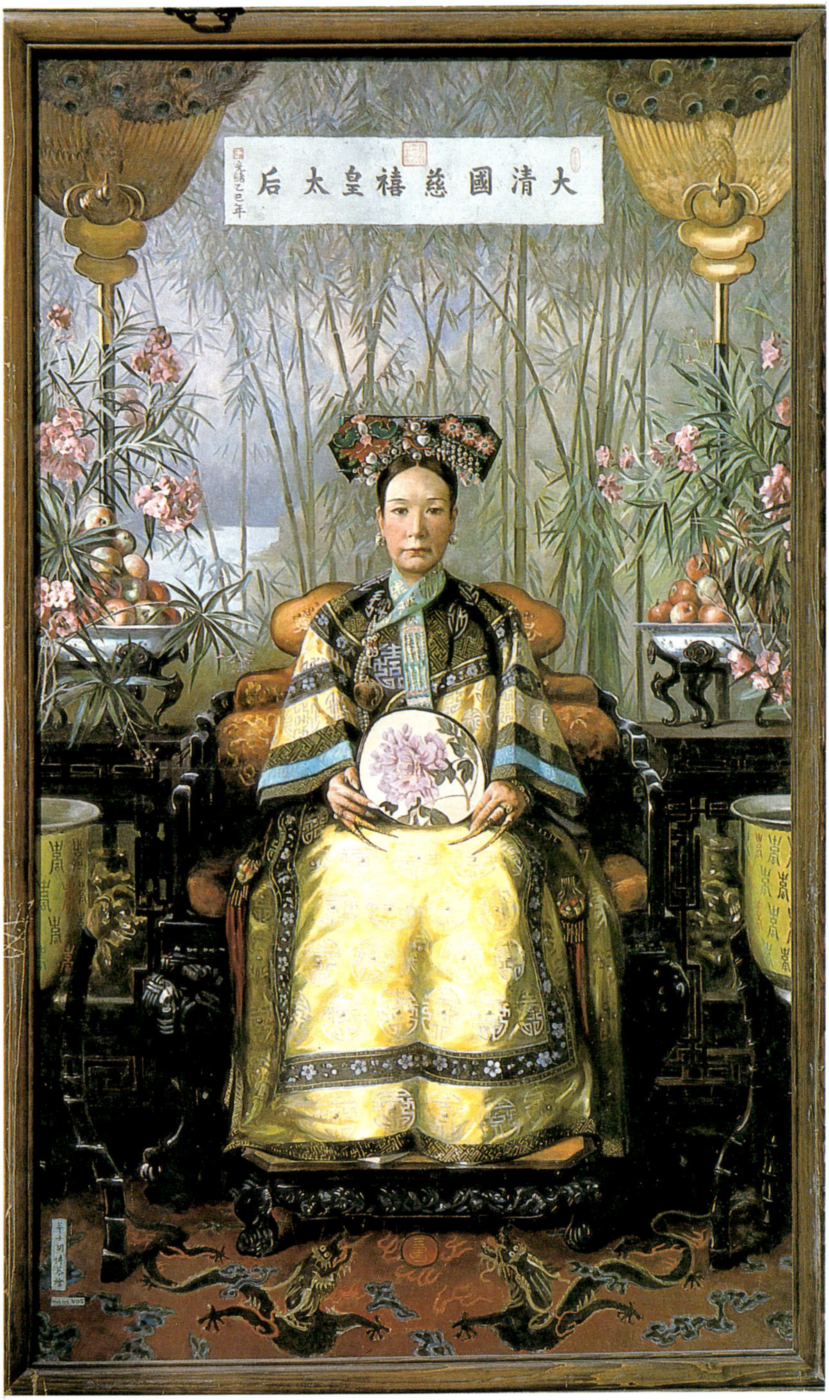

慈禧太后畫像 一九〇五年，荷蘭畫家華士·胡博(Hubert VOS)應聘爲慈禧太后畫像。那時的慈禧太后年已七旬，但畫像却顯得年輕，這顯然是畫家爲了討其歡心而故意這樣畫的。

Portrait of the Empress Dowager. In 1905, in her seventies, Cixi asked the Dutch artist Hubert Vos to do portraits of her. The artist painted her as a young woman in order to flatter her.

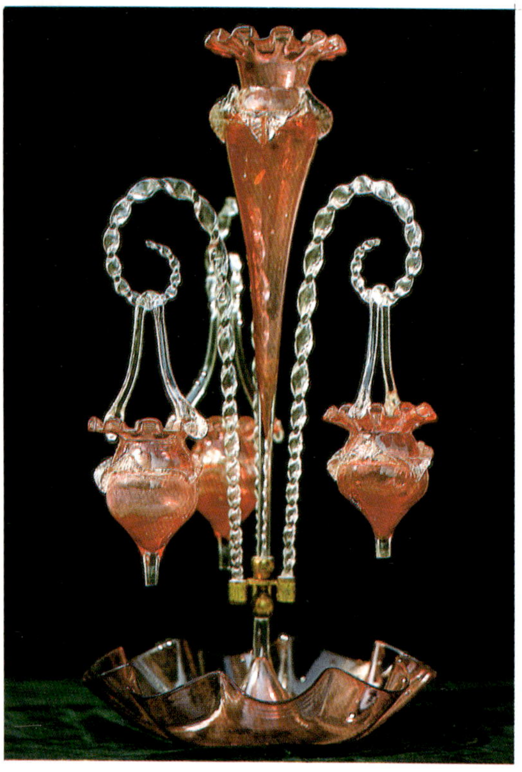

玻璃花籃 遠看紅白相間，近看呈淺紅色，典雅富麗，是外國送給慈禧太后的禮品，現陳列於展室。

Glass flower basket. This glass flower basket looks white and red when viewed from a distance but is pink when closely viewed.

遊客留影 遊覽德和園，遊客可與慈 禧太后蠟像合影，亦可着清代服裝留影。

When visitors come to the Garden of Virtue and Harmony, they would like to have a photo taken either with the waxwork of the Empress Dowager or in the Qing-Dynasty dress.

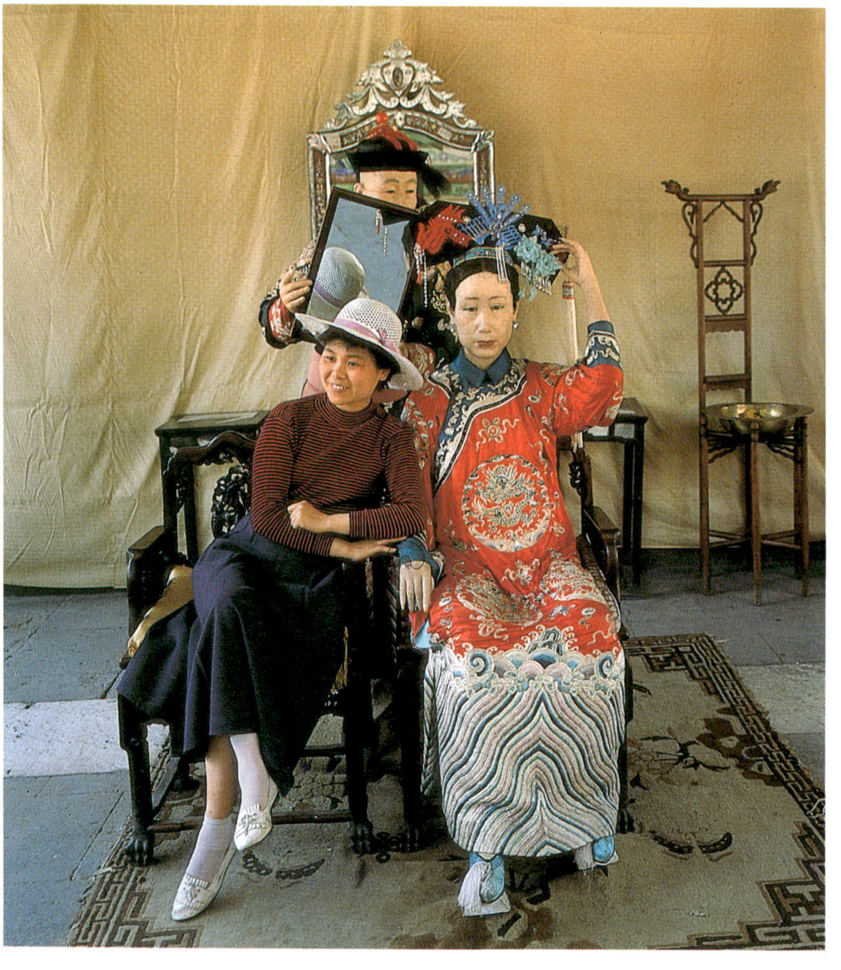

前山前湖景區

這一景區包括萬壽山前山和昆明湖，其面積約佔頤和園總面積的百分之九十。萬壽山前山景區由長廊、排雲殿、佛香閣以及分列於它們兩側的主要建築羣和重點建築物構成；昆明湖景區由西堤、南湖島以及堤和島上的主要點景建築構成。

建園匠師們巧妙利用前山的地勢和山形特點與建築佈局相結合，依山順勢，使那些建築羣體錯落有致，於嚴整中寓變化。在廣闊的昆明湖水面上修堤築島，並結合自然環境，又在堤上建有風格各異的數座橋亭。島上建築更是多種多樣，既有華麗的涵虛堂，又有肅穆的龍王廟。這種人工美與自然美的巧妙融合，達到了"雖由人造，宛自天成"的境界。極目眺望，景區內充滿詩情畫意，給人以鬼斧神工的藝術享受。

The Southern Slope and Lake Area

THIS scenic area includes the southern slopes of Longevity Hill and Kunming Lake, about ninety percent of the total area of the Summer Palace. The southern slopes consist of the Long Promenade, the Hall That Dispels the Clouds, the Tower of the Fragrance of Buddha, and the other towers and halls on both sides, while the lake area is formed by the West Dyke, the South lake Island and the buildings on it.

In an ingenious way the architects adapted the buildings to blend in with or accentuate the natural surroundings, making them a harmonious whole. The broad expanse of Kunming Lake is embellished with an island, a long causeway and several exquisitely built bridges. On the island are various buildings, among which the Hall of Forbearance and Humbleness and the Dragon King's Temple are most famous. The natural beauty is set off by a multitude of highly decorative halls, towers, galleries, pavilions and bridges; it is a poetic picture.

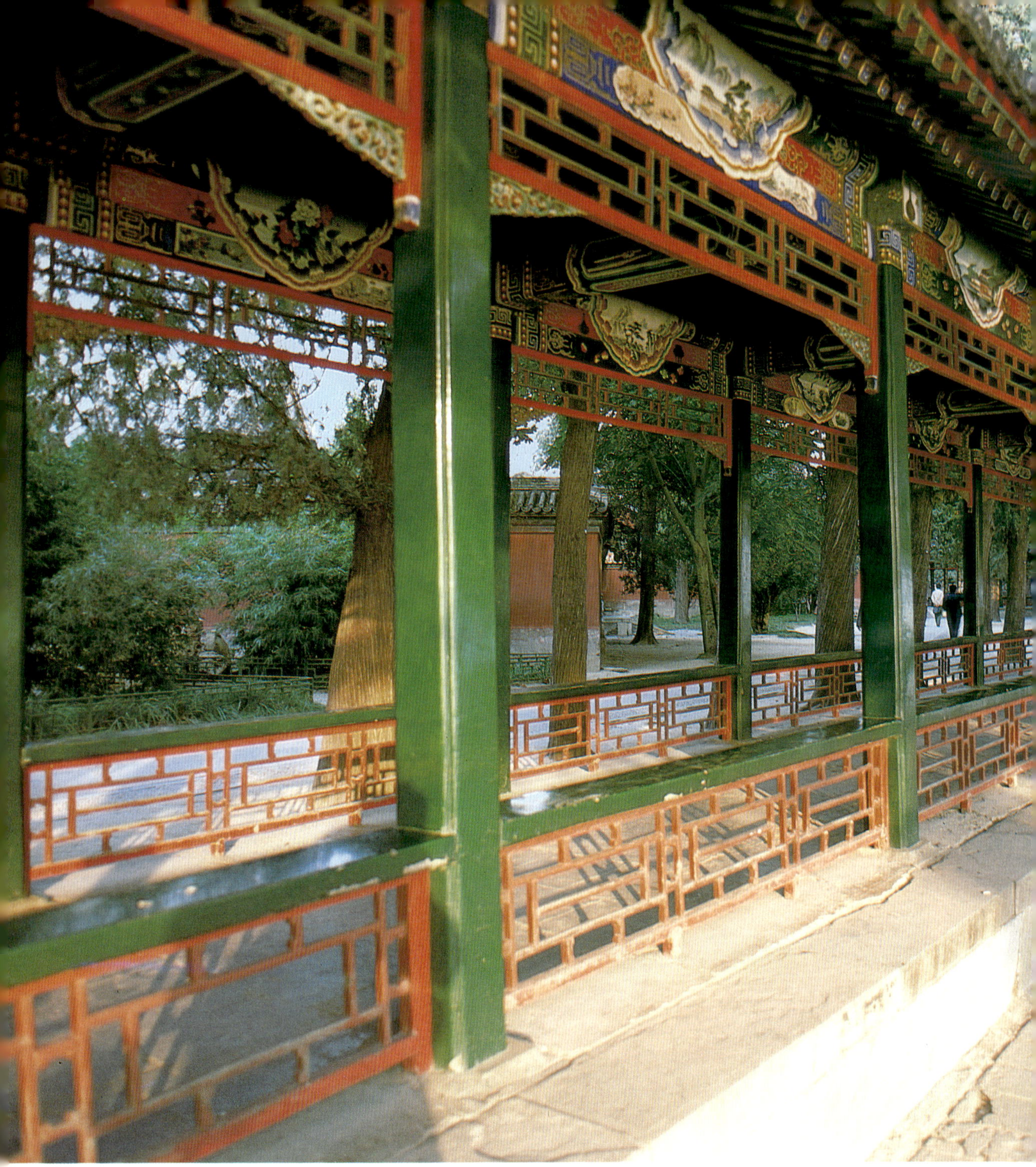

長廊　廊是組織園林景觀、分隔園林空間、聯絡點景建築和建築羣的一種帶屋頂的走廊，其形式多種多樣，最常見的是兩面透空的遊廊。中國的廊建築中，最大、最長、最負盛名的就是頤和園的長廊。

The Long Promenade. A promenade is a long covered corridor, which is used to accentuate a scenic spot, to separate different scenes, or to connect buildings in a garden. They vary in style and shape. The most popular one has two open sides. The promenade in the Summer Palace is the biggest and most famous one in China.

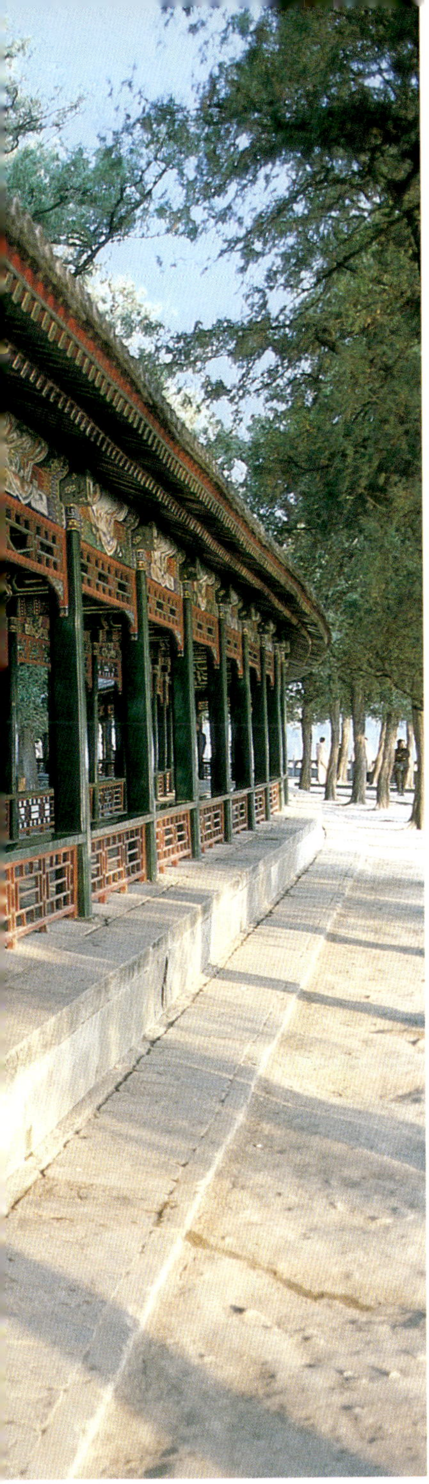

邀月門　長廊東起邀月門，西止石丈亭，中以排雲門分爲東西兩段，每段各伸出一截短廊連接對鷗舫和魚藻軒兩座臨水建築，全長七百五十多米，二百七十三間畫廊。

The Invite-the-Moon Gate. The Long Promenade begins at the Invite-the-Moon Gate in the east and ends at Ten-Foot Stone Pavilion and is divided into two symmetrical sections by the Gate That Dispels the Clouds. There are four large double-eaved octagonal pavilions along it. The 750-metre long promenade is divided into 273 sectors.

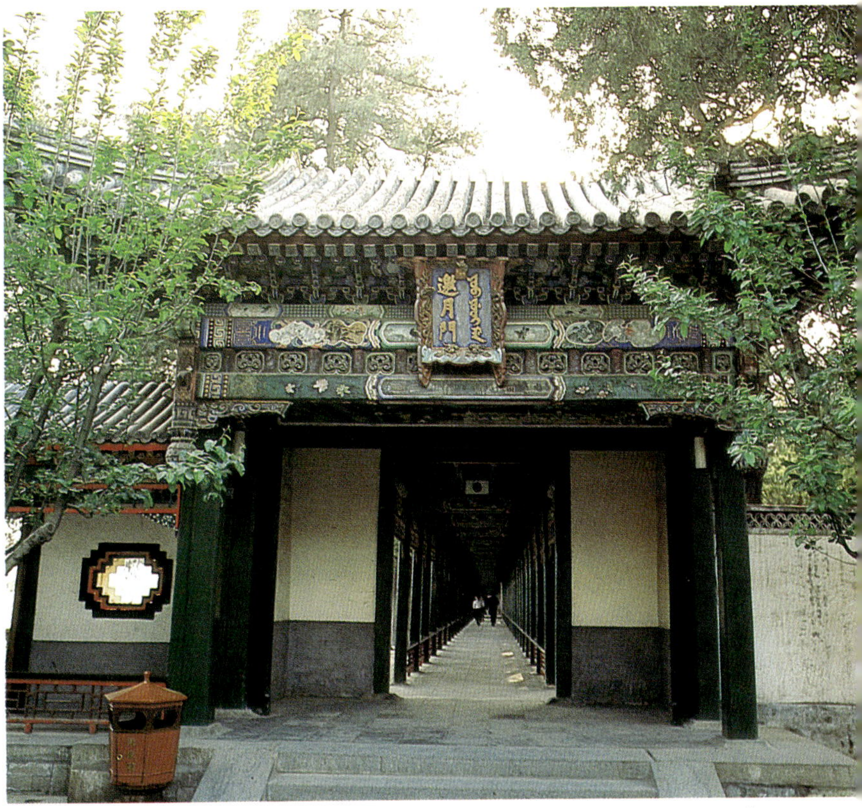

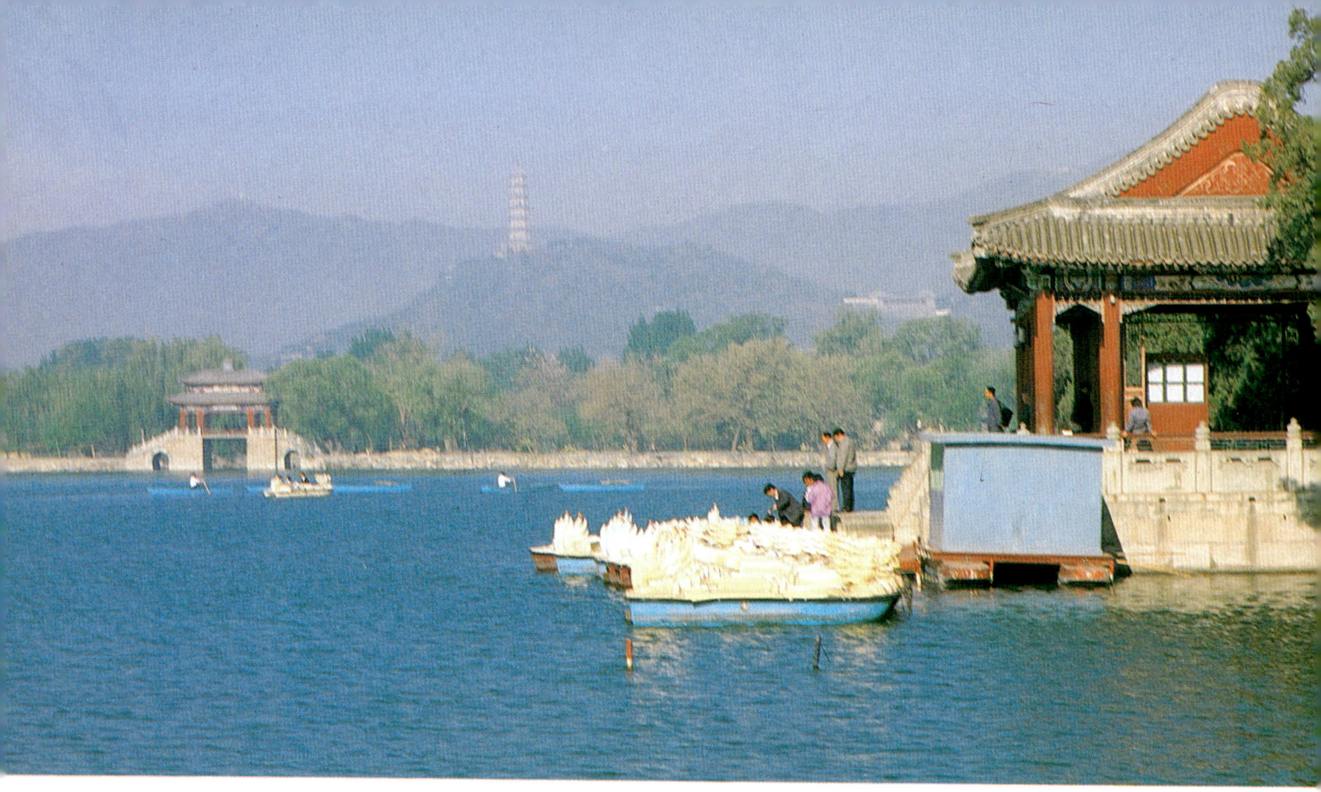

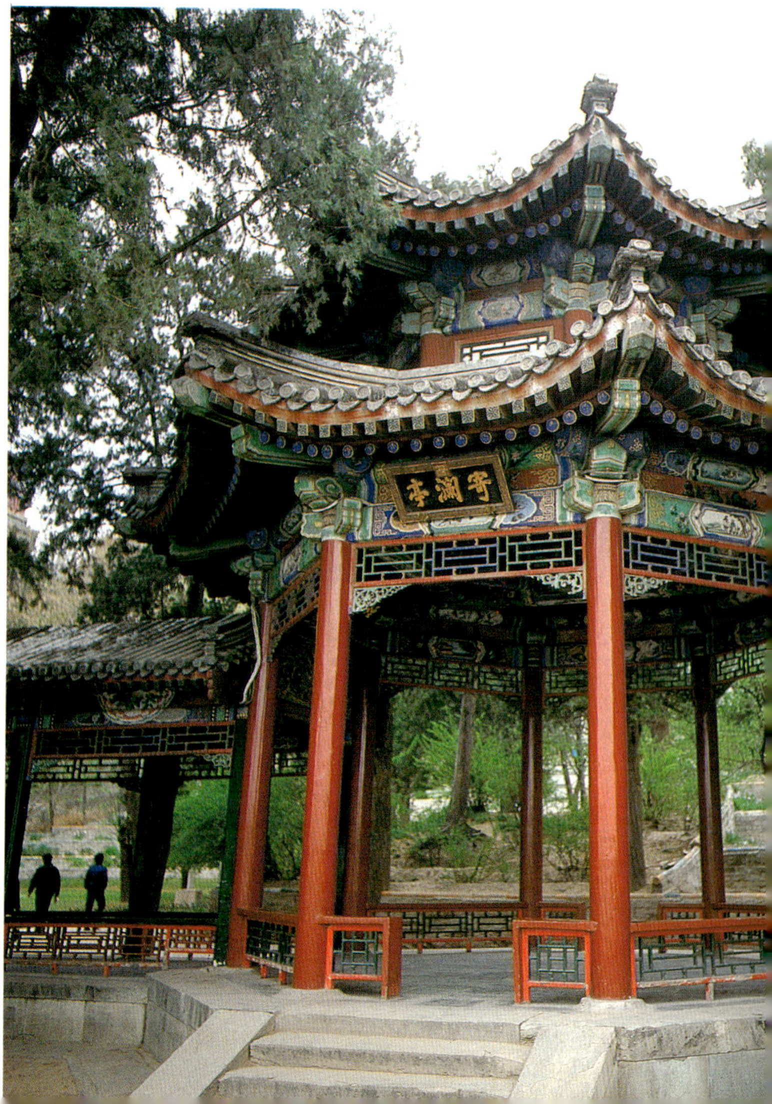

寄瀾亭 長廊共串連了“留佳”、“寄瀾”、“秋水”、“清遥”四座八角重檐亭，分別象徵春夏秋冬四季。亭不僅壯景，還起着支撑長廊的作用。

The Jilan Pavilion. The Long Promenade has four large double-eaved octagonal pavilions, namely the Liujia Pavilion (Retain the Good), the Jilan Pavilion (Living with the Ripples), the Qiushui Pavilion (Autumn Water) and the Qingyao Pavilion (Clear and Far), which symbolize the four seasons. These beautiful pavilions act as supports for the Long Promenade.

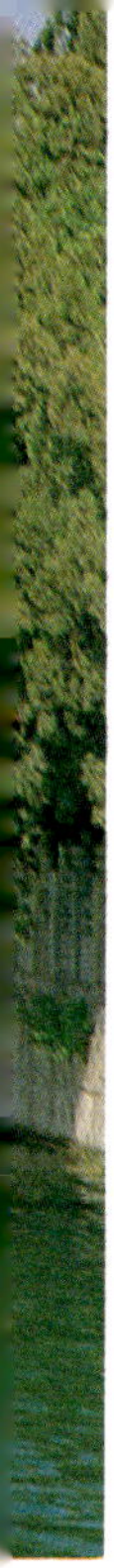

魚藻軒 位於長廊西段。名爲軒實爲榭，面湖而立。這裏有魚有藻，名副其實。

The Yuzao Pavilion. In the west section of the Long Promenade, the Yuzao Pavilion (Pavilion with Fish and Algae) faces the lake. There are really fish and algae here.

亭内藻井 藻井是中國木構架建築的常用手法，以樑枋桷椽叠架而成，由下上仰成“井”字形，故名藻井。

Caisson ceiling. This is a feature of ancient Chinese architecture.

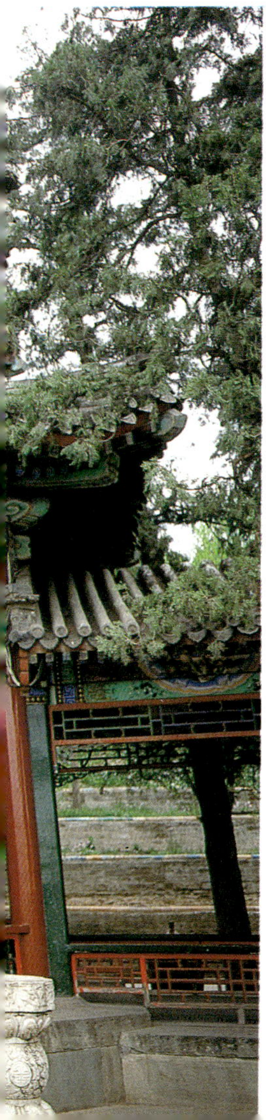

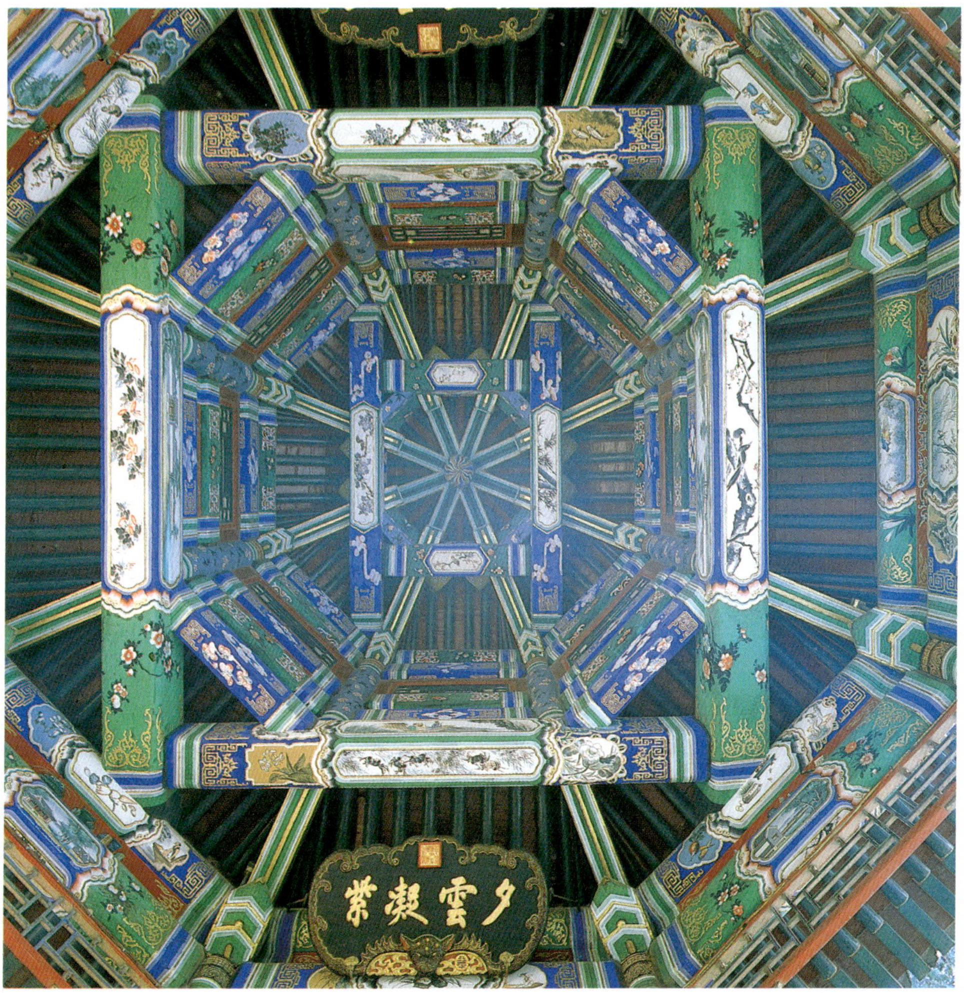

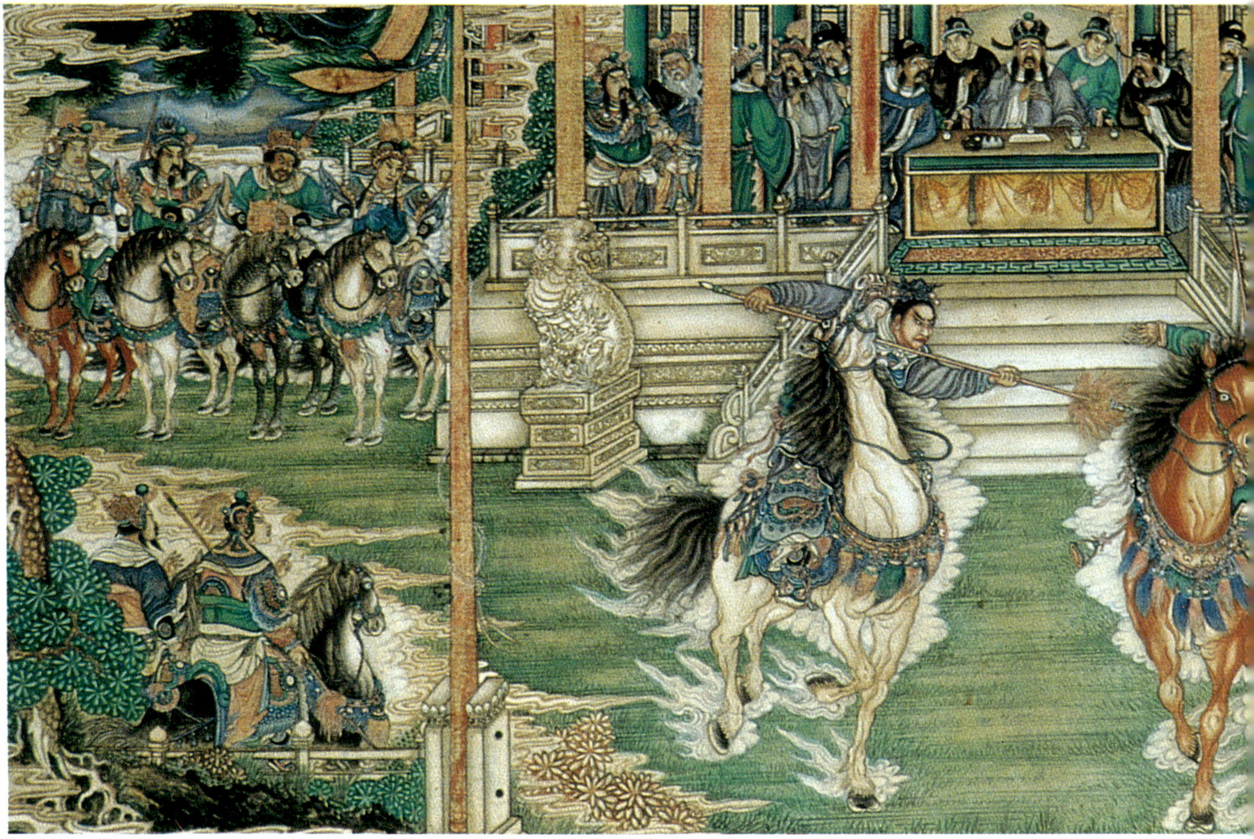

長廊彩畫 彩畫題材十分廣泛，有花鳥、樹石、山水、人物等。十八世紀中葉，乾隆皇帝曾派宮廷畫師到杭州西湖寫生，得西湖景五百四十六幅。這些湖景被悉數移繪到長廊二百七十三間畫廊的樑枋上。本世紀六十年代，中國政府不僅保留了西湖風景畫，還增繪了具有民族特色的彩畫一萬四千多幅，使長廊成爲名副其實的畫廊。圖爲中國古典小說《説岳全傳》中岳飛槍挑小梁王的故事。

Coloured designs. The paintings in the Long Promenade cover a wide range of subjects from birds, flowers, trees, mountains, rivers, and human figures. In the middle of the 18th century, Emperor Qianlong sent his court painters to do paintings of the West Lake in Hangzhou. They painted 546 different paintings and copied them on to the beams and pillars in the 273 sectors in the Long Promenade. In the 1960s, while keeping the original paintings of the West Lake, the Chinese government added 14,000 new paintings to the Long Promenade, making it a real art gallery.

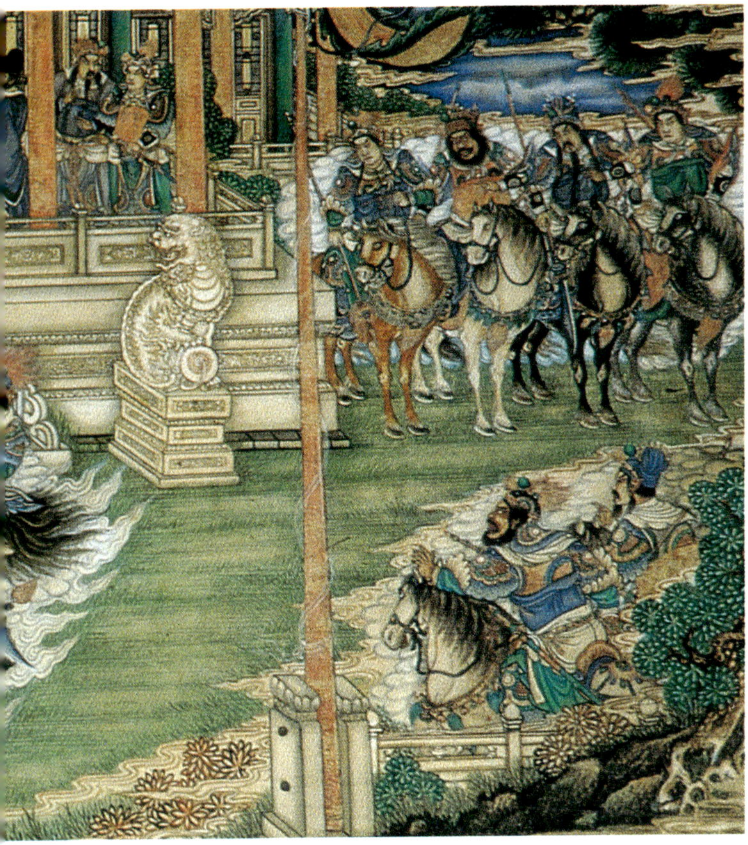

長廊山水畫 長廊的彩畫以中國傳統的工筆見長，筆觸工整、細膩。多數畫面被圈在大半圓的括綫内，稱爲“包袱”，分佈在凹凸不平的構件上，但給人的感覺却是平整而規則的。

Landscape painting. Most of the paintings in the Long Promenade are traditional pieces in meticulous brushwork. Painted in a semi-circle, they give a strong three-dimensional effect.

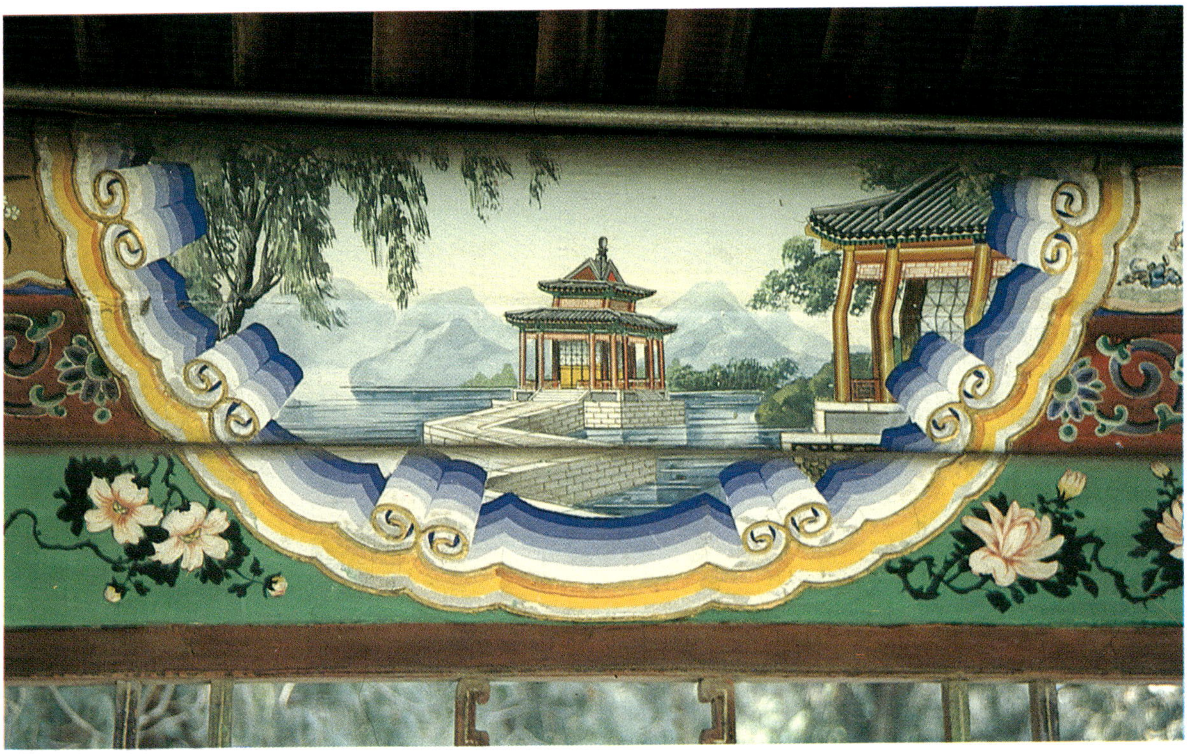

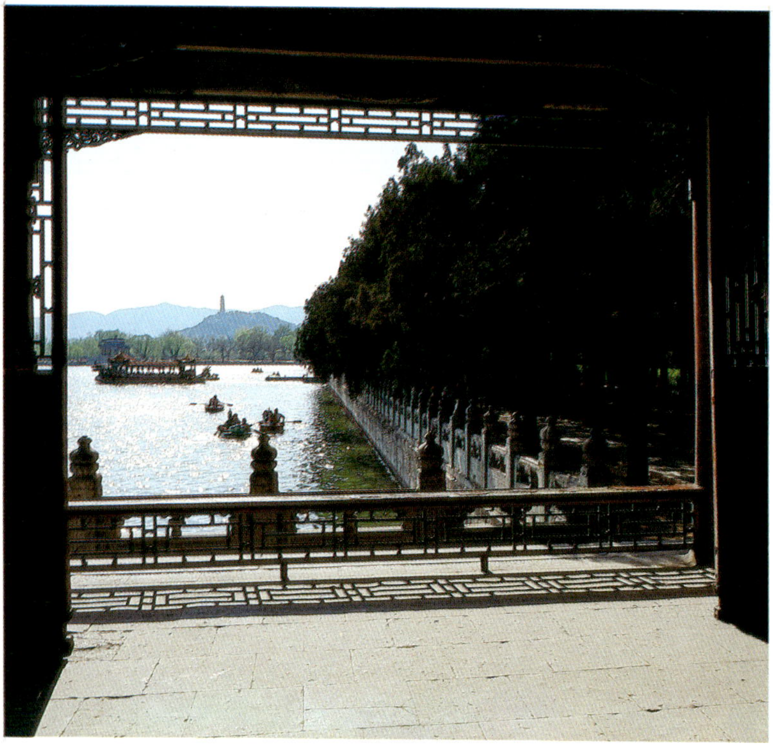

長廊觀景 從邀月門西行，向南可觀湖景，向北可覽山色。無論陰晴雨雪，均可在廊内遊憩賞景。圖爲從魚藻軒西眺。

Viewing from the Long Promenade. Starting from the Invite-the-Moon Gate, visitors walk westward along the promenade enjoying the scenery of the lake and the hill on the southern and northern sides. This can take place at any time rain or shine.

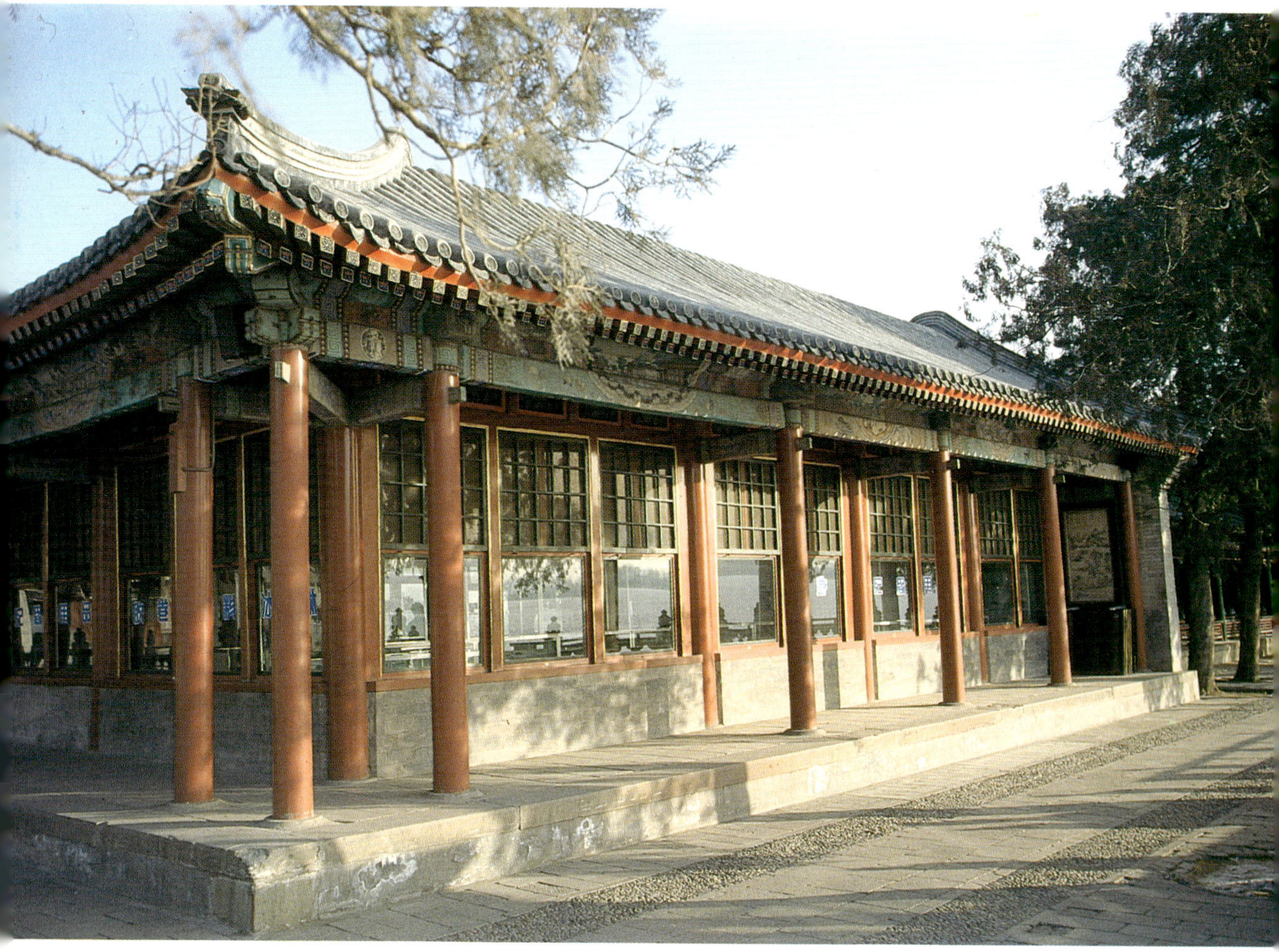

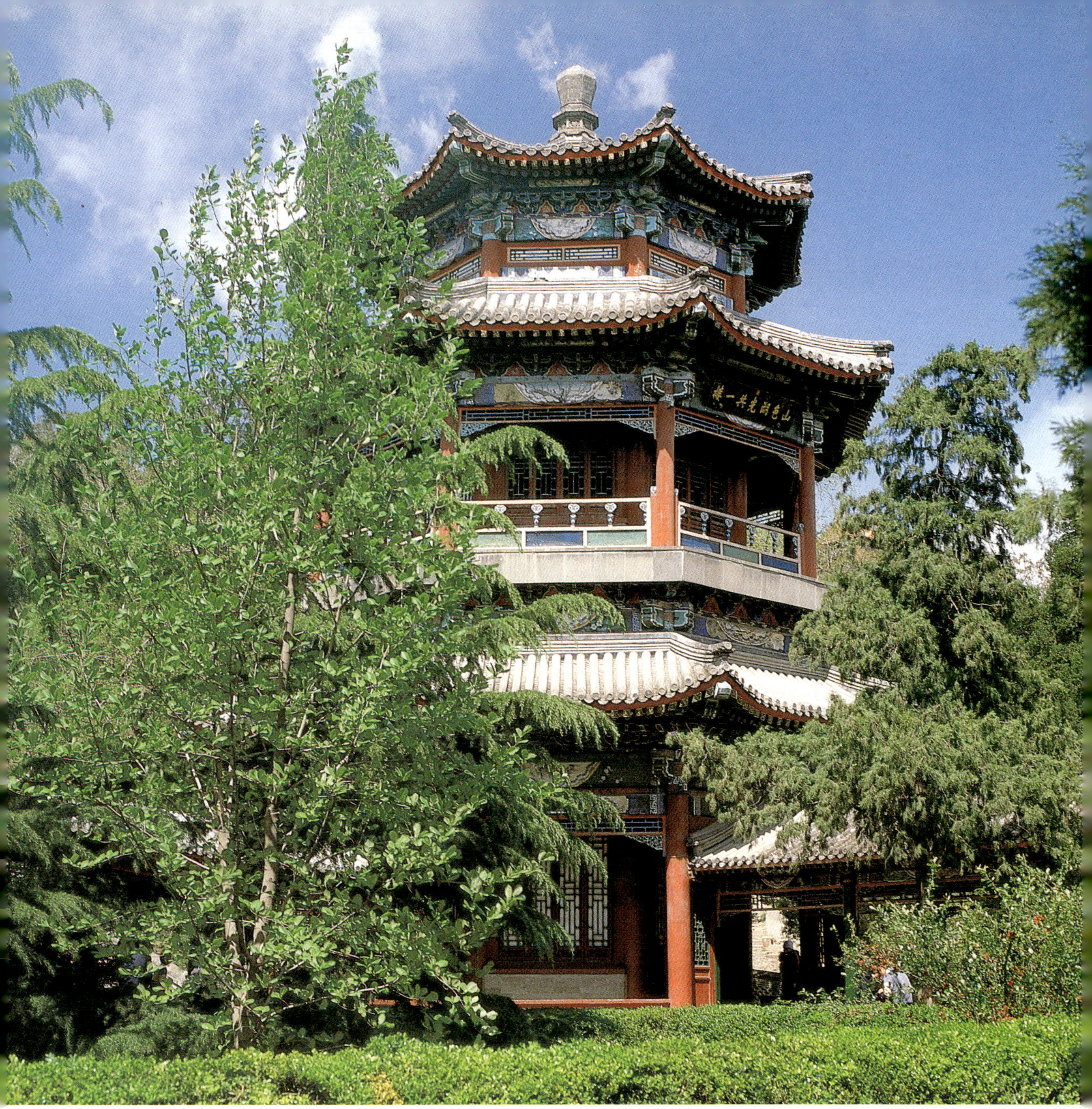

石丈亭 實際上不是亭而是殿，以院內石峰得名。石高丈餘，故名石丈亭。這是長廊的西止點。

Ten-Foot Stone Pavilion. This pavilion is named after the huge stone inside its courtyard. It is the west end of the Long Promenade.

山色湖光共一樓 西段長廊向北伸出一短廊連接此樓，登樓四望，山水盡覽，故此得名。

The pavilion converging the scenes of the hill and the lake. This pavilion is connected with the west section of the Long Promenade. When one ascends it and looks afar, the hill and the lake come into view.

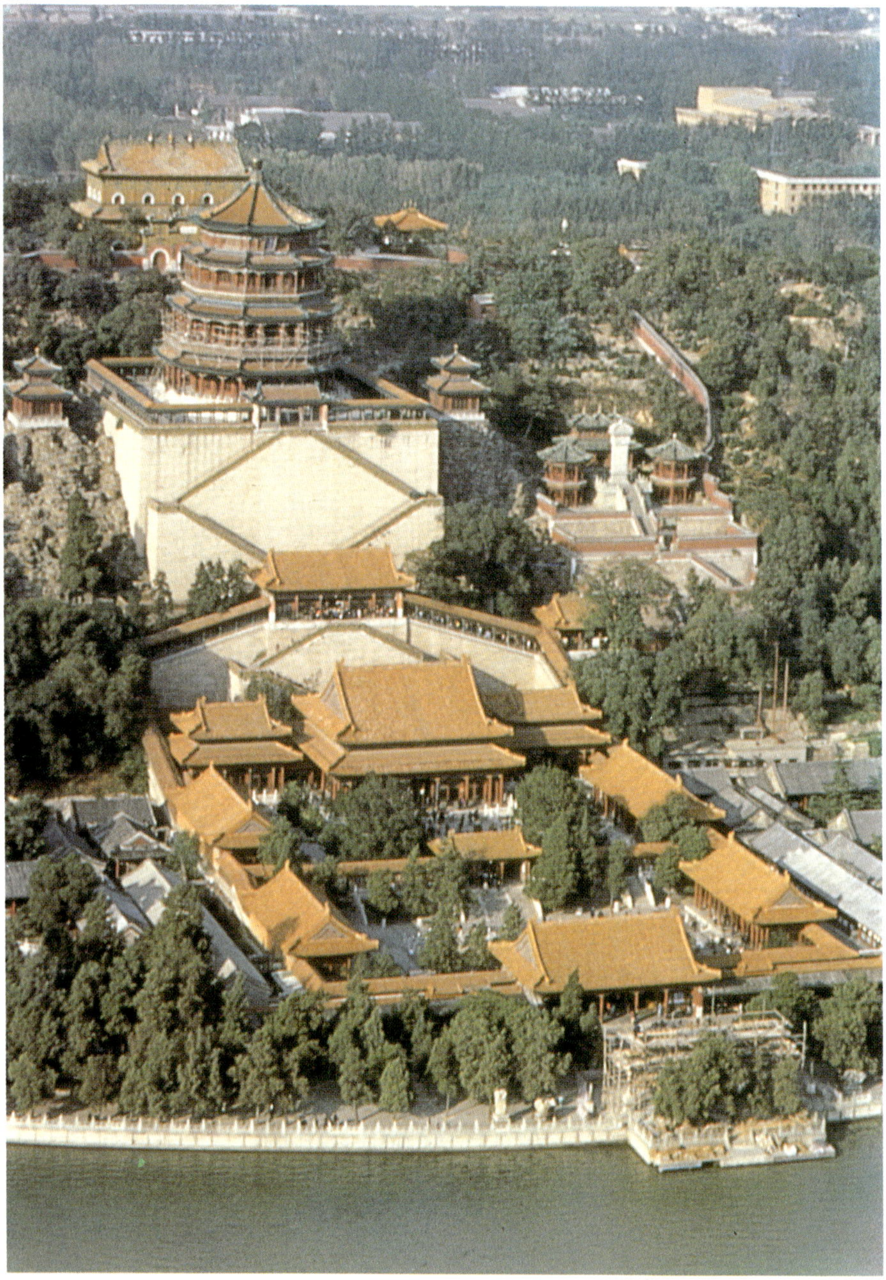

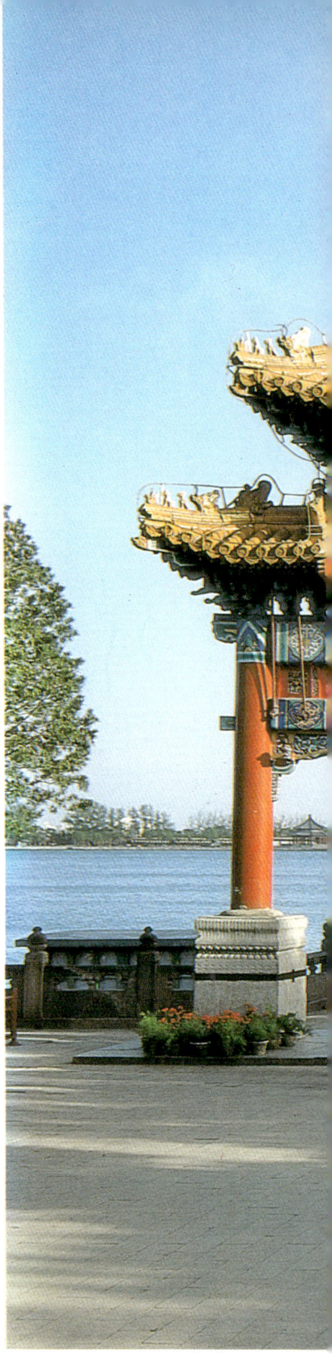

萬壽山中心建築羣 龐大的建築羣倚山而建，步步遞高，構成一條貫穿前山上下的中軸綫，這裏是總攬頤和園的構圖中心。

The massive buildings on the southern slope of Longevity Hill. This impressive group of buildings are arrayed on the slope one after the other along an axis from the hill's foot to its top. Here is the central area to view the Summer Palace.

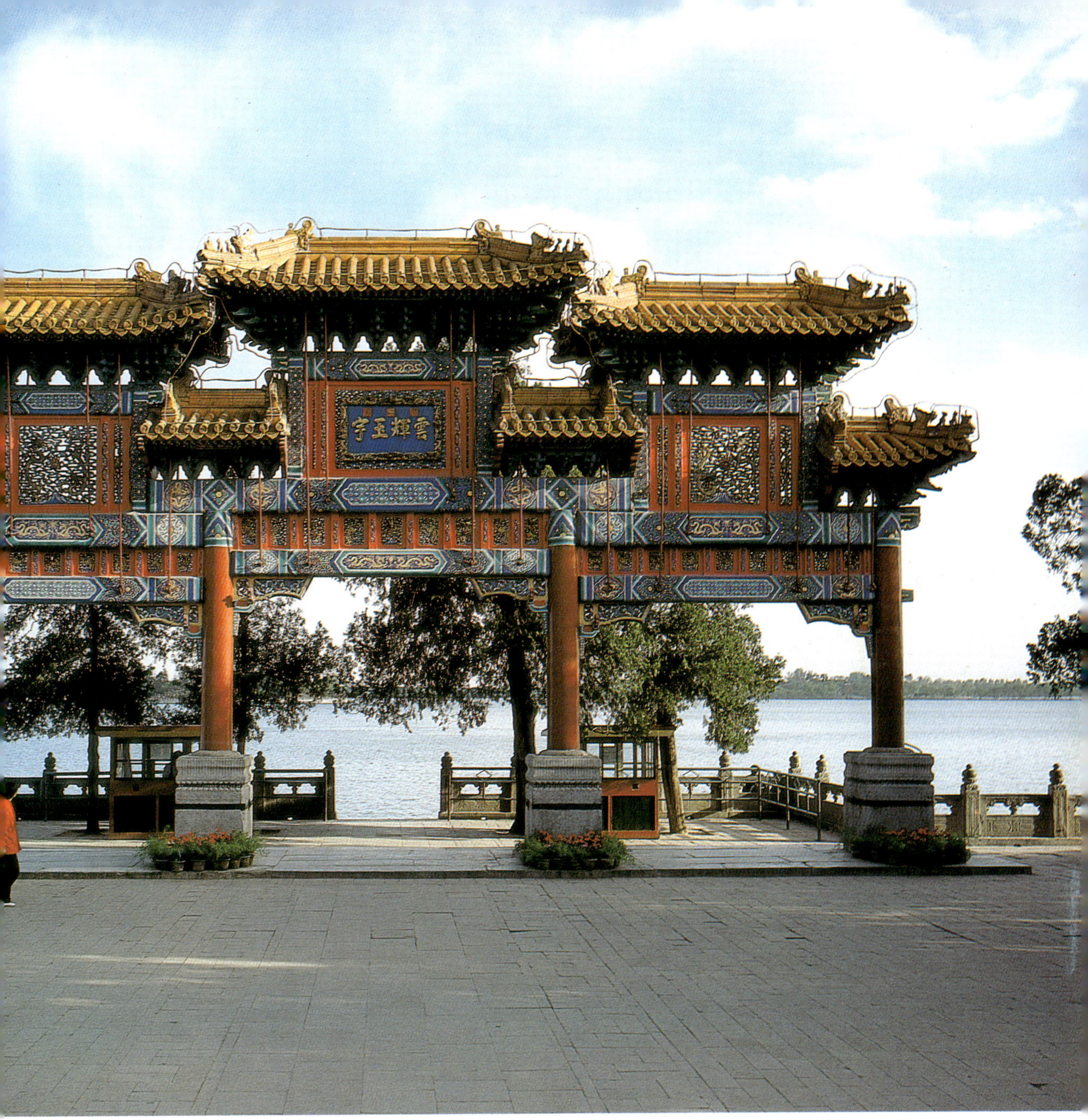

牌樓 濱湖而立。牌樓正背兩面分別書有“雲輝玉宇”、“星拱瑤樞”八字，意指這裏是九天仙界，玉宇瓊樓。

Pailou. This large arch stands close to the lake. On its front side was inscribed "Gorgeous Clouds and Jade Eaves" and on its back side "Stars Surrounding the Jade Hub", meaning that the place was a jewelled palace in the fairyland.

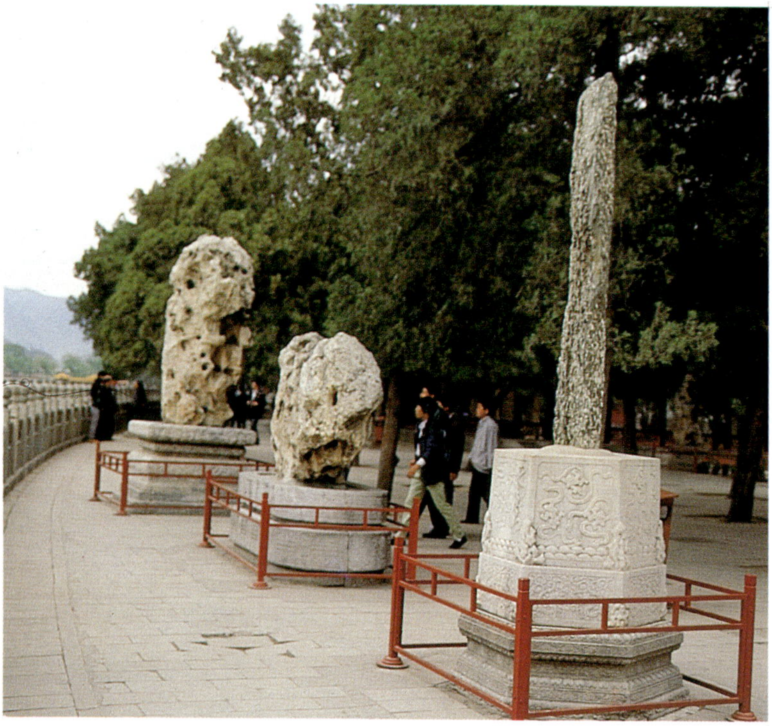

太湖石　俗稱“衙石”，共十二尊。據傳，建牌樓之初，慈禧太后嫌其勢孤不雅，故令人將原暢春園的十二塊風水壓石移置於此。乍看如亂石，細看如飛禽走獸，所以又有人稱它們爲“十二生肖石”。

Taihu rocks. These twelve grotesque rocks were known as “Court Rocks”. It was said that when the Gate That Dispels the Clouds was built, Empress Dowager Cixi thought it was not good to have the gate stand there alone, so she ordered these rocks brought here from Changchun Yuan. Each of the rocks is said to resemble some beast, real or mythical.

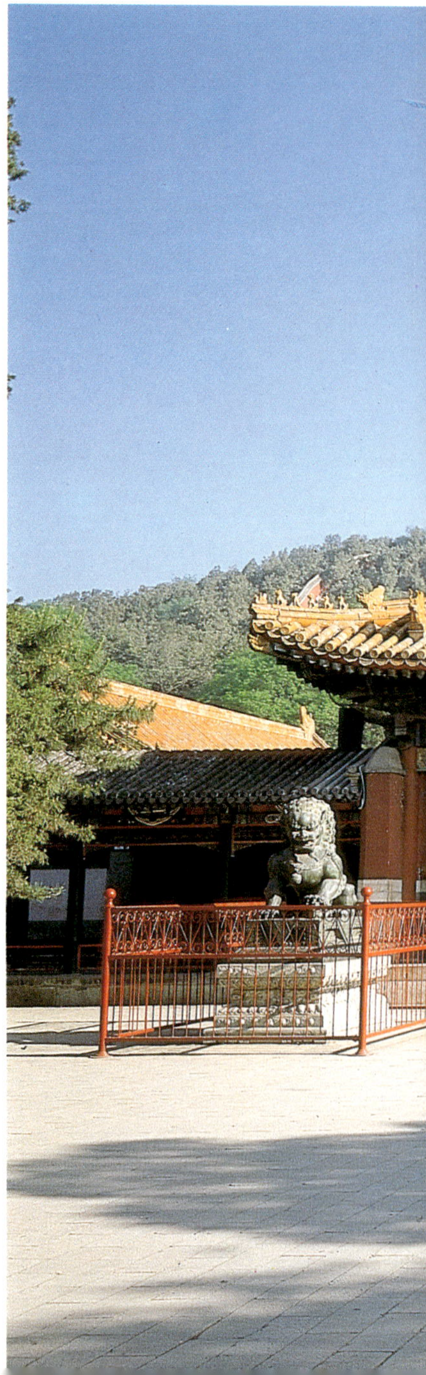

排雲門 排雲殿建築羣的正門。進門有兩座配殿，左爲“雲錦”，右爲“玉華”。

The Gate That Dispels the Clouds. This gate is the main entrance to the Hall That Dispels the Clouds. Behind it are two side halls: Yunjin Hall on the left and Yuhua Hall on the right.

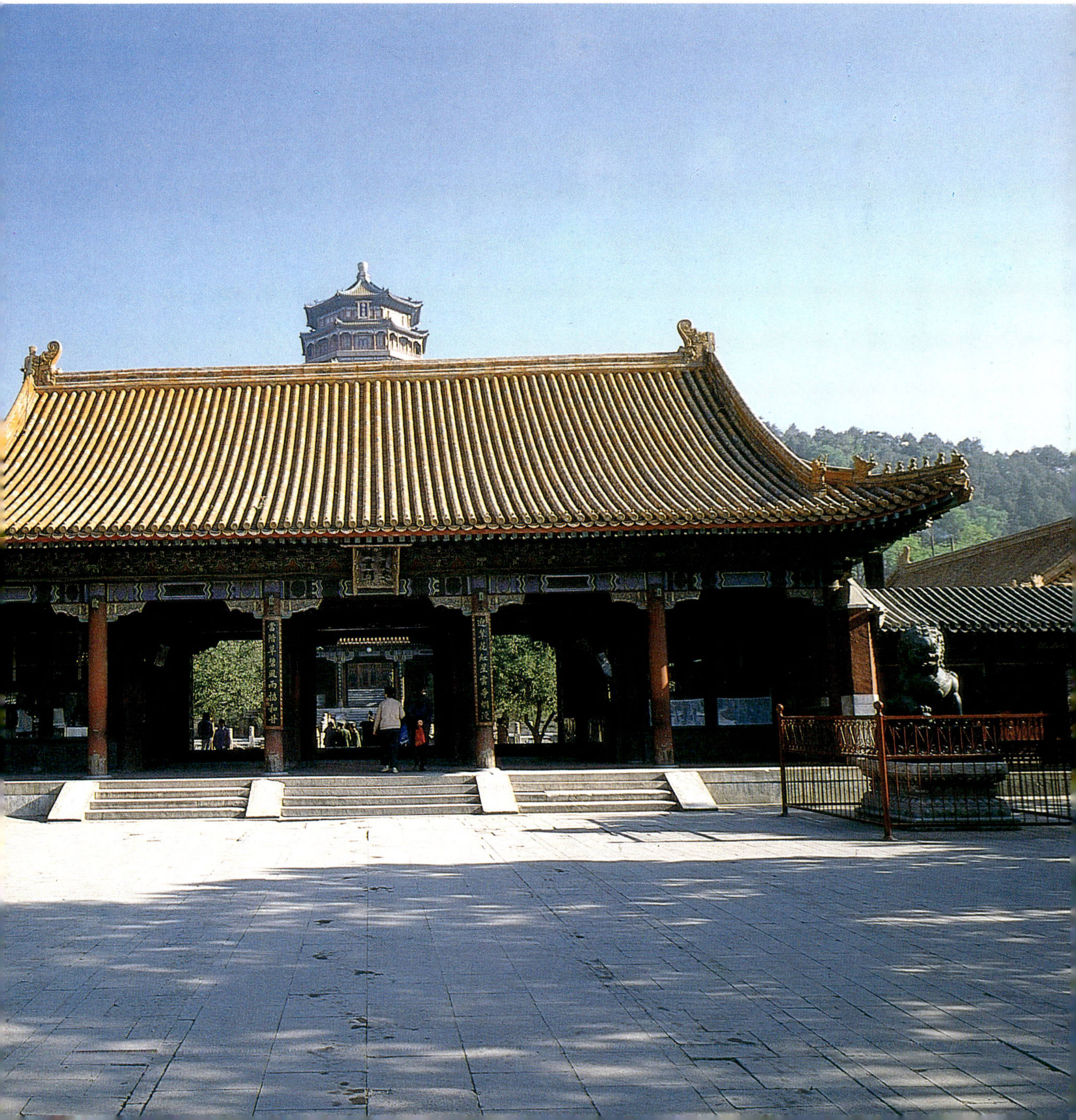

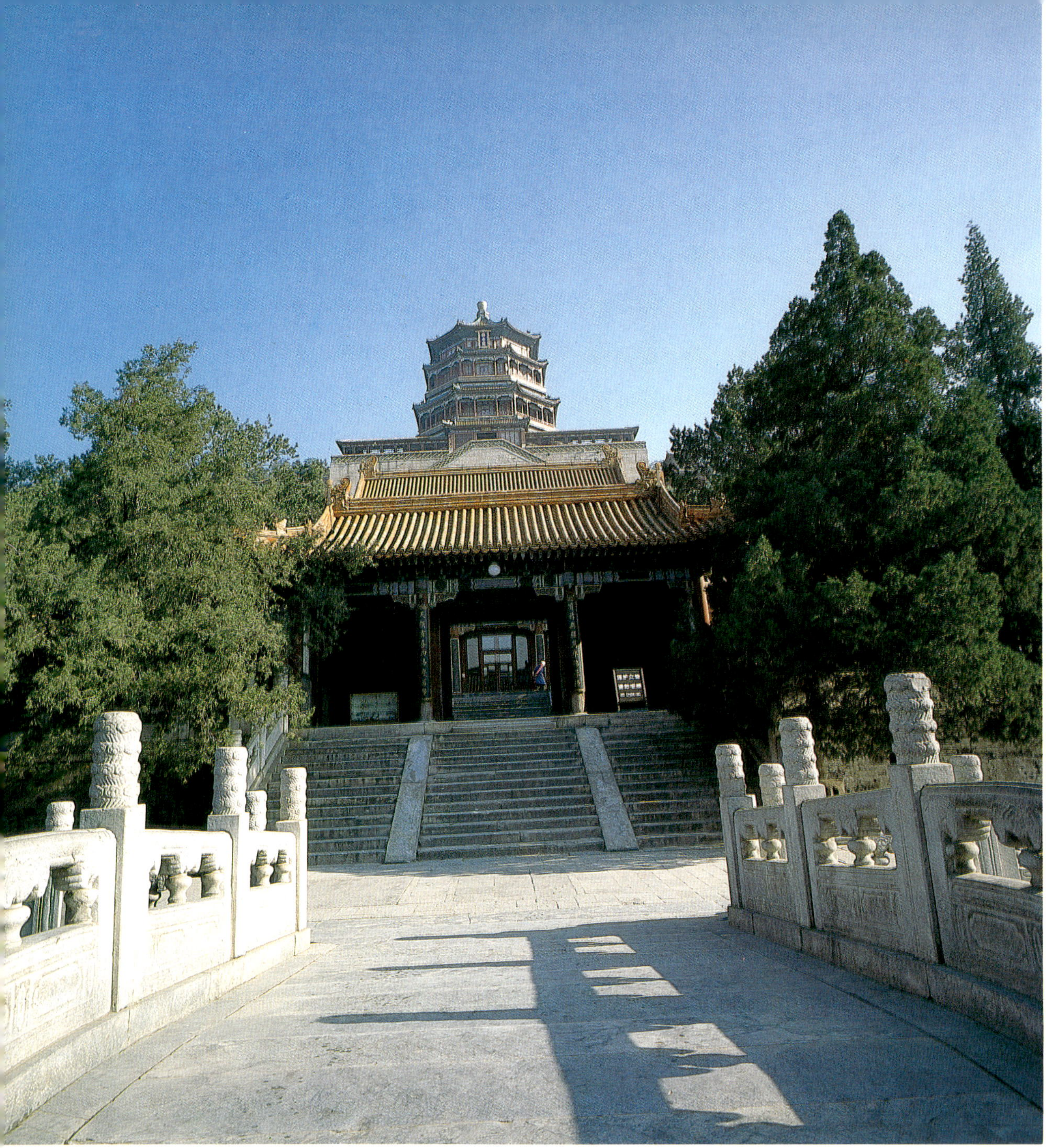

二宮門 隨山勢而築，門懸“萬壽無疆”匾，門前有金水池，上跨漢白玉石橋。進入此門，便是光緒皇帝爲慈禧太后祝壽時行大禮的地方；百官則在此門外跪拜。

The Second Palace Gate. Up a flight of stone steps stands the gate with a horizontal board inscribed with "A Long, Long Life" on it. Before the gate is the Golden Water Pond with a marble bridge across it. Entering the gate you come to the main building, where Emperor Guangxu kowtowed to Cixi on her birthday. High officials kowtowed outside the hall.

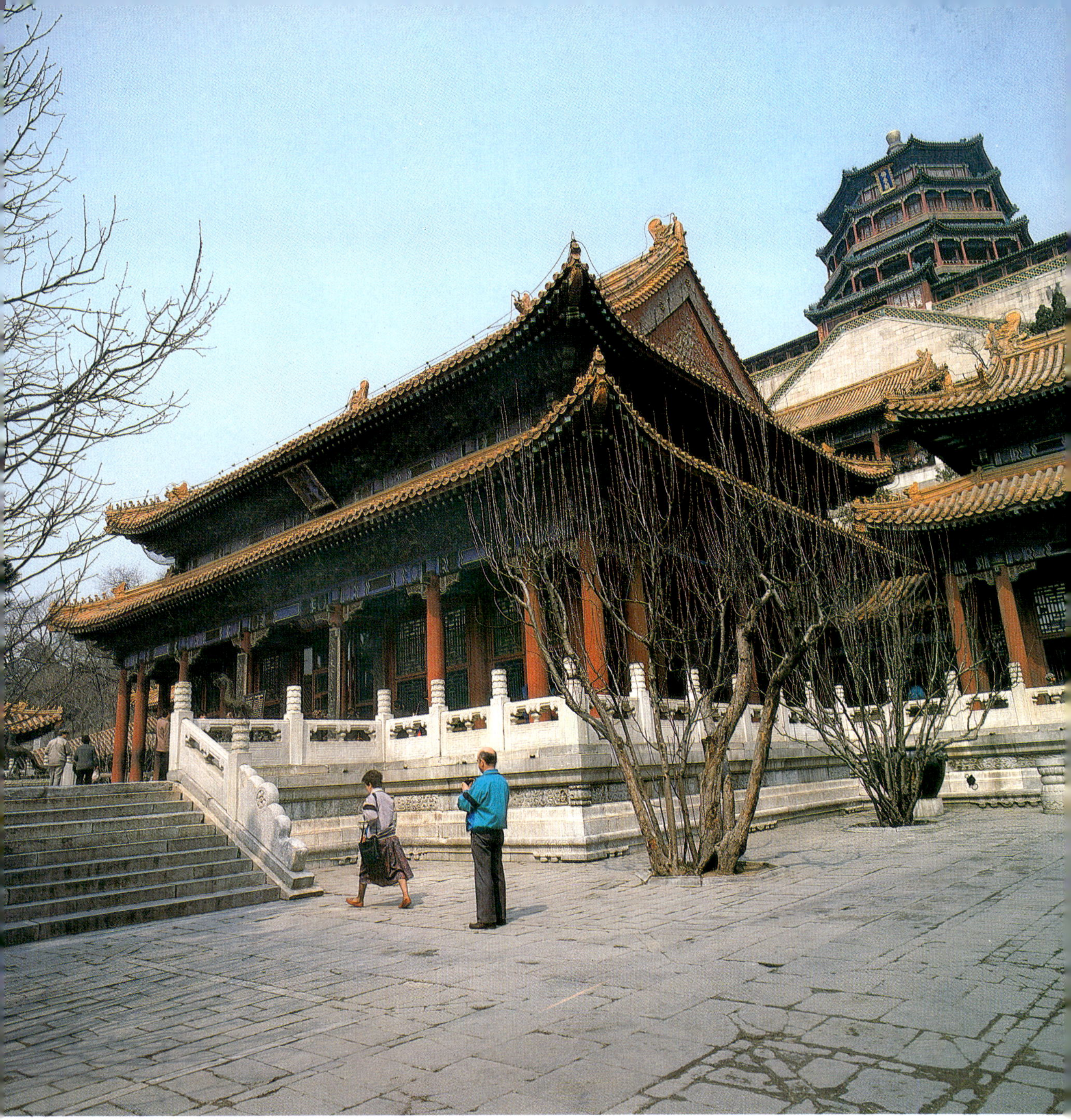

排雲殿 殿名出自東晉文學家郭璞（公元二七六——三二四年）“神仙排雲出，但見金銀臺”的詩句。這是專門爲慈禧太后過生日受賀而建的大殿。大殿橫列復道與左右耳殿相連，共二十一間，朱柱黄瓦，金龍眩目，氣勢宏大。

Hall That Dispels the Clouds. The hall was named after the poem "Excursion in Fairyland" by the Jin-Dynasty poet Guo Pu (276-324 AD):

When fairies dispel the clouds and emerge,
The gold and silver terraces appear.

It was built to hold Cixi's birthday celebrations. Connected with the side halls, it consists of 21 bays with red pillars and a golden tile roof.

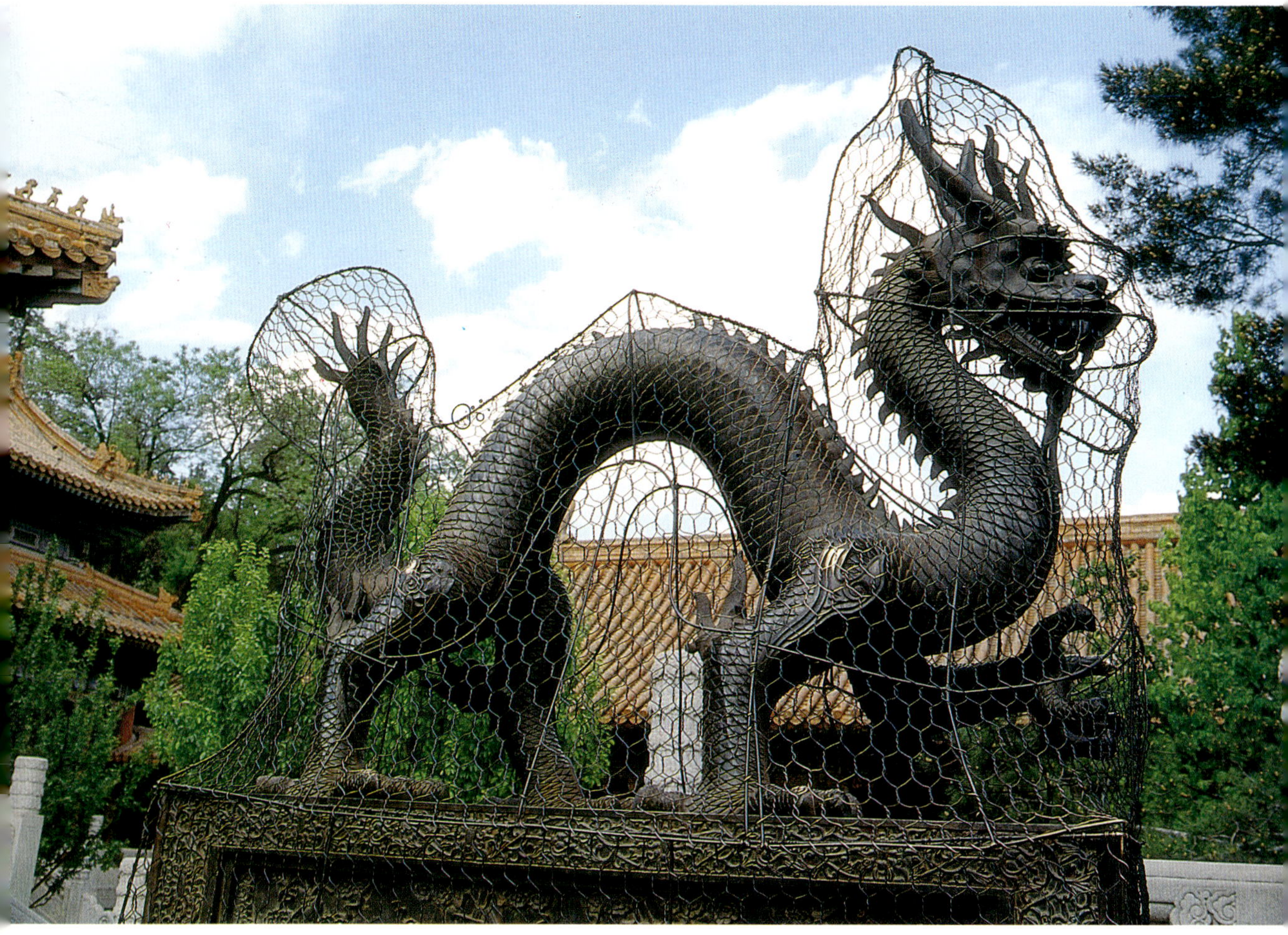

銅龍 分置於殿前月臺兩側，另有雙鳳相配。這些是皇家建築的獨特標誌。

Bronze dragon. Bronze dragon and phoenix are on the terrace before the Hall That Dispels the Clouds. They are special symbols of imperial buildings.

排雲殿内景　内設九龍寶座，座後爲朱漆底嵌珐琅博古圍屏，座旁有一對木雕大"壽"字，座前寶鼎成行，彩鳳成雙；殿内隔扇門裝飾着"萬"字不到頭的花紋，寓意長壽。殿内後間分立着高過真人的"麻姑獻壽"人形。大殿陳設如此奢華，但每年僅在慈禧生日時使用一次。

Interior view of the Hall That Dispels the Clouds. In the centre of the Hall stands the nine-dragon throne with a gilt lacquer screen behind, a wood sculpture of the word "Longevity" on either side and tripods and coloured phoenixes arrayed in front. On the doors are the decorations carved in the patterns of "Longevity" to symbolize a long life. At the rear of the Hall is a wood sculpture in the round — an image of one of the legendary Eight Immortals, the gods of longevity, holding longevity peaches. The Hall was lavishly furnished, but Cixi used it only once a year.

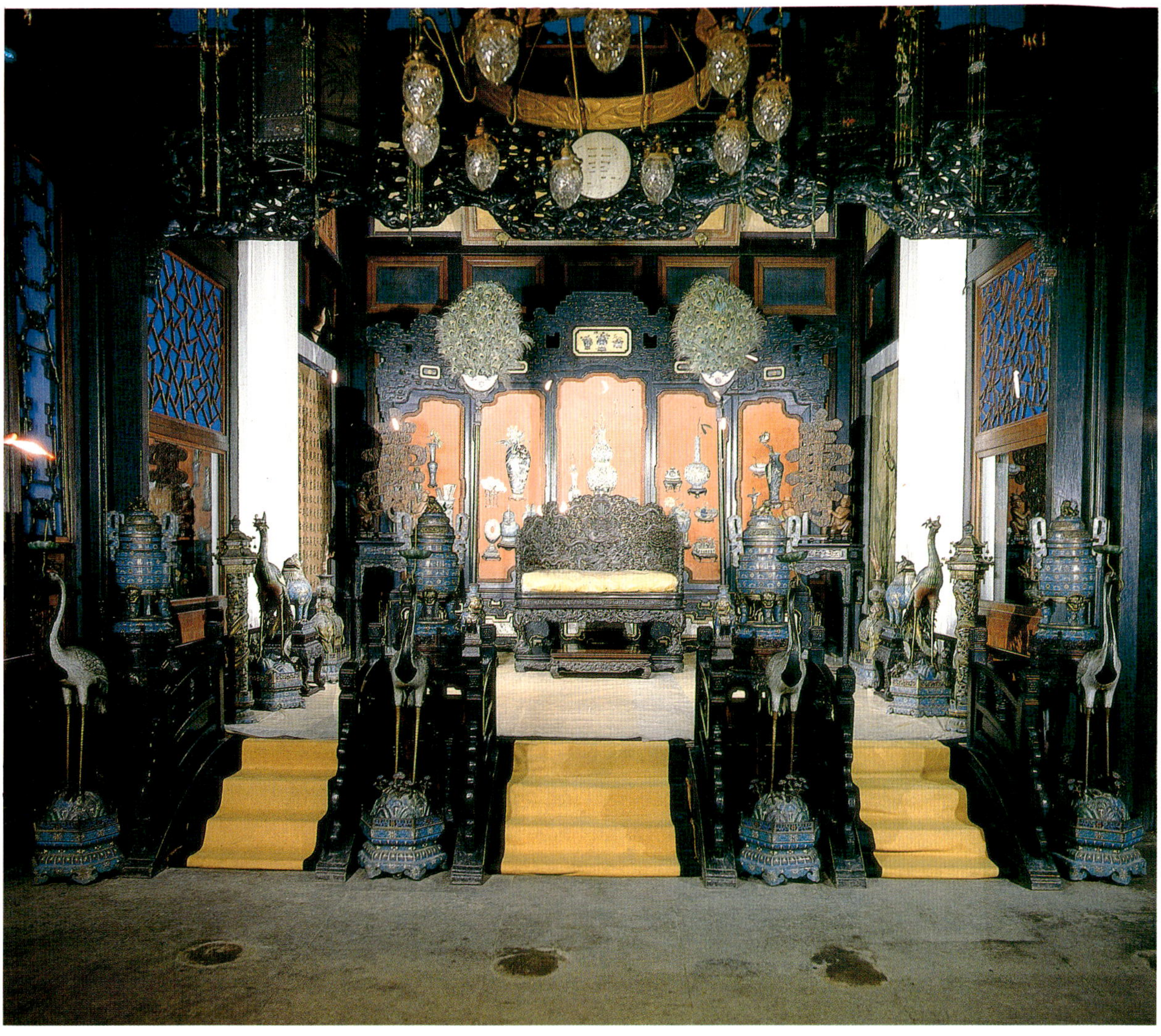

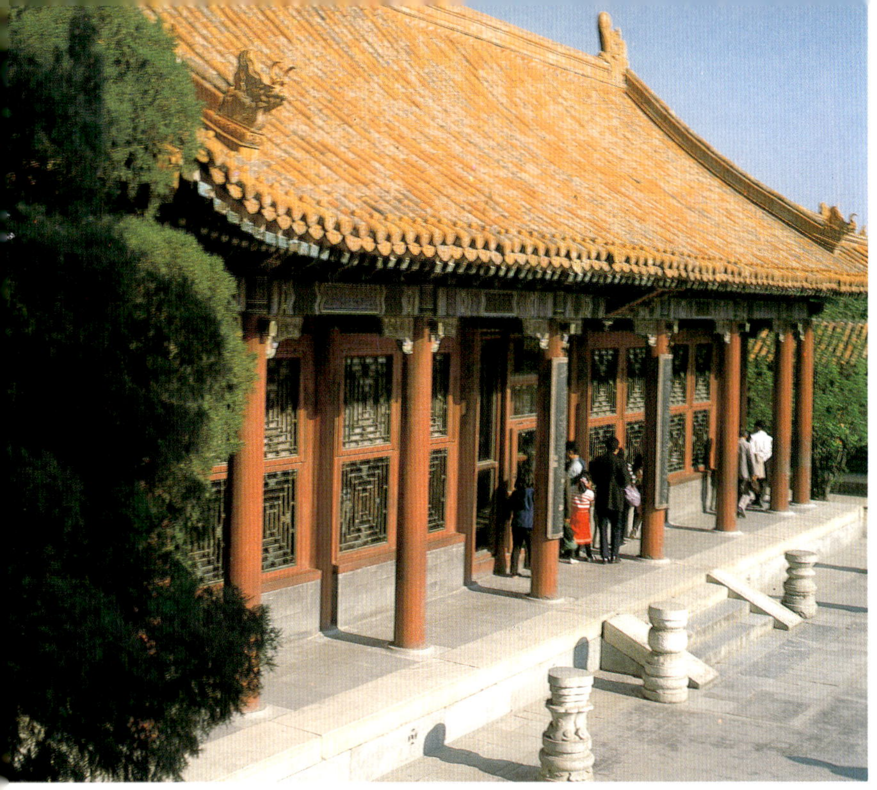

芳輝殿 二宮門的東配殿，是光緒皇帝賀壽時休息的便殿。

Fanghui Hall. The east side-hall of the Second Palace Gate, this was the place where Emperor Guangxu rested when he came to greet the Empress Dowager on her birthday.

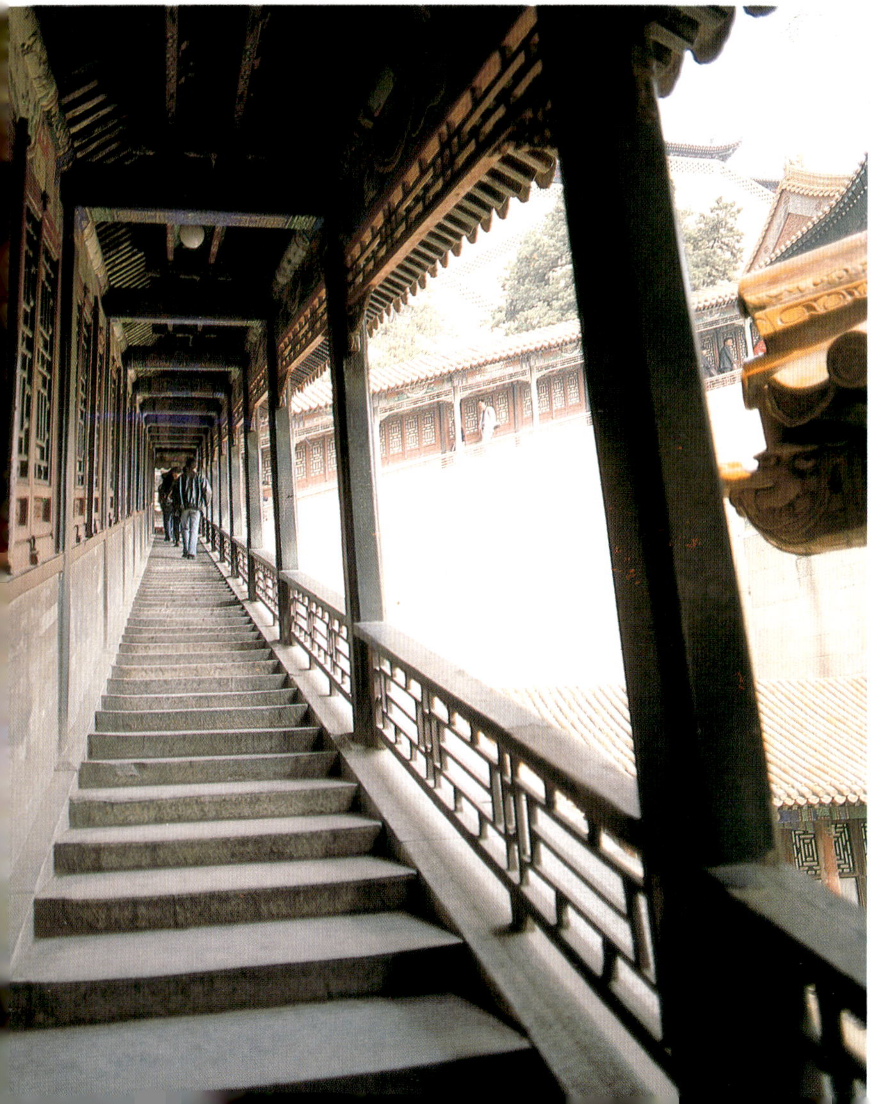

爬山廊 由排雲殿的左右耳殿雙向伸出，呈菱形，階梯狀上升，接德輝殿的東西兩端。遊人在廊的下半部可看到佛香閣熠熠生輝的閣檐，在上半部可盡觀各大殿雄姿，俯視仰望，盡得瓊樓仙閣之趣。

Mountain-climbing Gallery. Starting from the two side-halls of the Hall That Dispels the Clouds, two rhombic galleries wind their way upward to link the east and west sides of the Hall of Glorious Virtue. From their lower part visitors can see the resplendent and magnificent Tower of Fragrance of Buddha, and from their upper part can look down at golden roofed halls.

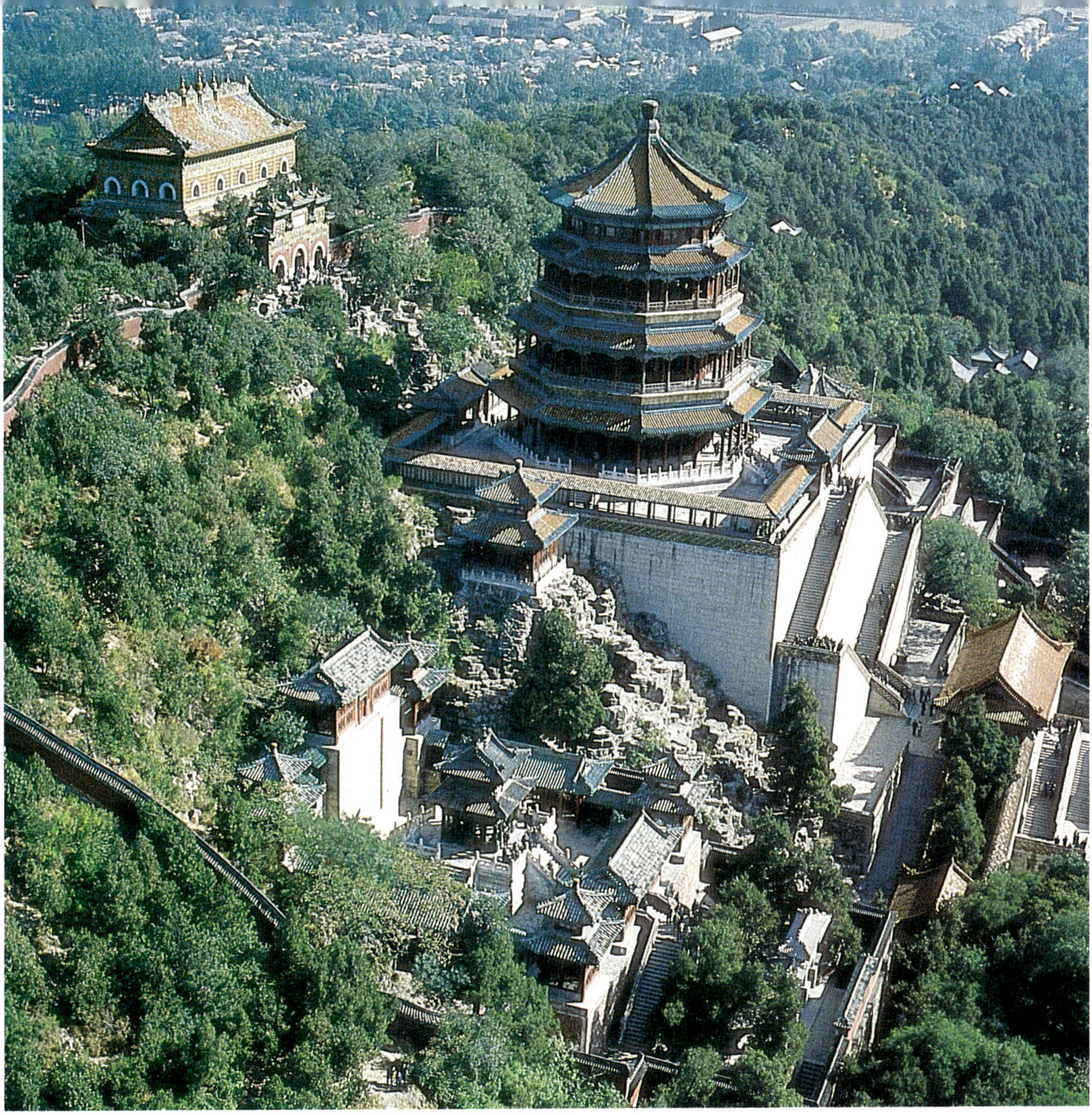

俯瞰佛香閣　佛香閣建在萬壽山前山陡坡高二十一米的巨石臺基上。它南對昆明湖，背靠智慧海佛殿，以它爲中心的各建築羣嚴整而對稱地向兩翼展開，彼此呼應，蔚爲壯觀。一八六〇年，佛香閣被英法聯軍燒毀，後照原樣重建，是座宗教建築。

Tower of the Fragrance of Buddha. The tower was built on a 21-metre high square platform of solid stones at the centre of the southern slope of Longevity Hill. With the Sea-of-Wisdom Temple behind its back, it faces Kunming Lake. From it other buildings fan out east and west in an orderly and symmetrical fashion. The tower was destroyed by the Anglo-French joint forces in 1860, and was rebuilt later according to its original form.

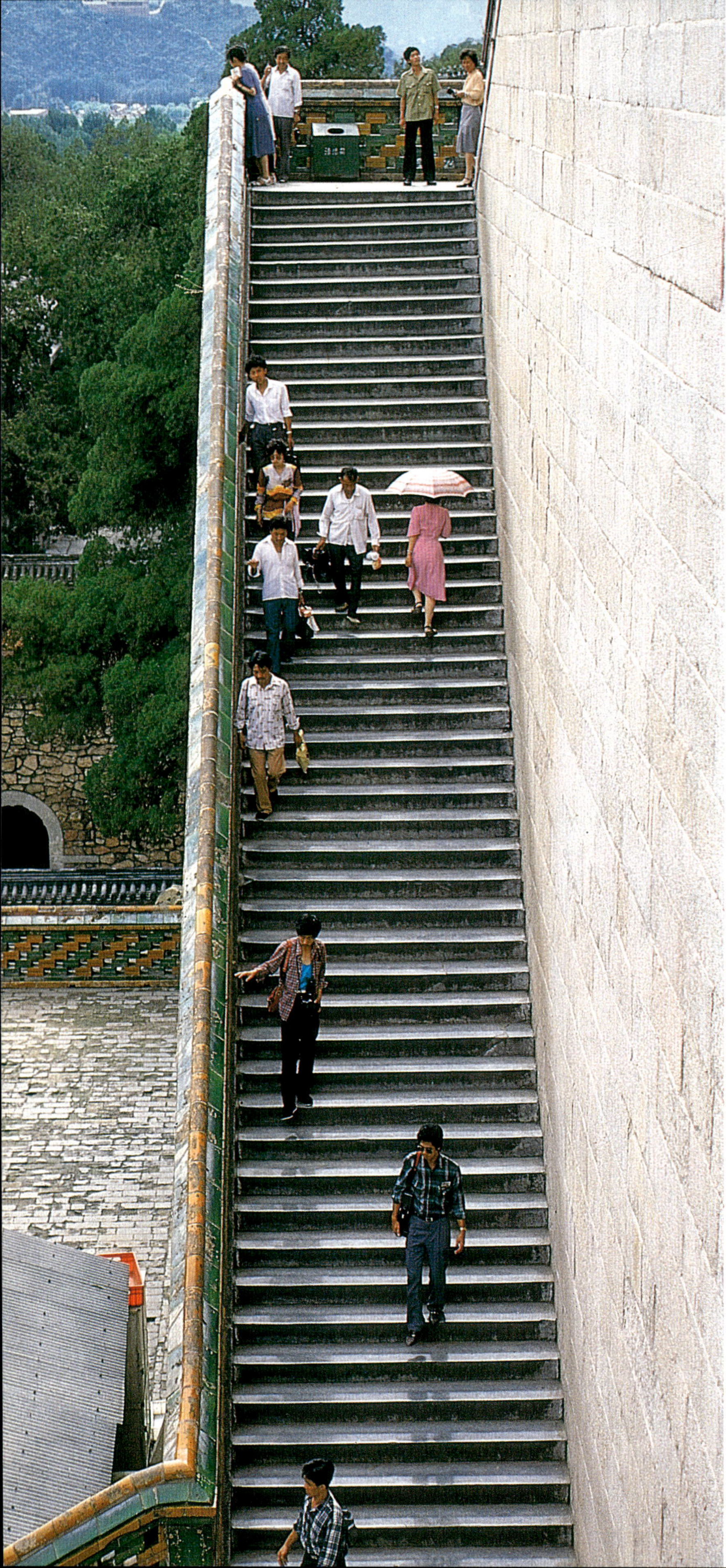

蹬道 緊貼臺基絶壁而築，高峻陡峭，共一百十四級臺階。

Stone stairways. Built closely to the platform, each of the two stone stairways has 114 steps.

佛香閣 高三十六點四八米，八面三層四重檐，頂覆黃綠琉璃瓦，飛檐翹角，鎏金寶頂，氣勢非凡。

Tower of the Fragrance of Buddha. The tower, 36.48 metres high, is a three-storeyed octagonal structure with four tiers of eaves. Architecturally, it is a major building.

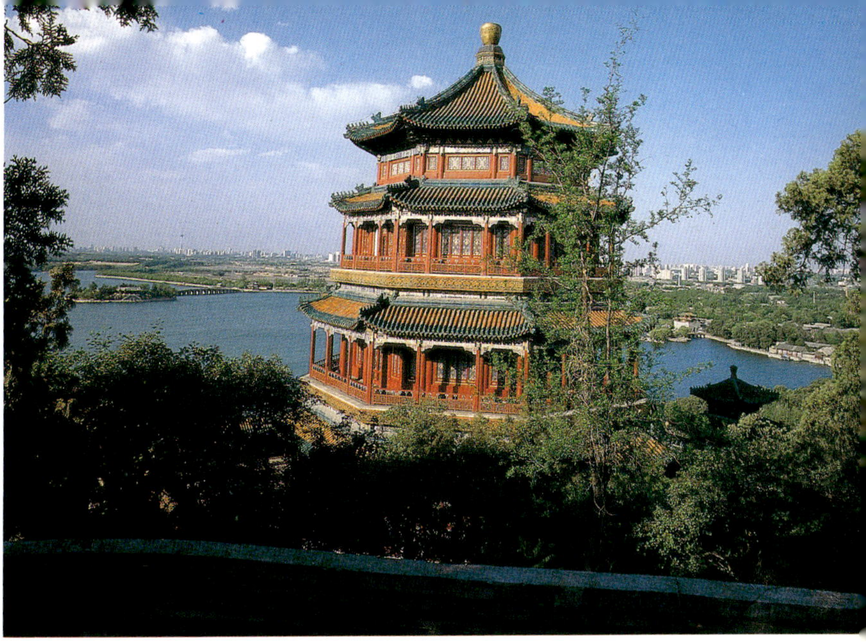

佛香閣夜景

Tower of the Fragrance of Buddha at night.

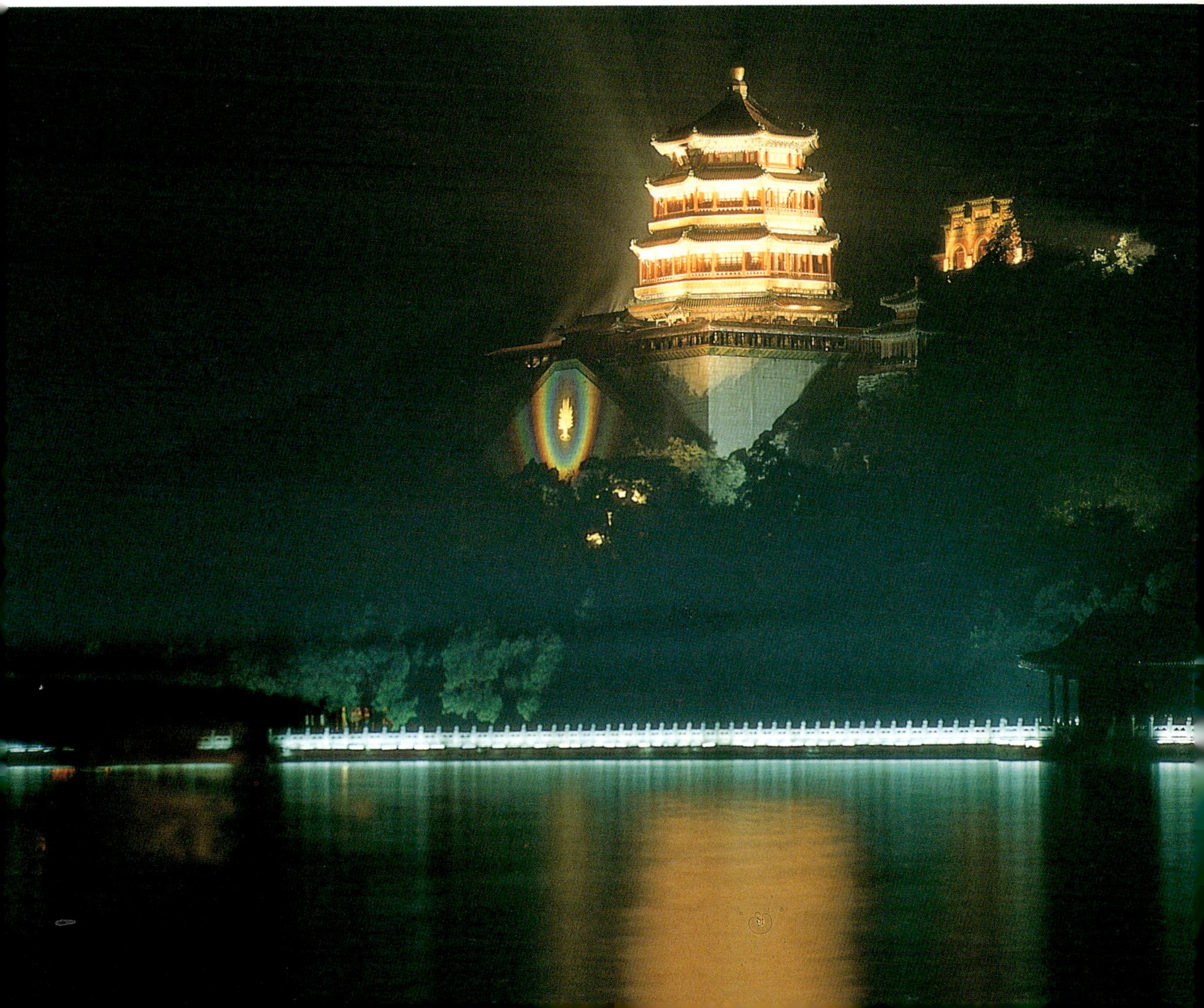

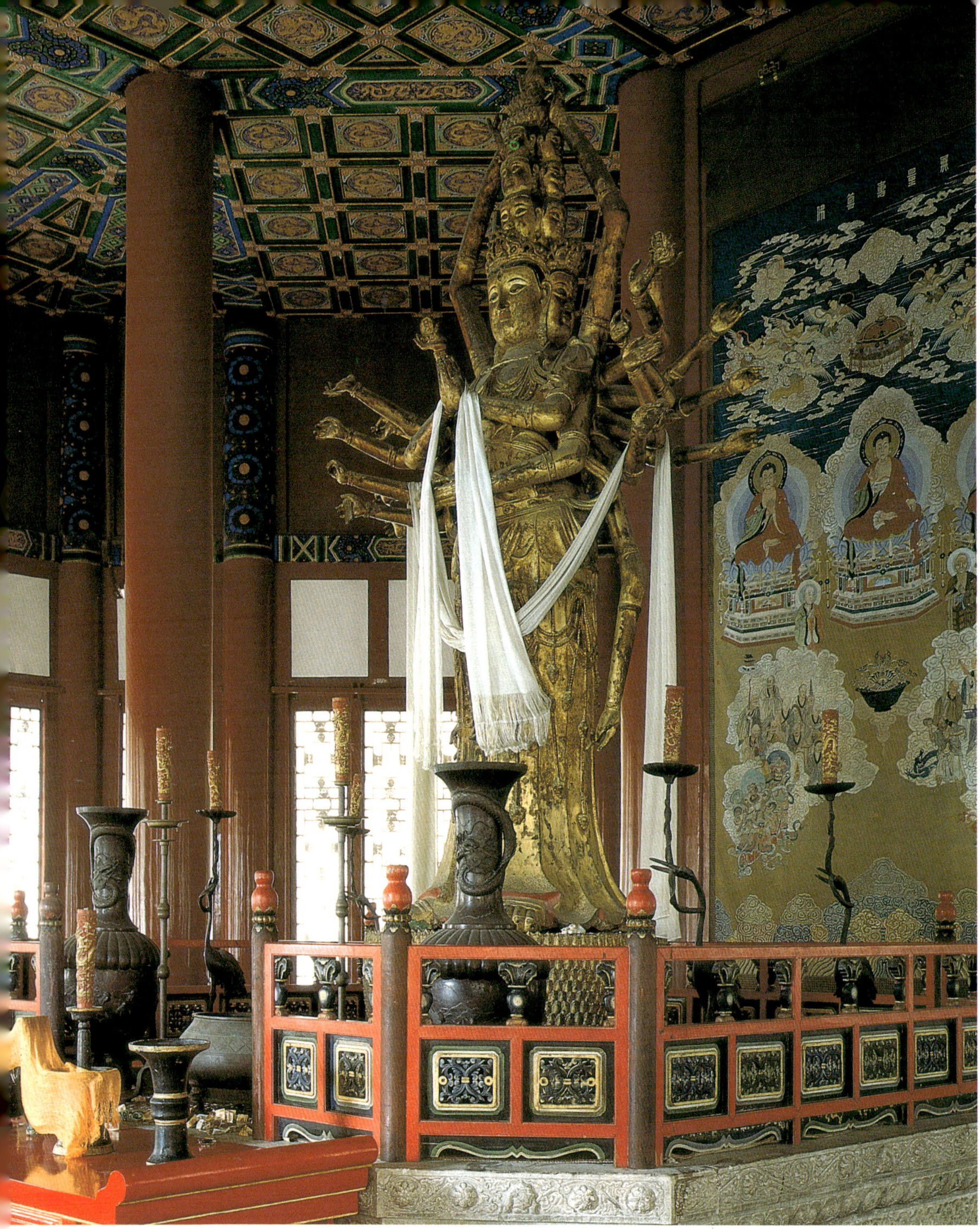

南無大悲觀世音菩薩 供於佛香閣一層，明萬歷二年（公元一五七四年）鑄造，高五米，重萬斤。佛像造型豐滿，神態安祥自然。

Statue of Bodhisattva. Enshrined at the first floor of the Tower of the Fragrance of Buddha, the statue was cast in the second year of Wanli Reign (1574). Five metres high, it weighs 10,000 catties.

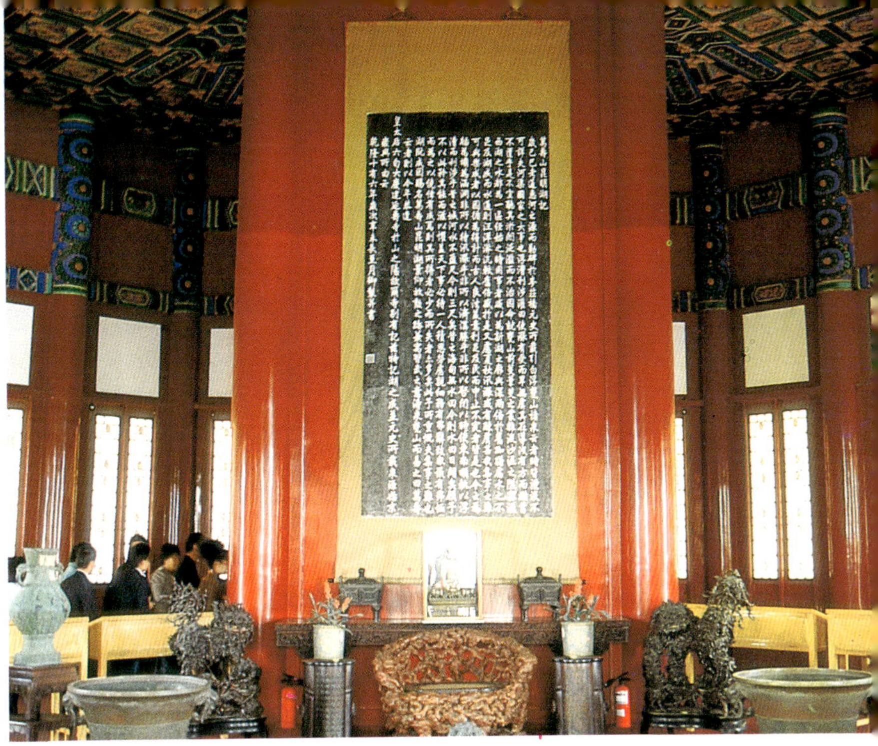

《萬壽山昆明湖記》拓片 碑文爲乾隆皇帝手筆，概述了京城西、北郊水系變化的歷史沿革。這幅拓片鑲裝於佛香閣二層正中。

"Note of the Longevity Hill and Kunming Lake". This huge note in Emperor Gianlong's handwriting is inlaid on the front side at the second floor of the Tower of Fragrance of Buddha. It records the history of the development of river system in the northwestern suburbs of Beijing.

佛香閣三層壁畫 共八幅，環貼於正中天井井壁。壁畫以天仙神女爲內容。三層樓還存放着有關佛香閣的建閣史料和不同季節的景觀圖片，供遊人閱讀和觀賞。

Mural paintings. These murals, eight all together, are on the walls on the third floor of the Tower of Fragrance of Buddha, depicting fairies and goddesses. Also on the third floor are historical materials about the building of the tower and pictures about the changes of the four seasons.

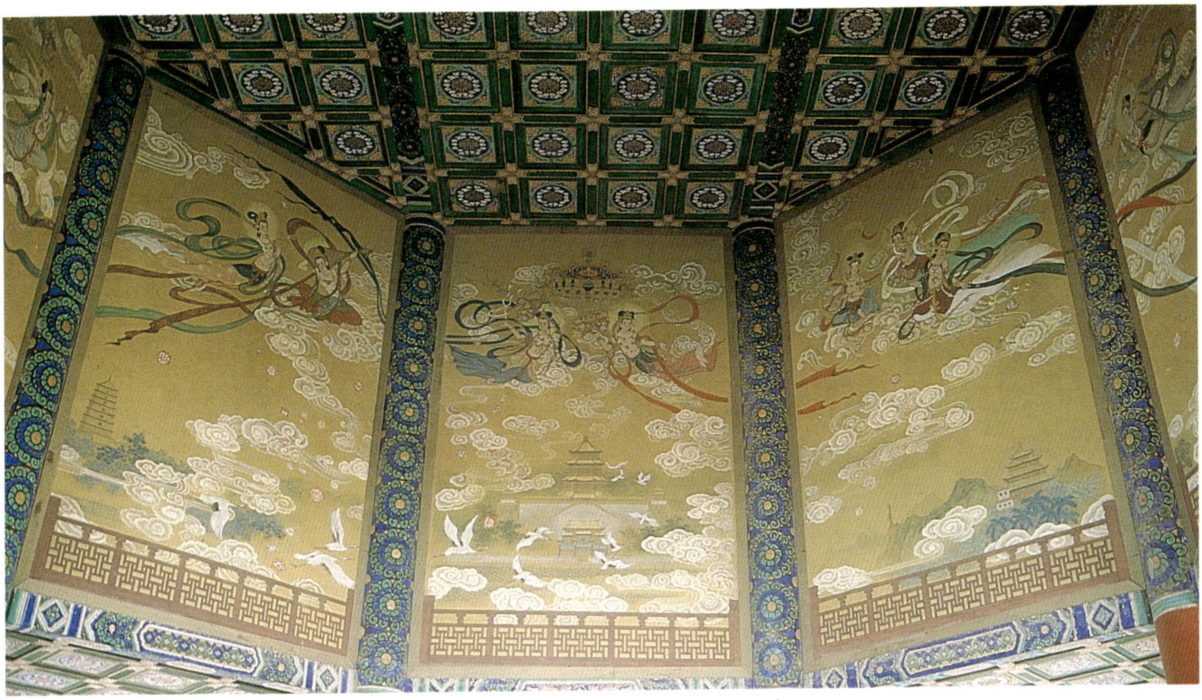

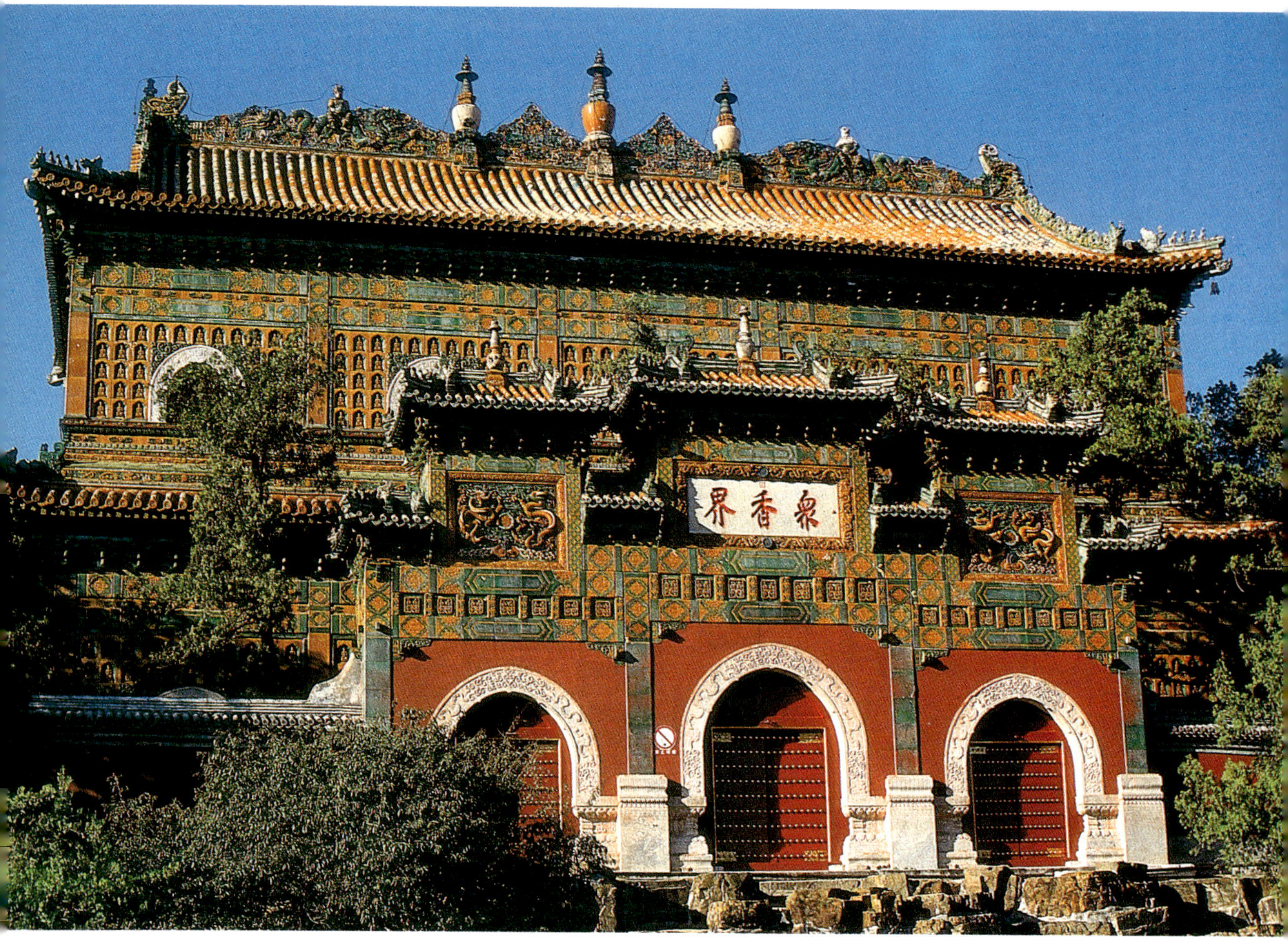

衆香界　磚石結構，表面用五色琉璃瓦件裝飾。這是座宗教牌坊，在牌坊的正、反面石額和智慧海的前後石額上，都刻着這樣一句話:“衆香界，祇樹林；智慧海，吉祥雲。”這首三字偈語巧妙地把這裏比作佛門福地。

The Boundary Stone of Popular Fragrance. This arch of five-coloured glaze with three doorways is a structure of bricks and stones. On the front and back sides of this arch and on that of the Sea-of-Wisdom Temple are carved the words: "Boundary Stone of Popular Fragrance; Venerable Forest of Trees; the Sea of Wisdom; and Auspicious Clouds."

智慧海 爲萬壽山的制高建築。"智慧海"語出佛經，意思是如來佛智慧如海。整座建築不施寸木，全用磚石發券砌成，俗稱"無樑殿"。其表面全部用五色琉璃構件鑲貼並嵌有一千多尊無量壽佛。殿内供有觀世音菩薩坐像。

Sea-of-Wisdom Temple. This temple at the top of Longevity Hill built entirely of brick and stone, without a single beam or rafter is popularly called the "beamless hall". Its plainness is relieved by green and yellow glaze on the outside. The outer walls have rows of over one thousand exquisitely carved Buddha statuettes. Inside the temple is enshrined the statue of Guanyin.

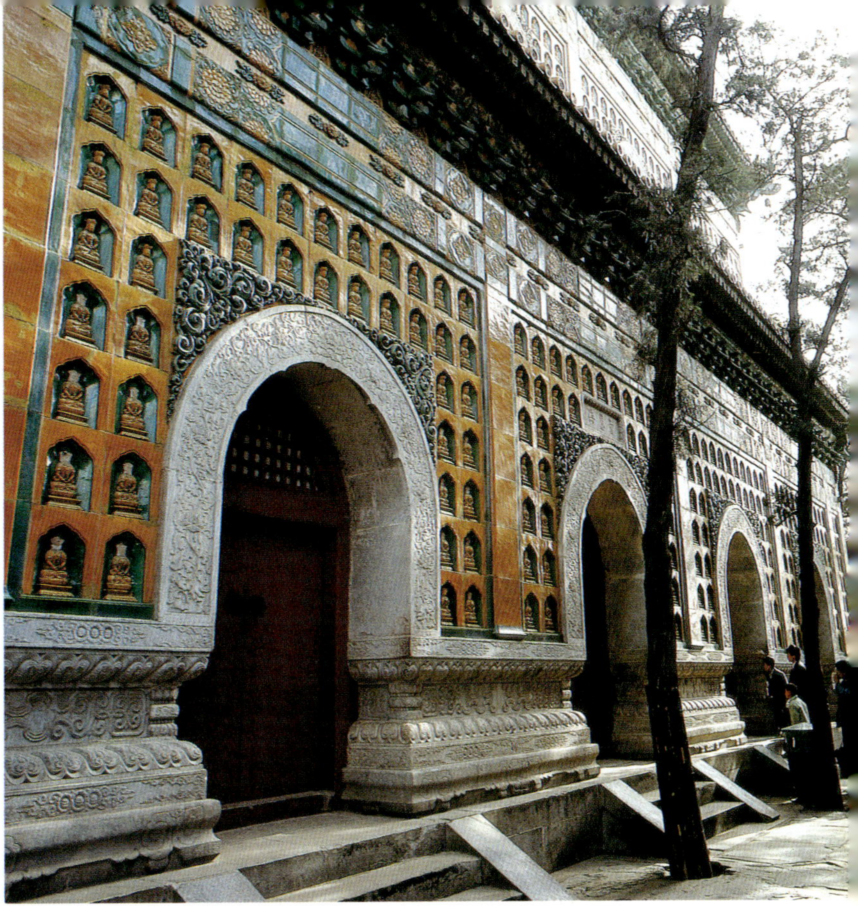

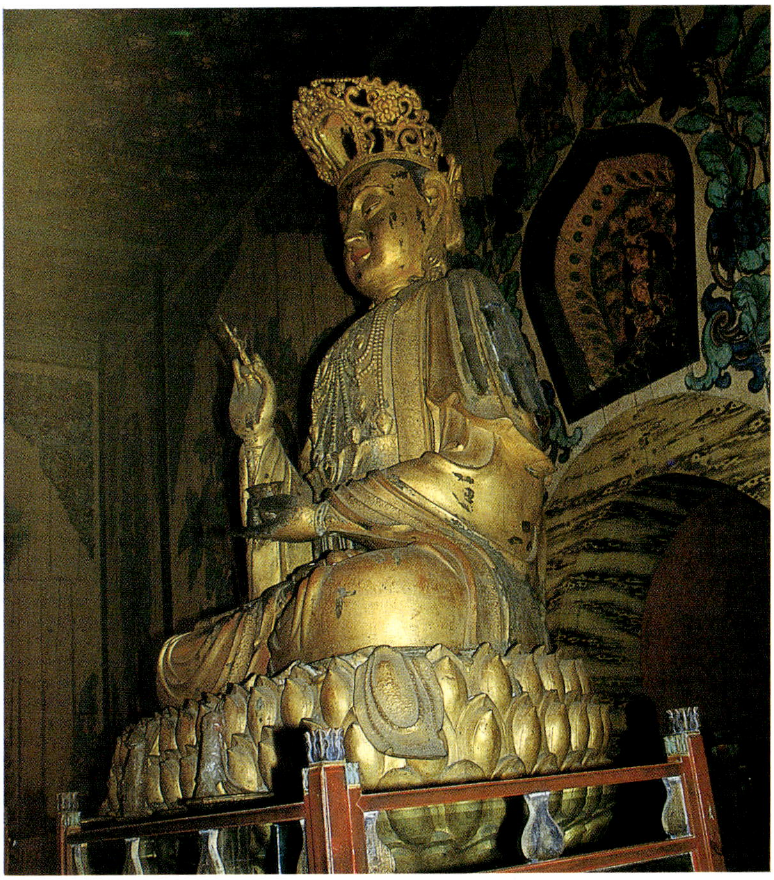

菩薩坐像 供於大殿正中。據佛教傳説，此佛是南海普陀山觀世音菩薩。她左手托甘露寶瓶，右手持楊柳枝，法力無邊。這尊菩薩像通身貼金箔，安坐在蓮花寶座上，神情慈善安祥。

Statue of Guanyin. This statue is placed in the centre of the temple. According to mythology, Guanyin with a precious bottle in her right hand and a willow branch in her left hand has boundless magic power. This statue of Guanyin covered with goldleaf sits at ease on a lotus throne.

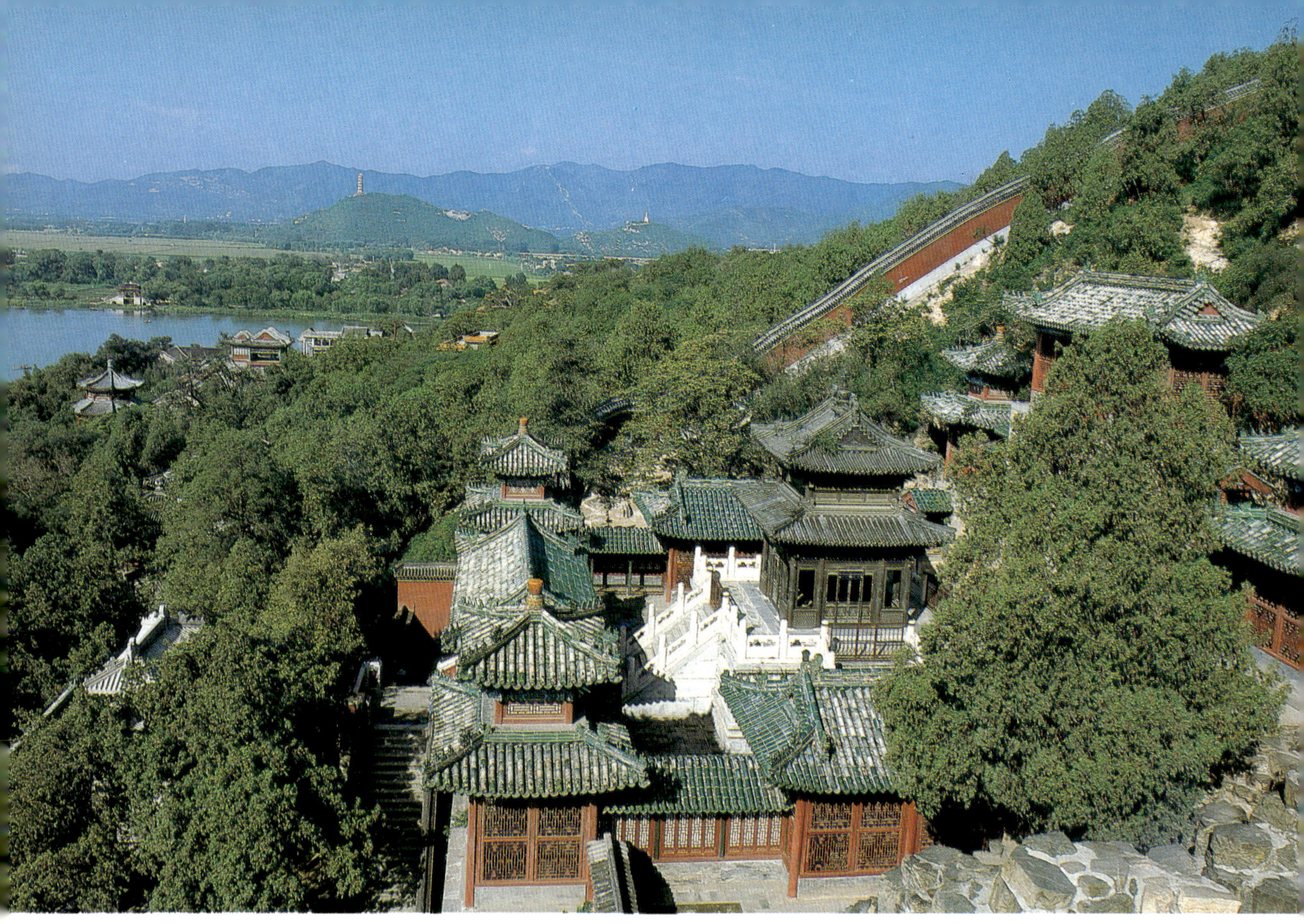

五方閣 位於佛香閣西側，是一組方形建築，在其中心漢白玉石臺基上聳立着聞名遐邇的銅亭。“五方”係佛家語“五方色”的意思，“五方閣”意爲聚五方之色的高閣，寓意天下太平，四海昇平。

Five-Square Pavilions. West of the Tower of the Fragrance of Buddha is a cluster of buildings, with galleries on all four sides and four small pavilions in the four corners. In the centre is the famous Bronze Pavilion resting on a base of carved white marble. Five-Square Pavilions means it embodies the colours from all sides, symbolizing peace and prosperity in the world.

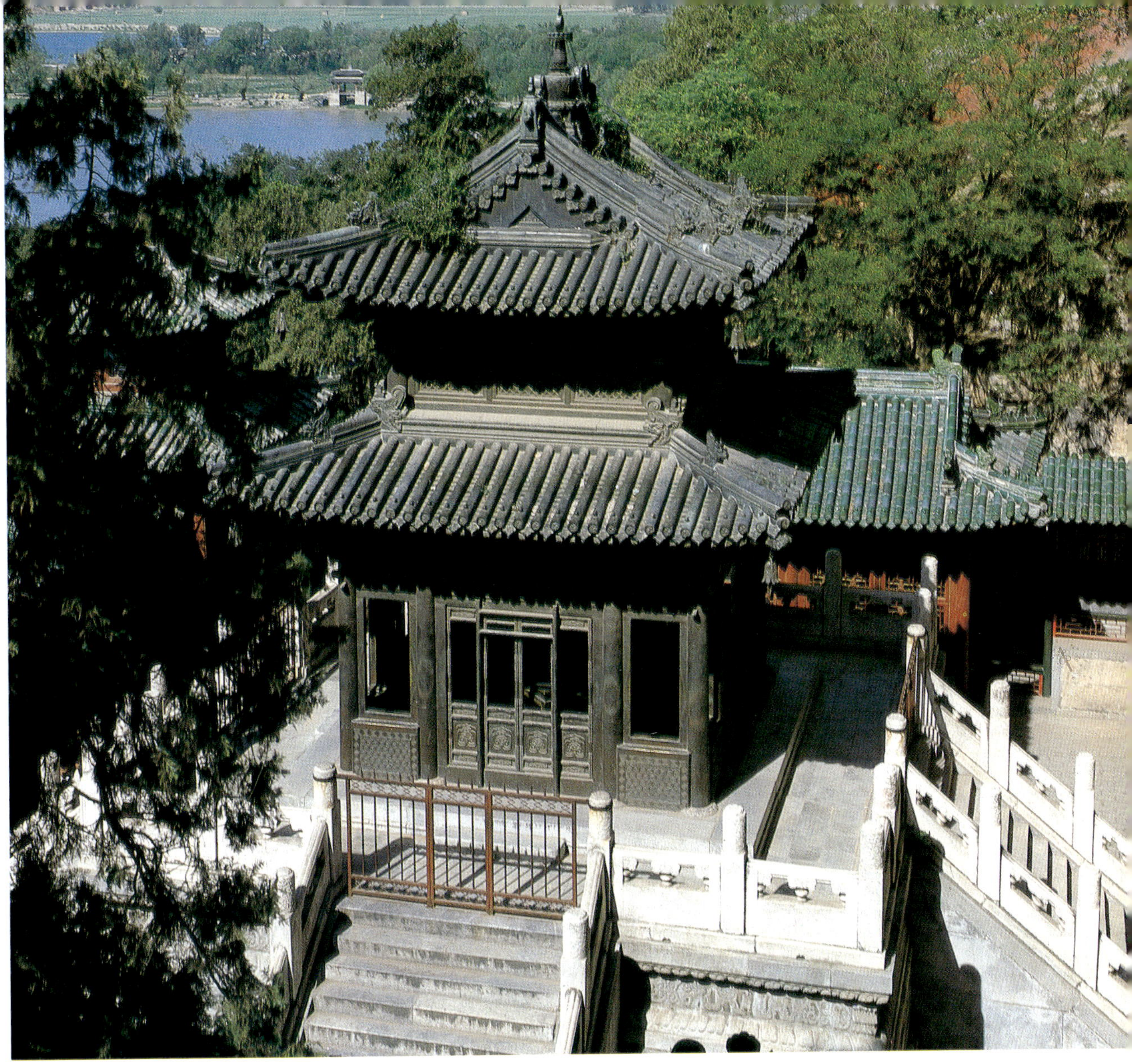

寶雲閣 俗稱銅亭，內供佛像，但兩次遭受浩劫，佛像及亭的部分構件被偷運海外。銅亭鑄造於一七五五年，高七點五五米，重二百零七噸。據史料記載，鑄造時爲磨光表面，僅銼下的銅屑就重五噸多。銅亭爲重檐方頂，亭身的菱花隔扇、柱、樑、斗拱、椽、瓦以及九龍匾、對聯等，都同木結構一模一樣，通體呈蟹青冷古銅色。銅亭造型精美，是世界上罕見的青銅建築精品。

Pavilion of Precious Clouds. Also called the Bronze Pavilion, it had a statue of Buddha in it, but twice it met with catastrophe. The statue of Buddha and some parts of the bronze pavilion were taken abroad by foreign invaders. The Bronze Pavilion, cast in 1755, is 7.55 metres high and weighs 207 tons. According to historical record, it had a polished surface and the bronze fillings amounted to five tons. The double-eaved roof, the partitions with waterchestnut designs, the beams, columns, lintels, rafters, brackets, tiles and pinnacle, the couplets and nine-dragon plaque, are exactly the same in form and design as those of a wooden pavilion, but all are of bronze and of a greenish-grey hue. It is a superb piece of architecture rarely found anywhere in the world.

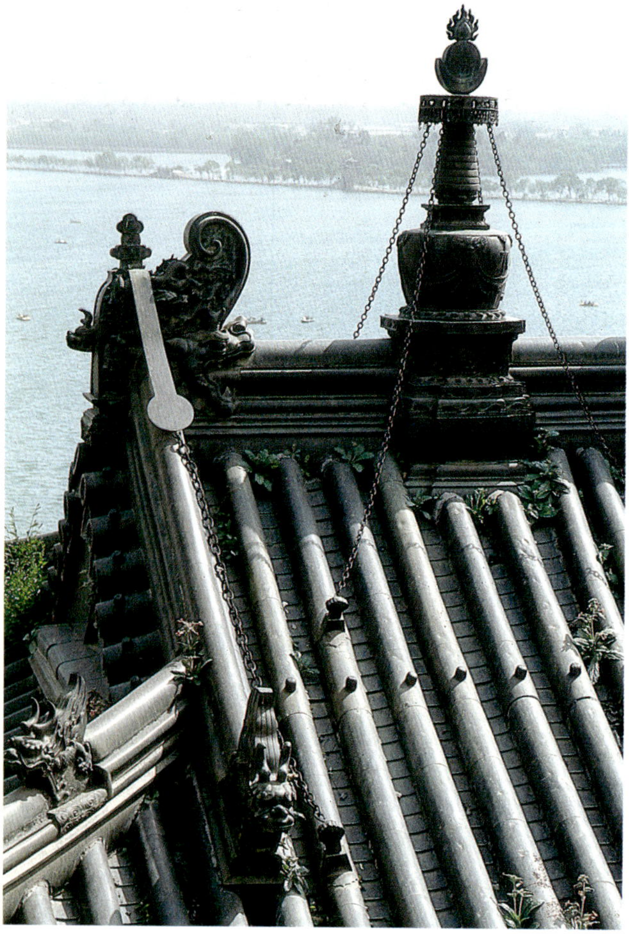

亭脊一角 寶塔和龍頭製作精細，説明在二百多年前中國的鑄造工藝已經十分精湛。

The pavilion's ridge. The pagoda and the dragon's head are examples of fine casting craftsmanship. They show the maturity of China's casting art two hundred years ago.

亭壁花紋 用中國傳統的鑄造工藝——“撥蠟”法製成，即先雕刻蠟模，外面用泥做範，熔金屬注入泥範而成。爲作紀念，亭内南墻上刻有參加這項工程的工匠的名字，這是珍貴的史料。

Designs on the pavilion. These designs were cast from wax moulds, a process requiring a very high degree of skill. The names of the artisans appear on the southern wall inside the pavilion.

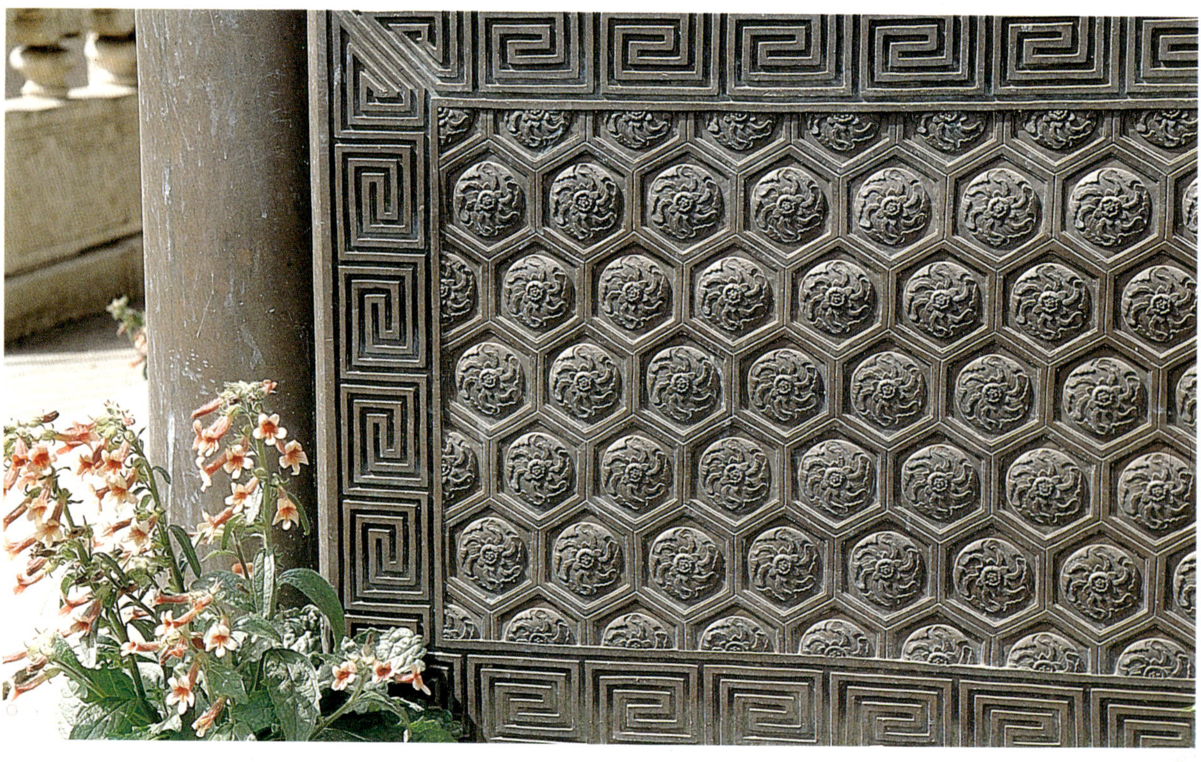

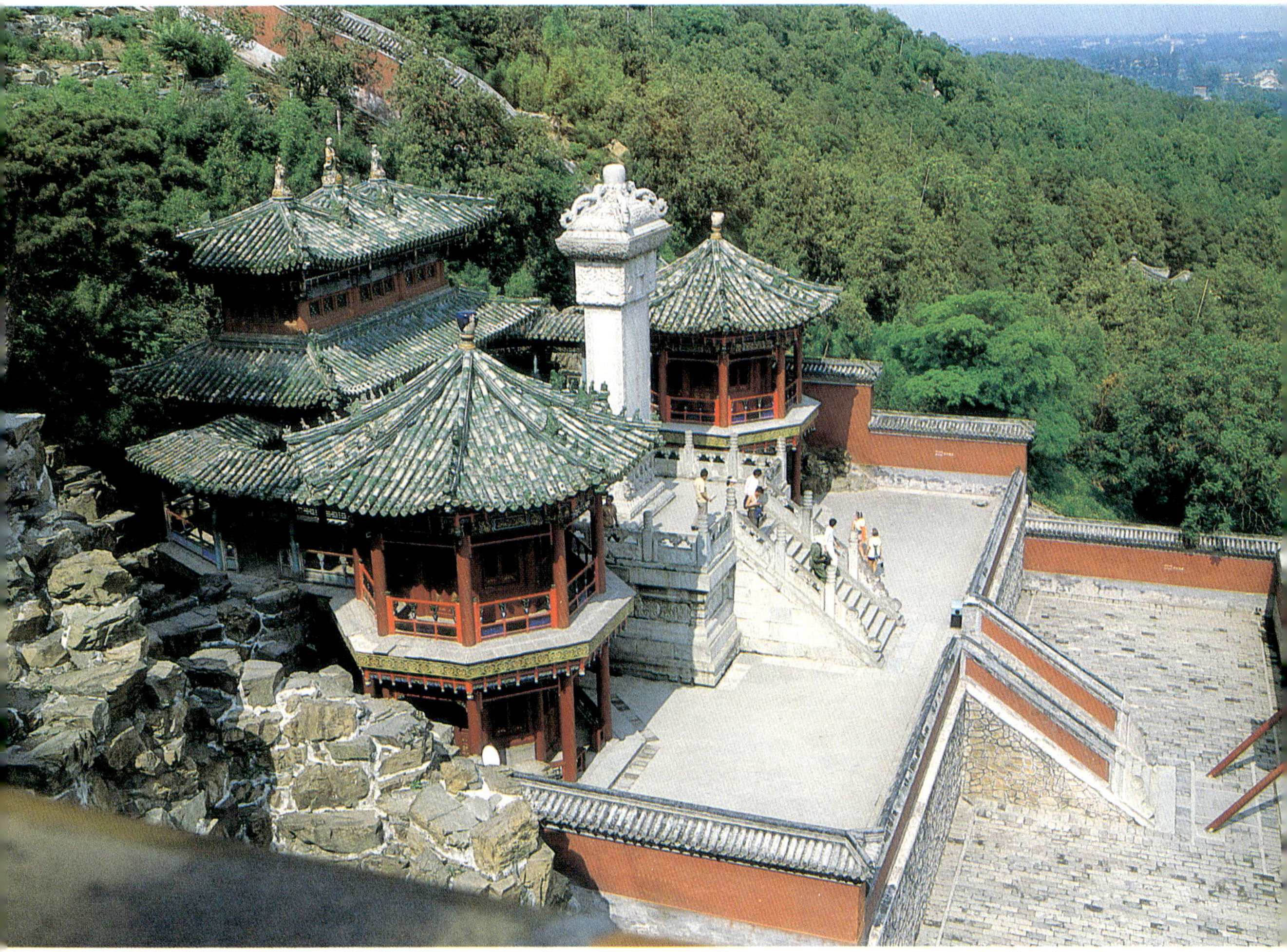

轉輪藏　是佛香閣東側山坡上的一組建築物，由正殿、配亭和“萬壽山昆明湖”石碑組成。這裏是帝、后貯藏經書、佛像和念經祈禱的地方。

Revolving Archive. Zhuanluncang (Revolving Archive) is a group of buildings east of the Tower of the Fragrance of Buddha, consisting of the main building, the side-pavilions and the large stone tablet bearing the inscription "Longevity Hill, Kunming Lake". This was where the emperors and empresses kept copies of Confucian classics, Buddhist scriptures and Buddha portraits, and where they chanted scriptures and said their prayers.

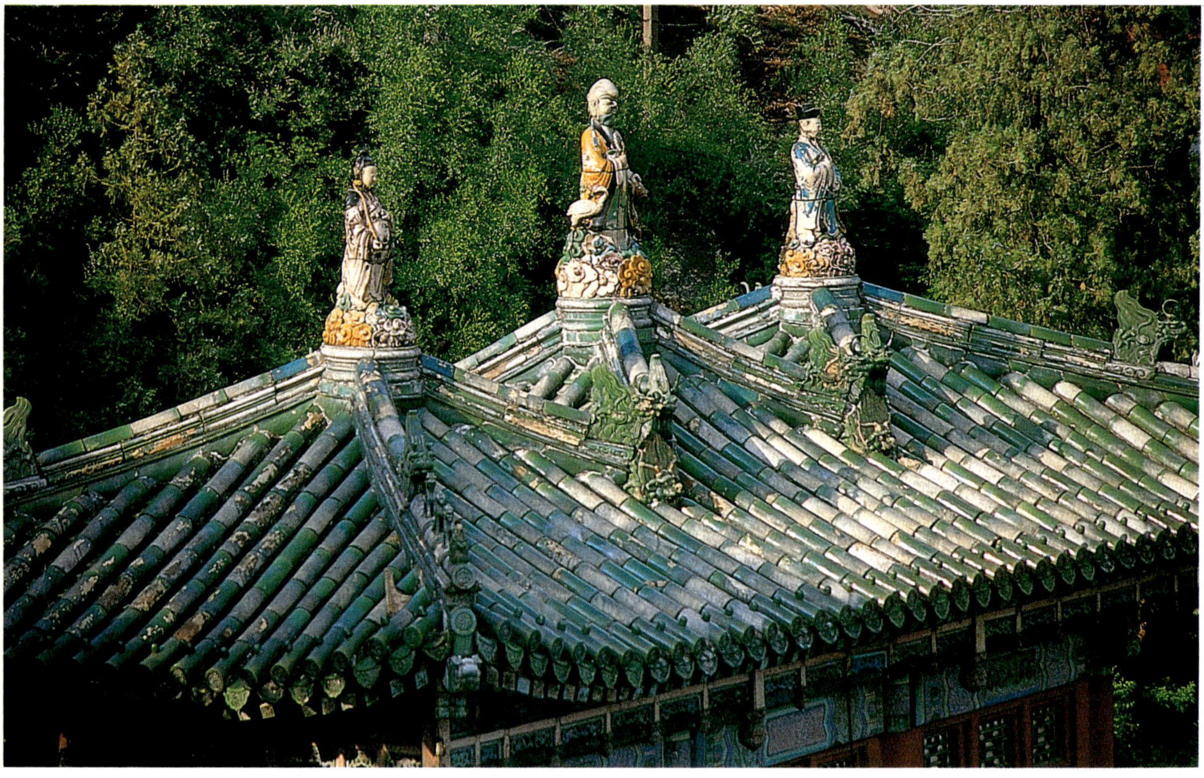

殿脊神像 正殿殿脊上的琉璃像是福、禄、壽三星神像。

Glazed figures. On the roof of the main hall of the Revolving Archive stand three glazed figures representing happiness, emolument and longevity.

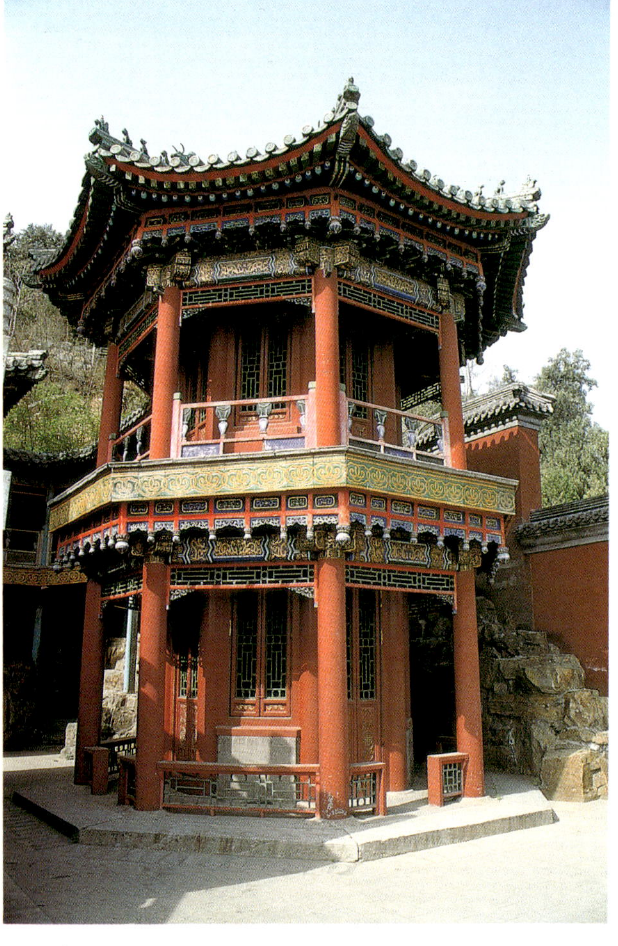

藏經亭 亭中設有八面可藏經書和佛像的木塔，塔有中軸，推之可轉動。帝、后入亭祈禱，衹須輕輕轉動木塔，就算把經書念了一遍，所以叫“轉輪藏”。

Archive towers. The octagonal wooden towers, one each in the two side pavilions, once held Buddhist scriptures and Buddha portraits. They revolved about a central axis controlled by a mechanism below. When emperors and empresses came to chant scriptures and say their prayers, they just turned the towers. Hence the name Revolving Archive.

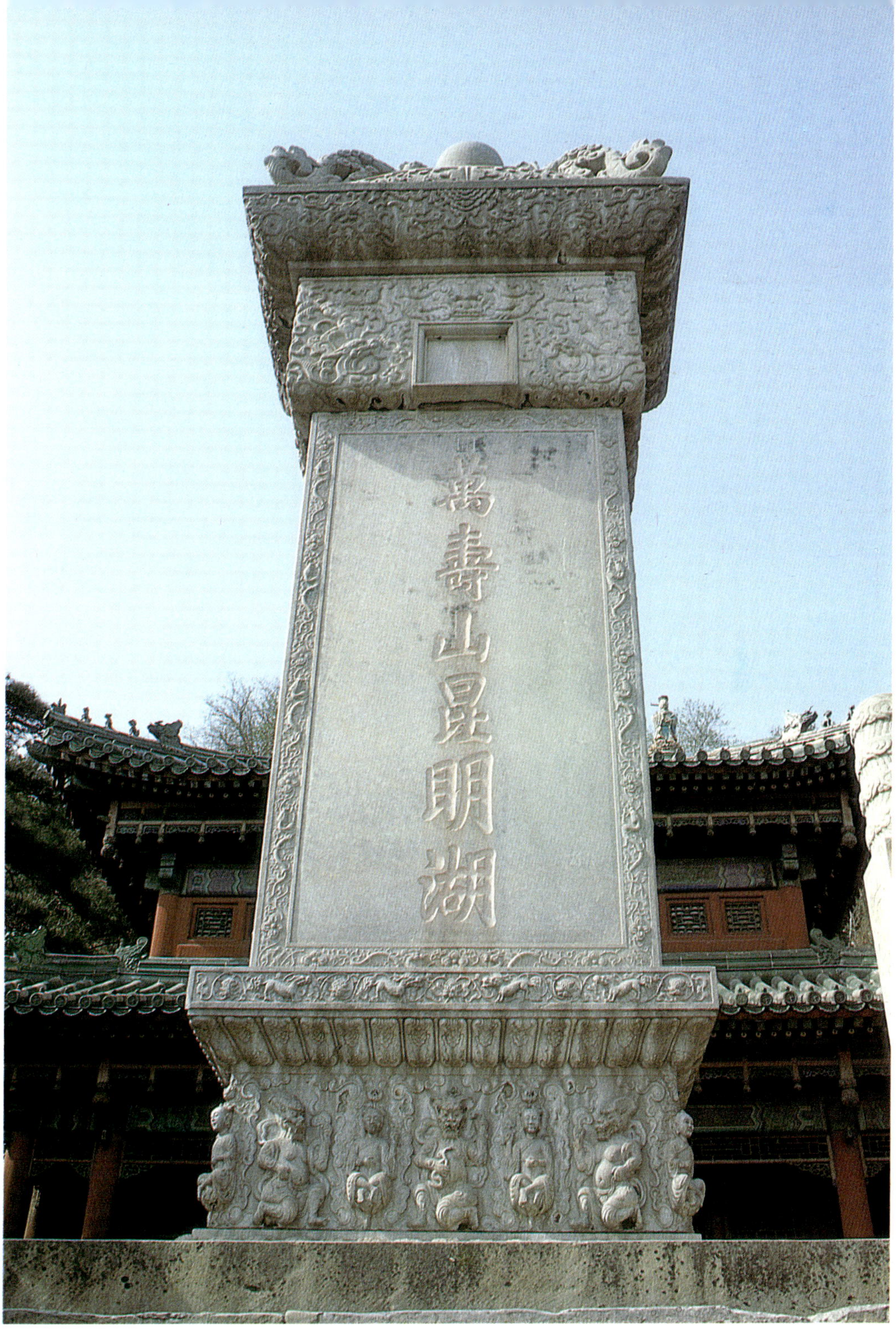

石碑　建於一七五一年。正面刻“萬壽山昆明湖”六個大字，背面刻《萬壽山昆明湖記》碑文一篇，均爲乾隆皇帝御筆。

The stone tablet. This beautifully carved tablet was erected in 1751. On its front side are the words "Longevity Hill; Kunming Lake" and on its back side is an essay entitled "Notes on Longevity Hill and Kunming Lake", both of which are in Emperor Qianlong's handwriting.

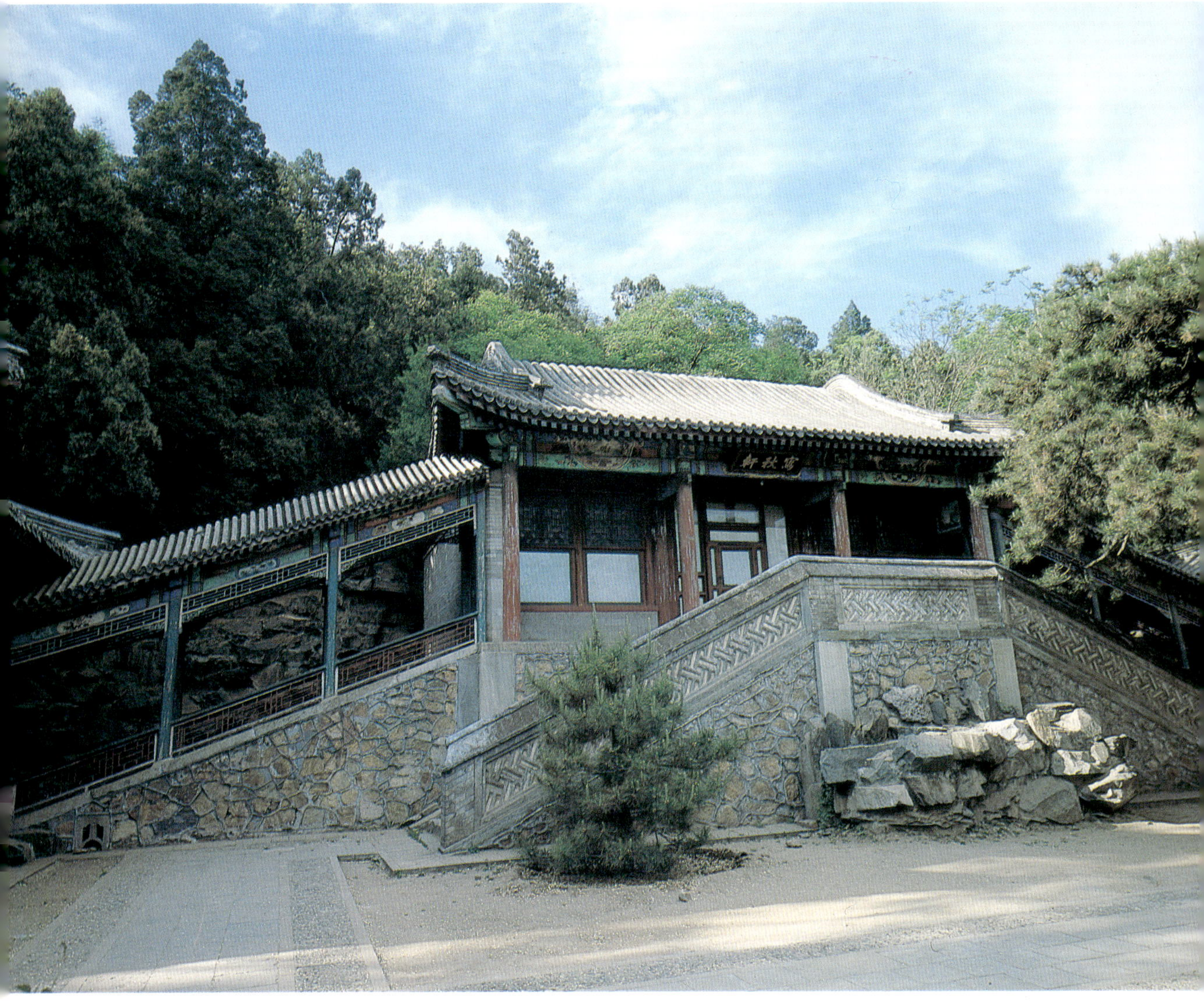

寫秋軒 背山而建，左右以小廊下接尋雲、觀生意二亭，是一處點景建築。乾隆年間這裏遍植黄櫨樹，深秋紅葉映軒，景色迷人。

Pavilion for Writing about Autumn. Built on the slope of the hill, this pavilion is connected with two towers through a small corridor. Smoke trees were planted around here in the Qianlong Period. In late autumn, when the tree leaves turn red, the red leaves and the pavilion form a fascinating picture.

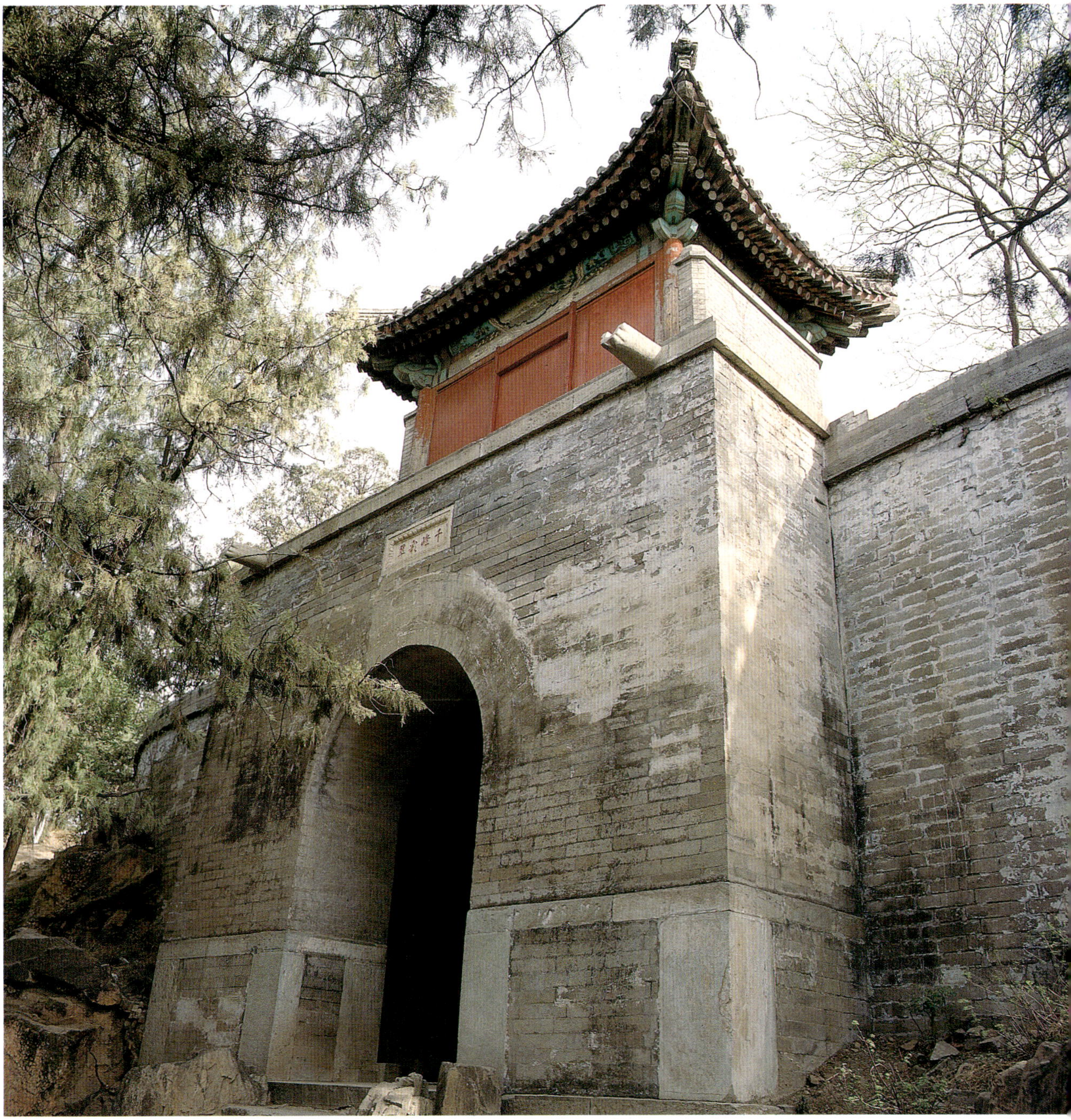

千峰彩翠 位於萬壽山東部山頂，爲城關式建築。據民間傳説，一八八八年重建頤和園的工程行將結束時，風鑑家認爲山頂太空，可望見園外的六郎莊，而漢字“郎”“狼”諧音，慈禧太后屬相爲羊，一羊遇一狼尚且不敵，何况如今一羊遇六狼，所以内憂外患頻仍。於是建議修這座城關式門樓以鎮六狼，並把六郎莊改名爲太平莊。

Thousand Green Peaks Tower. Located on the eastern top of the hill, this tower is in the style of a city gate. According to a folktale, when the rebuilding of the Summer Palace was about to complete in 1888, the geomancer found that there were very little buildings on the top of the hill, from where Liulang Village outside the park could be seen. "Liulang" is the homophony of "six wolves" in Chinese. The geomancer thought: as the Empress Dowager was born in the year of sheep, how can sheep stand against six wolves? This probably is the reason why the country is besieged with domestic trouble and foreign invasion. So he ordered the tower built here and changed the name of the village from "Liulang Village" to "Pacific Village".

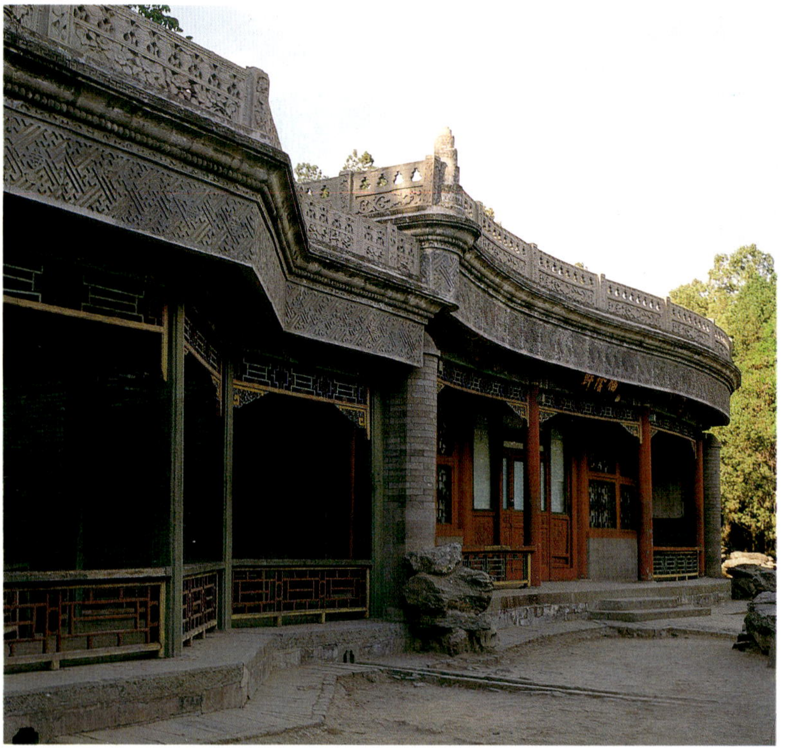

福蔭軒　俗名書券殿，三間。在它西面巖石間刻有"燕臺大觀"四字。由此可南望昆明湖，煙雲蒼溟，雲水盡覽。

Pavilion of Blessed Shade. Also known as Juandian, this pavilion consists of three bays. On the rock west of the pavilion is carved "Yantai Grand View". From here there is an excellent view of the misty Kunming Lake.

蕾亭　爲兩個六角亭套合而成，形似蝙蝠，既是點景建築，又是觀景亭。在此遠眺近觀，各有樂趣。

Tower of Luxuriant Growth. Formed with two hexagon towers in the shape of a bat, this tower also provides excellent views of the landscape.

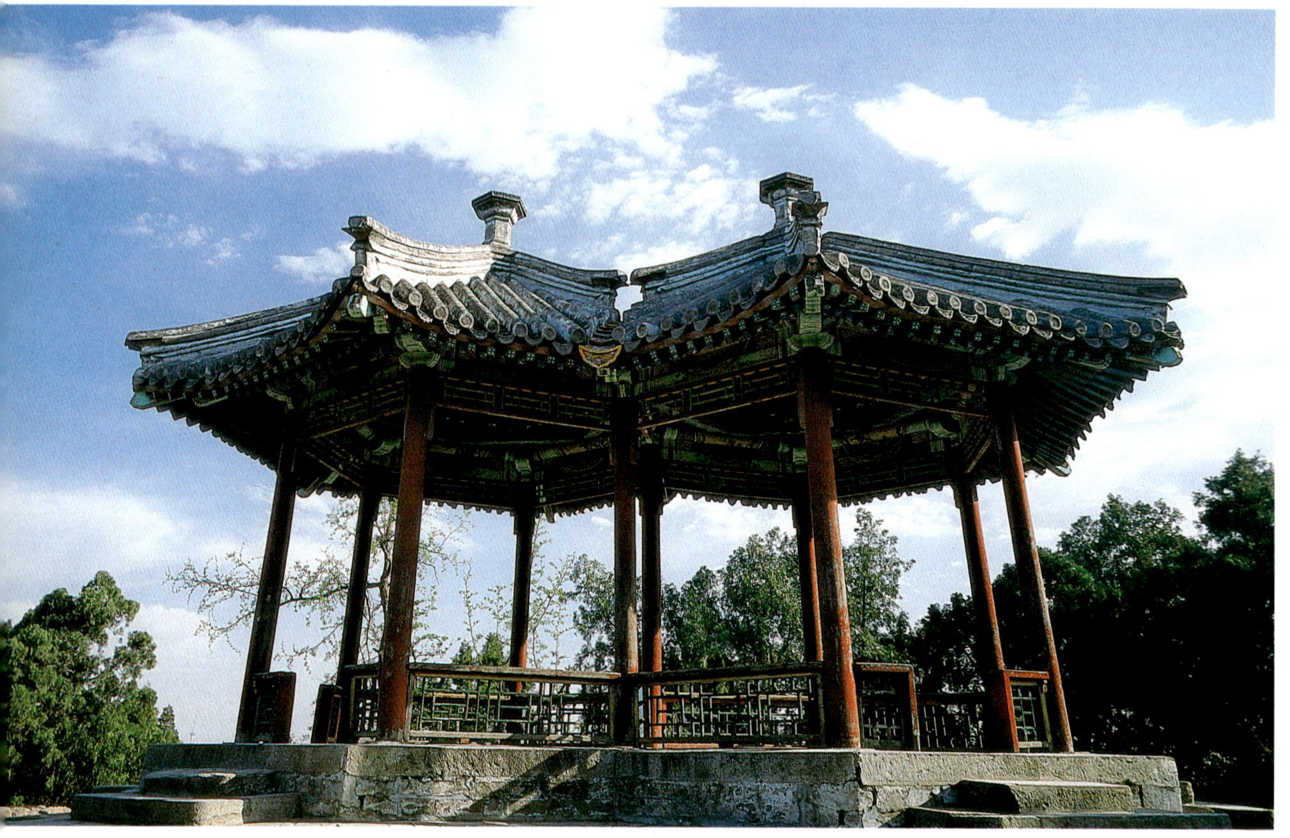

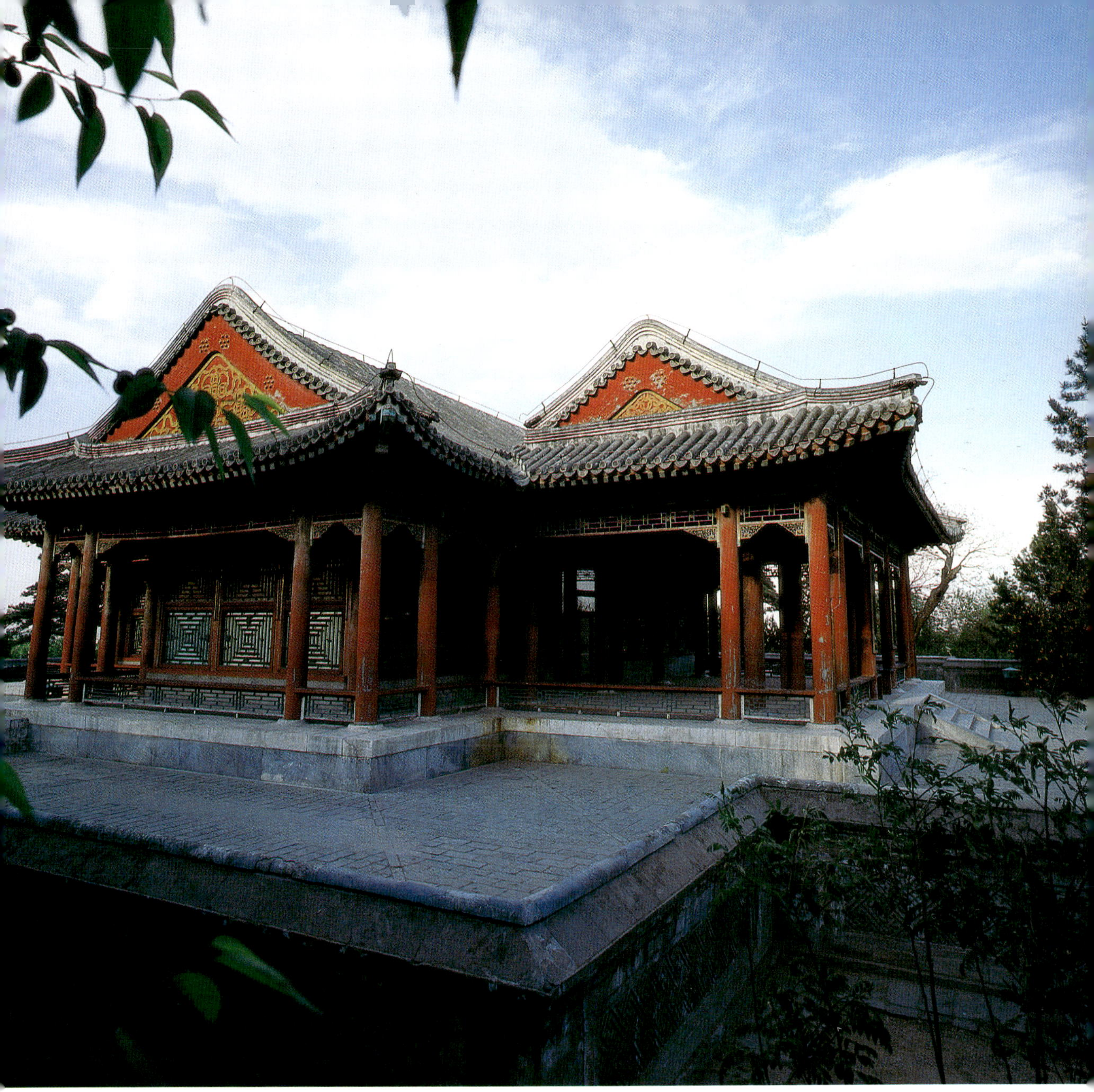

景福閣 前後各五間，有曲廊相通。憑欄四望，湖光山色美不勝收。慈禧太后每年七月初七在此祭牛郎織女，八月中秋在此賞月，九月重陽在此品嘗野味，盛夏常在此和后、妃、宮女們押寶、推牌九。

Pavilion of Blessed Scenery. This pavilion is a relatively large building with three interconnected *juanpeng* (rolled-mat) roof pieces and a spacious open hall facing south. It commands a good view of the lake and its surrounding landscape. The old Empress Dowager came here to worship the Cowherd and the Girl Weaver on the seventh day of the seventh month every lunar year; enjoy the moon at the Mid-August Festival; eat rare dishes at the Double-Ninth Festival; or play cards with empresses, consorts and palace maids in the summer time.

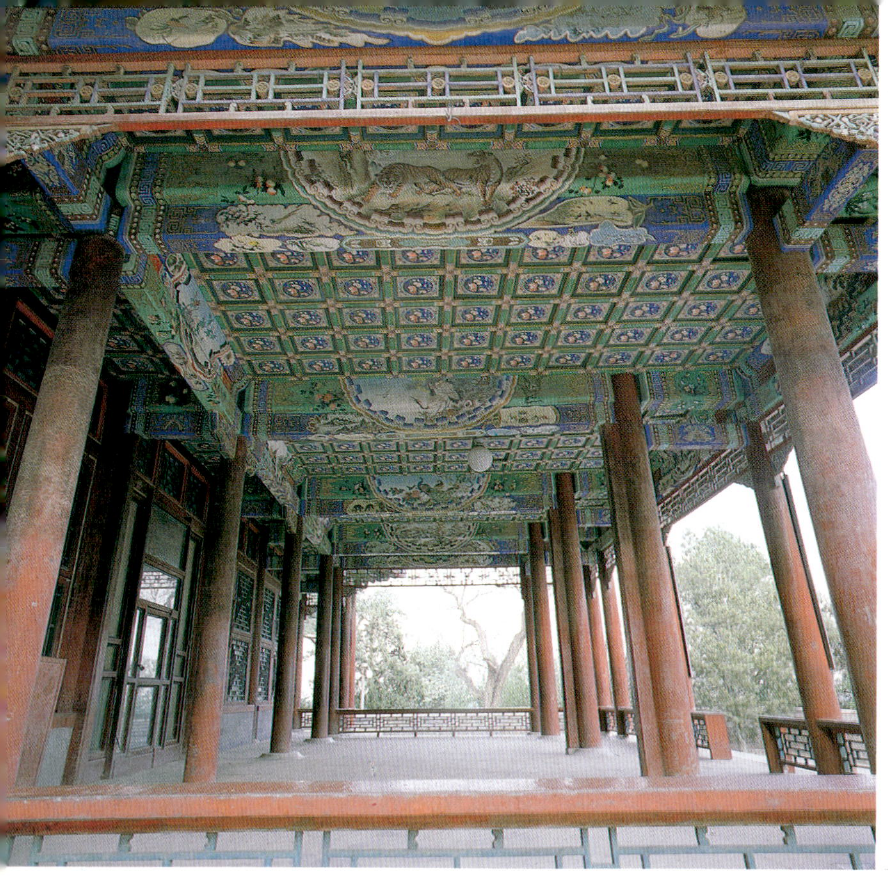

景福閣敞廳 實爲抱厦。天花板及樑枋繪滿彩畫。廳三面寬敞明亮，是賞景的理想之所。

The open hall of the Pavilion of Blessed Scenery. With painted beams and ceilings, the hall is very spacious, providing a good view of the lake and the landscape around it.

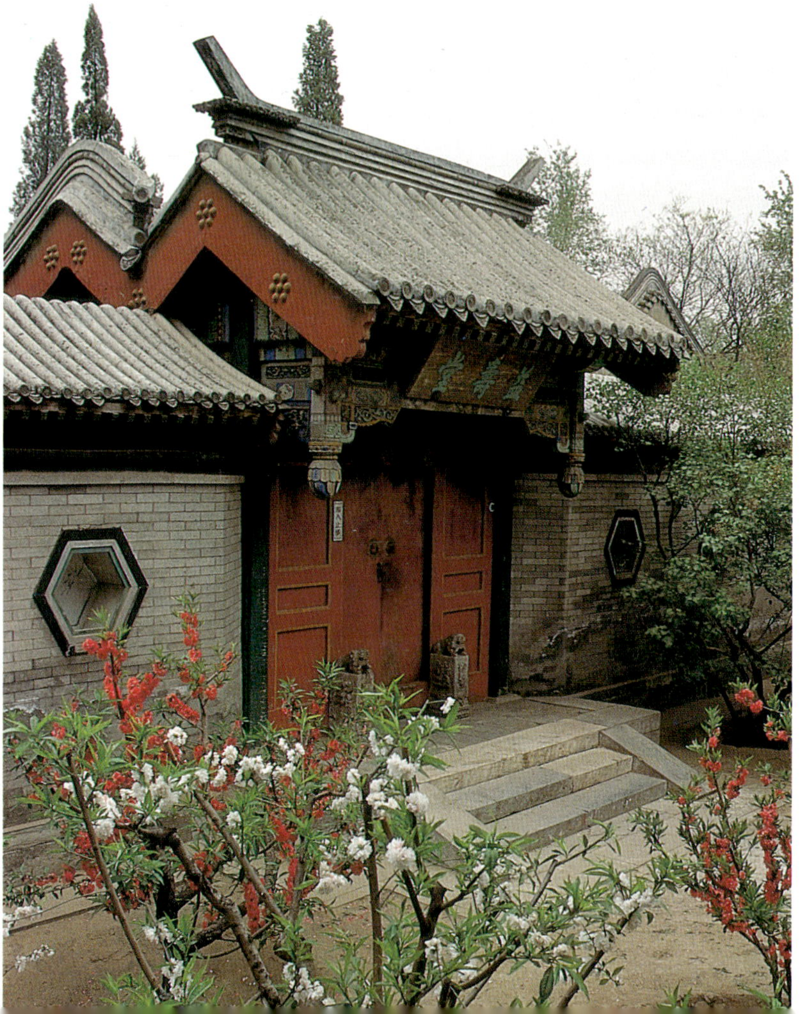

益壽堂 爲一四合院。内有正堂五間，配堂兩座，四周圍以磚墻，墻上刻滿花紋圖案。一九四九年春三月，毛澤東主席曾在此宴請在京的民主人士。隨後，在《和柳亞子先生》的詩中寫下了"莫道昆明池水淺，觀魚勝過富春江"的著名詩句。

Hall of Benefit and Longevity. This is a courtyard with a main hall of five bays and two side-halls. Their four walls are carved in various patterns. In March, 1949, Chairman Mao Zedong held a banquet here to entertain democratic personages, after which he wrote a poem entitled "To Mr Liu Yazi". Two lines run as follows:

Do not say that the waters of Kunming Lake are too shallow;
For watching fish they are better than Fuchun River.

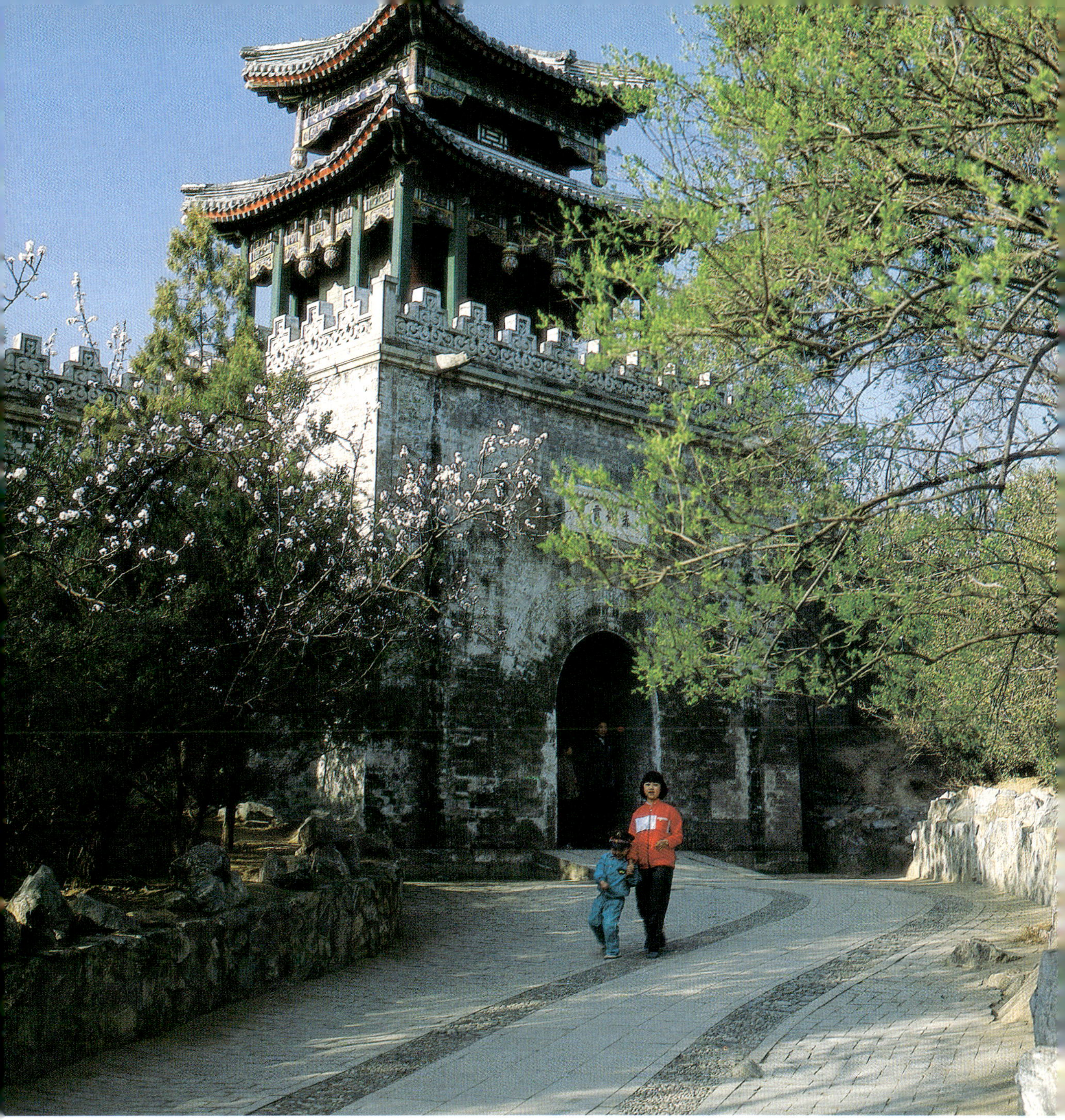

紫氣東來 位於萬壽山東麓，爲一雙層四角飛檐關樓。"紫氣"多指祥瑞之氣。清晨至此，旭日初照，晨霧升騰，確有紫氣繞身之感。

Tower of Violet Clouds Coming from the East. This is a two-storeyed building with double-eaved roof on the eastern slope of Longevity Hill. Violet clouds mean auspicious clouds. In early morning at sunrise, the tower is covered in mist as if everything is surrounded by violet clouds.

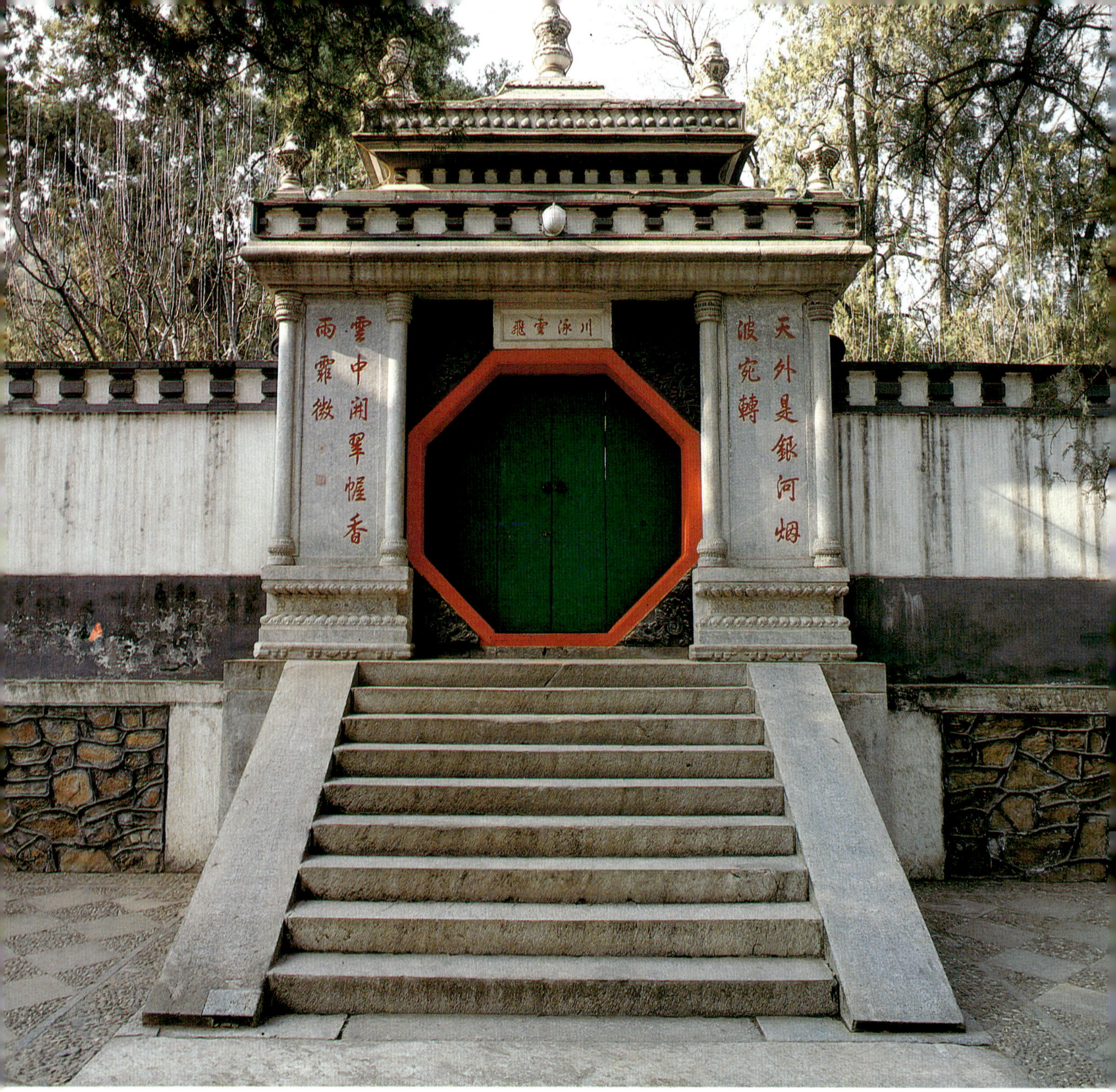

養雲軒 位於長廊東首之北，門如鐘形。額上"川泳雲飛"四字爲乾隆皇帝御題。門前有荷塘，形如葫蘆，所以也稱"葫蘆河"，上架石橋。門內有軒五間，爲清代妃嬪休息之所。

Clouds Gathering Pavilion. North of the eastern end of the Long Promenande, the pavilion has a door in the shape of a bell. Above the door were carved the words "Winding Stream and Flying Clouds" in Emperor Qianlong's handwriting. In front of the pavilion is a lotus pond in the shape of a gourd with a bridge across it. The five halls inside it were the resting place of imperial consorts.

國花臺　建於一九〇三年，又名牡丹臺。　爲倚山壘土而成，臺上廣種牡丹。慈禧太后常以富貴花牡丹自比，特定牡丹爲國花，並命人將“國花臺”三字刻於石上。

National Flower Terrace. Built in 1903, it is also known as Peony Terrace. The old Empress Dowager often compared herself to the gorgeous peony. She was so fond of the peony that she named it the national flower and ordered "National Flower Terrace" carved into the rock on the terrace.

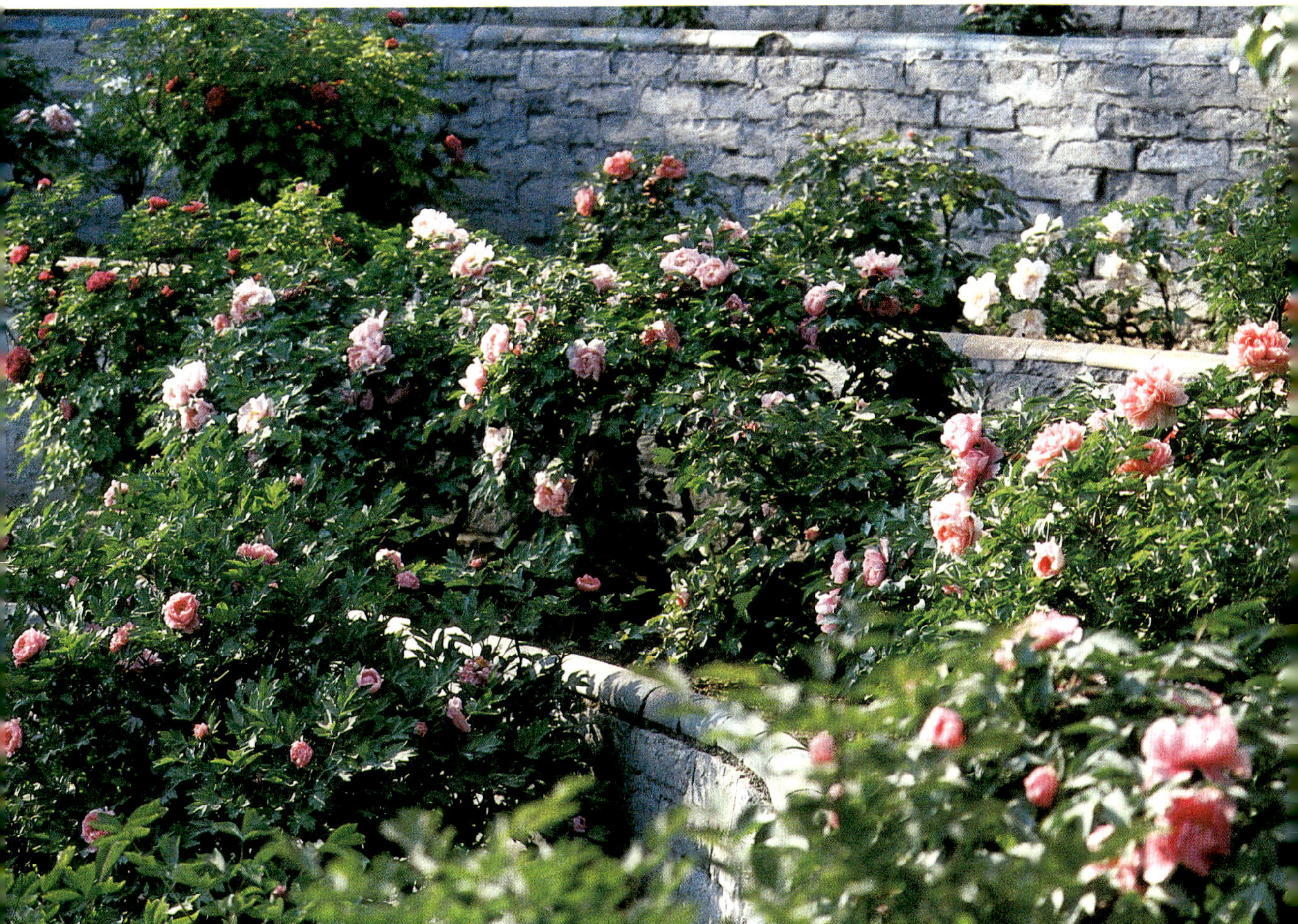

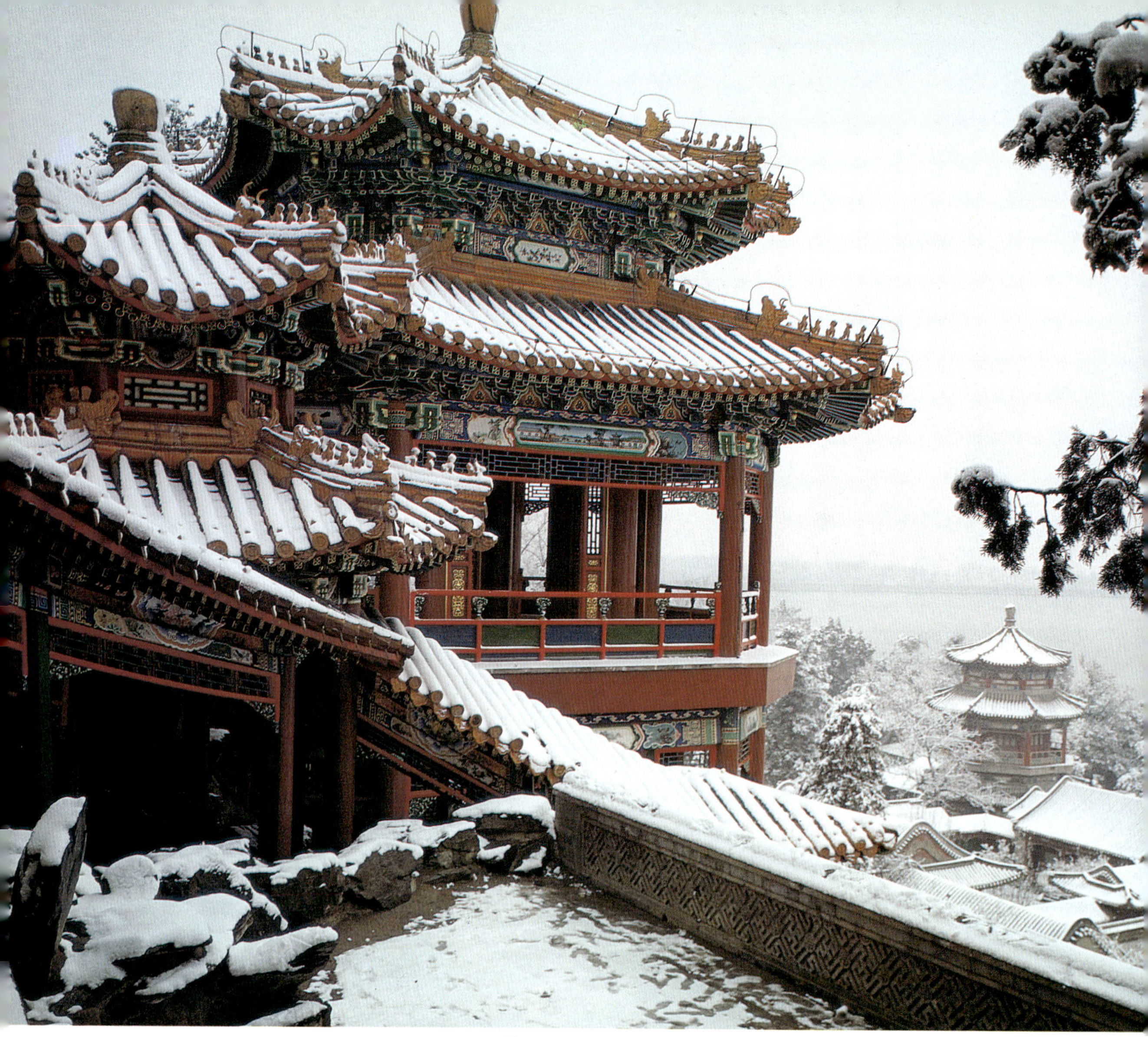

畫中遊　爲佛香閣西側較大的點景建築，共有三亭二樓一齋一牌坊。主建築是雙層八角重檐的大敞亭。此組建築倚山高築，遊人至此，居高臨下，循廊觀景，一步一趣，彷彿置身於畫中，故名“畫中遊”。

Strolling Through a Picture-Scroll. This complex of buildings stands on the hillside west of the Tower of the Fragrance of Buddha. It has three towers, two pavilions, a gallery and an arched gateway. The main building is a large octagonal two-storeyed open pavilion with a double-eaved roof of green and yellow glazed tiles. It was intended to give the visitor a feeling of strolling through a picture.

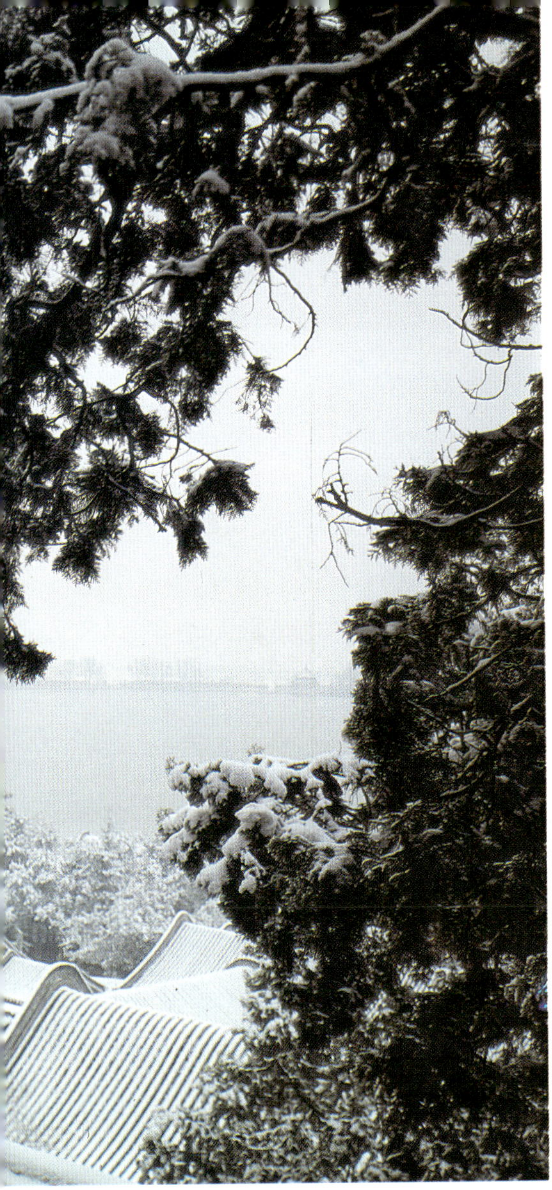

借秋樓　畫中遊大敞亭的東面有愛山樓，西面有借秋樓，好似一主二僕，相伴相隨。二樓後有曲廊、小徑與其他建築相通。循徑登石，爬廊鑽洞，其樂無窮。

Tower for Borrowing Autumn. To the east of the complex of buildings of Strolling Through a Picture-Scroll stands the Tower for Loving the Hill and to the west is the Tower for Borrowing Autumn. Behind the two towers are serpentine galleries and paths leading to other buildings. Strolling through the galleries, paths and grottoes can be an enjoyable experience.

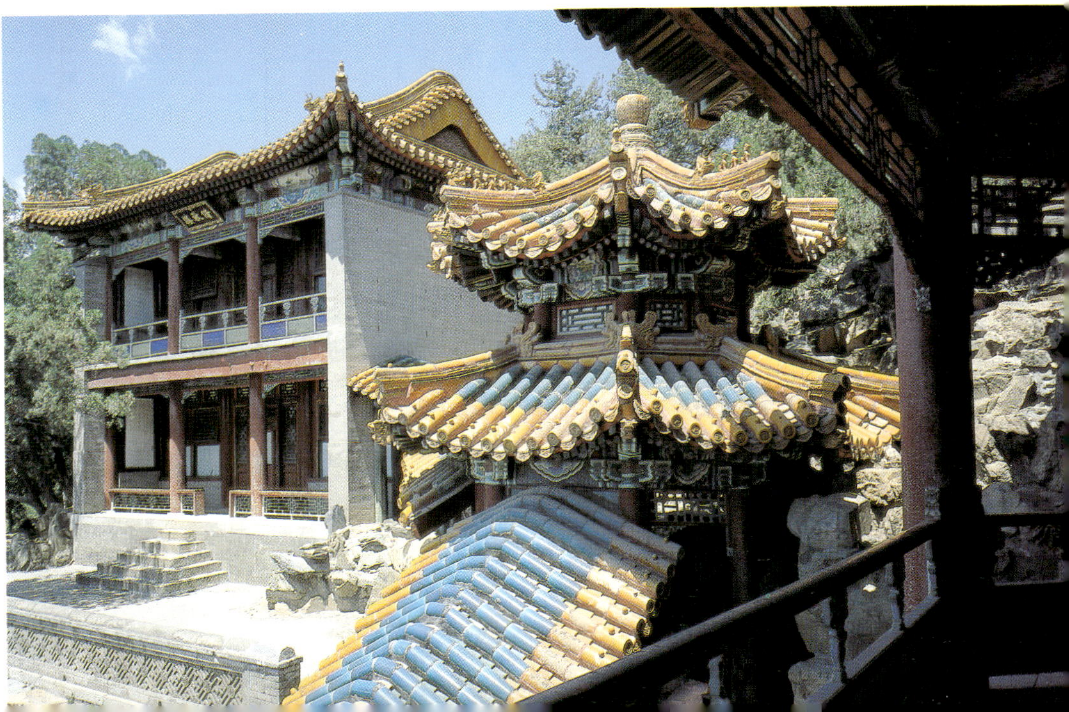

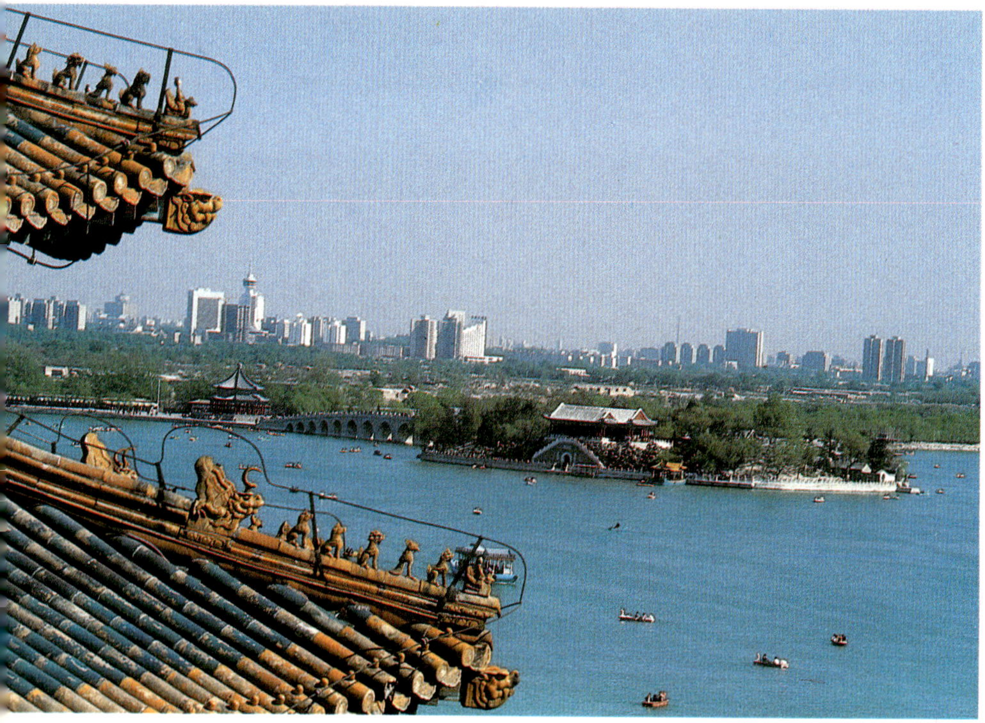

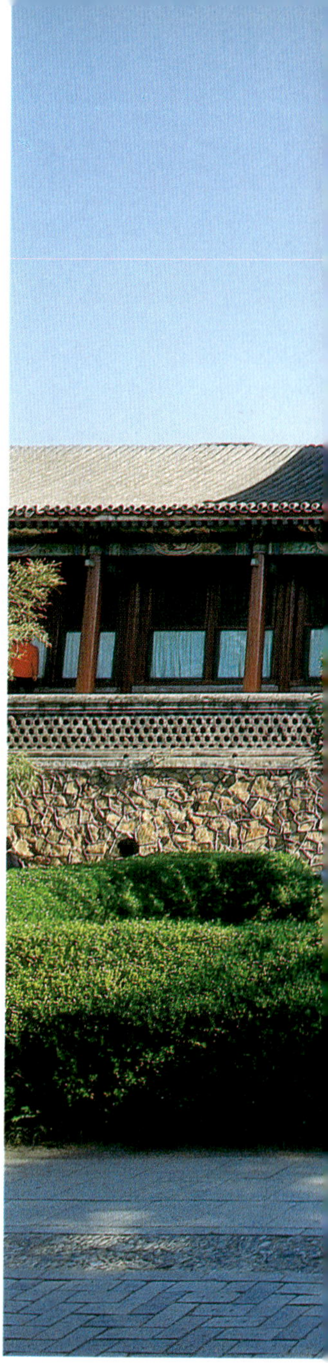

畫中遊觀景　南望昆明湖碧水似玉，南湖島翠黛如屏，正如乾隆皇帝在畫中遊牌坊上所題："山川映發使人接應不暇，身所履歷自欣得此奇觀。"

View from the two-storeyed open pavilion. Viewed from the pavilion, the water of Kunming Lake looks like jade, South Lake Island becomes a green screen. It is indeed a marvellous view.

小戲臺　在德和園大戲樓建成前，慈禧太后常在此看戲。

Small stage. Empress Dowager Cixi was fond of operas. She often came here to enjoy performances before the much larger Great Stage in the Garden of Virtue and Harmony was completed.

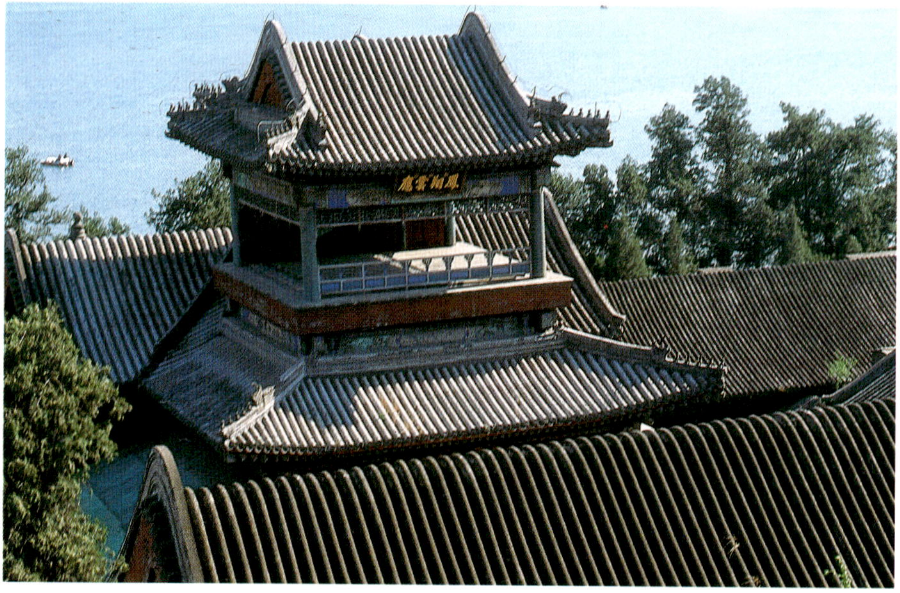

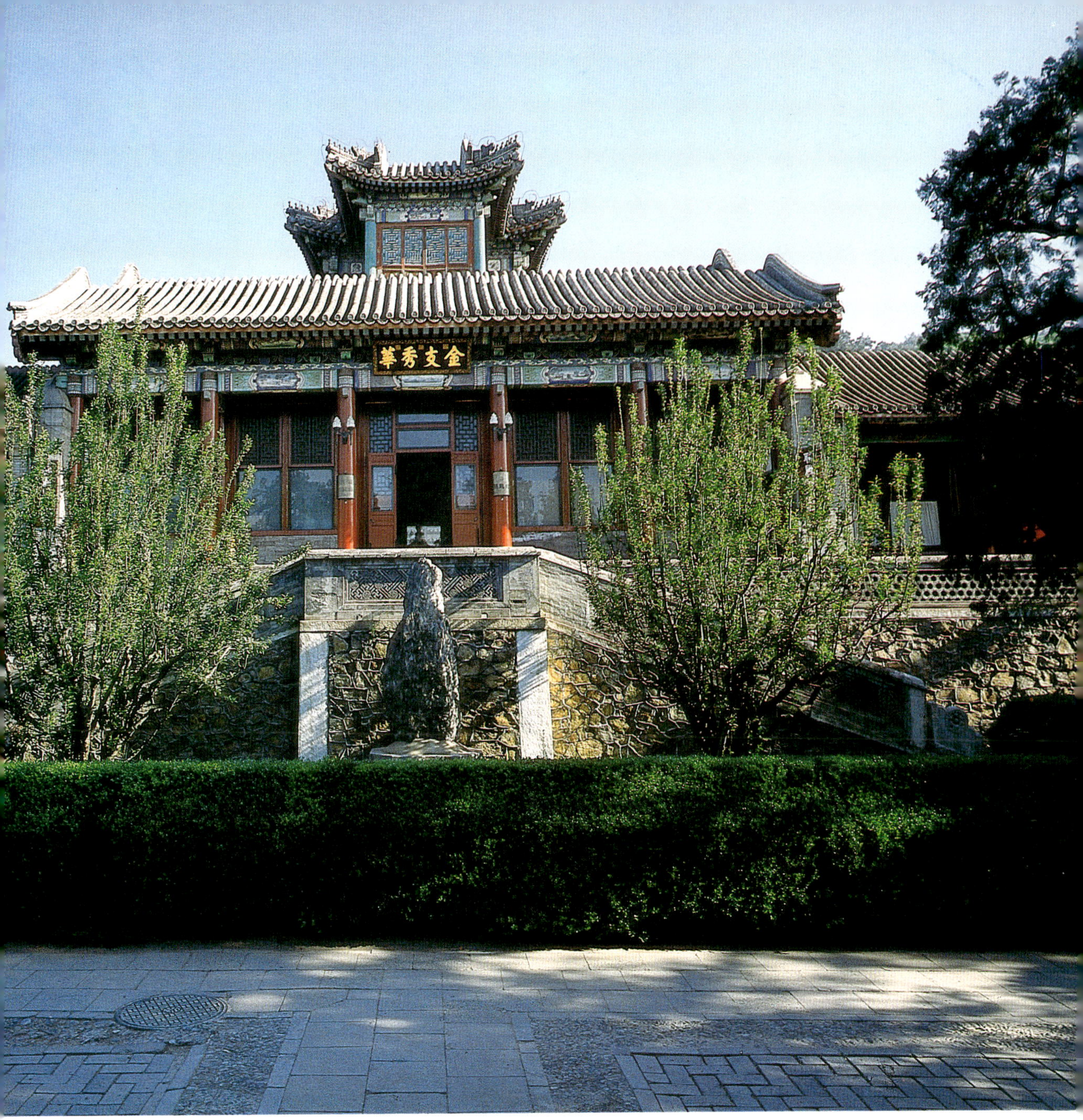

聽鸝館　内設戲臺。正門門匾“金支秀華”原指古樂器上飾的金花，這裏喻宮廷藝術猶如金枝麗花。現在，聽鸝館已闢爲旅遊餐廳，遊客可在此品嘗宮廷佳餚。

Pavilion for Listening to Orioles. Inside the pavilion there is a two-storeyed stage for theatrical performances. Above the front gate of the pavilion is the inscription "Golden Branches and Beautiful Flowers". Today, the pavilion has been transformed into a large restaurant serving many of the famous dishes once prepared in the imperial kitchen.

清晏舫 又名石舫，建於一七五五年，舫身係用巨石雕造而成。通長三十六米，有上下兩層艙房。取意“水能載舟，亦能覆舟”，喻示清王朝堅如磐石，水不能覆。

Boat of Purity and Ease. Popularly known as the Marble Boat, the boat was built in 1755. It is 36 metres long, with a hull and upper deck made of massive stone slabs. The saying goes: "Water can carry a boat, and it can also capsize a boat." By following the allusion, the marble boat was built to mean that the Qing Dynasty would be as solid as rock and never fall.

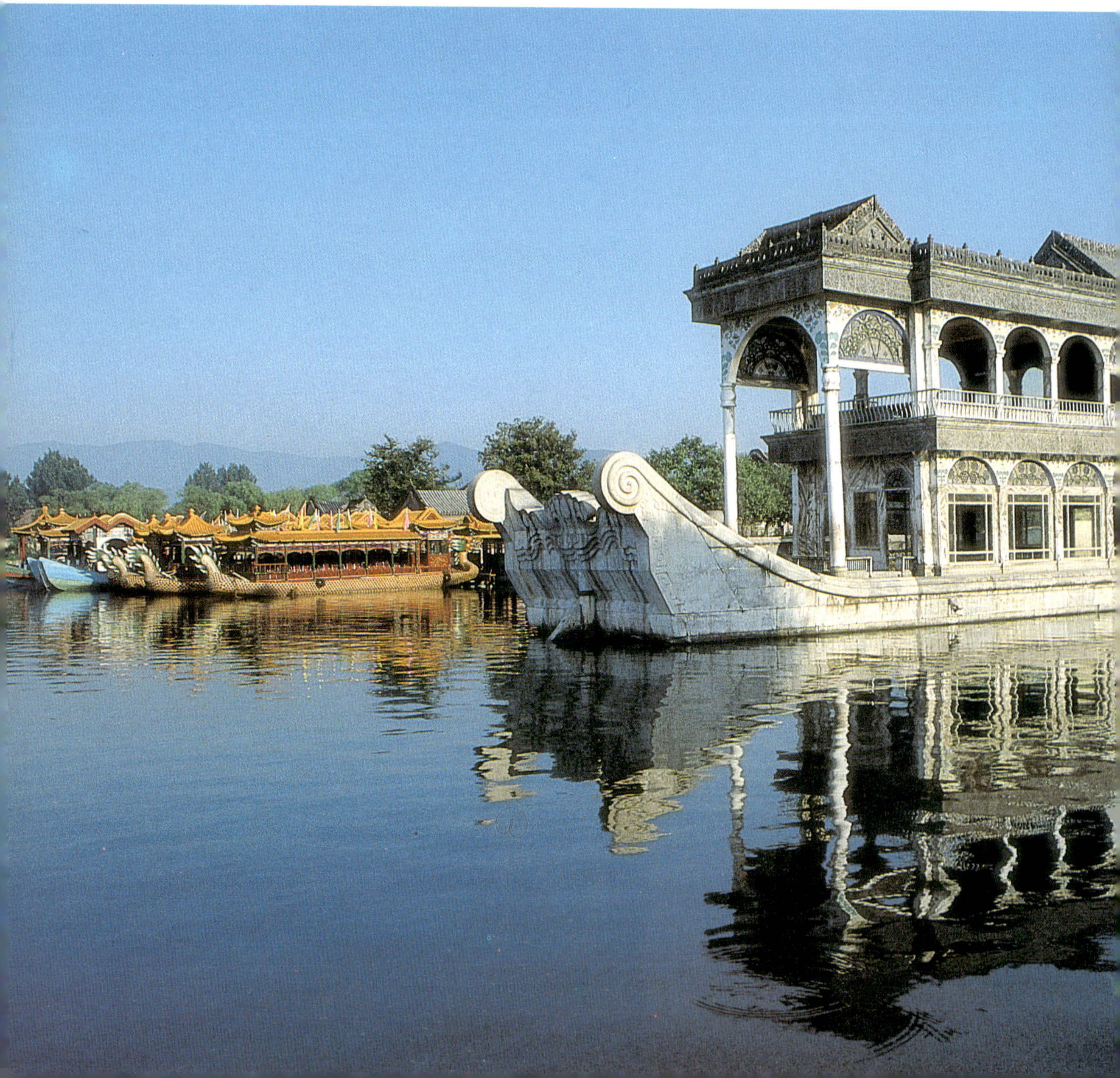

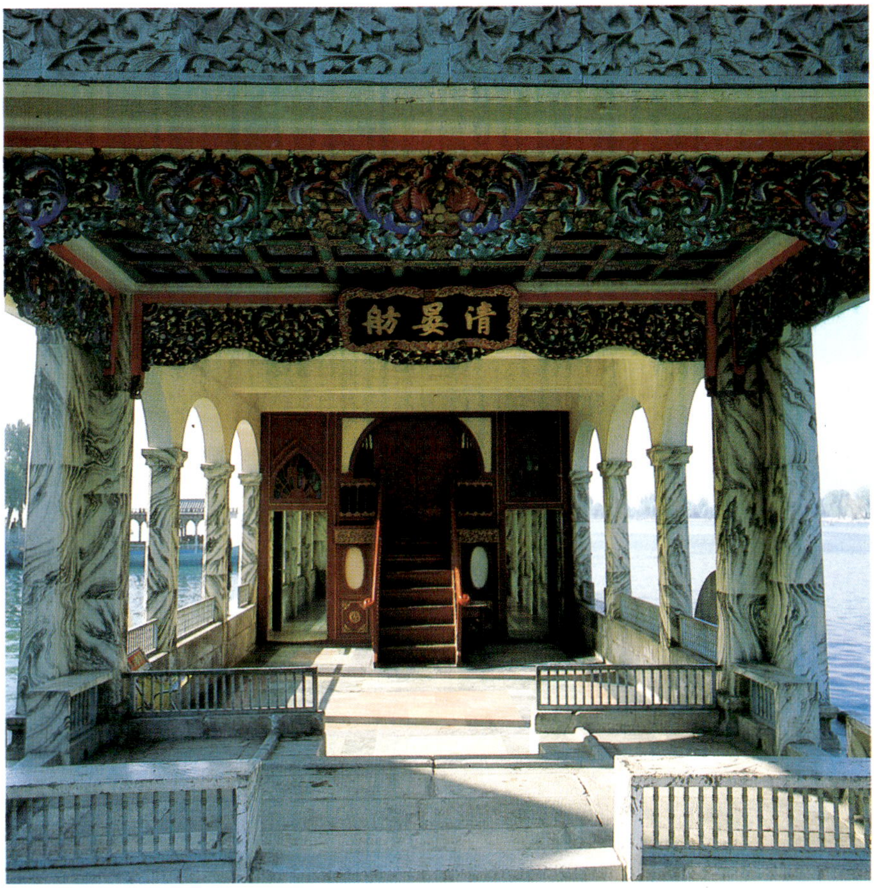

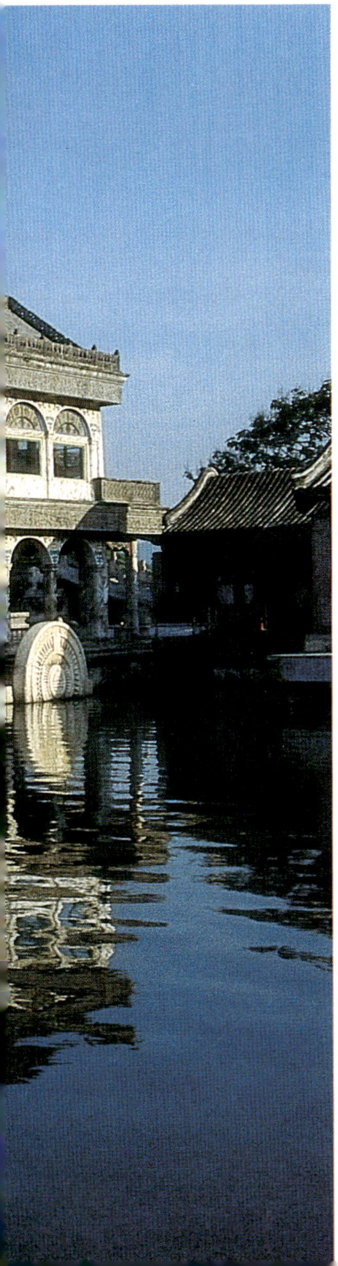

石舫底艙 艙爲木結構，地墁花磚，窗嵌五色玻璃。盛夏時慈禧太后常在艙内用早點、吃夜宵，故將石舫命名爲“清晏舫”。據另説，“海清河晏”爲中國成語，是比喻天下太平的意思，取其爲石舫名，寓意清王朝國泰民安。

The cabin of the boat. The cabin is made of wood, the lower deck is paved with floral bricks, and the windows are of stained glass with mosaic design. The old Empress Dowager often had her breakfast and dinner in the cabin in the summer time.

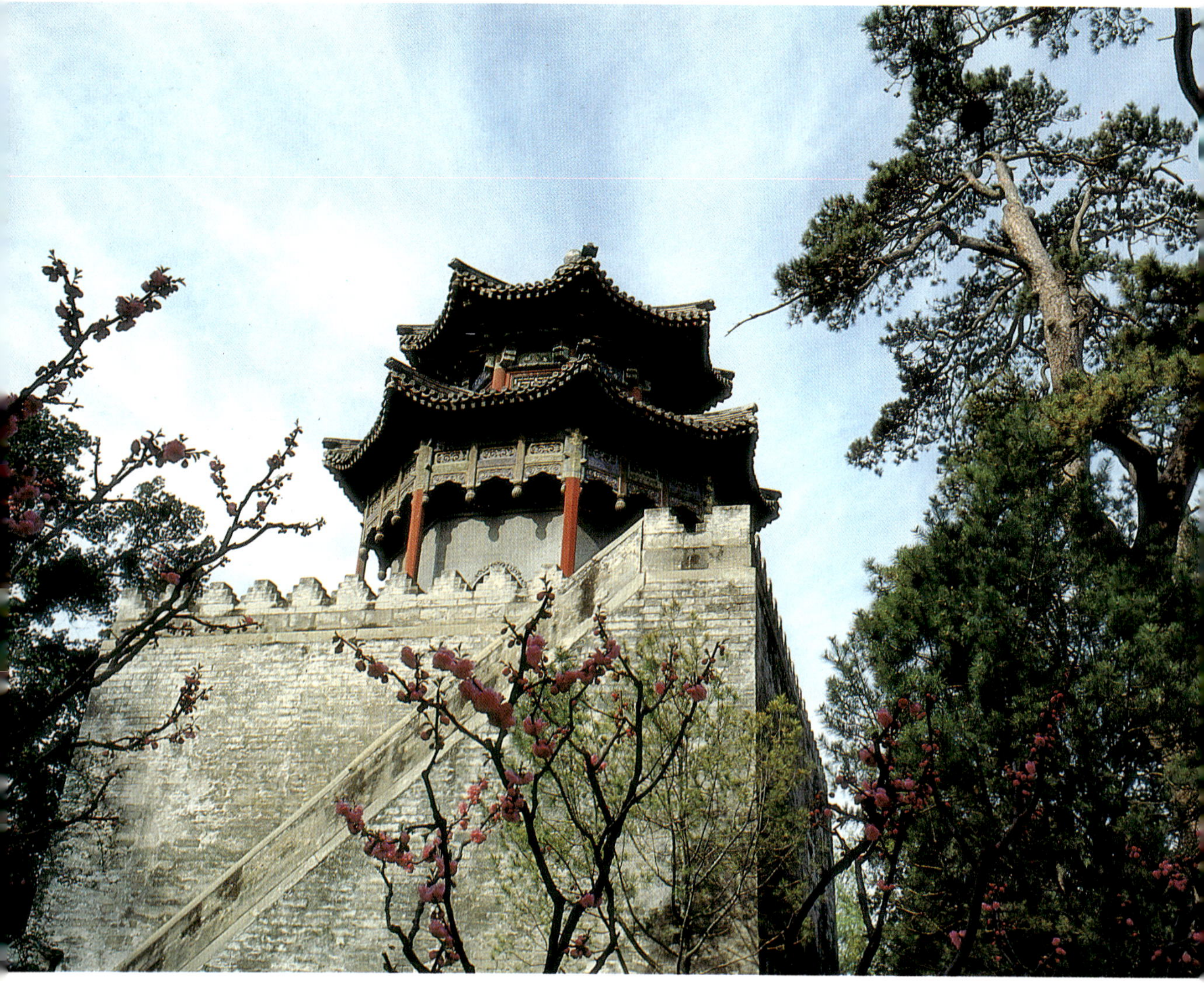

宿雲檐 爲一獨立無靠的城關。城上原有樓，内供三國時代（公元二二〇——二八〇年）蜀漢名將關羽的塑像，後改爲亭式建築，已無供像。登關南望，可見西所買賣街（小蘇州街）遺址。

Suyunzhan. This is an independent tower. Originally, inside the tower there was a statue of Guan Yu, a hero during the Three Kingdoms period (220-280 AD), but later the statue was removed. From the tower one can see the ruins of the little Suzhou Street.

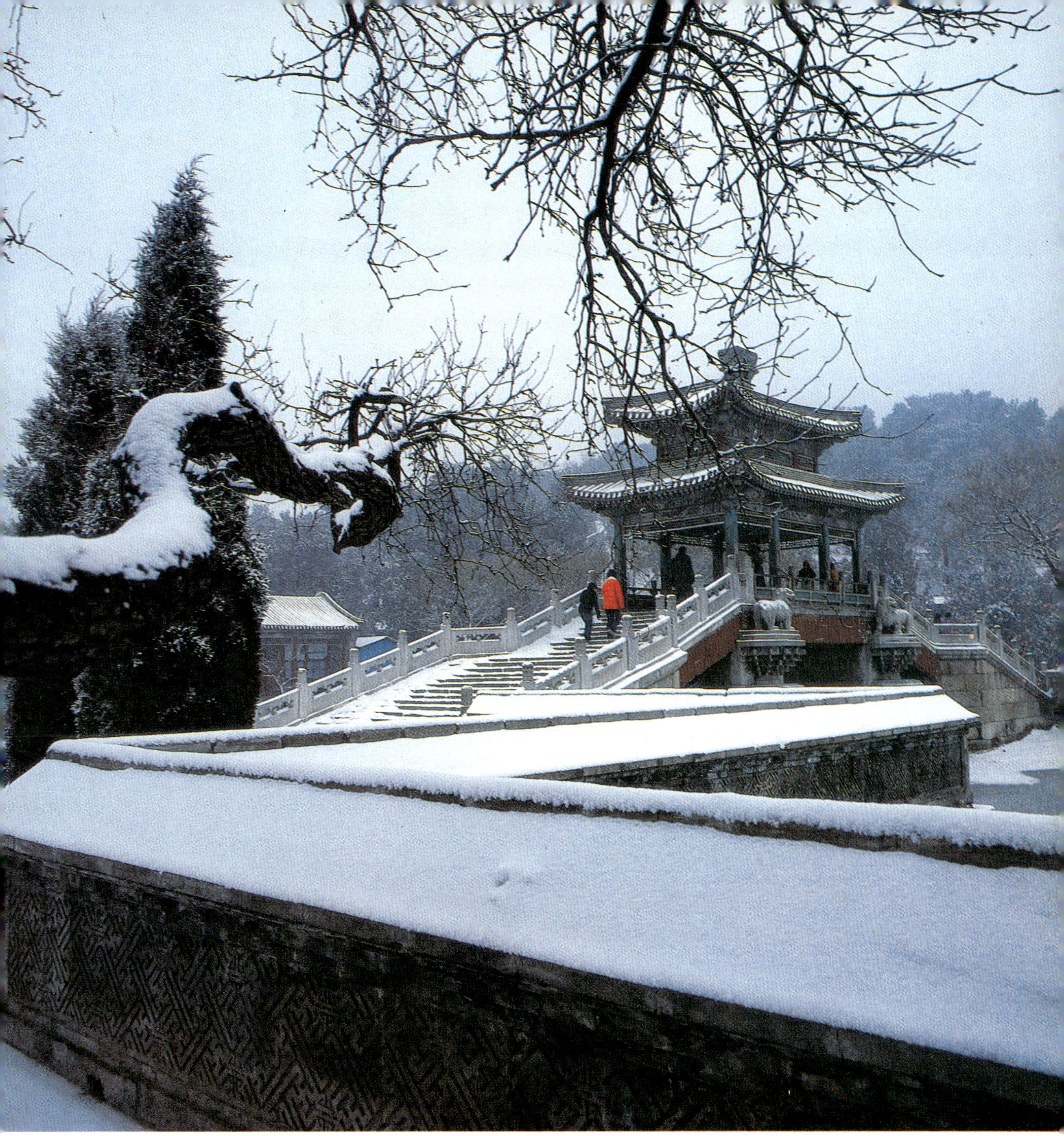

荇橋 位於石舫北。橋上置雙層四角方亭，橋墩兩端有石獅，設計和建造很有特色。

Bridge of Floating Hearts. North of the Marble Boat is a stone bridge with an open pavilion above it, called the Bridge of Floating Hearts. The pavilion has a double-eaved roof and the bridge has exquisitely carved lions on its piers. The design and building are very unique in style.

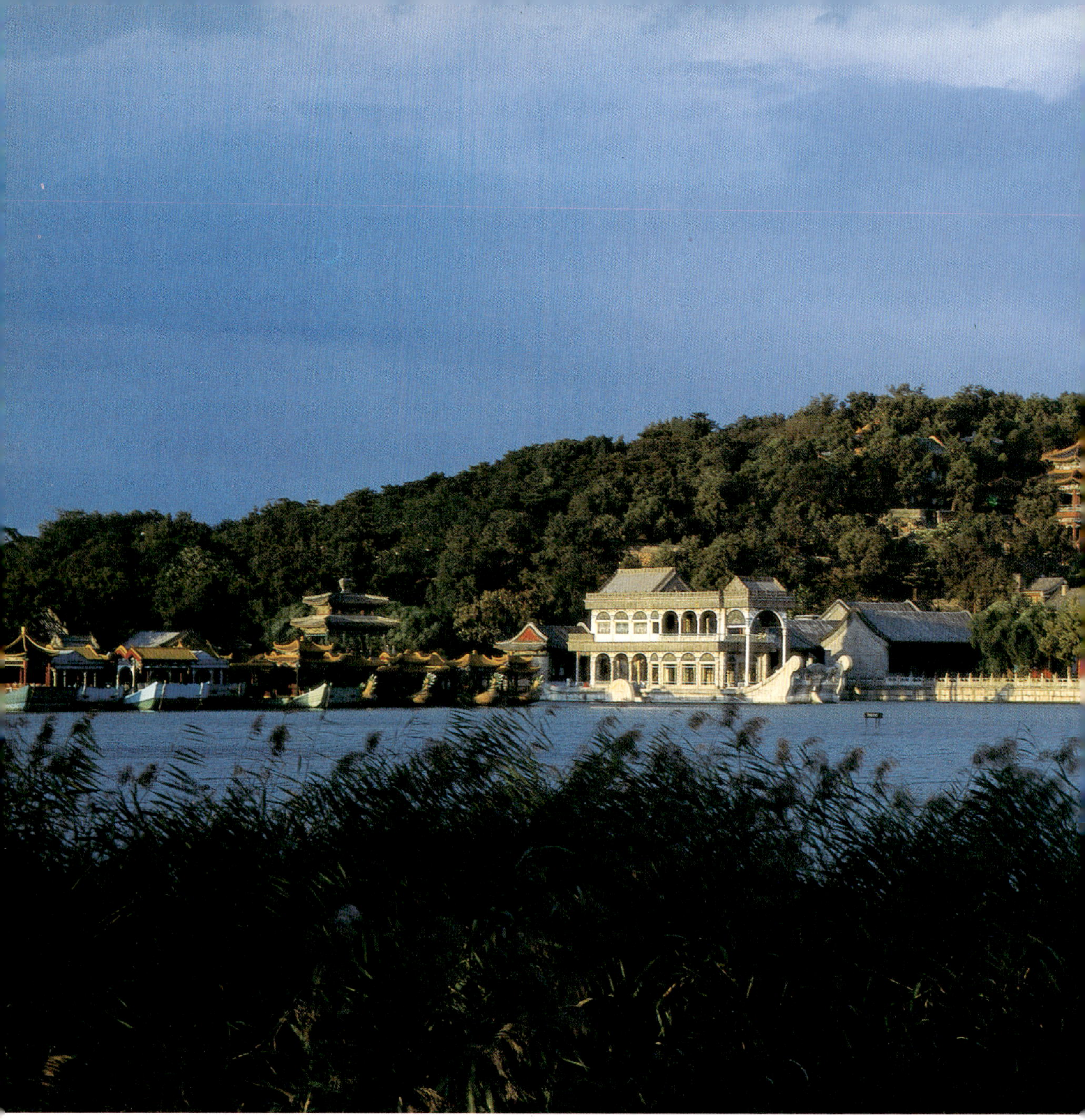

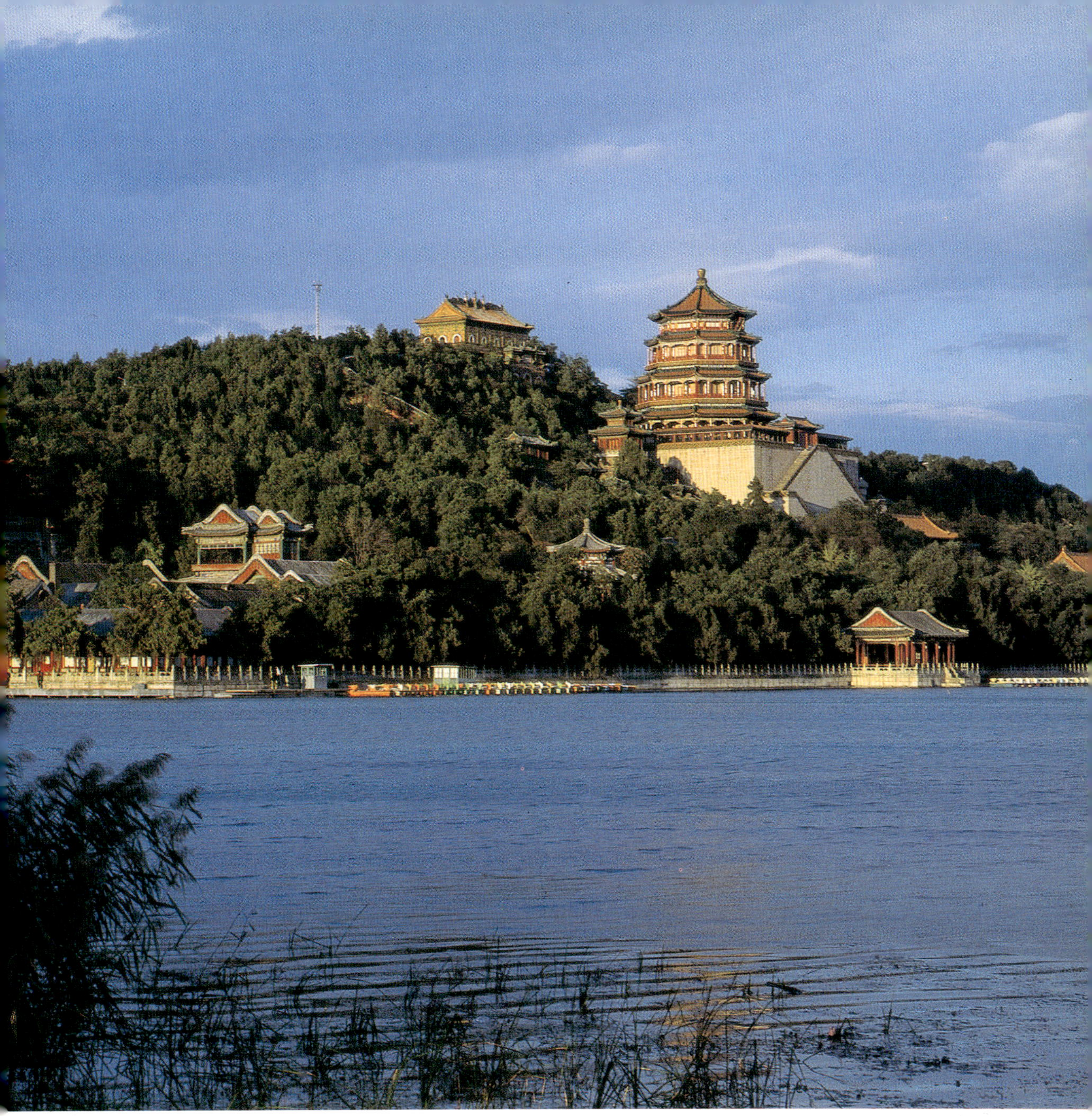

從西堤看萬壽山

A view of Longevity Hill from the West Dyke.

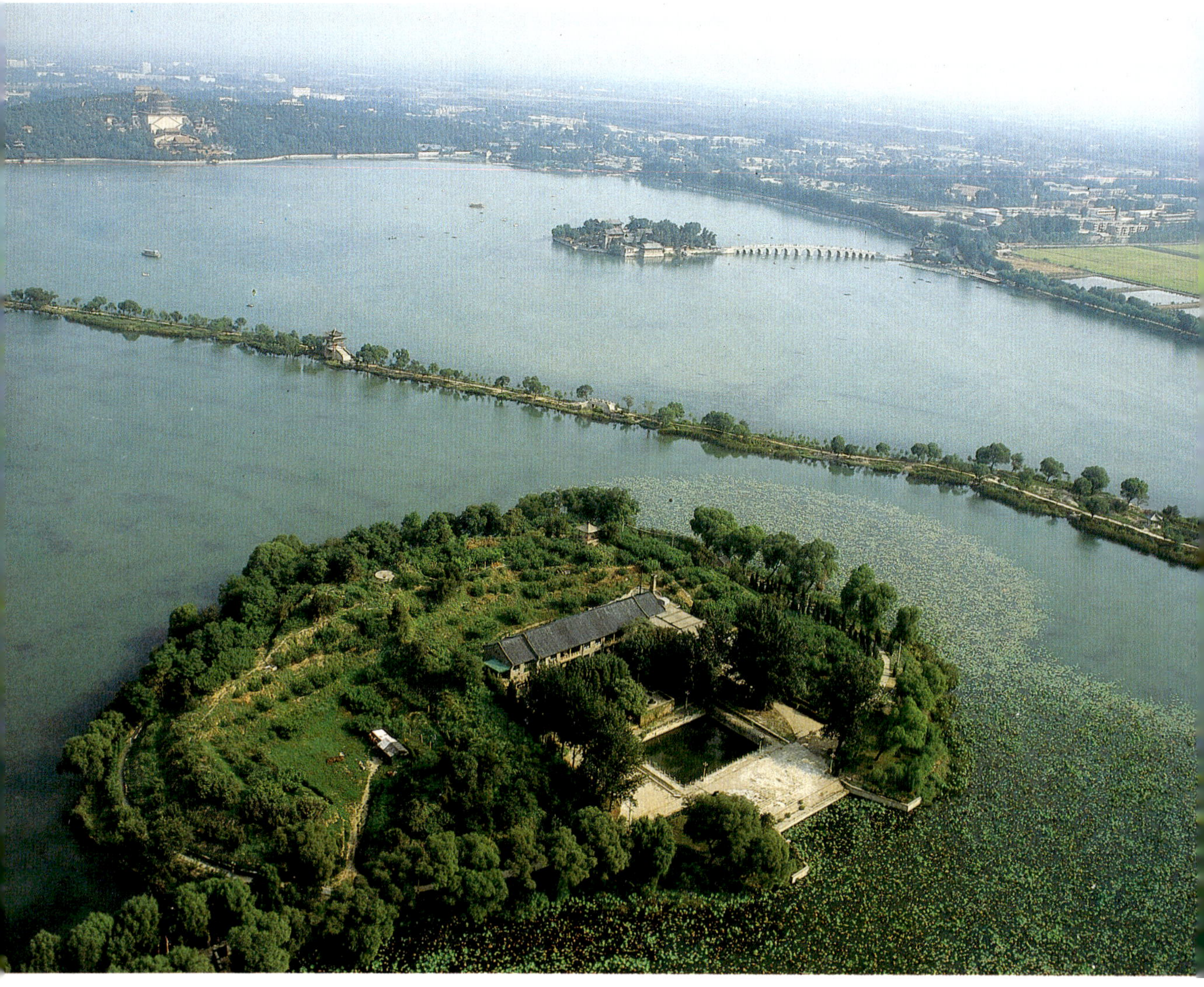

俯瞰昆明湖 湖面上有一條長達數里的湖堤，這就是仿杭州西湖蘇堤建造的西堤。堤上除六座小橋外，没有任何高大建築，顯得深邃沉静，與前山熱烈濃密的情景構成强烈的景觀對比效果。

Kunming Lake. At the lake there is a long causeway. This is the West Dyke, patterned after the Su Dyke in West Lake in Hangzhou. With only six small bridges, it has no tall buildings. Its tranquillity sets a striking contrast to the magnificent buildings on the front slope of Longevity Hill.

景明樓 建於清代乾隆年間，其名出自宋代范仲淹《岳陽樓記》"春和景明，波瀾不驚"詩句的意境。主樓兩側各有一座兩層樓的配樓，是昆明湖西堤上重要的景觀建築。

Jingming Hall. Built in the qianlong Period of the qing Dynasty, the name of the hall was taken from a line in the essay "Yueyang Pavilion" by Fan Zhongyan of the Song Dynasty. The main hall is flanked by two side halls. It is an importaht signt on the western bank of Kunming Lake.

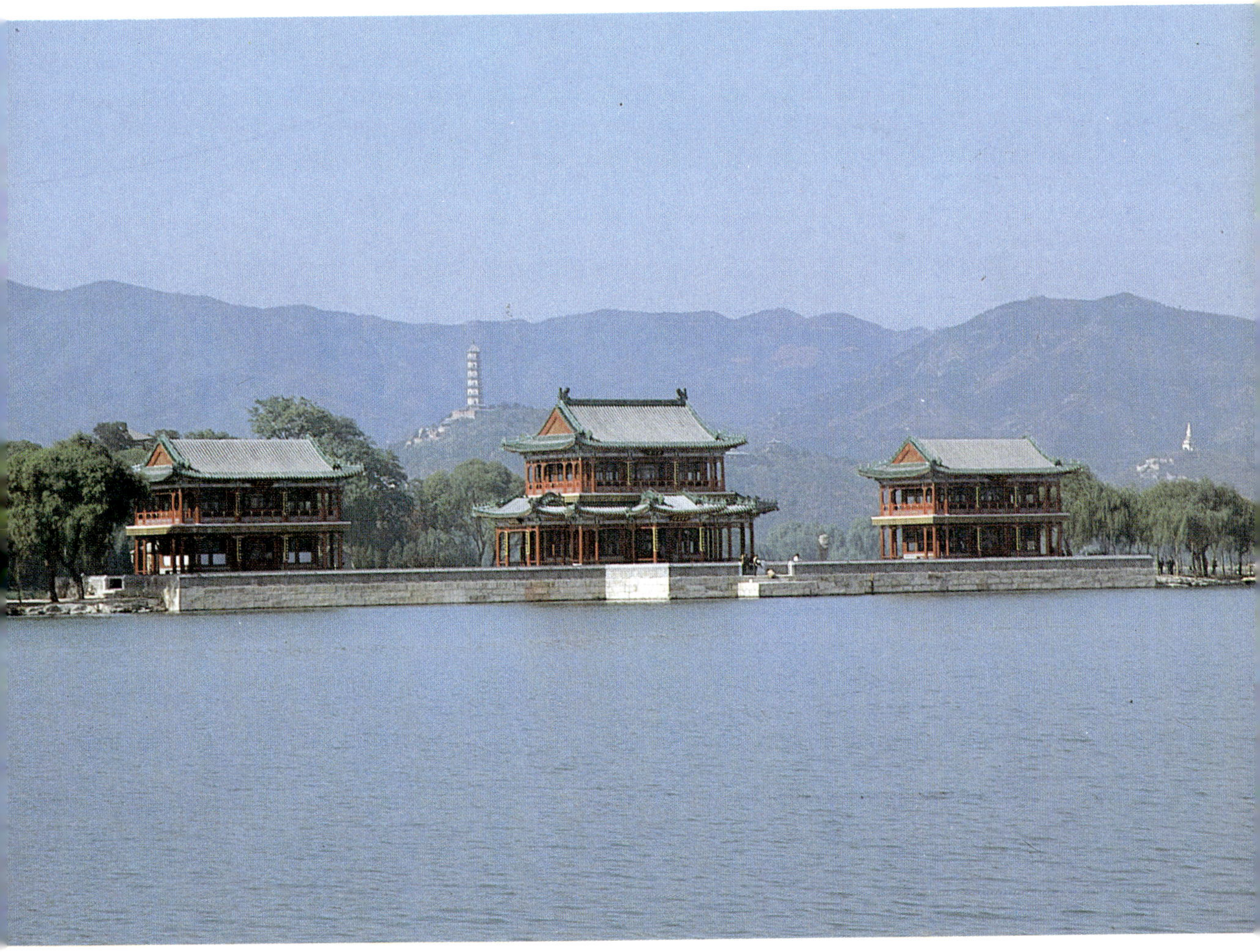

豳風橋 橋名源於二千多年前中國第一部詩歌總集《詩經》中的"豳風"詩。豳風記録的是奴隸生産的詩歌，以此名橋，大約是想表明帝王們對農事的重視。

Binfengqiao (State Song Bridge). This bridge was named after the title of a poem from the *Book of Songs,* China's first collection of poetry dating from two thousand years ago. The poem was about slave labour. The reason it was chosen for the name of the bridge was probably because the emperor wanted to show he cared about agriculture.

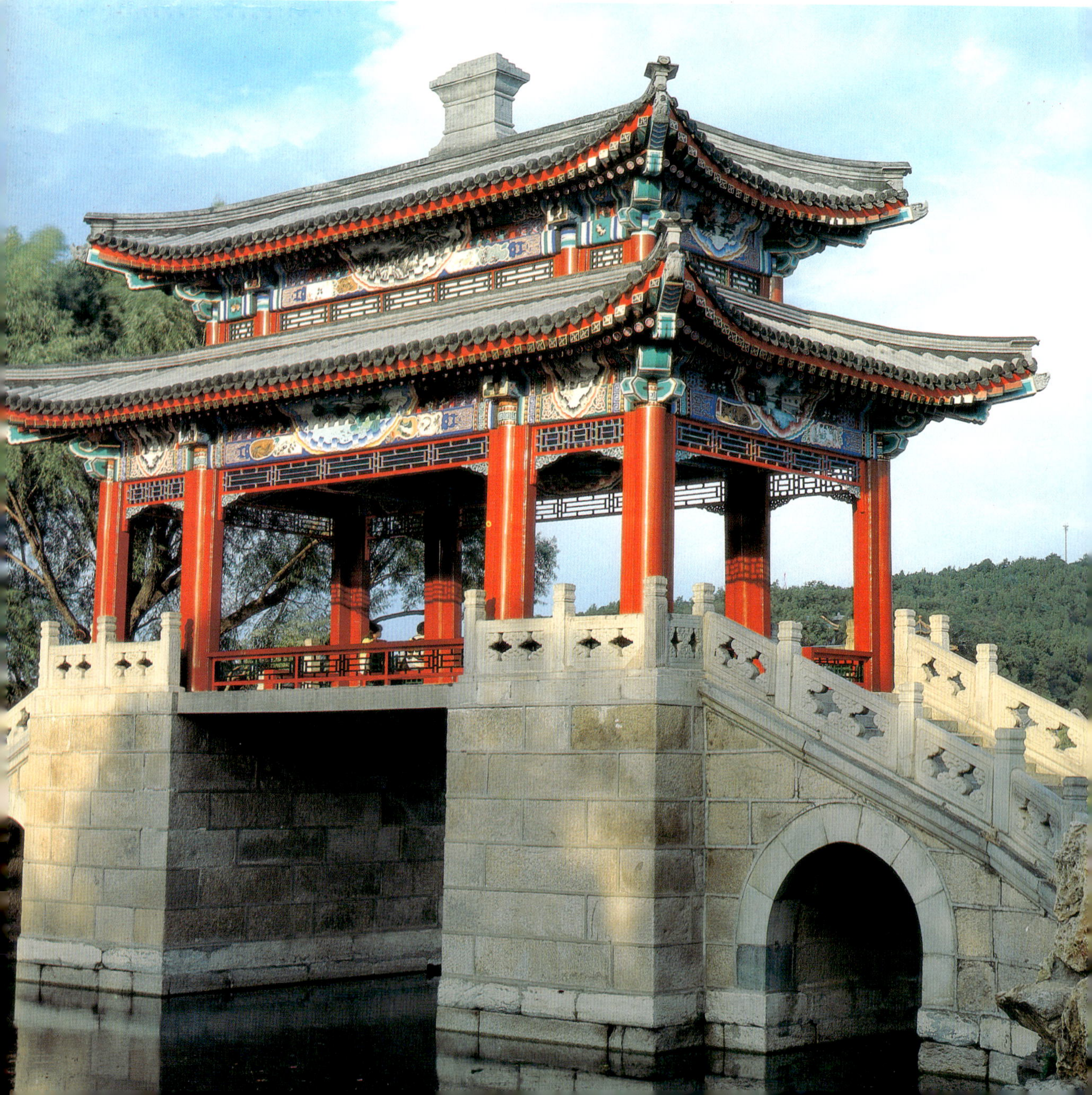

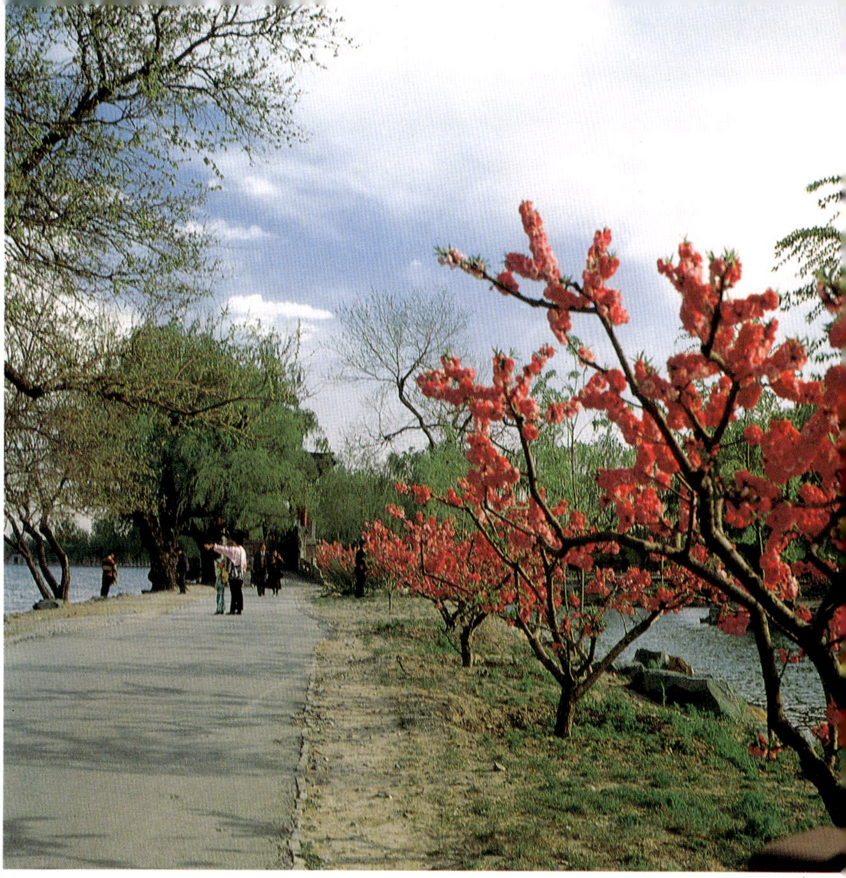

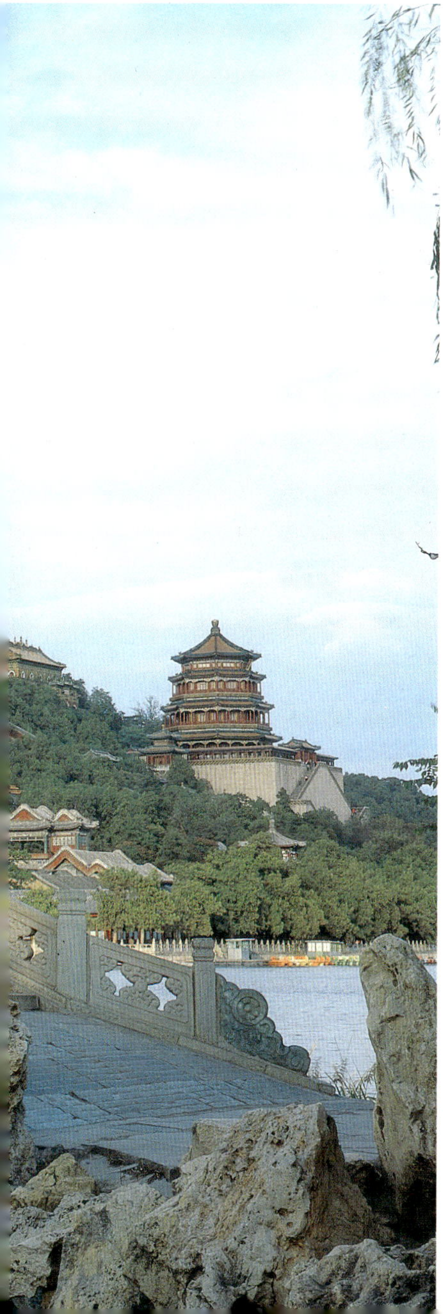

春到西堤 西堤兩側遍種楊柳桃杏。每至春天，柳綠花香，在堤上散步，令人流連忘返。

Spring Comes to the West Dyke. The dyke is lined with weeping willows and pink mountain peach trees. One can forget oneself in the beauty of the scenery.

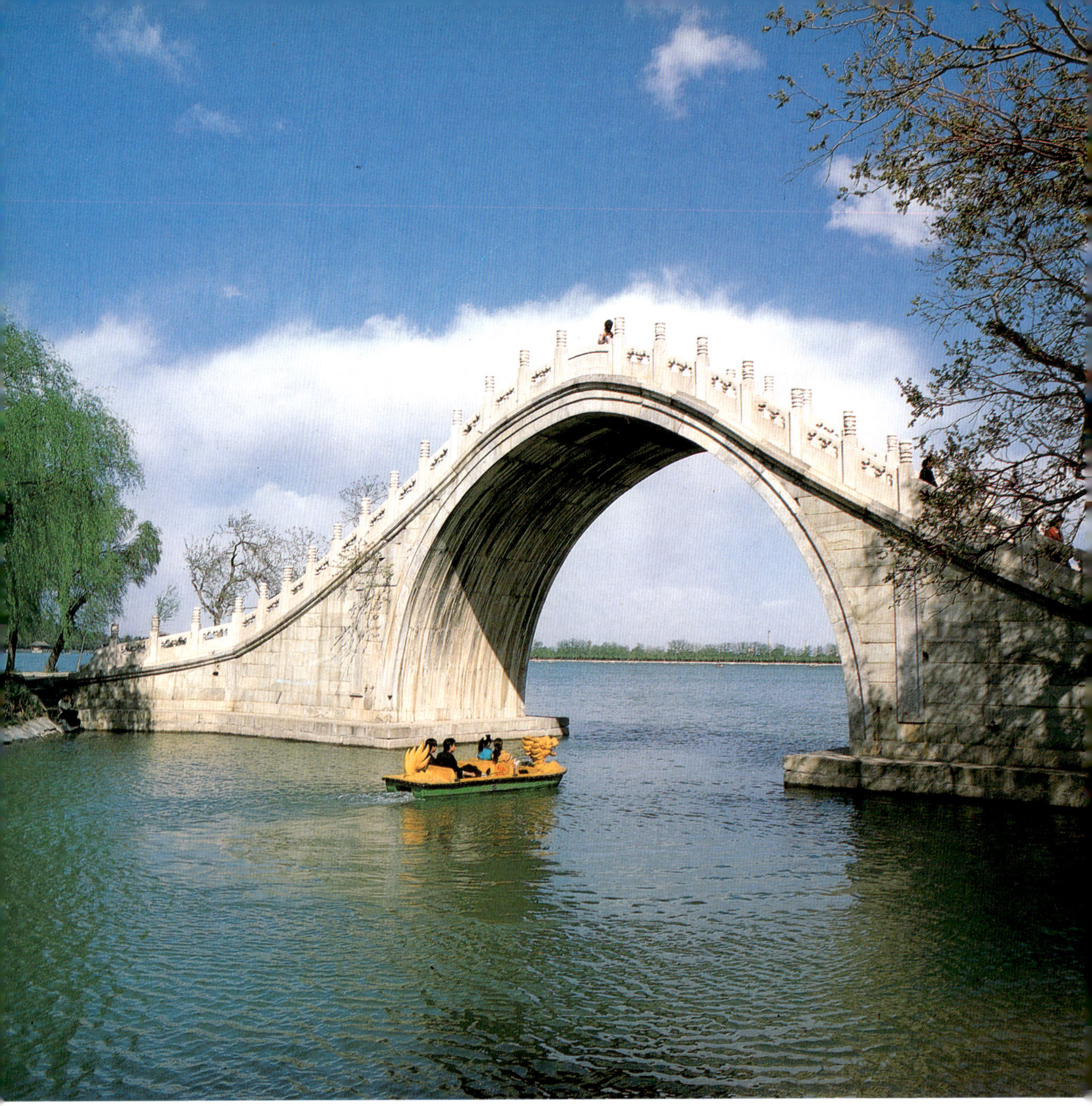

玉帶橋 拱高而薄，橋身、橋欄用青白石和漢白玉石雕砌，呈曲綫形，宛若玉帶。它是西堤六橋中唯一具有實用功能的橋。橋下爲昆明湖的入水口，當年帝、后走水路去玉泉山，必經此橋。

Jade Belt Bridge. The bridge is of white marble and granite, with a thin high-arched body resembling a jade belt and balustrades with carved designs of "fairy cranes" flying into the clouds. The imperial boats used to pass this point when the emperor and empress went from Kunming Lake to Jade Fountain Hill by water.

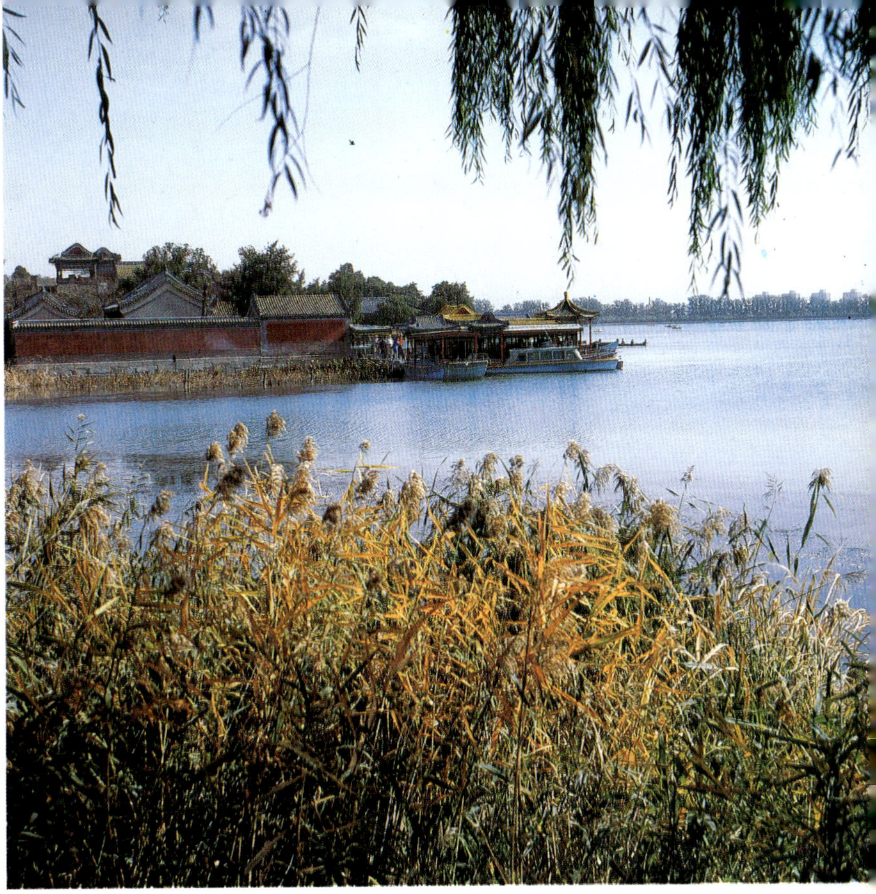

西堤秋色 深秋，昆明湖蘆葦染黄，柳葉飄零，湖上顯得格外寂静。遊人至此，頓覺這裏的秋風、秋色、秋景别有一番意境和情趣。

The West Dyke in Autumn. The scenery here is most beautiful in late autumn when reeds grow thick and the catkins are out.

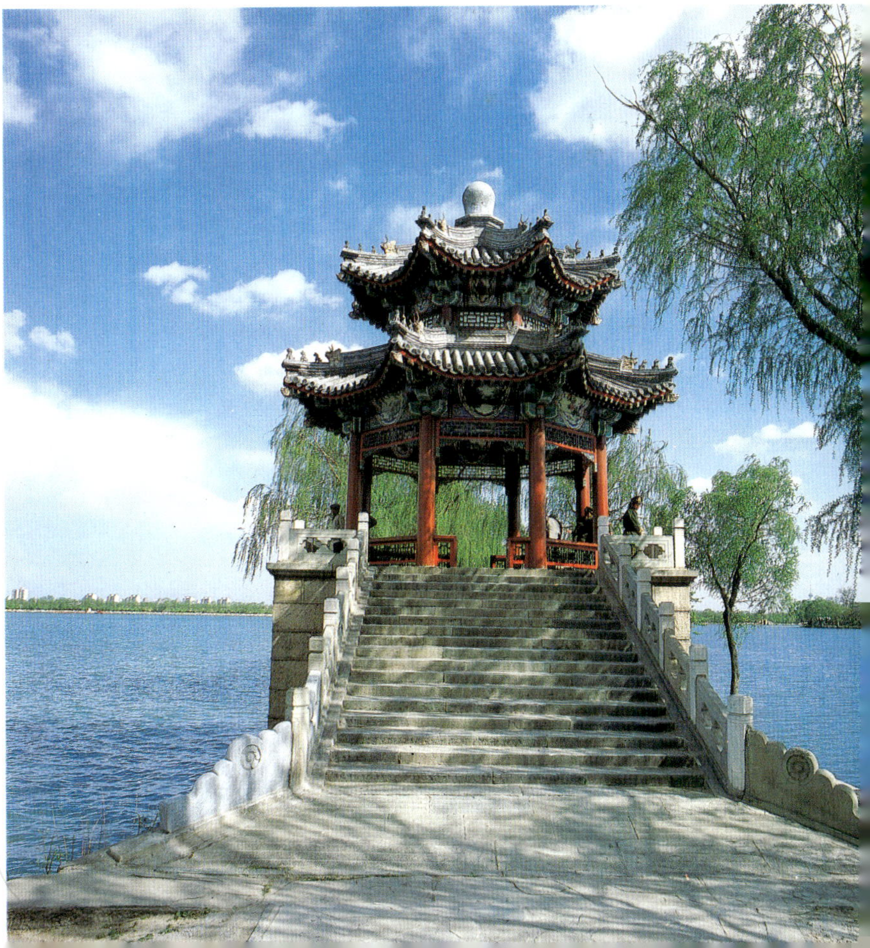

鏡橋 橋名出自李白“兩水夾明鏡，雙橋落彩虹”的詩句。乾隆皇帝也賦詩道：“若道湖光宛是鏡，阿誰不是鏡中人。”

Mirror Bridge. The bridge takes its name from two lines of poetry by the Tang poet Li Bai: "A mirror between two bodies of water; a rainbow beneath two bridges." Emperor Qianlong also wrote a poem for it with two lines running like this: "If the lake looks like a mirror, who'd be the people who don't want to be in it?"

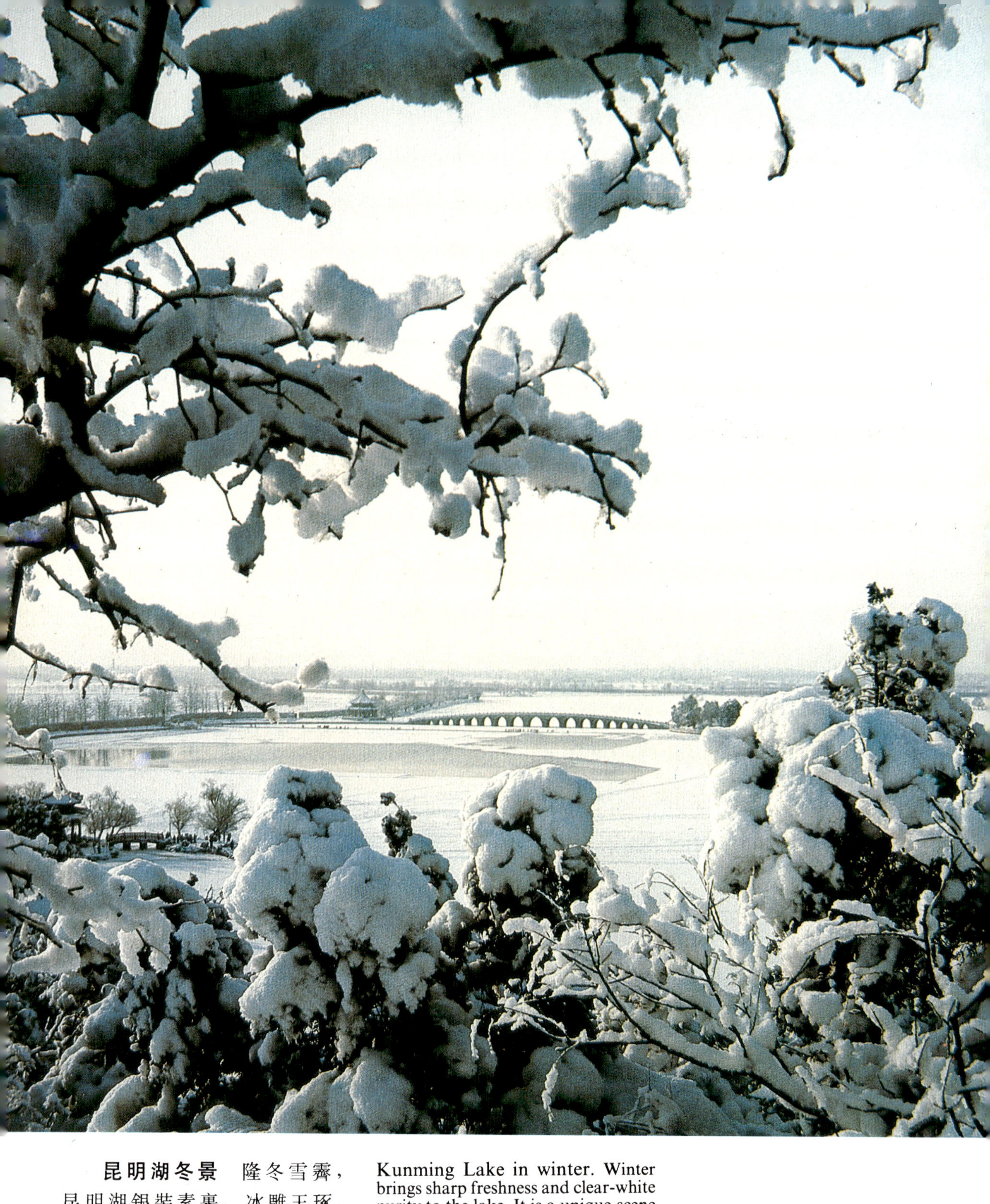

昆明湖冬景 隆冬雪霽，昆明湖銀裝素裹，冰雕玉琢，呈現出一派北國風光。

Kunming Lake in winter. Winter brings sharp freshness and clear-white purity to the lake. It is a unique scene of north China.

柳橋　橋名取自“柳橋清有絮”的詩句。一到夏天，這裏堤柳成蔭，荷葉蓋湖，葦草青青，加之玉峰寶塔如畫，西山羣峰似屏，有如江南清麗的景色。

Willow Bridge. The bridge's name comes from a line in a poem: "Willow bridge is bright, covered with catkins." The dyke here is lined with hanging willows. The area of the lake is covered by lotus leaves where green reeds grow thick. Jade Fountain Hill and the pagoda can be seen from here as well as the peaks of West Hills looming like a screen in the distance, together forming a beautiful scene of south China.

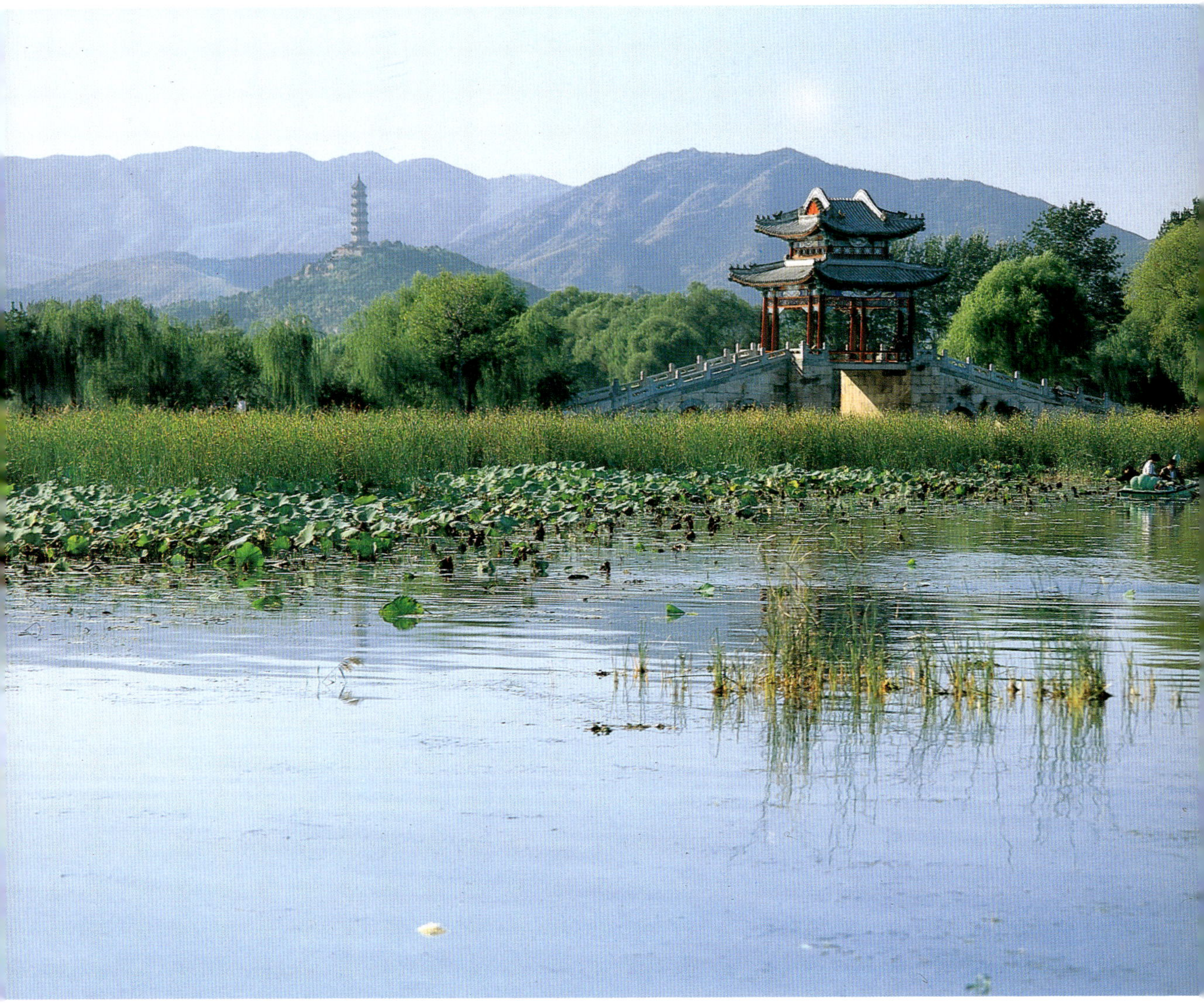

俯瞰南湖島　南湖島位於昆明湖東水域，由十七孔橋與東堤連接。島上松柏森森，樓閣如畫，清宮太監們稱它爲“蓬萊島”。其景色之美，確如神話中的東海蓬萊仙島。

South Lake Island. Located in the eastern part of Kunming Lake, this island is linked with East Dyke by the Seventeen-Arch Bridge. On it are ancient pines and cypresses, exquisitely built halls, pavilions and towers. The eunuchs of the Qing court called it the Penglai Isle as it is as beautiful as the mythical isle of Penglai, the home of immortals.

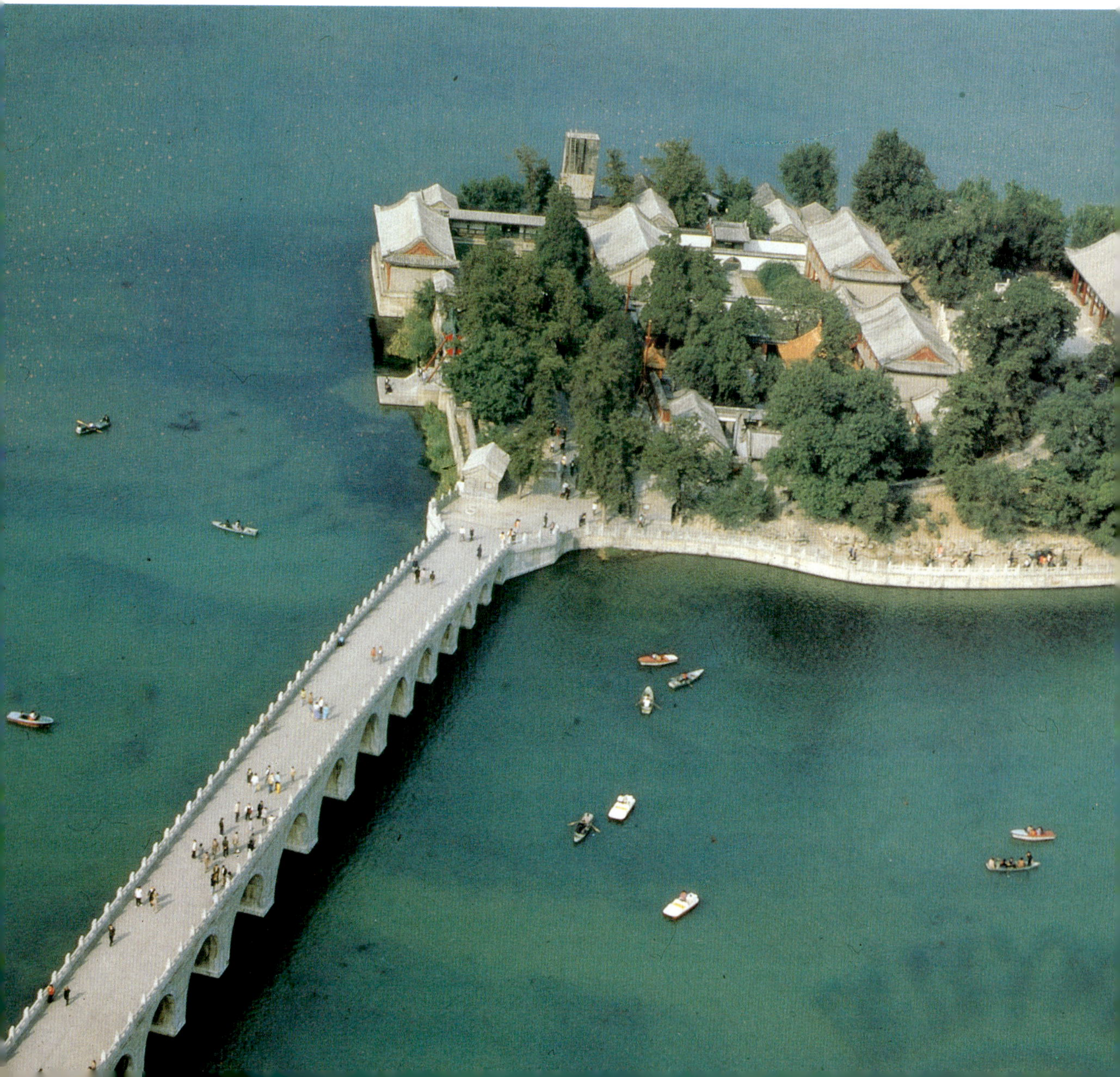

涵虛堂 高居於島北岸臨湖石臺上，隔水與佛香閣遥相呼應。慈禧太后曾率光緒皇帝和后妃們在這裏觀看海軍演習水操。

The Hall of Forbearance and Humbleness. This hall stands on the artificial hill of heaped rocks in the northern part of South Lake Island. It faces the Tower of the Fragrance of Buddha across the wide expanse of Kunming Lake. This is where Empress Dowager Cixi led Emperor Guangxu, the empress and consorts to watch naval exercises on the lake.

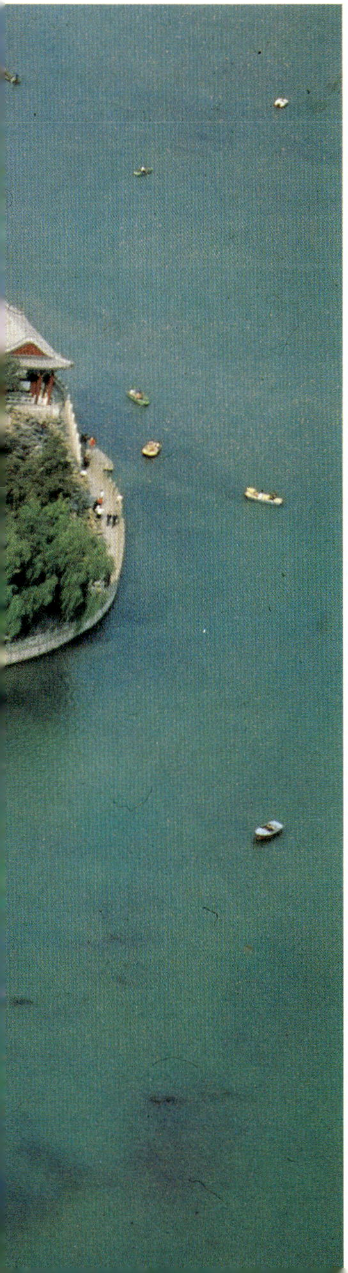

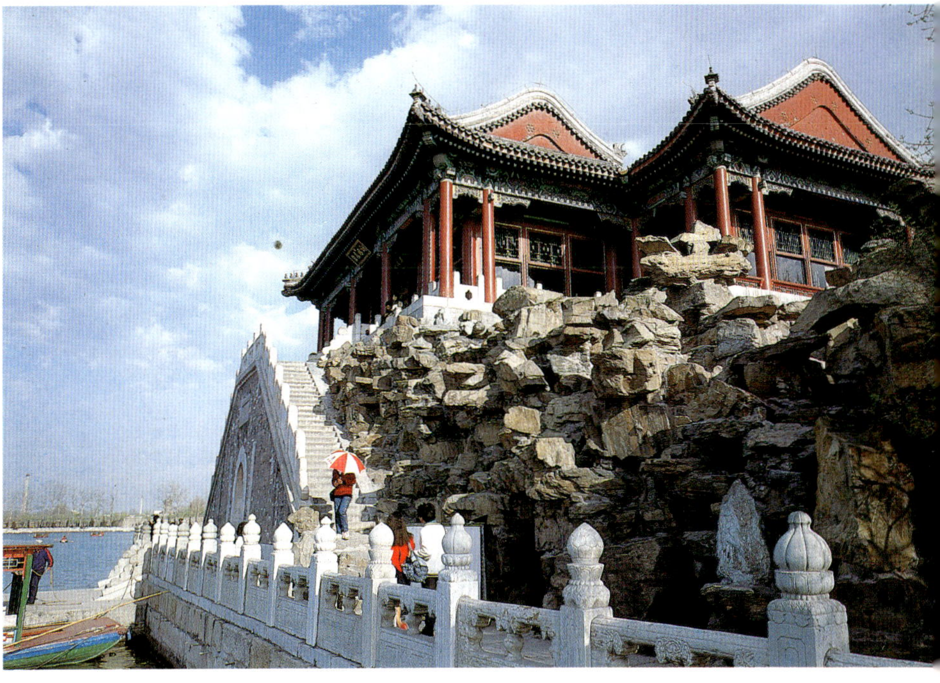

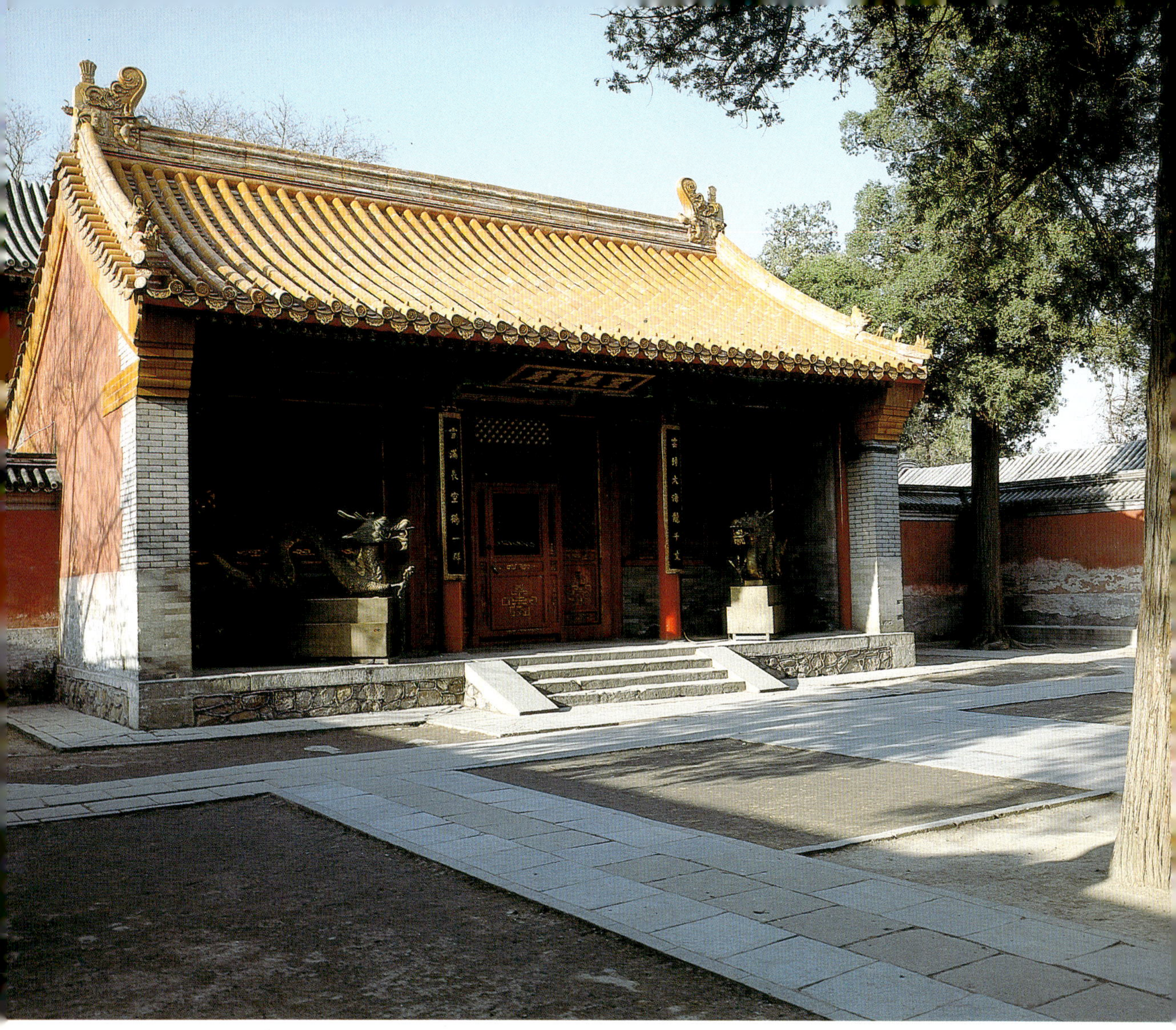

龍王廟　即廣潤靈雨祠，因宋代真宗皇帝（公元九九八——一〇二二年在位）曾封西海龍王爲廣潤王，昆明湖前身名西海，故取此名。龍王廟正南有一小島名鳳凰墩。墩上原有鳳凰樓，内置銅鳳。龍鳳是帝、后的象徵，北龍南鳳既成對景，又有龍鳳呈祥的寓意。

The Dragon King's Temple. This temple is also called the Temple of Beneficial and Blessed Rain. Emperor Zhenzong (reigned 998-1022) of the Song Dynasty made the Dragon King of the West Sea the Prince of Beneficial and Bless Rain, and Kunming Lake was formerly called the West Sea. Hence the present name of the temple.

龍王塑像 金面綠袍，人身龍像。中國人自古就有在河岸湖畔建龍王廟以鎮水害的習俗。這裏的龍王廟以點景爲主，也有鎮水之意。

Statue of the Dragon King. The Dragon King in golden green robe has a human body and a dragon's head. Since ancient times Chinese people have had the customs of building the temple of the Dragon King on the bank of a river or a lake to control water. The Dragon King's Temple here was built with the purpose to decorate the island as well as to control water.

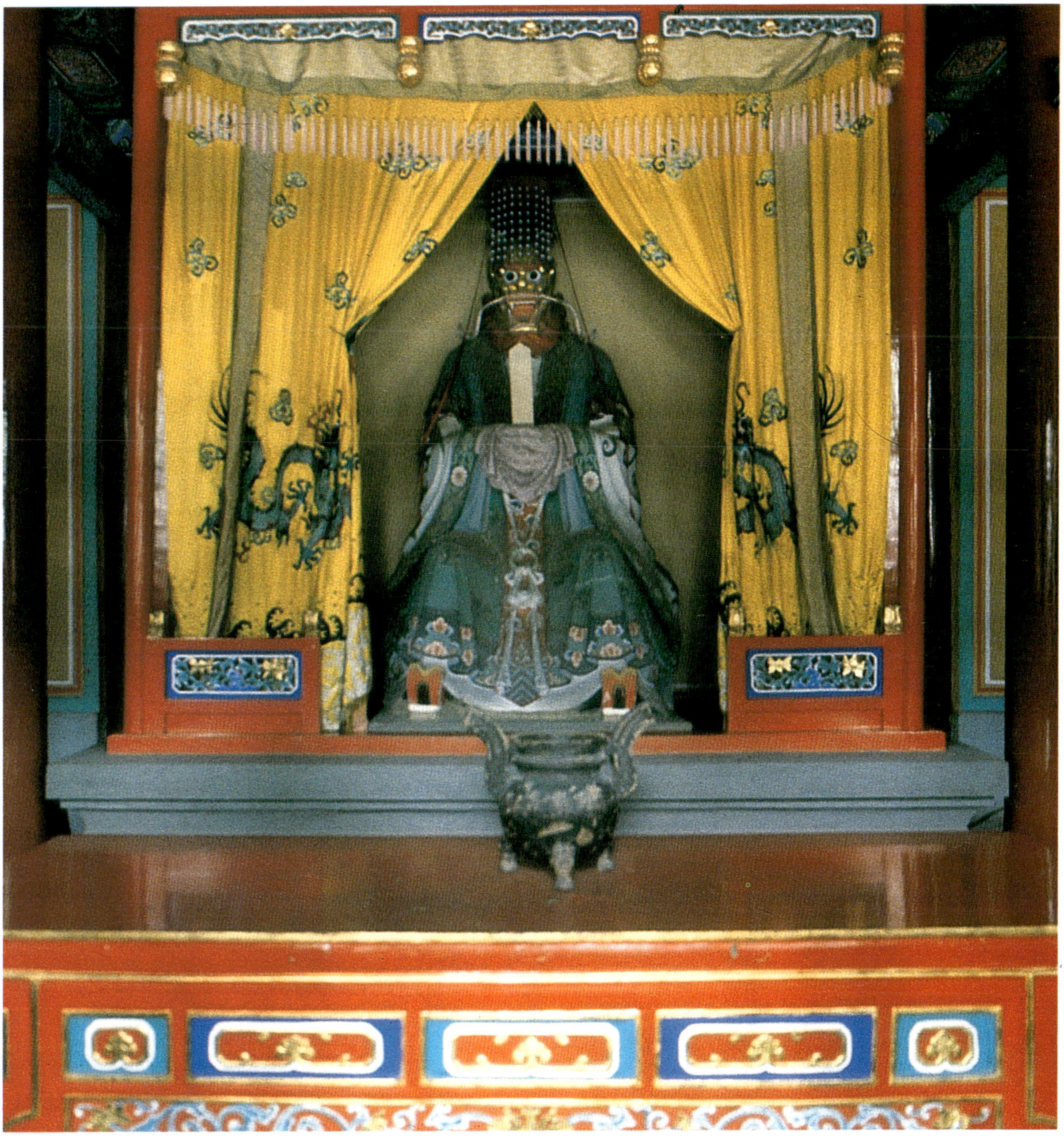

十七孔橋　東接東堤，西連南湖島，長一百五十米，有如長虹卧波，蔚爲壯觀。

Seventeen-Arch Bridge. This bridge links East Dyke at its eastern end and connectes South Lake Island at its western end. It is 150 metres long and looks like a rainbow on the lake.

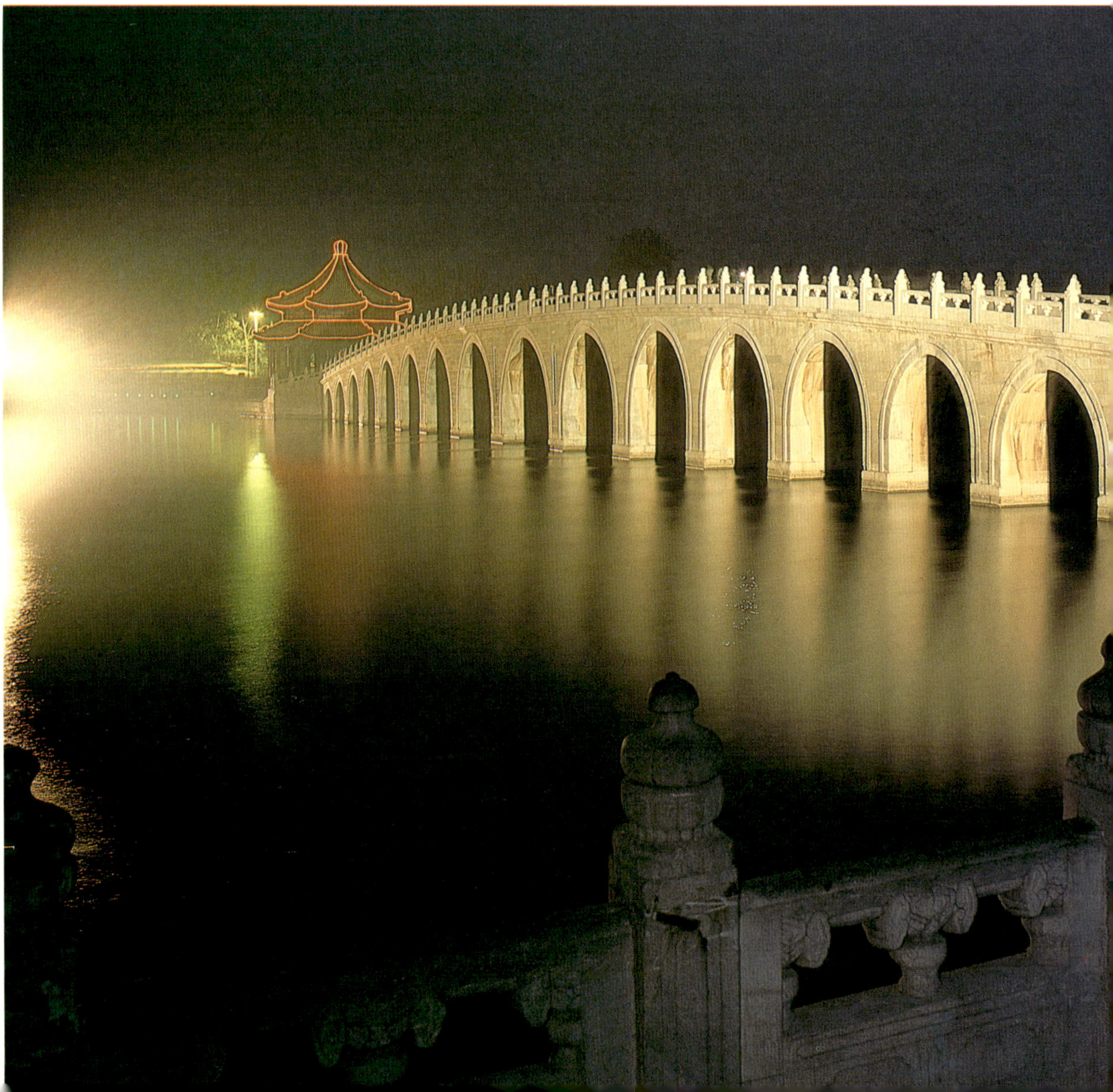

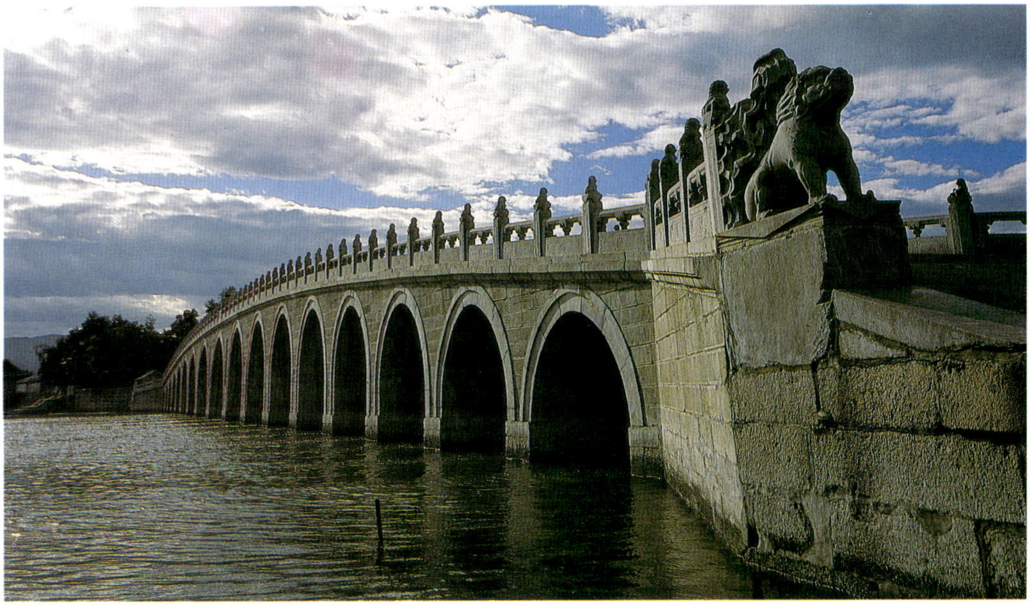

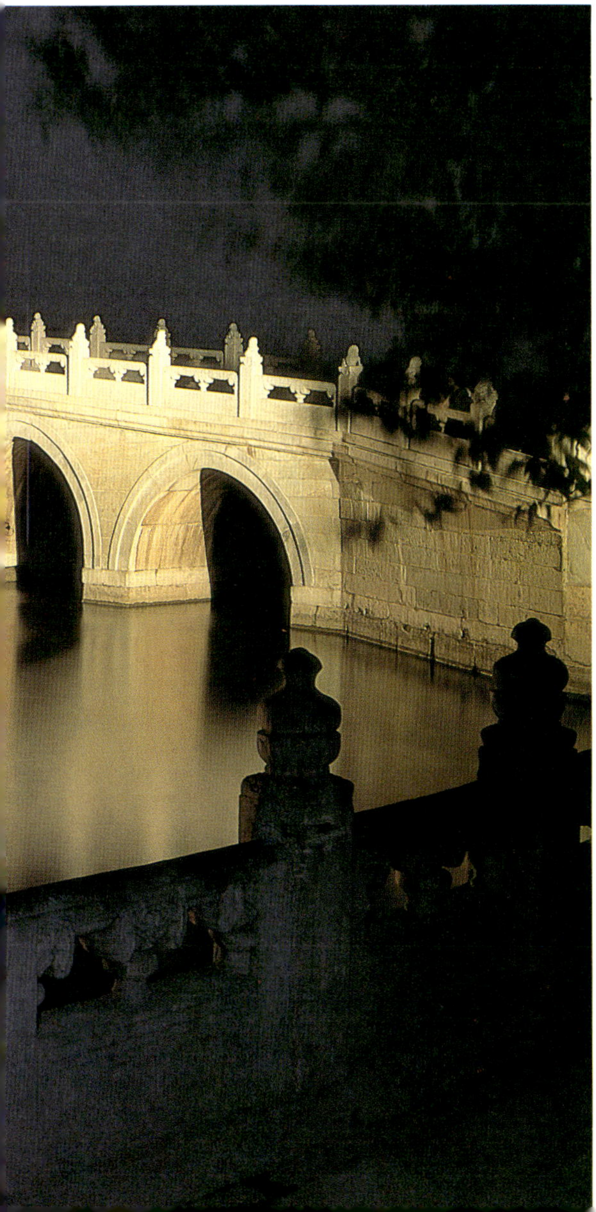

石獅　橋頭及橋欄望柱上共雕有五百四十四隻石獅，形態無一雷同。

Stone lions. The Seventeen-Arch Bridge has 544 different stone lions on the top of balusters.

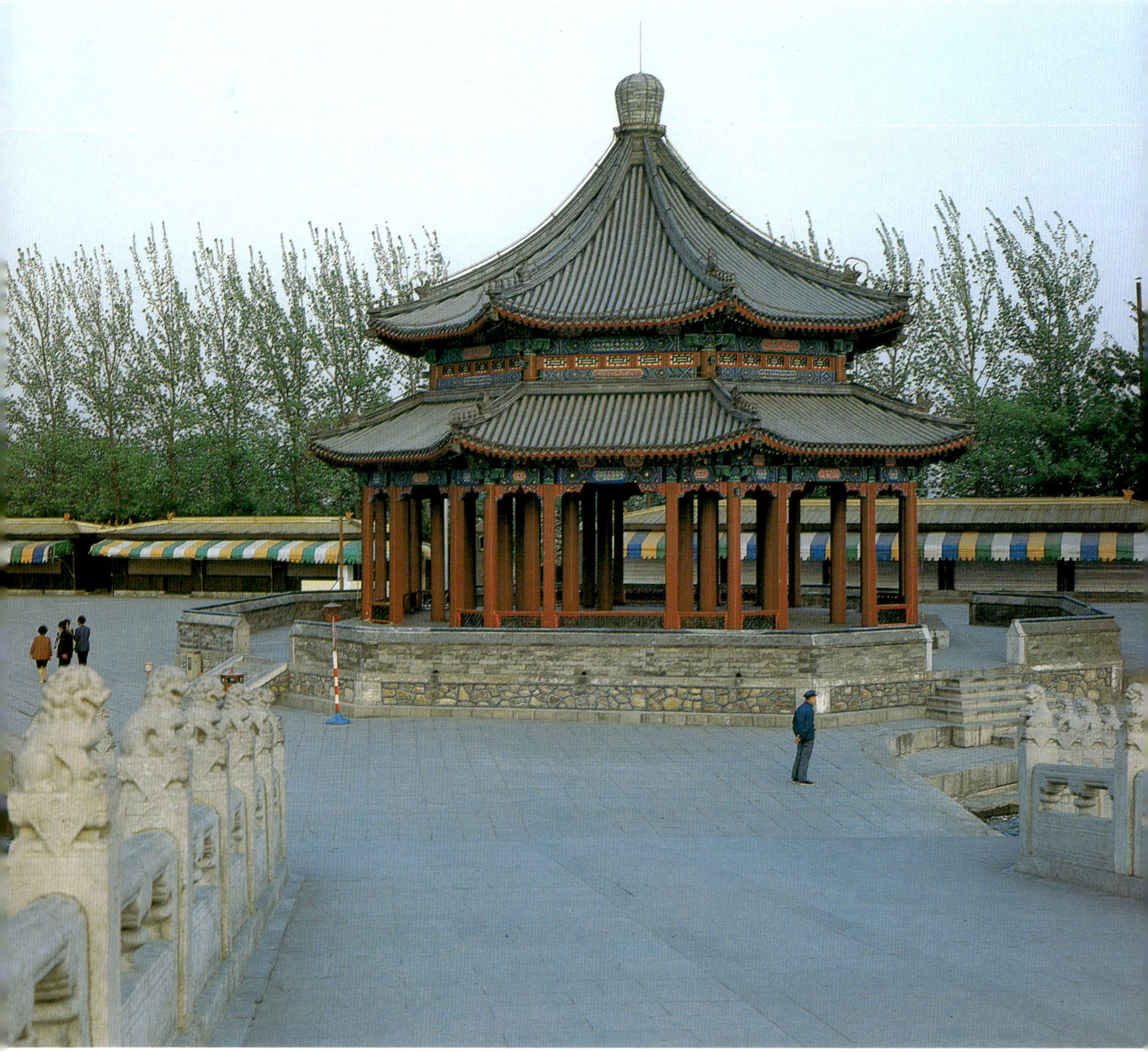

廓如亭 爲八角重檐亭，面積一百三十多平方米，由内外三層二十四根圓柱和十六根方柱支撑。亭體舒展穩重，氣勢雄渾，是中國亭建築中最大的一座。

Kuoruting (Spacious Pavilion). This pavilion of unusual size is eight-sided and double-eaved, with an area of over 130 square metres. It has 24 round pillars and 16 square pillars, making it the biggest pavilion of its kind in China.

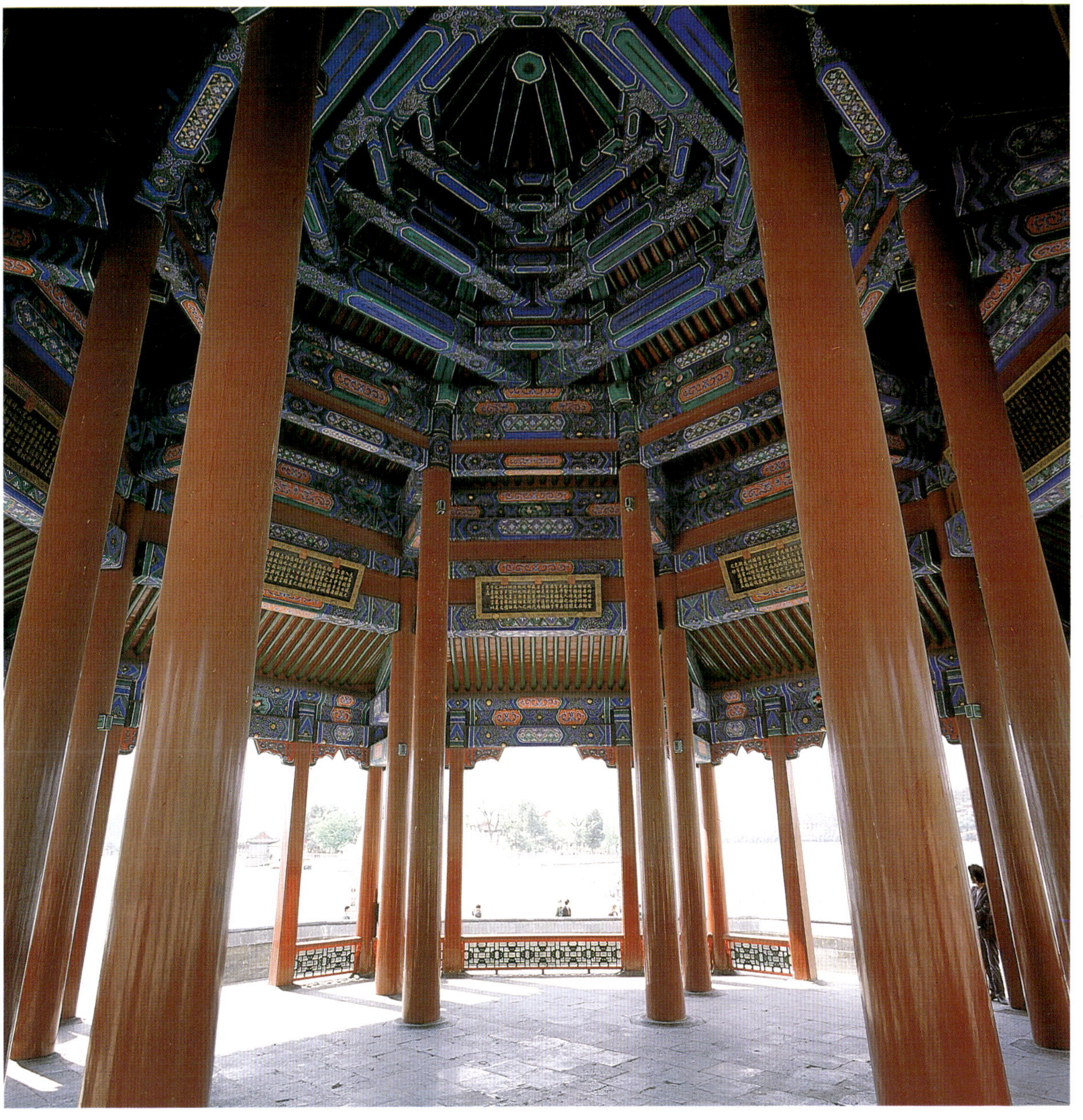

廓如亭藻井　藻井層層上疊，視之眩目。藻井樑枋遍施彩畫。彩畫以藍緑爲主，間以少許紅黄，素雅清麗。在清代，帝后們常在亭内飲宴，或與文人學士們會酒賦詩。亭内懸掛的詩匾，多爲乾隆皇帝詩文和“文心雕龍”。

Caisson ceiling of the Spacious Pavilion. The beams and panels are dazzlingly painted, mainly in blue and green together with red and yellow. The pavilion is very tastefully done. During the Qing Dynasty, the emperor and empress often held banquets here, and sometimes the emperor and his scholars would drink wine and compose poetry here. Tablets with Emperor Qianlong's poems and couplets written by the scholars in response to his verses still hang in the pavilion.

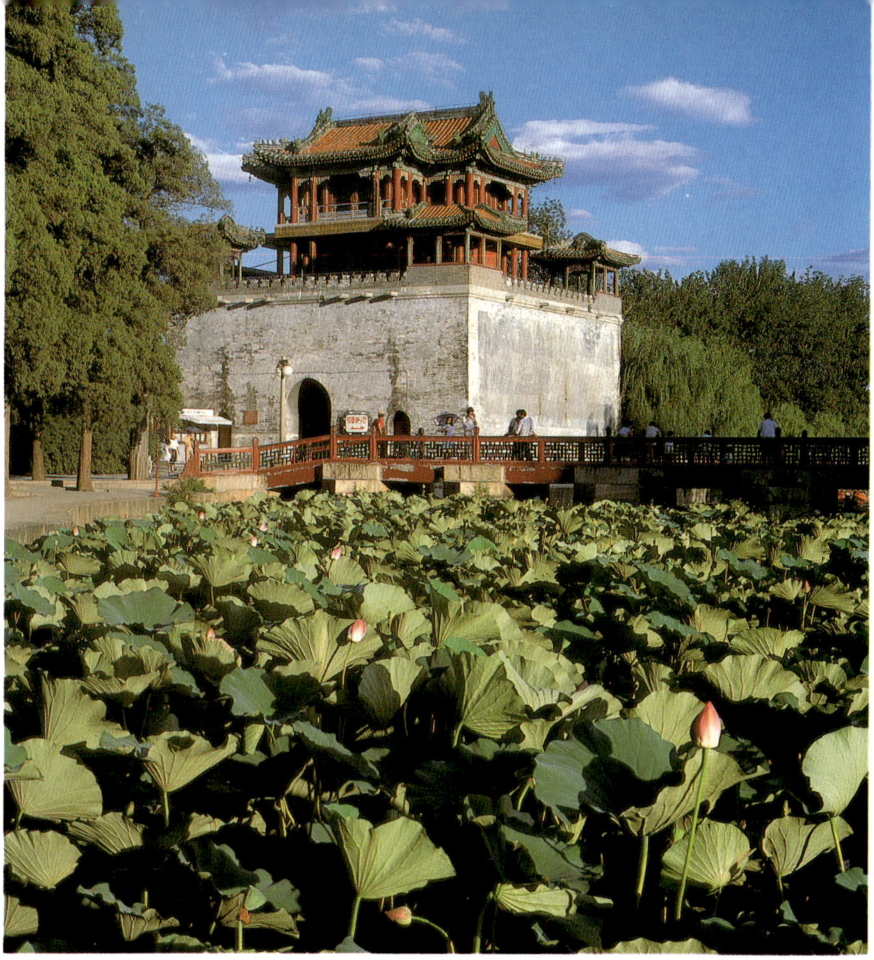

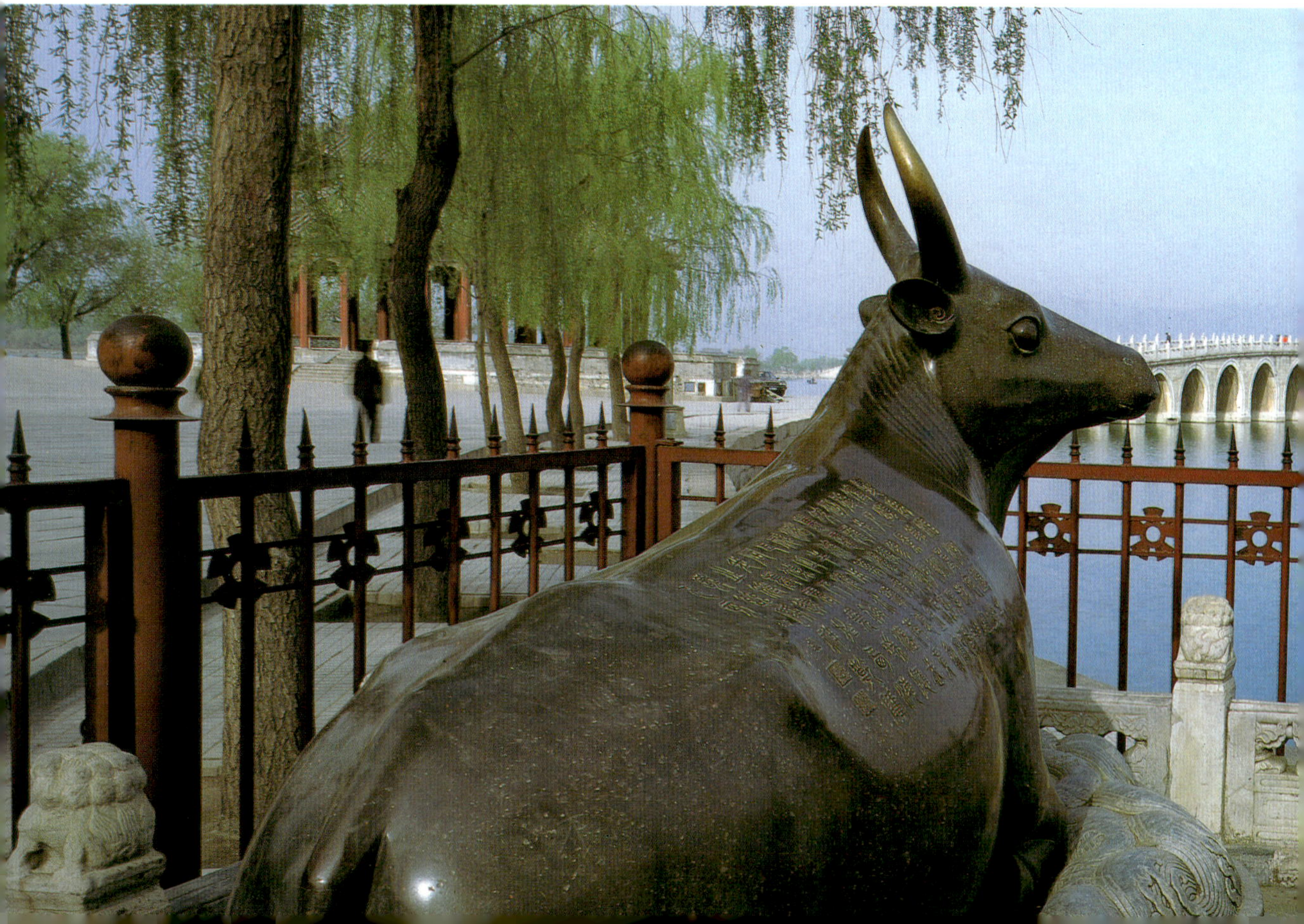

文昌閣 位於東堤北端，城關式建築，上有十字形二層樓閣，内供文昌帝君銅像。“文昌”本是星名，星相家認爲此星主大貴，道教則尊它爲功名利禄之神。文昌閣居昆明湖東，供文神；宿雲檐位於昆明湖西，供武聖，象征文武顯聖。這裏妙不在寓意象徵，而在建園師的巧妙對景。

Studio of Literary Prosperity. Standing at the northern end of East Dyke, the Studio of Literary Prosperity is a building in the shape of a city gate. Inside the two-storeyed building is enshrined the bronze statue of the God of Literary Prosperity. This building stands east of Kunming Lake with a civil god in it, while the Suyunzhan Tower stands west of the lake with a military god in it. It symbolizes that the two gods make their presence felt. This reflects the ingenuity of the architects in designing the park.

銅牛 鑄造於一七五五年。它兩角聳立，雙耳竪起，目光炯炯，形象十分逼真。牛背上鑄有八十字篆體銘文，説明它是用來鎮水的。

Bronze ox. Cast in 1755, the ox has its head raised, its horns turned upward and its eyes fixed ahead. On its back is cast an eight-word inscription to explain its presence. It was also used to control water.

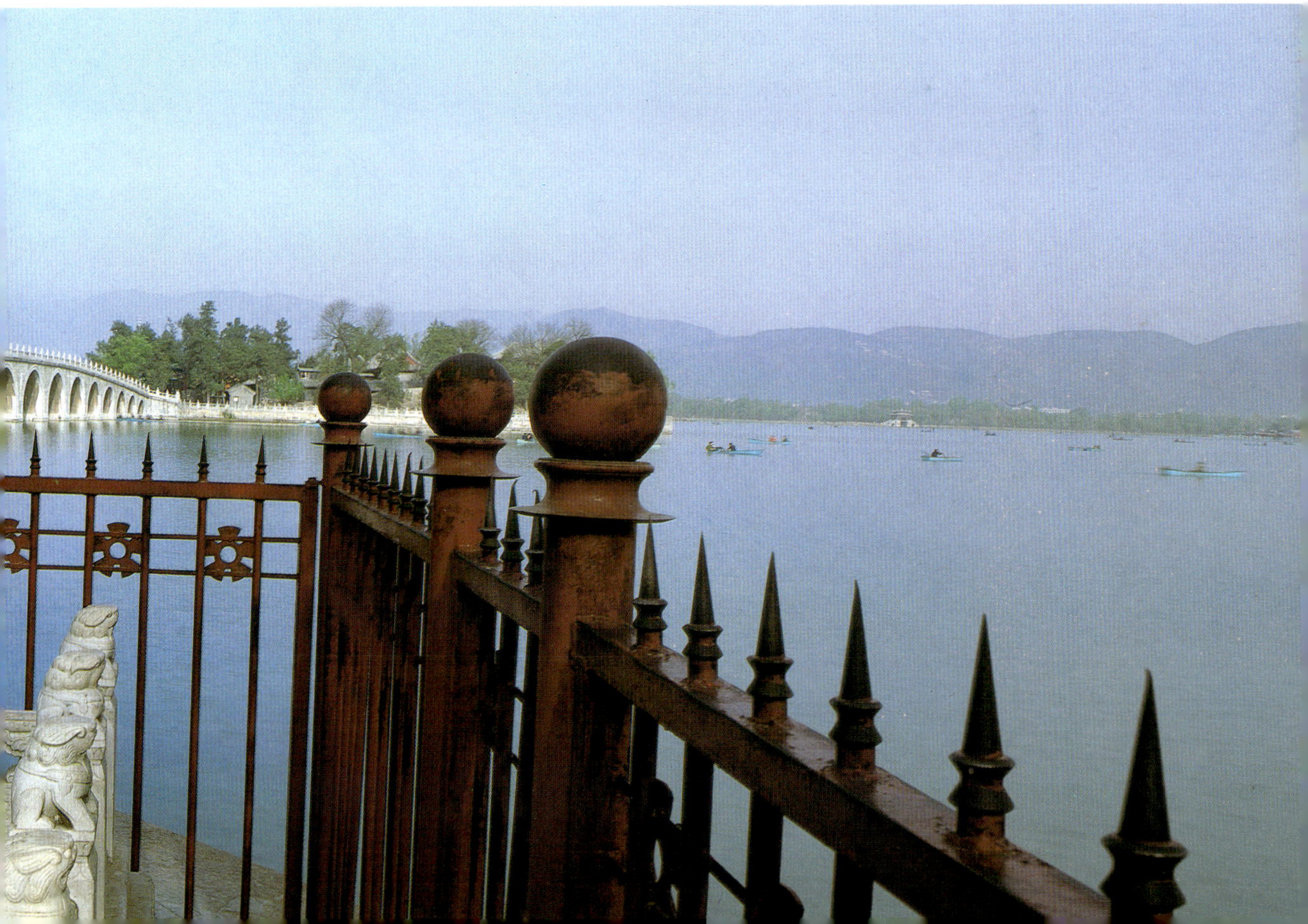

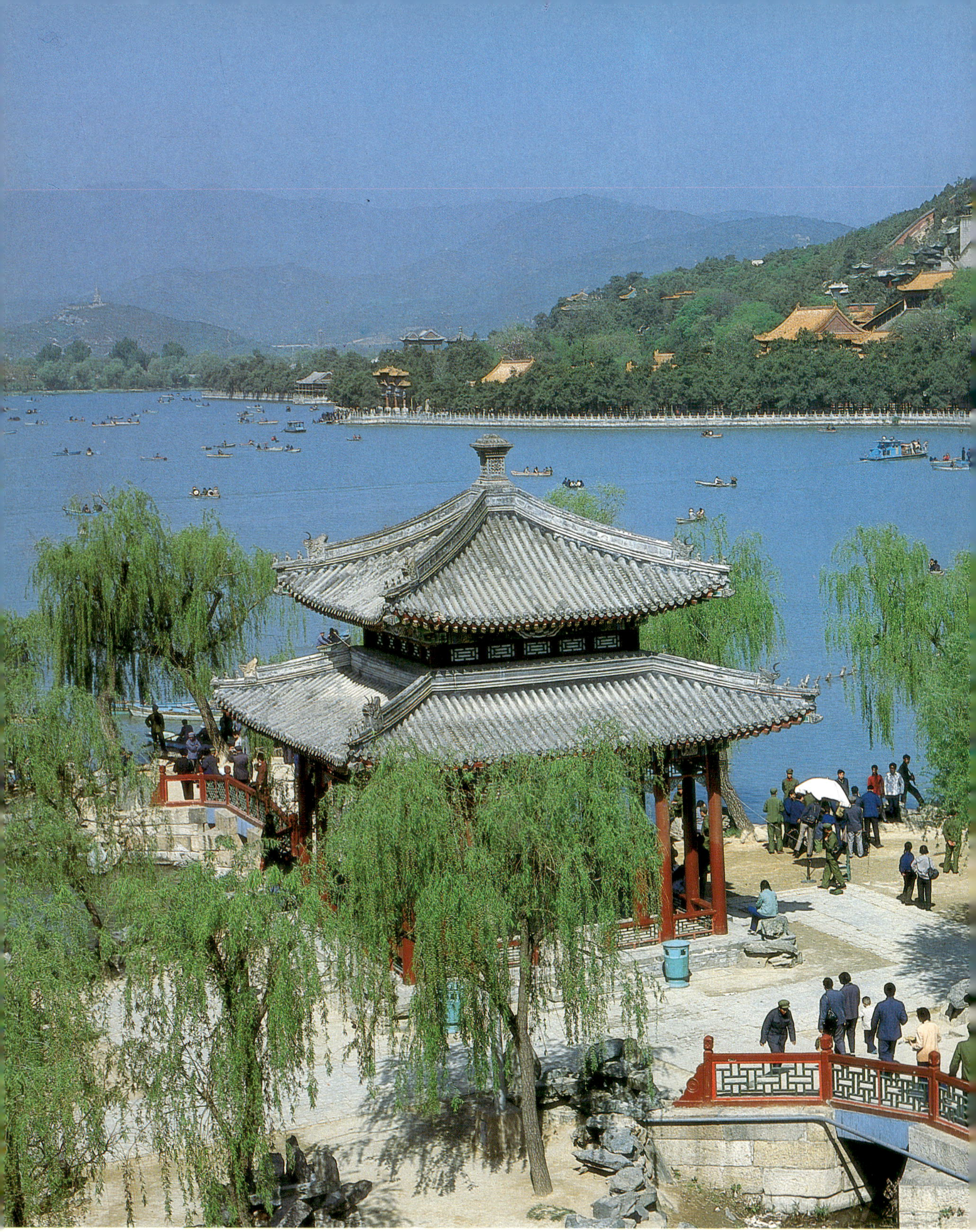

知春亭 四面臨水，亭畔點綴着山石。冬去春來，湖冰最早在這裏消融，告知人們春已來臨。

Pavilion Heralding Spring. The pavilion stands on an islet in Kunming Lake and is connected to the shore by a bridge. It has intricate rockery and is

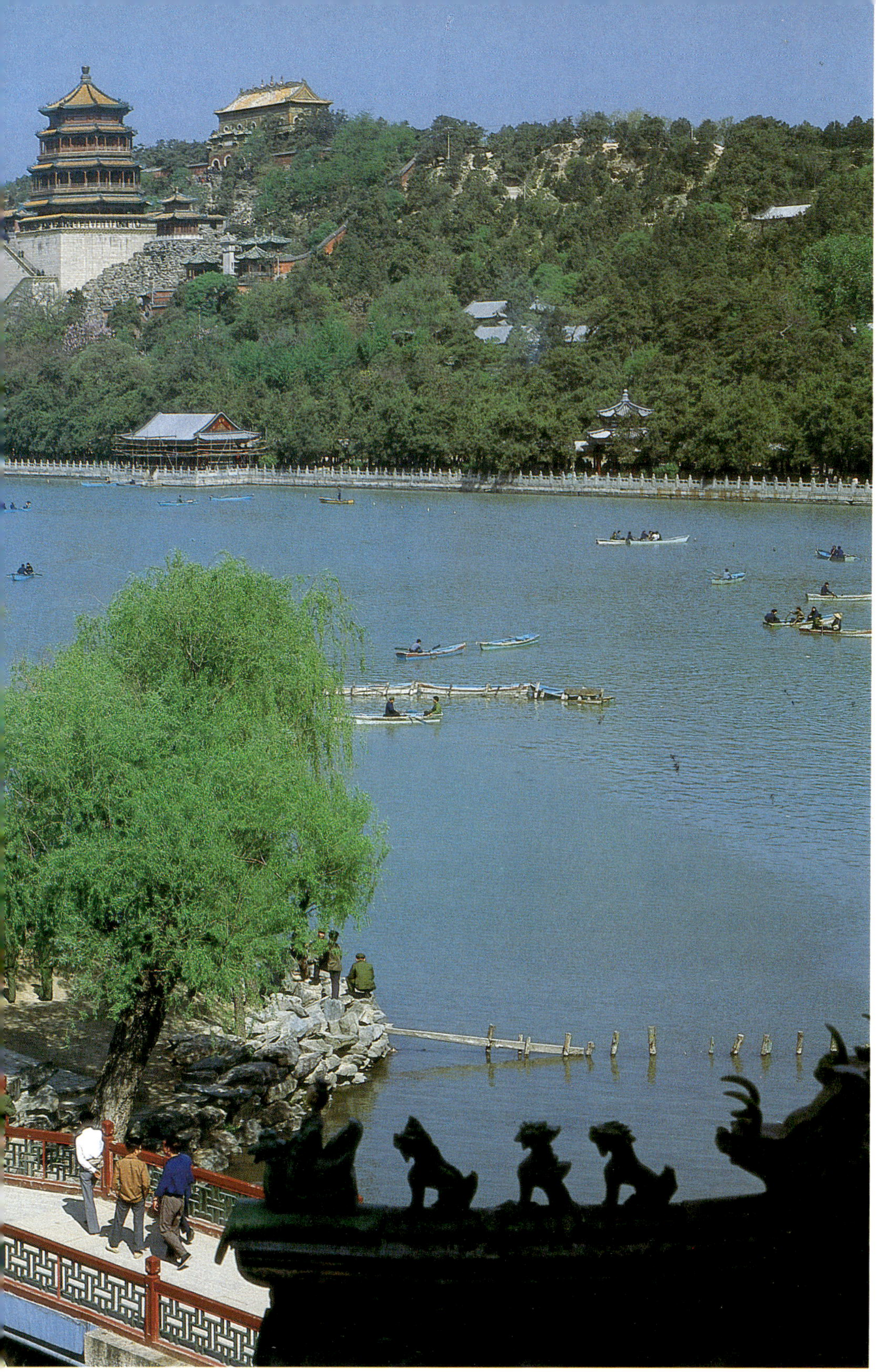

planted with poplars, willows, peach and apricot trees. In early spring, when the ice begins to thaw, the peach tress send forth a mass of pink blossoms and the willows turn a tender green, signalling that spring has returned.

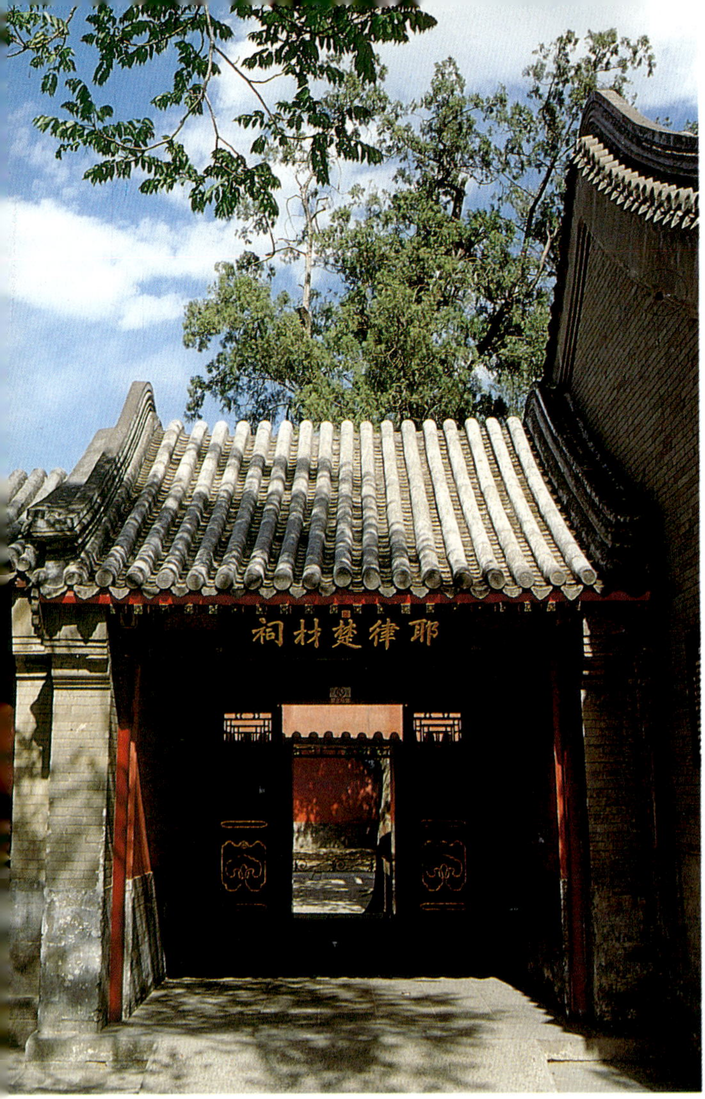

耶律楚材祠 耶律楚材是契丹族人，元代著名政治家，官至中書令（宰相）。他爲維護中華民族的利益做出過重大貢獻。他死後，根據其遺願安葬於燕京故里的瓮山脚下。清代保留了他的墓塚，並建祠紀念。

Yelu Chucai Temple. Yelu Chucai, a Khitan, was a famous politician of the Yuan Dynasty. During his lifetime he greatly contributed to the preservation of China's interests. After he died he was buried at the foot of Jar Hill. In the Qing Dynasty his tomb was left intact and a temple was built to commemorate him.

耶律楚材塑像 爲清代塑造的彩色坐像。

Statue of Yelu Chucai. This statue was sculpted in the Qing Dynasty.

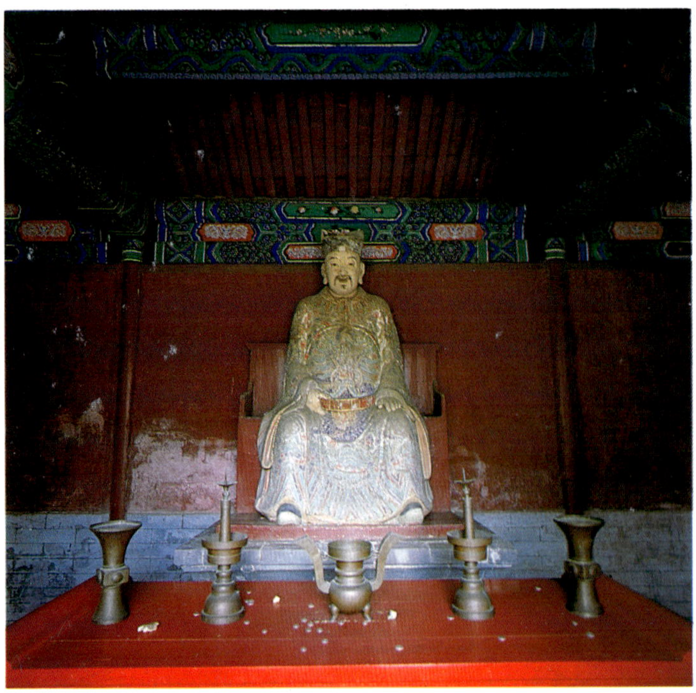

後山後湖景區

這一景區包括萬壽山北坡和一條人工開鑿的後溪河（後湖），面積約三十多公頃。

後山溝壑縱橫，地勢起伏，水清山幽。據史料記載，乾隆年間，後山曾分别建有八處風格各異的小園式風景點。一八六〇年英法聯軍入侵後，後山後湖除一座多寶琉璃塔外，所有建築蕩然無存。光緒年間重修頤和園時，因財力不足，採取拆東補西的辦法，將後山有用之材用於修補前山景點，衹在香巖宗印之閣原址改建了一座佛殿。致使後山後湖在長達一個多世紀的時間裏荒蕪不堪，遊人不願涉足。

自本世紀六十年代後，中國政府花費大量人力物力，在後山植樹造林，栽花種草，並重建了規模宏大的四大部洲寺廟羣，恢復了具有江南水鄉情趣的蘇州街，使後山後湖重放異彩。

The Back Hill and Back Lake Area

THE Back Hill and Back Lake Area encompasses the northern slope of Longevity Hill and the man-made Back Lake. It covers a space of over 30 hectares. The Back Hill is an undulating slope criss-crossed by small valleys and ditches. It is a very quiet place. According to historical records, there were eight gardens of different sizes built on the slope during the Qianlong period. Unfortunately, with the exception of the Glazed Tile Pagoda of Many Treasures, all these elegant little gardens were reduced to ashes by the Anglo-French Allied Forces. When the Summer Palace was rebuilt during the Guangxu period, because of the shortage of funds, only a Buddhist temple was constructed at the former site of the Pavilion of Fragrant Rocks and Ancestral Seals. For over a century the Back Hill and Back Lake lay waste, where no one dared to visit. After the 1960s, the Chinese government began to plant trees, plants and flowers on the back hill. The massive temple buildings of the Four Great Regions were rebuilt and Suzhou Street, typical of the riverside street in south China, was restored.

諧趣園 位於後山東麓。大園林中包含小園林，是清代大型皇家園林的特徵之一，被稱爲"園中之園"。諧趣園就是運用此種造園方法，仿江南名園——無錫惠山脚下的寄暢園而修建的。園内有五處軒堂，七座亭榭，百間遊廊，五座小橋。所有建築環繞荷池展開，極富江南園林柔媚清秀的特色。

Garden of Harmonious Pleasures. On the eastern side of the Back Hill, this garden is a reproduction of a famous South China garden called Jichangyuan in Huishan, Wuxi. Also known as "the Garden within a Garden", it is typical of the large imperial gardens of the Qing Dynasty. It has five halls, seven pavilions, a hundred bays of promenades and five small bridges. All the buildings are around a lotus pond. The South China atmosphere inside the garden is palpable.

涵遠堂 諧趣園的主體建築，是慈禧太后在諧趣園遊樂時休息的便殿。

Hall of Magnanimity. This hall is the main building in the Garden of Harmonious Pleasures, the resting place of the old Empress Dowager.

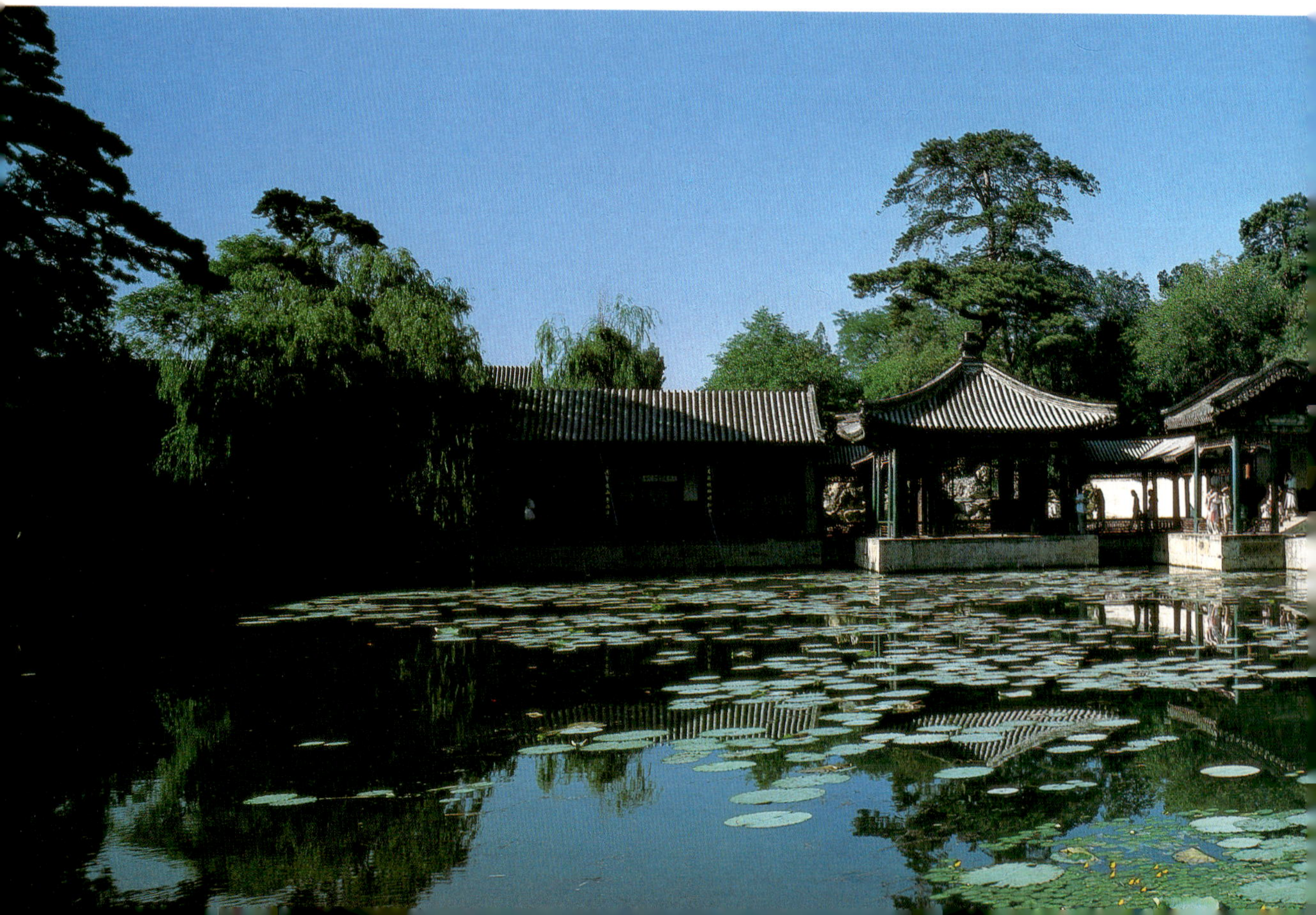

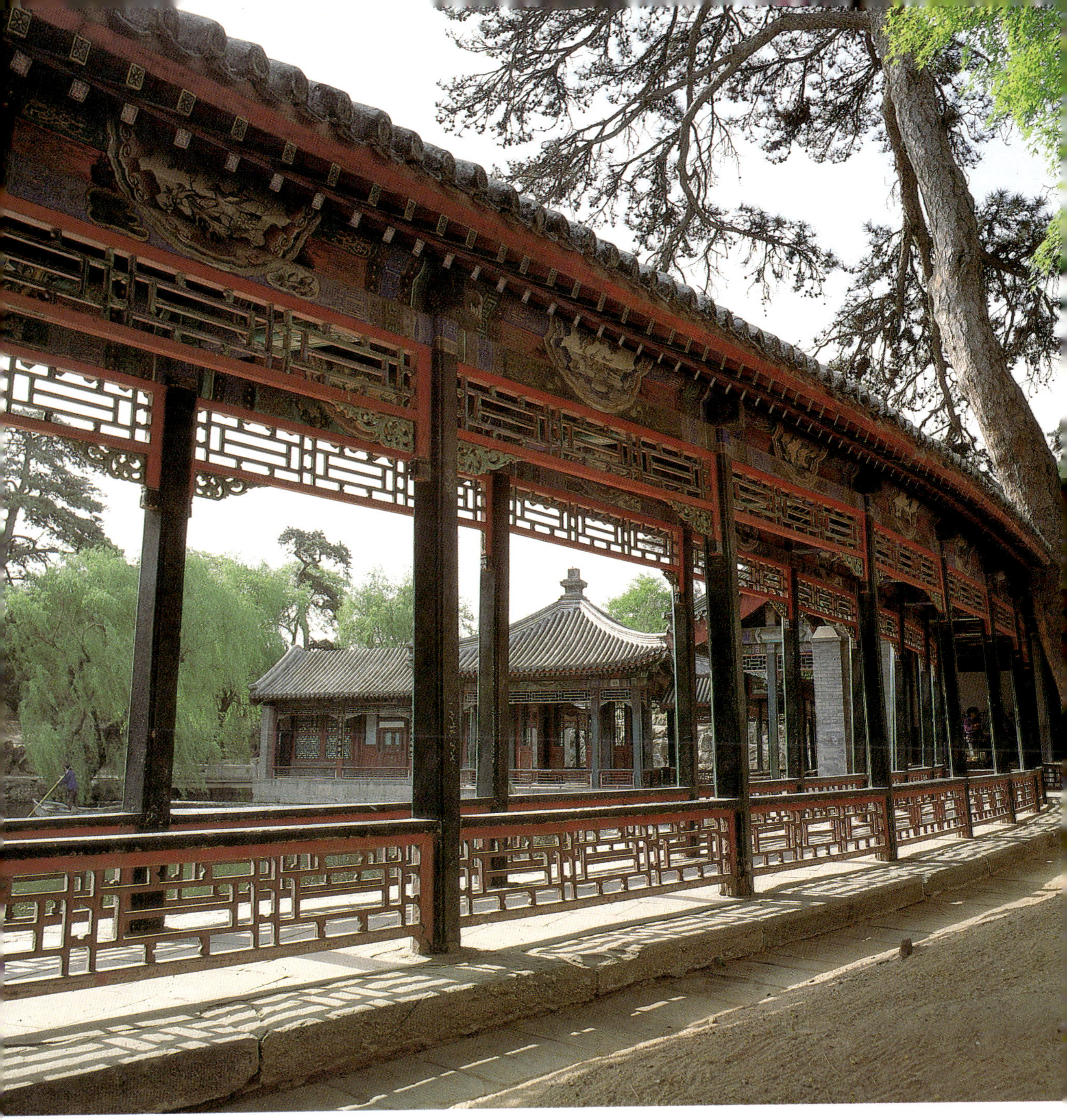

曲廊　三步一迴，五步一折，婉轉與亭榭相連。遊人漫步廊中，可觀魚戲，可賞芙蓉，着實別有一番情趣。

Zigzag gallery. These zigzag galleries are linked with halls and pavilions. Walking along them, one can watch the fish and lotus flowers in the pond.

飲綠水榭　臨水而建，是慈禧太后垂釣的地方。

Pavilion That Takes in the Green. Close to the pond, the pavilion is where the old Empress Dowager fished.

半廊 爲一邊透空、一邊有墻的廊。墻上的什錦窗造型各異，憑窗觀望，一窗一景。

Half-Open Promenade. This promenade has one side open and the other closed by a brick wall. In the wall are windows of different shapes, from which one can see different views.

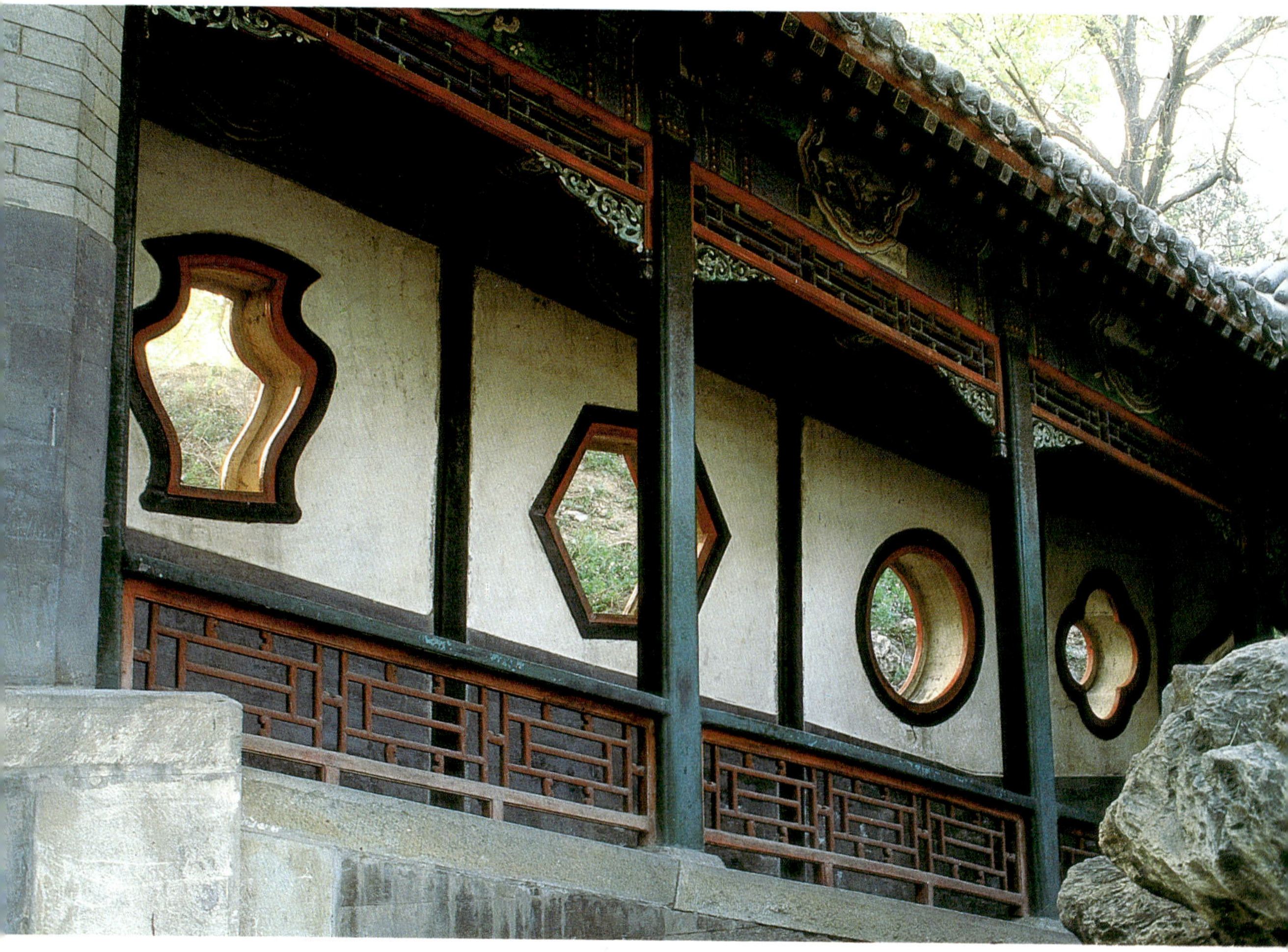

尋詩逕　置於園內蘭亭中，碑正面書“尋詩逕”三字，背面爲抒情五言詩，均爲乾隆皇帝御筆。

Tablet of Looking for Stone Path. This tablet stands in a tower in the garden. On its front side are carved the words "Looking for Stone Path" and on its back side is a lyric poem. Both the inscription and the poem are in Emperor Qianlong's handwriting.

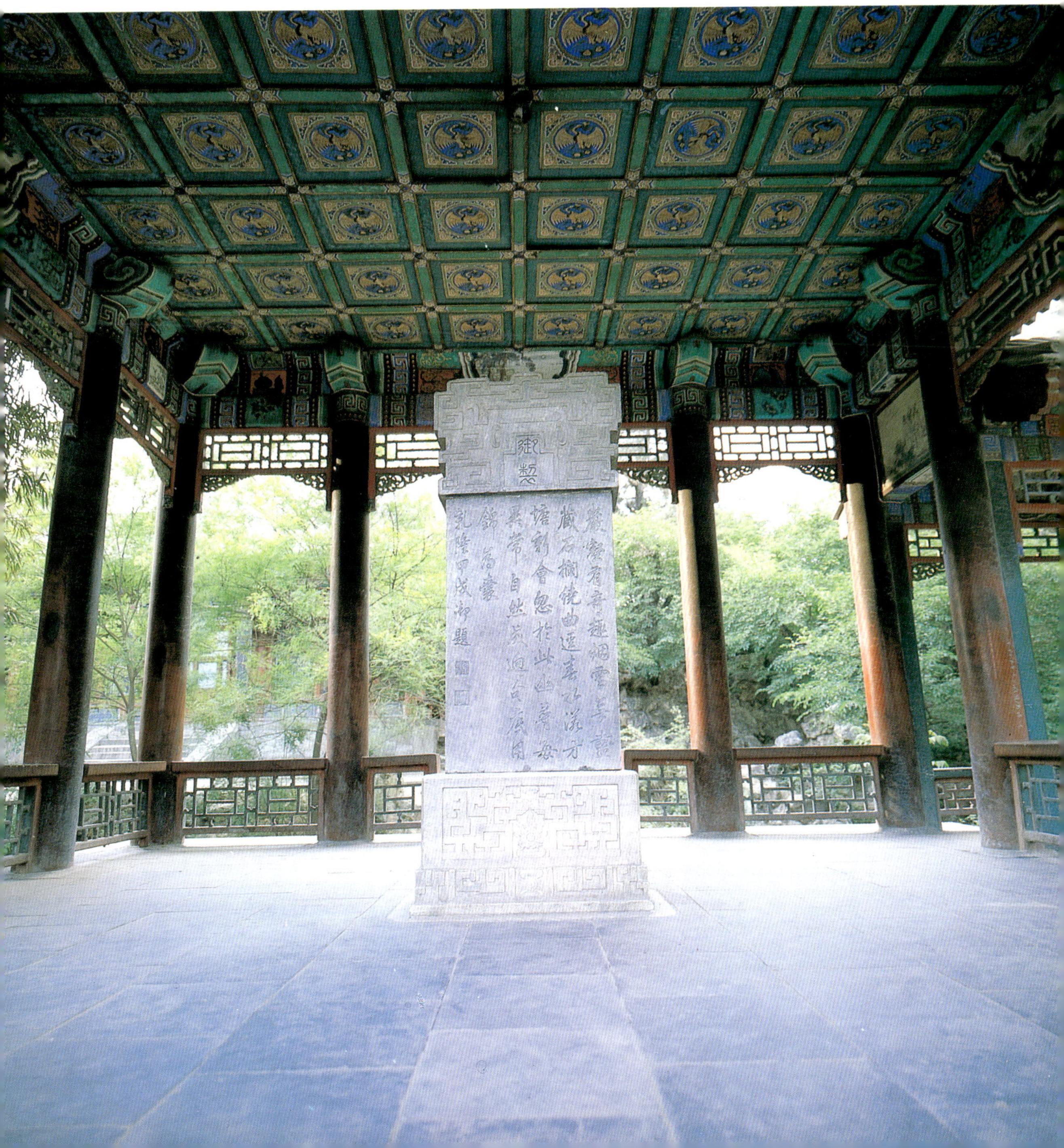

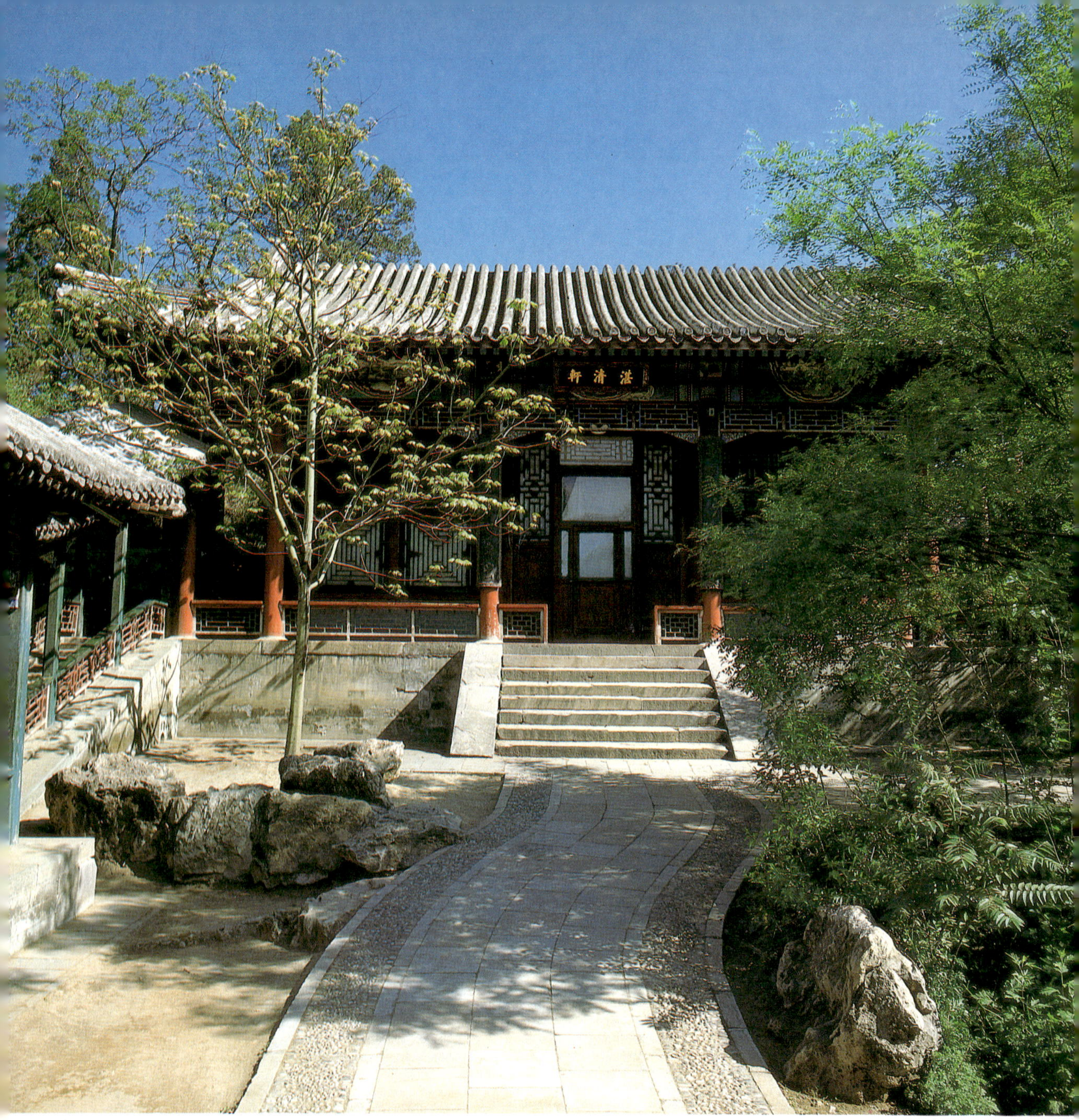

湛清軒 軒前有花圃、太湖石，軒東有曲徑、假山。佈置典雅，環境清幽。

Pavilion of Profound Purity. The pavilion has a flower nursery and rockery on its front side with a winding path and rockery on its eastern side. It is very elegant and peaceful.

玉琴峽　位於諧趣園西北角。人們將山石鑿成寬一二米、長約二十多米的曲折的石峽，引後湖之水層層跌落而下，水聲猶如琴聲，故名。

Jade Zither Gorge. The gorge is in the northwestern corner of the Garden of Harmonious Pleasures. The sound of water flowing in from the back lake is said to resemble the music of a zither.

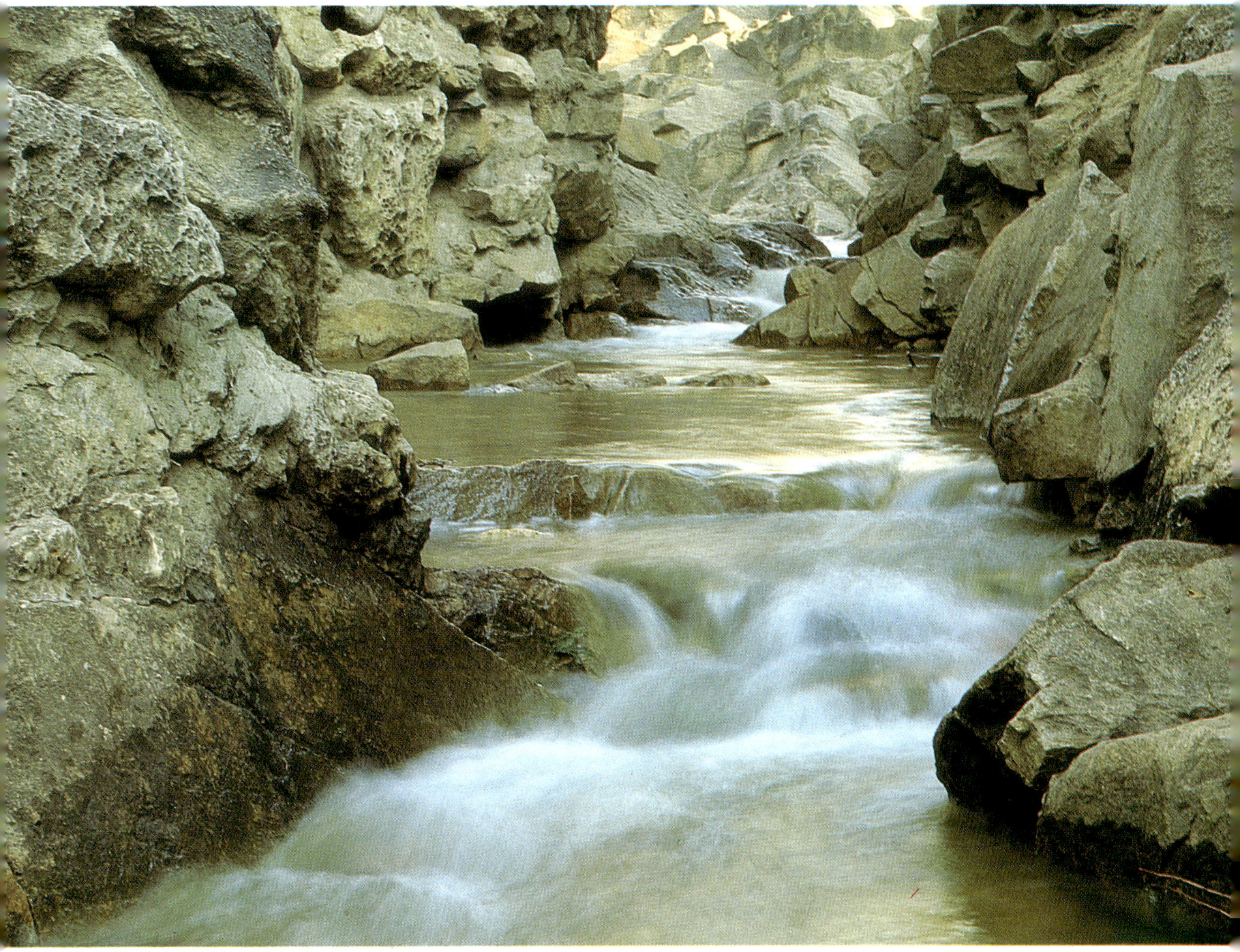

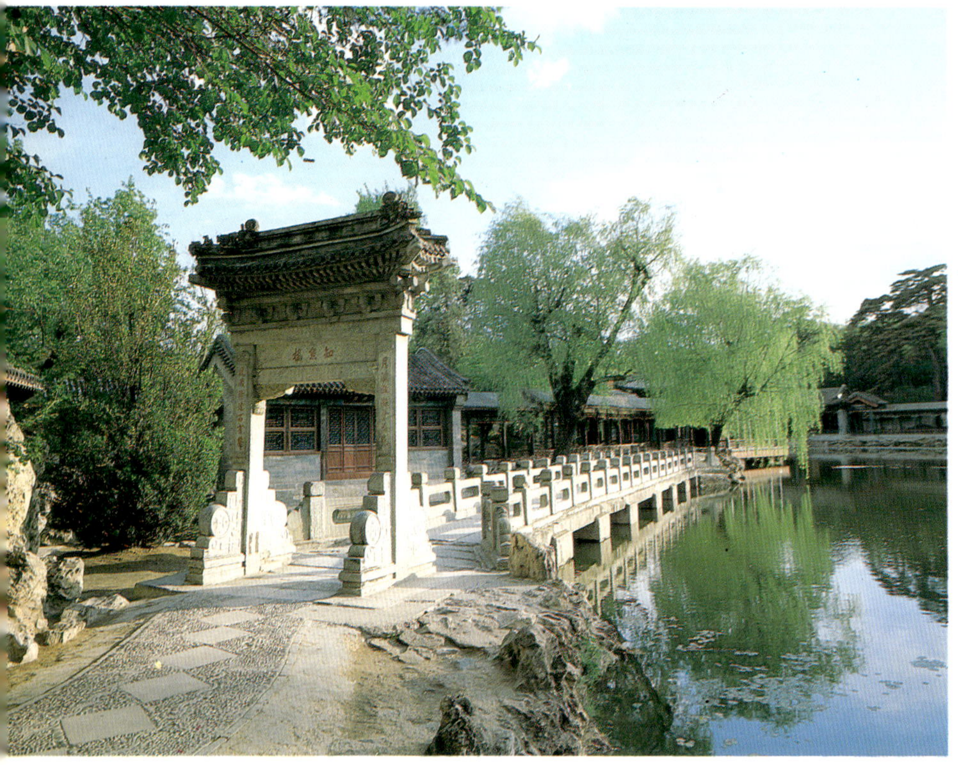

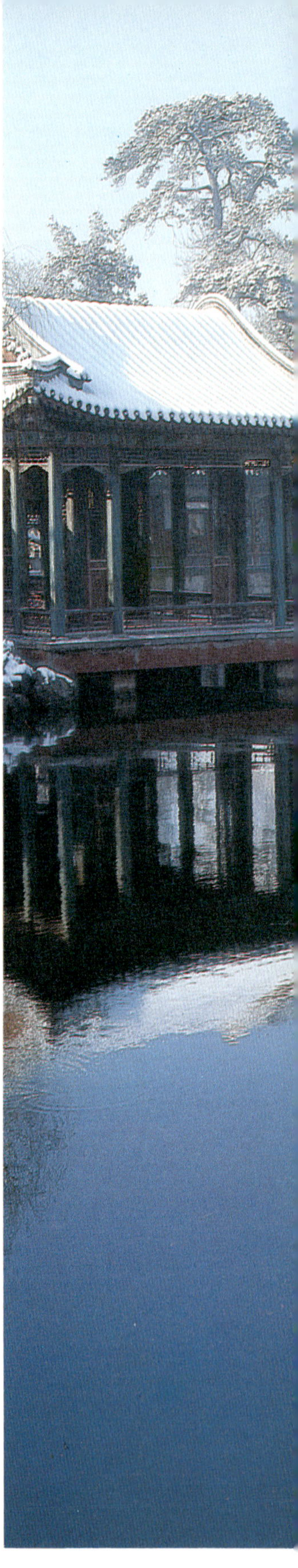

知魚橋 橋身貼近水面，極便觀魚。橋名來源於公元前中國兩位哲學家莊子和惠施的一次觀魚對話。莊子說："魚兒出來了，魚兒真快樂。"惠施問道："你不是魚，怎知魚之樂？"莊子反駁說："你不是我，怎知我不知魚之樂？"

Know-Your-Fish Bridge. The bridge is built close to the surface of the water, enabling a person standing on it to clearly see the fish at play. The bridge's name comes from an amusing dialogue between two ancient philosophers, Zhuangzi and Huizi. Zhuangzi said: "The fish is really happy." Huizi asked: "You are not a fish, how do you know fish is happy?" Zhuangzi asked back: "You are not me, how do you know I don't know the fish is happy?"

諧趣園雪景 雪後初晴，踏雪賞景，頗富詩意。

Garden of Harmonious Pleasures in Snow. The buildings and trees are mantled in silver.

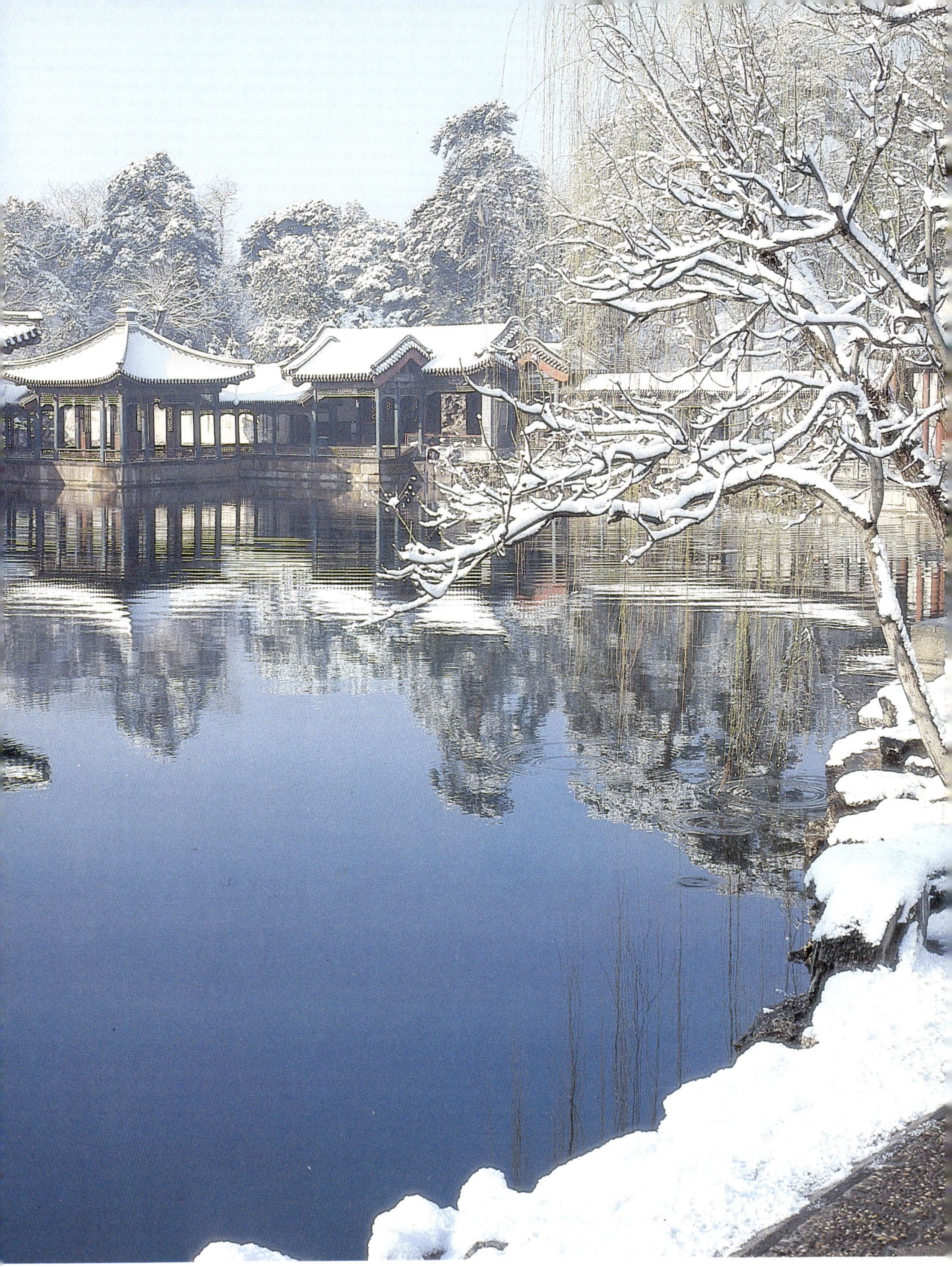

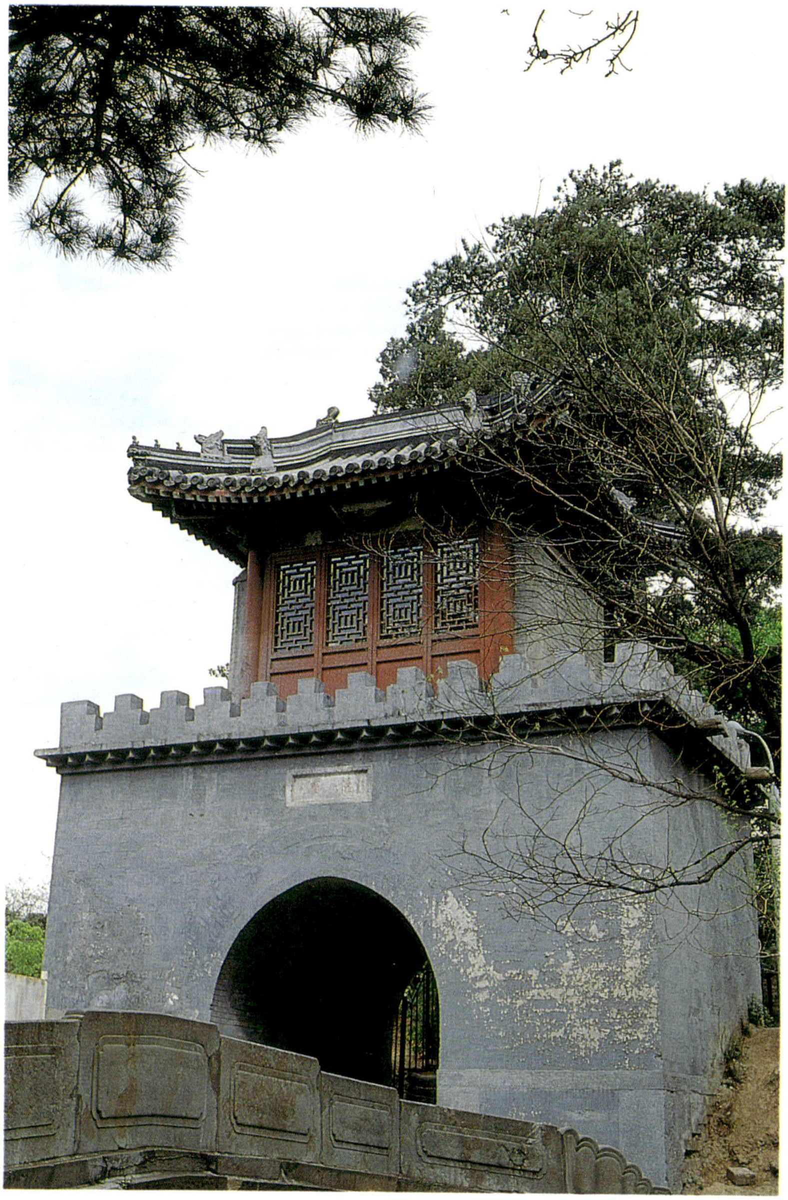

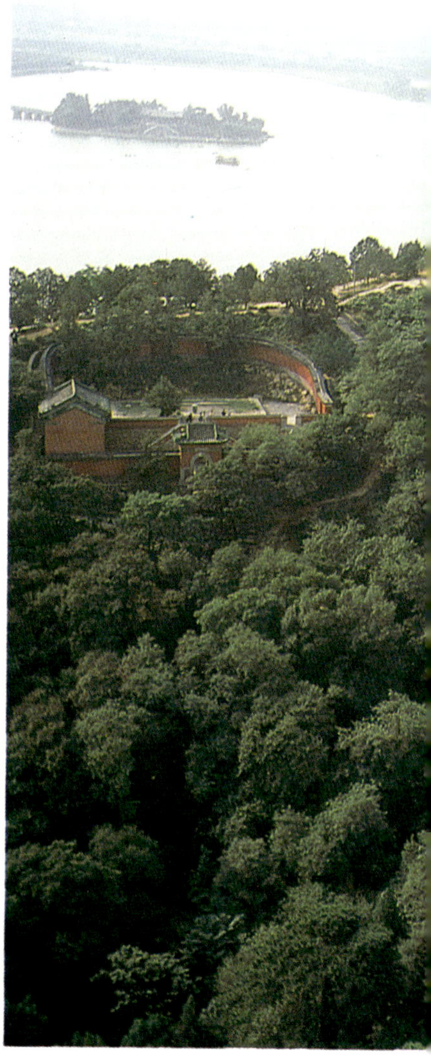

寅輝城關　位於後山東部，突兀而立。東邊石額刻"寅輝"二字，西邊刻"挹爽"二字。城關左控山谷，右臨後湖，關前石橋橫跨山澗，儼然雄關要塞。

Tower of Early Morning Light. A representation of a city gate, the tower stands on the eastern side of the Back Hill like a sentinel guarding the slope overlooking the lake. It is across a stone bridge built over a gully, which gives the place the appearance of a mountain fortress. A stone tablet on the east wall bears the words "Early Morning Light", a similar one on the west wall is inscribed "Exuding Pleasures".

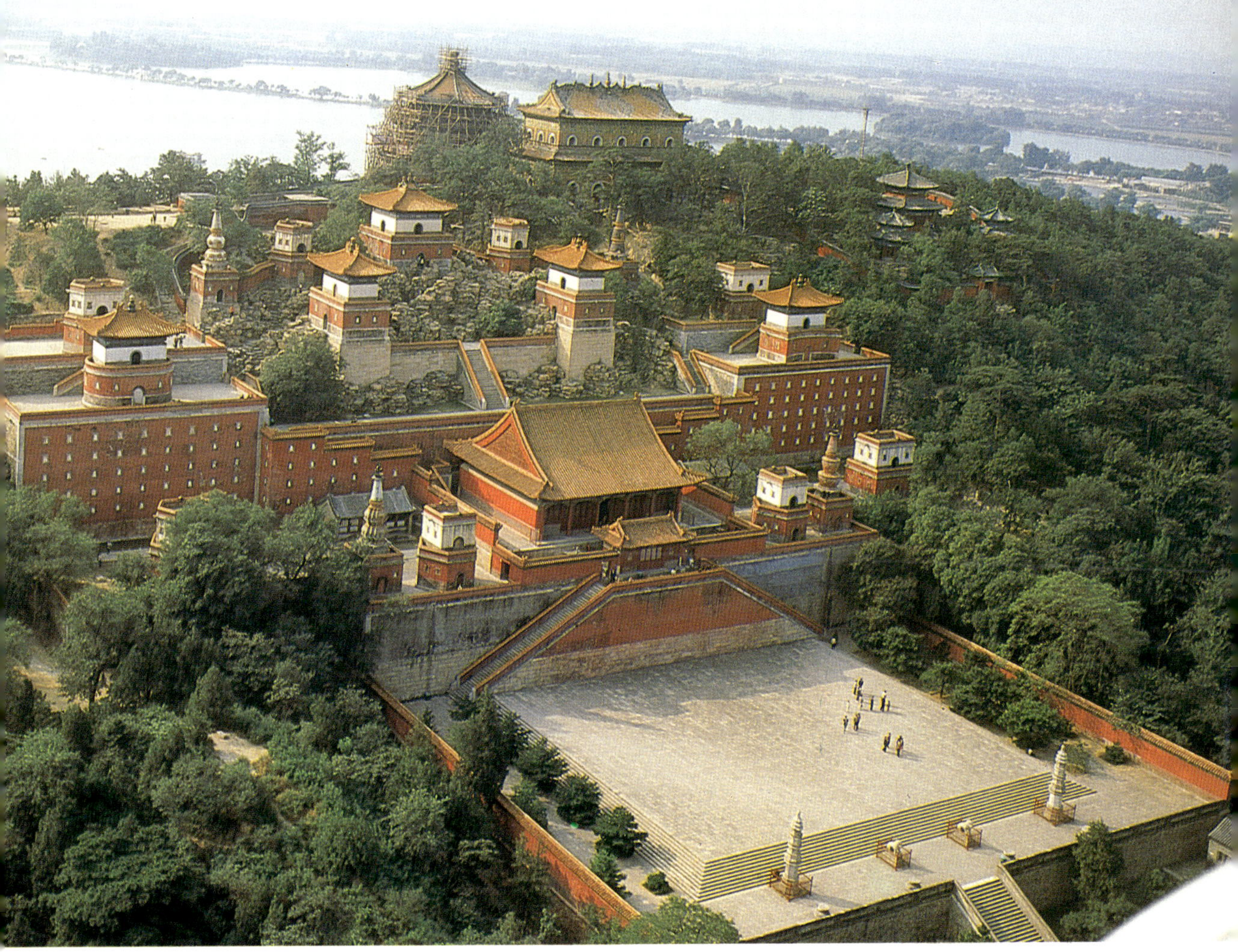

鳥瞰後山　古木蒼翠，梵宇放彩，龐大的寺廟建築羣因山順勢，錯落佈置，氣勢宏偉。

A bird's-eye view of Back Hill. On the slope of the hill are ancient trees and massive temples. It is a grand view.

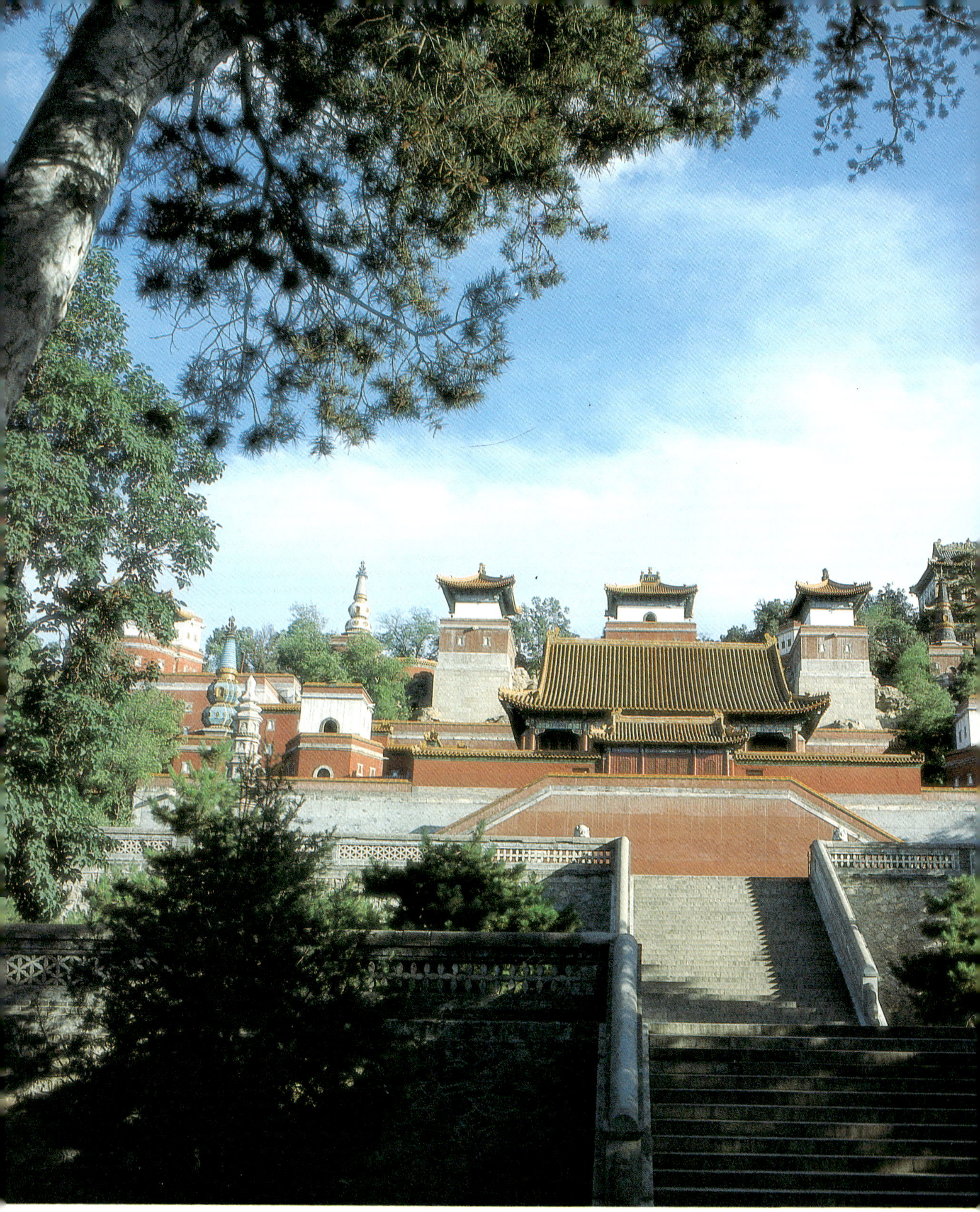

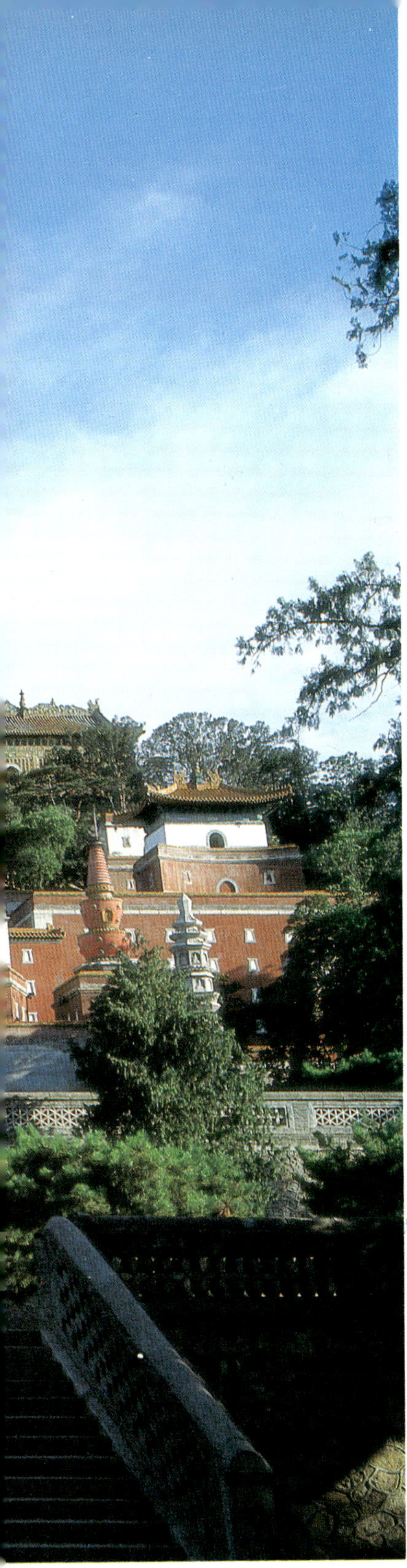

四大部洲　是乾隆年間興建的一座藏式宗教建築，曾毁於一八六〇年戰火，近年重建，基本恢復了原貌。

Four Great Regions. This is a massive complex of buildings forming a Tibetan-style temple. It was built in the Qianlong period, but was devastated in war in 1860. Reconstruction of these buildings has begun in recent years.

四大部洲佛殿　原建築的香巖宗印之閣，象徵佛教中的須彌山。光緒年間重修頤和園時改爲佛殿，内供佛像。

Buddhist Hall of the Four Great Regions. Originally known as the Pavilion of Fragrant Rocks and Ancestral Seals, it symbolized the Buddhist Mount Xumi. After the Summer Palace was rebuilt in the Qianlong period, the hall was changed to a temple with a statue of Buddha inside.

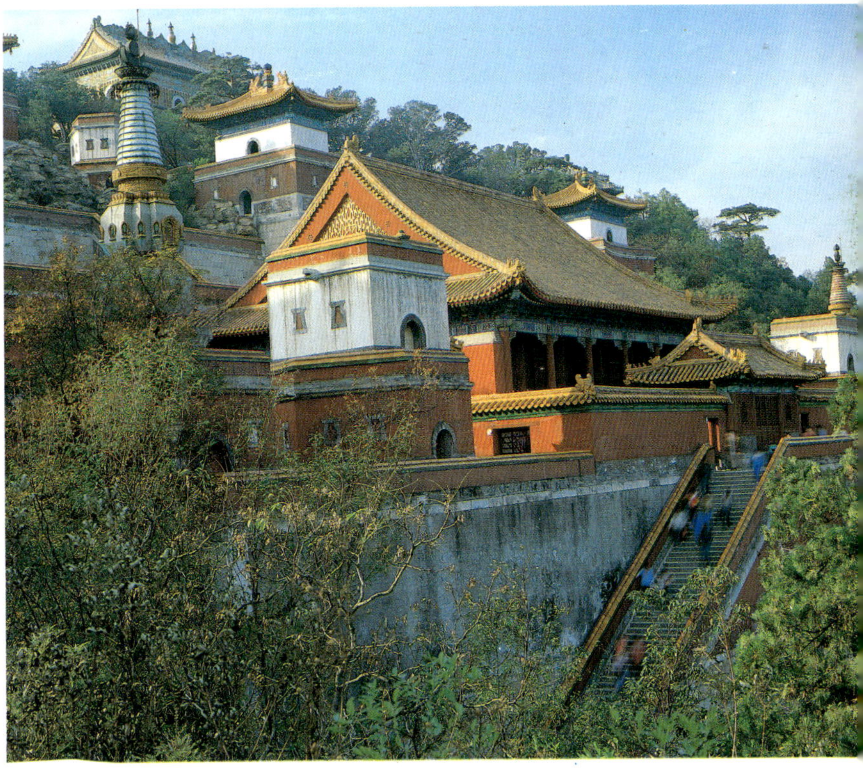

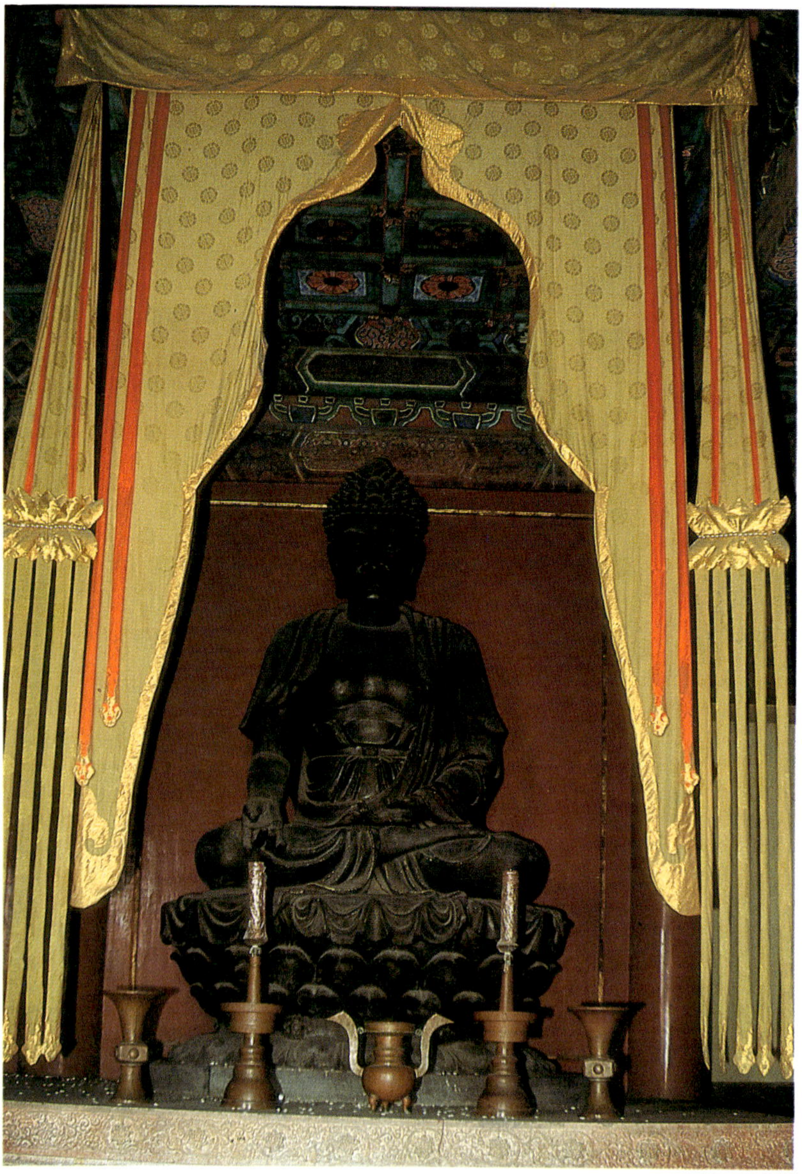

大殿主佛　殿内供有三尊佛像，造型雷同，祇是手勢有别。圖爲居中的釋迦牟尼像。

Statue of Buddha. There are three statues of Buddha in the hall. Pictured is the statue of Sakyamuni.

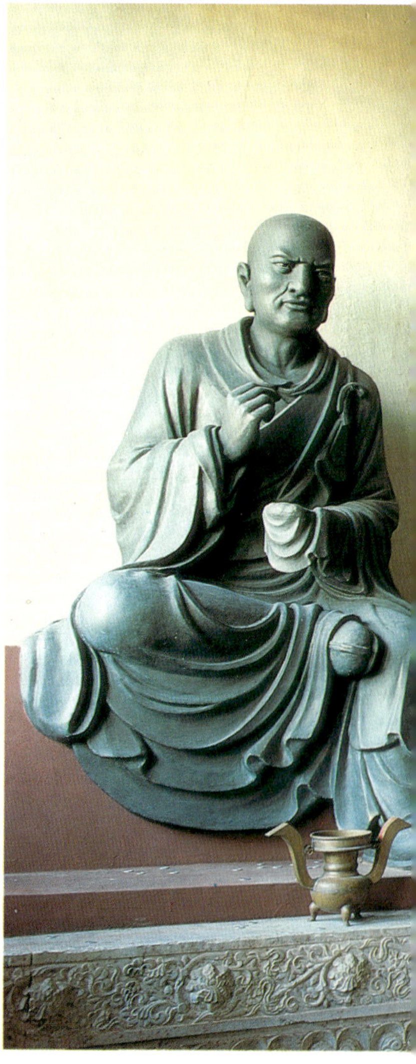

十八羅漢 供於三尊主佛的東西兩側，每側九尊。圖爲西側羅漢。

Eighteen arhats. These eighteen arhats stand on either side of the three statues of Buddha. Pictured are the nine arhats on the western side.

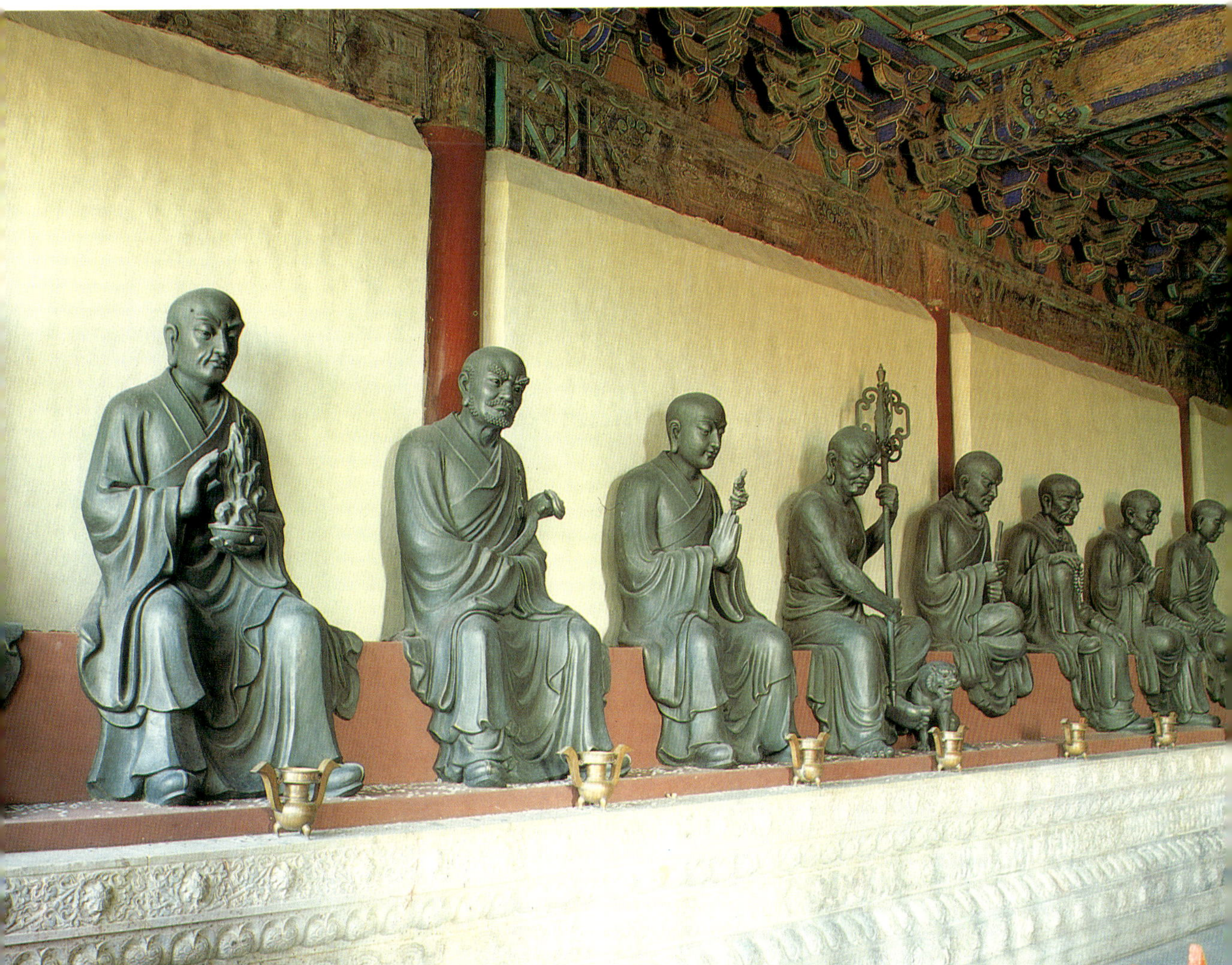

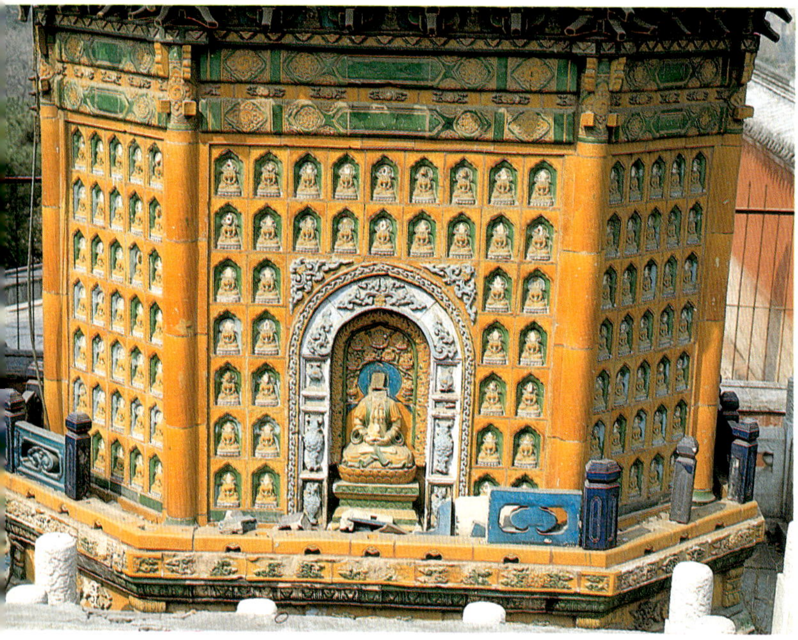

塔身佛像　塔身八面嵌砌琉璃小佛像。一八六〇年佛塔雖幸免於戰火，但許多佛像被破壞，至今仍有傷痕。

Statues of Buddha. These small statues of Buddha are engraved on the glazed walls on eight sides of the pagoda. Although they survived the war of the 1860 foreign invasion, many of them were damaged. The damage is still visible today.

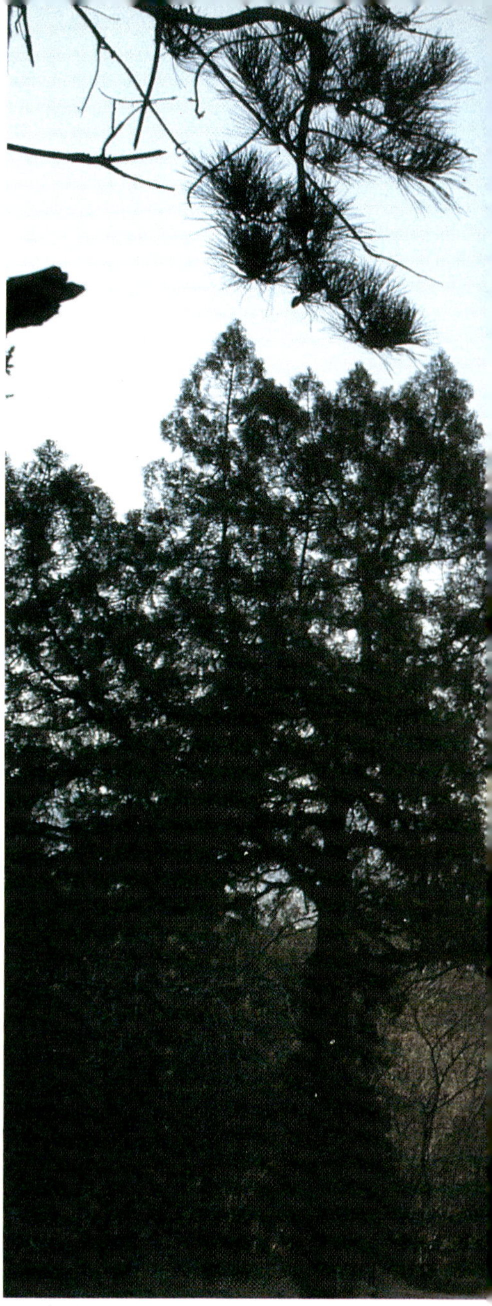

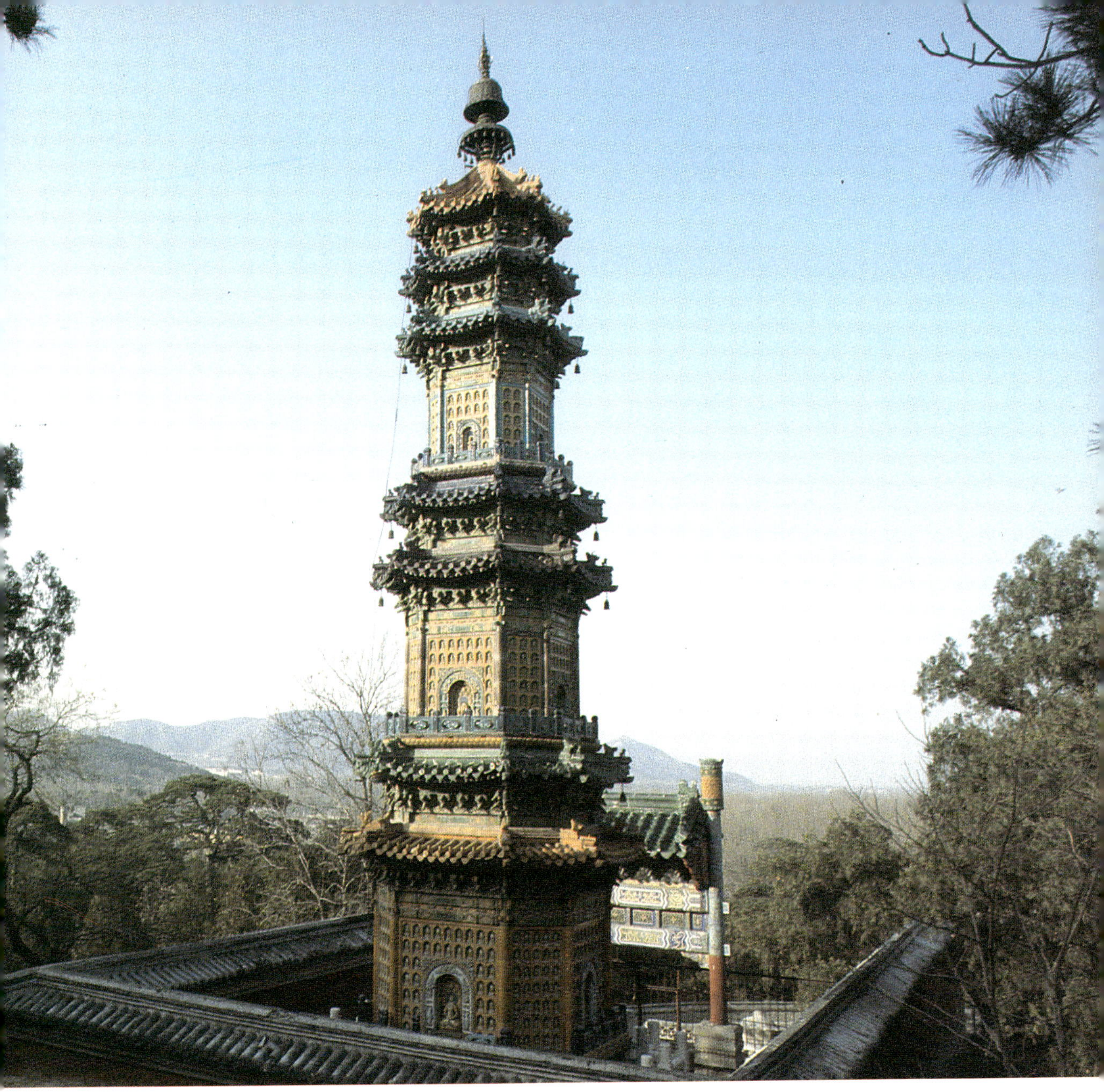

多寶琉璃塔 塔高十六米，八面七級，全部用琉璃磚砌成。下爲白石須彌座，上爲鍍金塔刹。頂部懸銅鈴，風吹鈴響，疑是梵聲入耳。塔前立有石碑，碑上用漢、滿、蒙、藏四種文字刻着乾隆皇帝《御製萬壽山多寶佛塔頌》。

The Glazed Tile Pagoda of Many Treasures. This pagoda is a seven-storeyed, eight-sided building over 16 metres high, inlaid from top to bottom with glazed bricks alternately of blue, green and yellow, on which are engravings of Buddha. It rests on a white stone platform and is crowned with a gilded pinnacle. From the top of the pagoda are hung bronze bells, which produce a melodious sound in the wind. In front of the pagoda stands a stone tablet, on which is carved "Ode to the Imperially Built Pagoda of Many Treasures of Longevity Hill" in Chinese, Manchu, Mongolian and Tibetan.

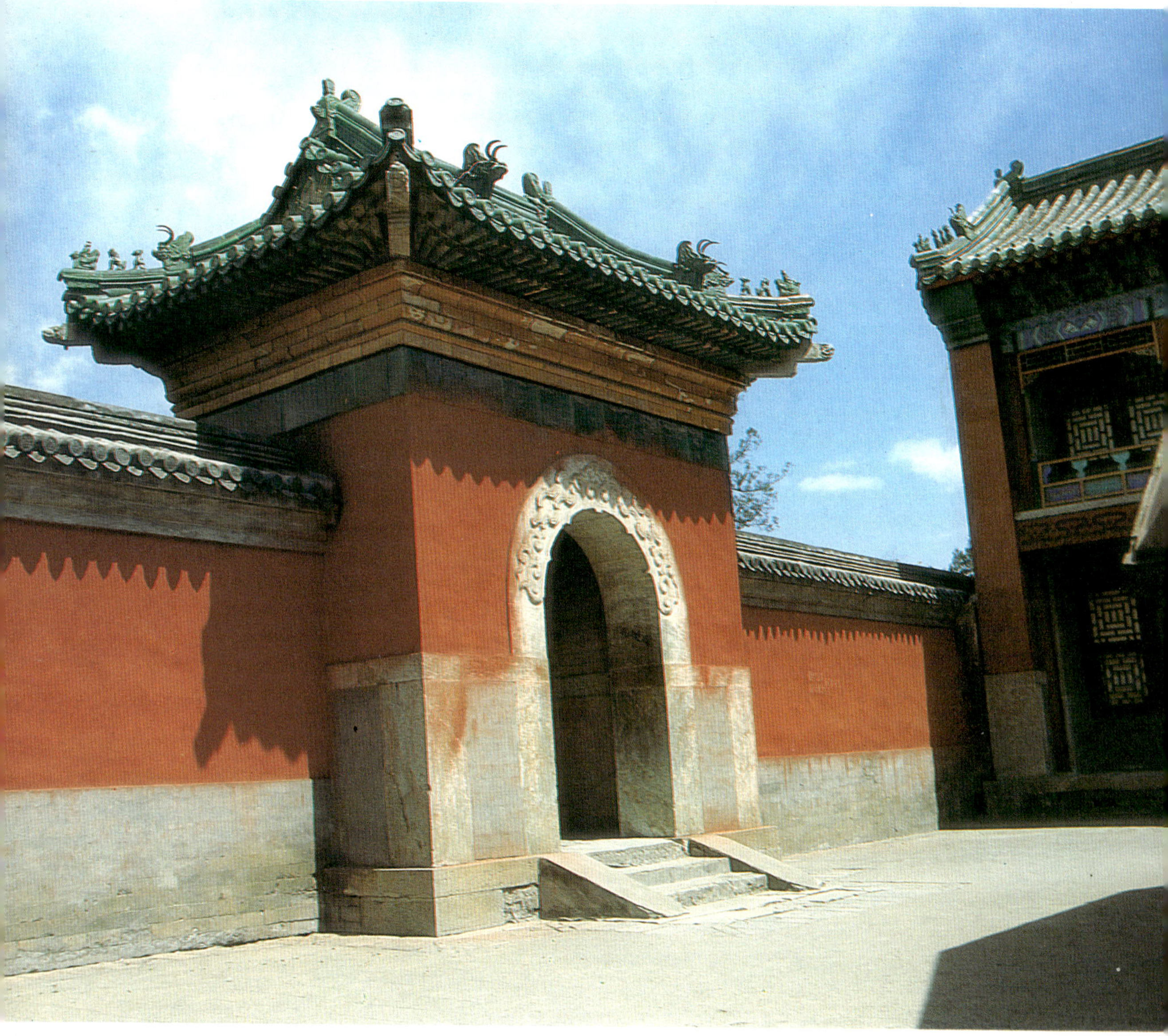

善現寺山門　位於香巖宗印之閣東側，現僅存山門和一配樓。"善現"即梵語"須菩提"，相傳爲釋迦牟尼十大弟子之一，以論證"諸法性空"著稱。

Gate of Shanxian Temple. The temple was on the eastern side of the Pavilion of Fragrant Rocks and Ancestral Seals. Only its gate and a side hall remain today.

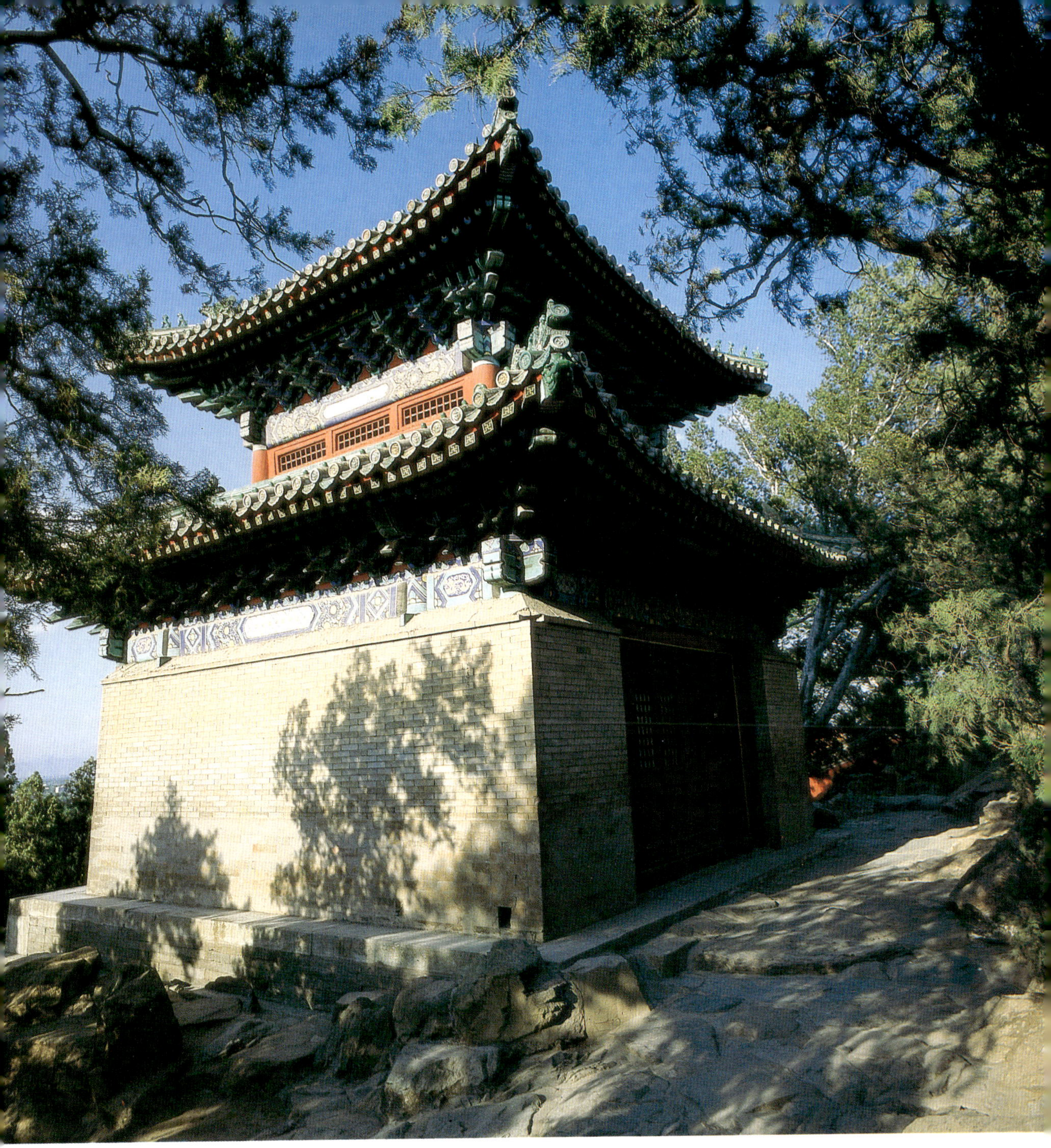

雲會寺 爲雙層方形亭式建築，内供毗盧佛銅像。寺院内松柏參天，坡路曲折，幽雅清静。

Temple Where Clouds Gather. This temple is a two-storeyed building in the shape of a tower. Inside it is a bronze statue of Buddha. The temple courtyard is quiet and secluded, shaded by tall pines and cypresses. It is accessible only by a tortuous path.

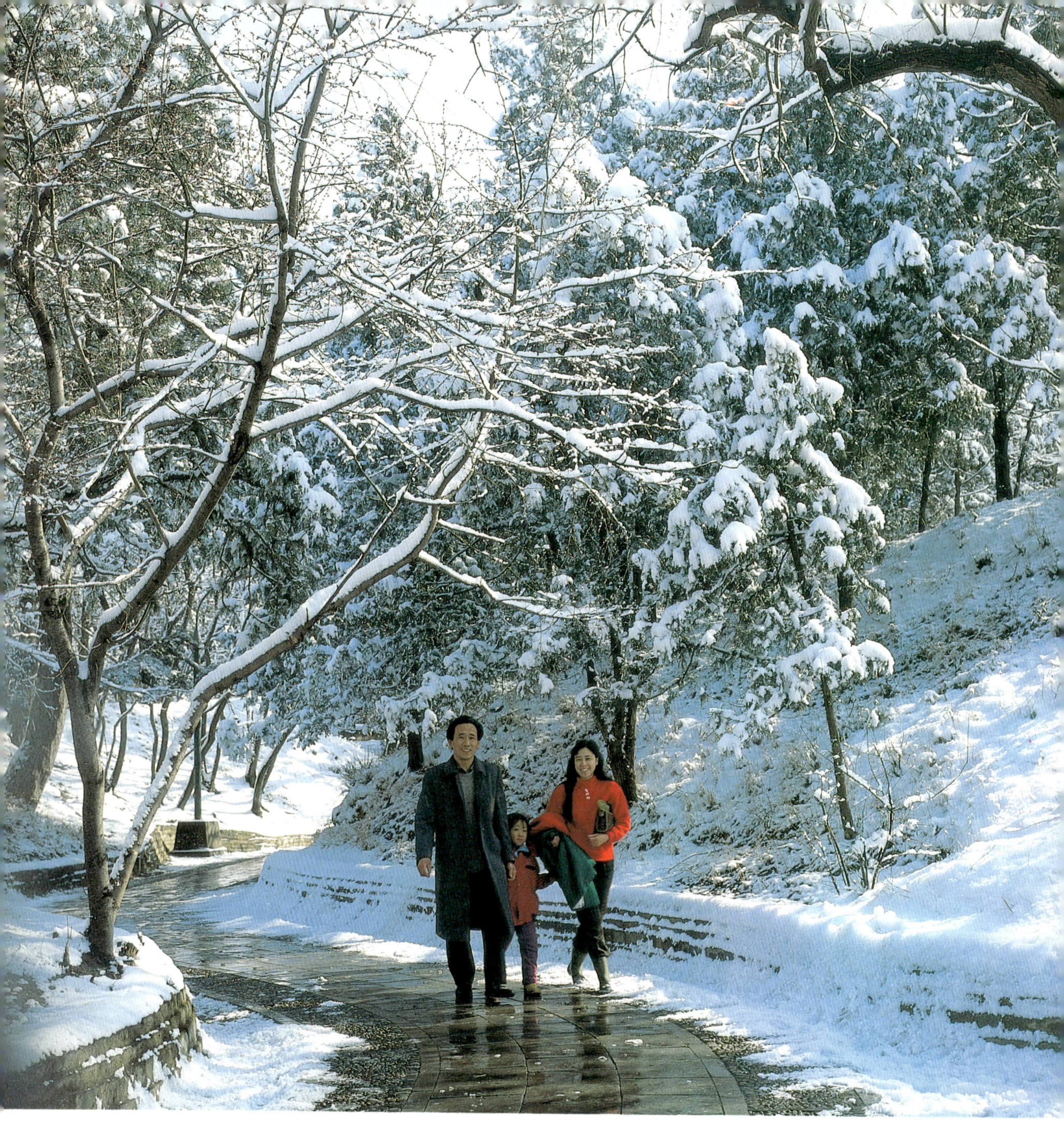

中御路 當年帝、后御用的主幹道，與湖平行，直中寓曲，時起時伏。雪後沿路賞景，如密林探勝，頗有北國林海雪原的意境。

The Central Imperial Path. This path, which the emperor and empress used to stroll, runs parallel to the lake. Walking along it after snow, one can see a landscape of the northern country.

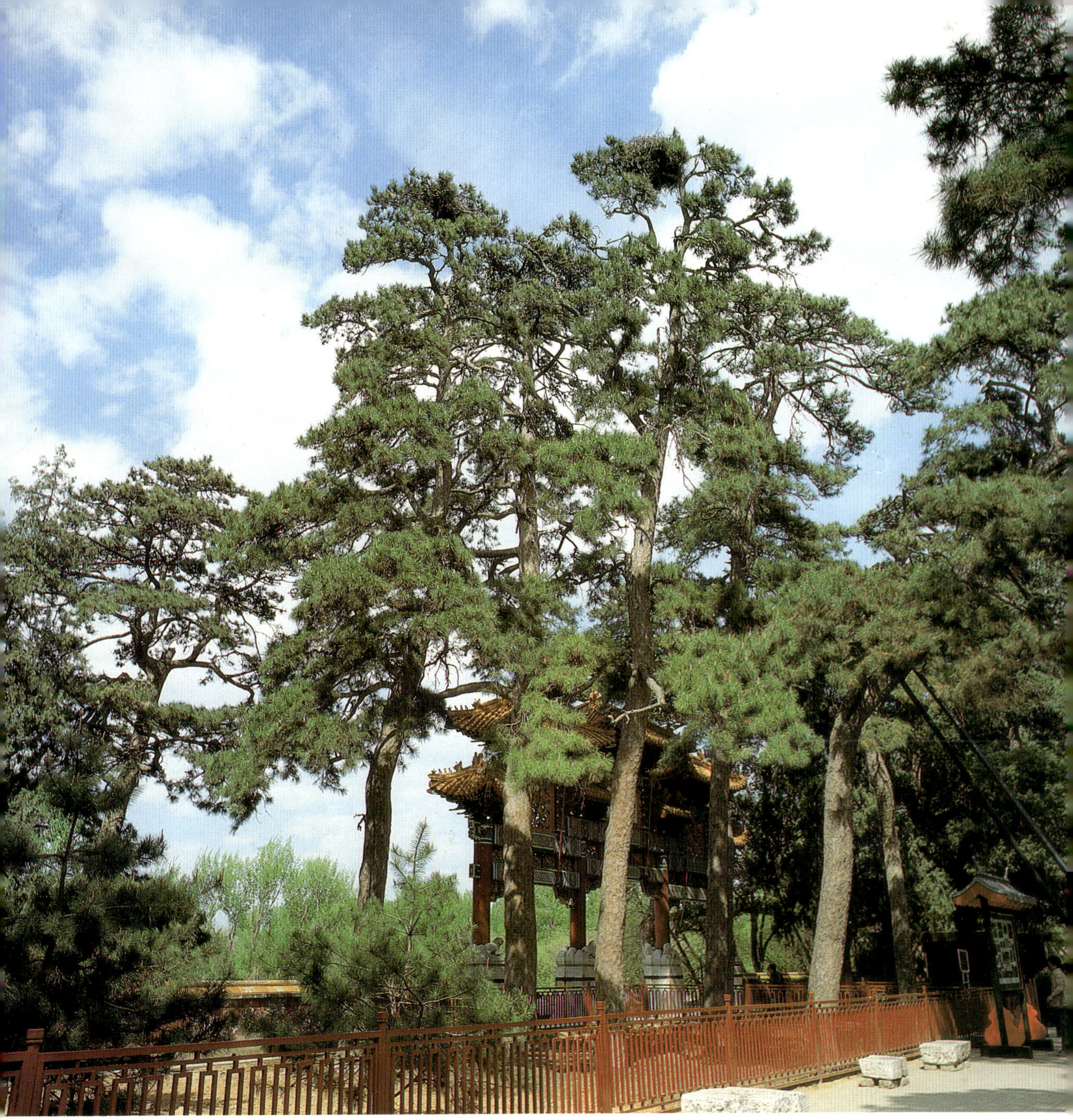

松堂　爲一大庭院，院内古木扶疏。庭院東、西、北三面原有牌樓，除北面牌樓已恢復外，另兩座僅存雕刻精美的夾柱石。

Hall of Pines. It used to be a large courtyard with many ancient trees. Originally there were archways on its east, west and north sides. Now only the archway on the north has been restored. The other two remain unrestored with their exquisitely carved pillar stones lying on their original sites.

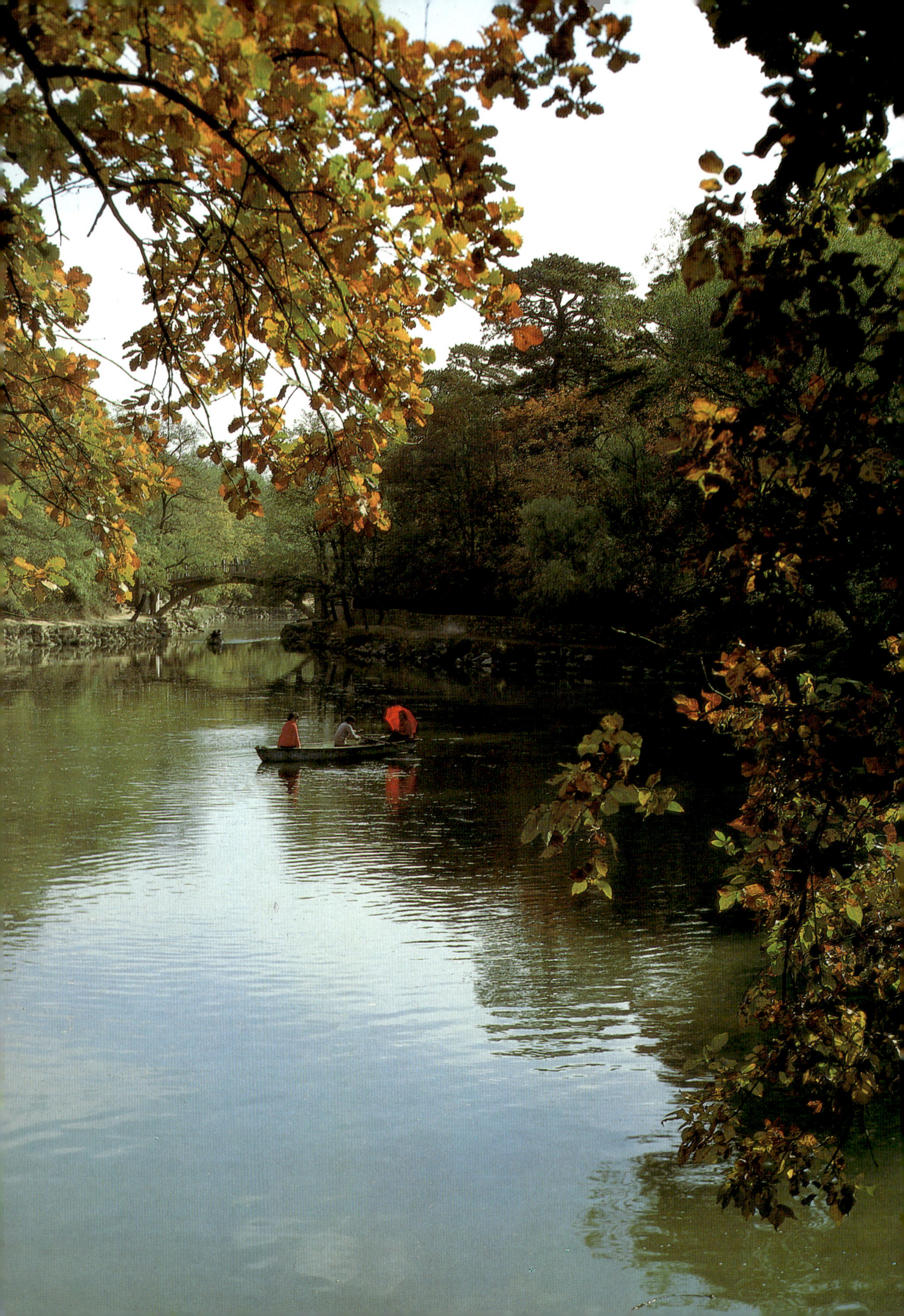

後湖 西起昆明湖的荇橋，東止諧趣園的玉琴峽，全長千餘米，乍寬乍窄，最寬處六十米，窄處僅十米。河岸松柏蒼翠，楊柳依依，野花自開自落，頗具江南園林風韵。

Back Lake. From Xingqiao Bridge on Kunming Lake in the west to the Jade Zither Gorge in the Garden of Harmonious Pleasures, the Back Lake is over 1,000 metres long. At some places it is 60 metres wide and at some places it is only 10 metres wide. On its two banks are tall green pines, cypresses, weeping willows and wild flowers.

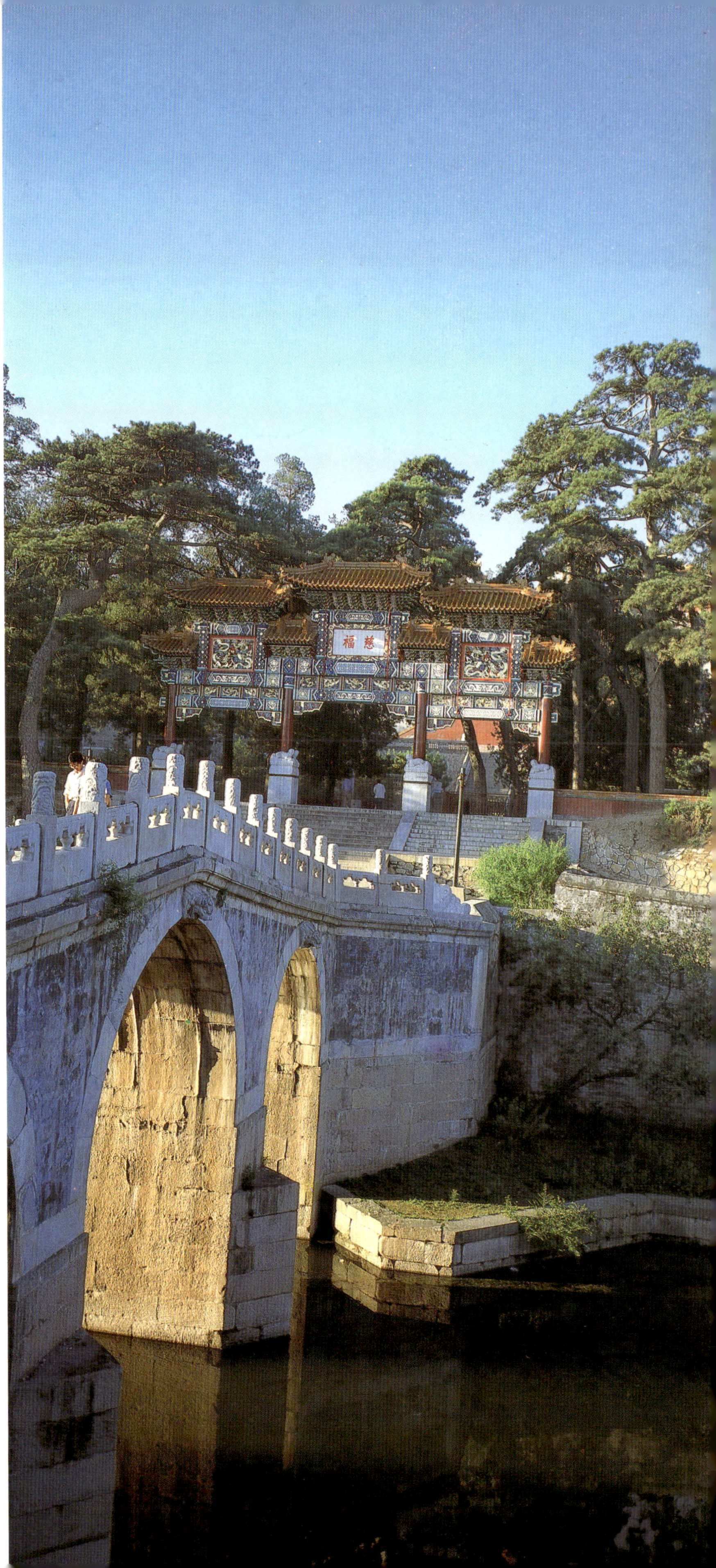

慈福牌樓和三孔石橋 牌樓金碧彩繪，堂皇華美。三孔石橋橫跨後湖中段，是連接北宮門和後山主體建築的樞紐，橋下湖兩岸即爲蘇州街。

Archgate of Kindness and Happiness and the Three-arch Stone Bridge. The archgate is resplendent and magnificent. The Three-Arch Stone Bridge across the middle section of Back Lake connects the North Palace Gate with the main buildings on Back Hill. Below the bridge is Suzhou Street.

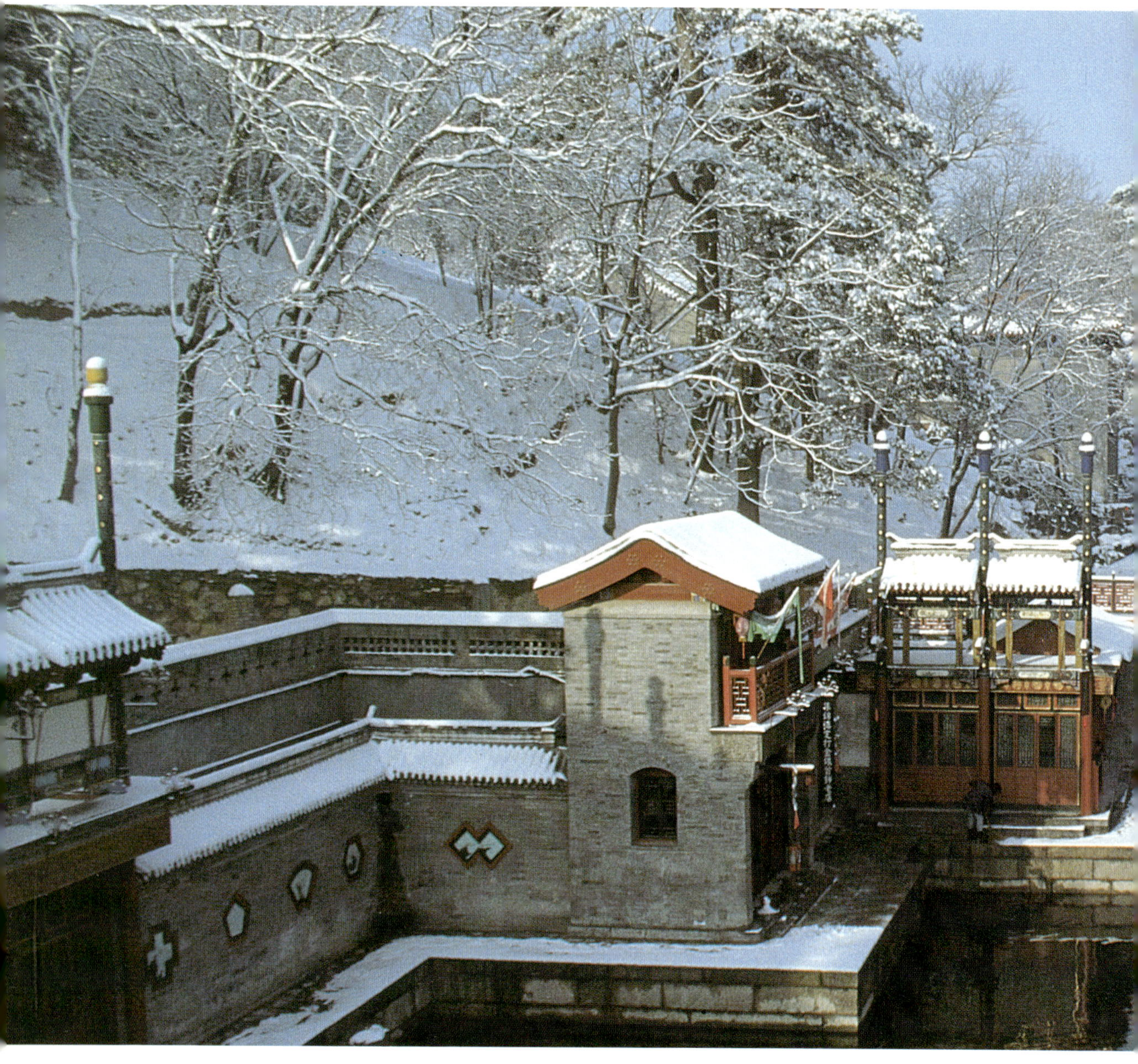

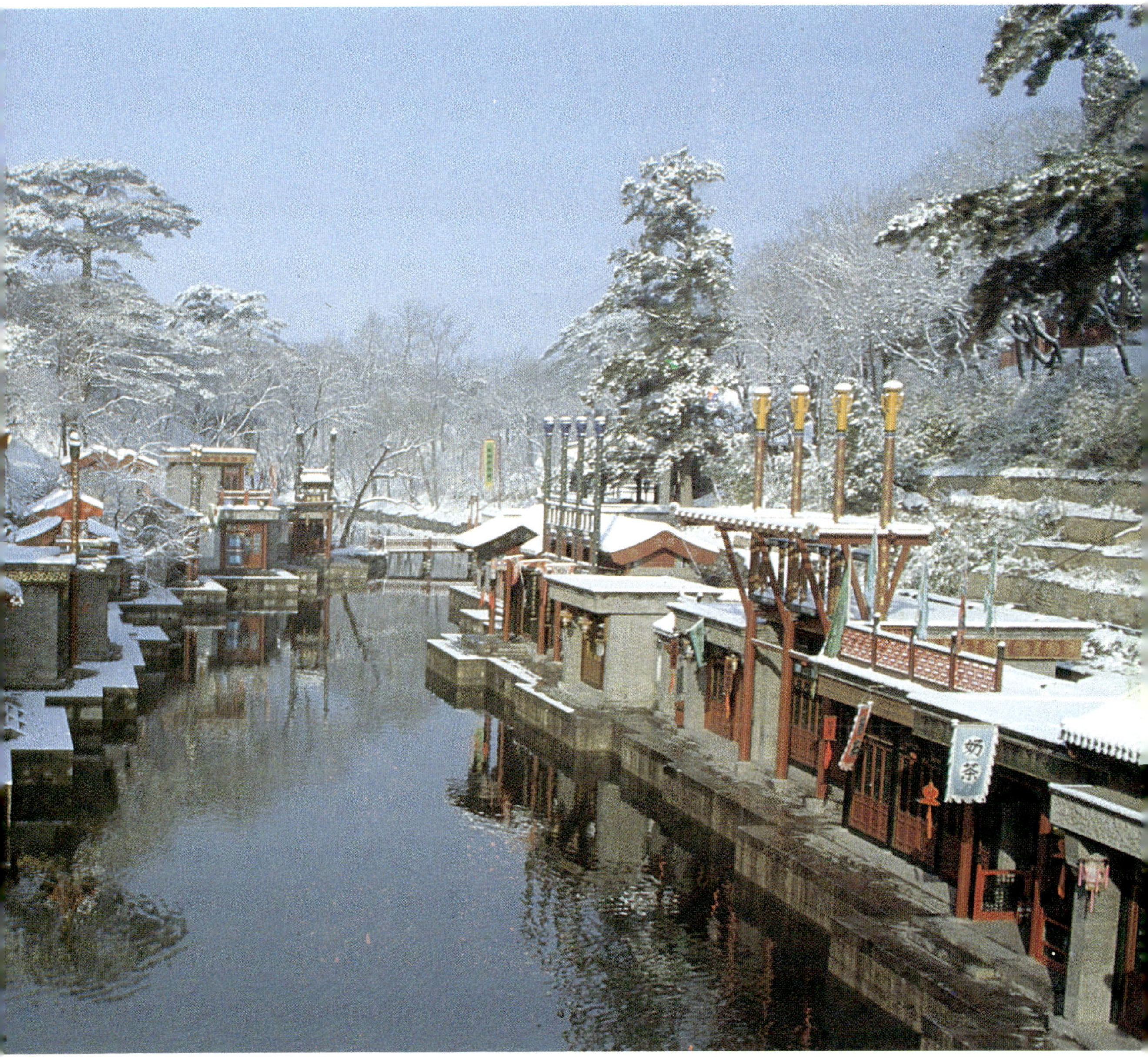

蘇州街 位於後湖中段，蜿蜒曲折三百餘米，建築面積近三千平方米。列肆於宮苑，始於漢代。蘇州街和它上方的四大部洲寺廟羣形成了“以廟帶肆”的商業模式。它以水當街，以岸作市，共有六十四座鋪面，十四座牌樓、牌坊，八座小橋。

Suzhou Street. The street in the middle section of Back Lake runs for over 300 metres along the lakeside, covering a building space of 3,000 square metres. It has 64 shops, 14 gateways or archways and 8 small bridges. The shop assistants wearing clothes in the style of the Qing Dynasty warmly welcome customers from all over the world. The street really looks like a South China fair.

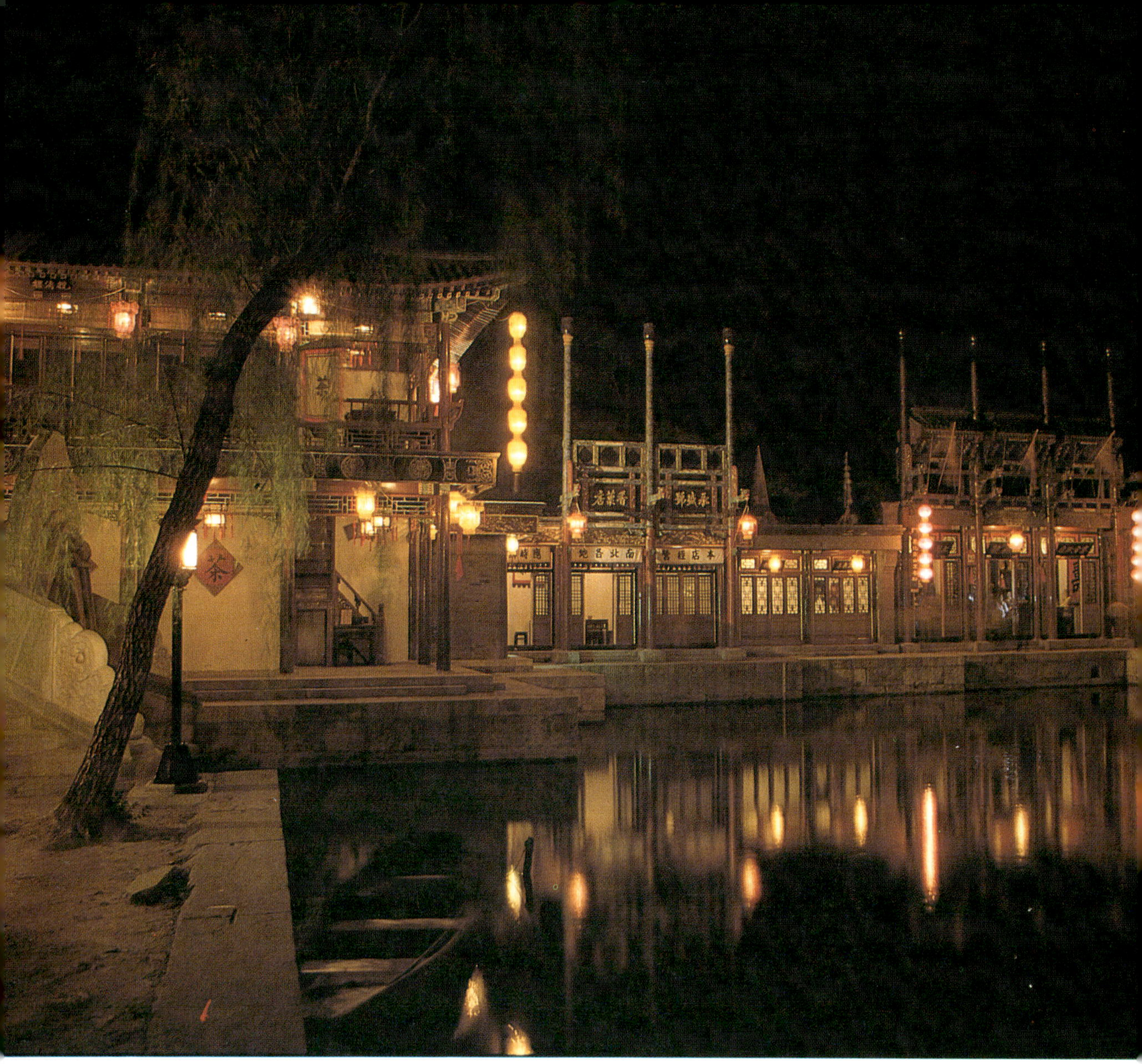

蘇州街夜景　Suzhou Street at night.

泰來號綢緞鋪　是中國民間老字號店鋪，以經營綢緞聞名。當年這裏的商店並不經銷商品，而是慕名設店，作爲街面點綴。

Tailaihao Silk Shop. Tailaihao is a famous traditional silk shop. But the shops here throughout their history have never done any real business. They were established simply to embellish the street.

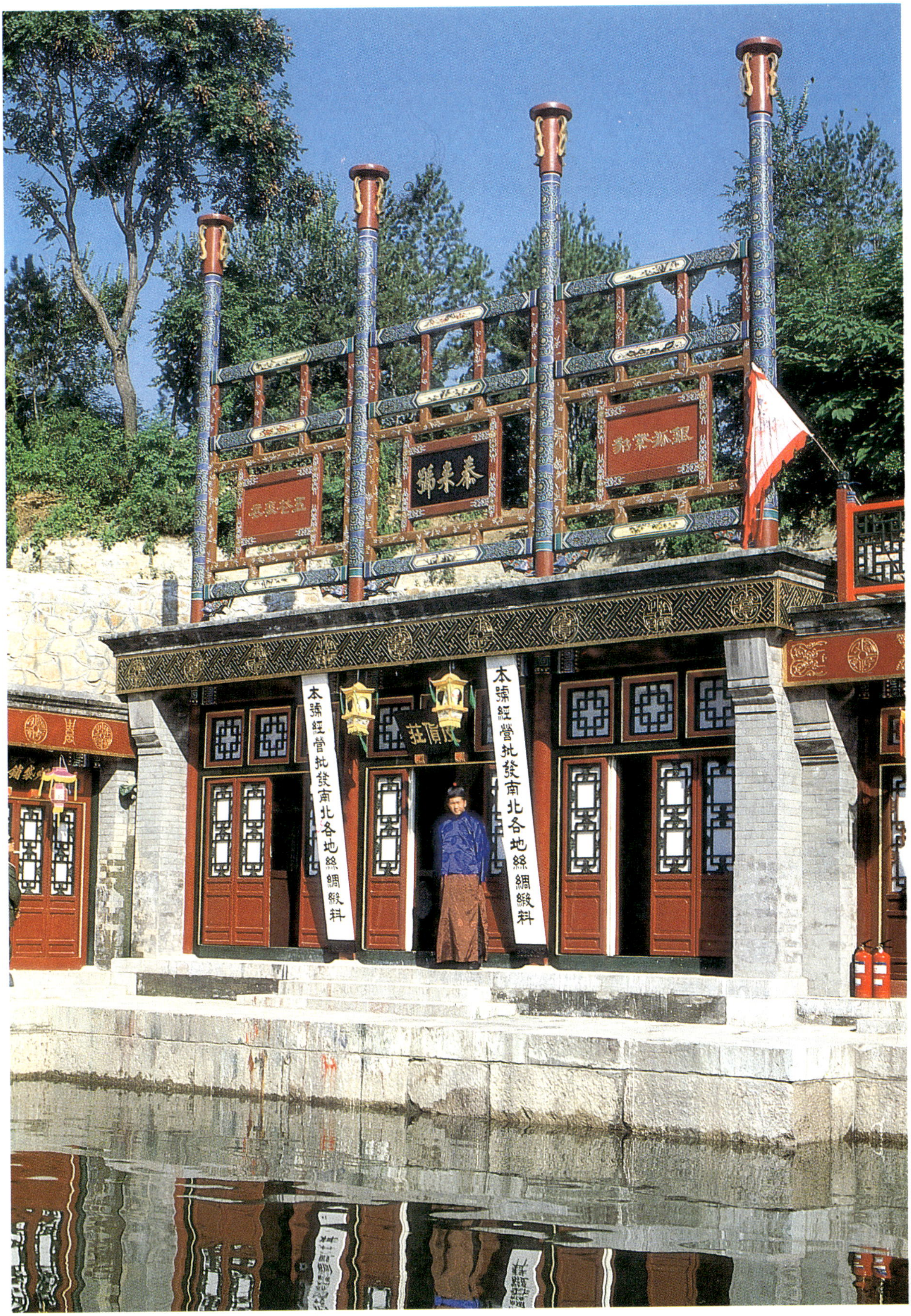
本號經營批發南北各地絲綢緞料
本號經營批發南北各地絲綢緞料

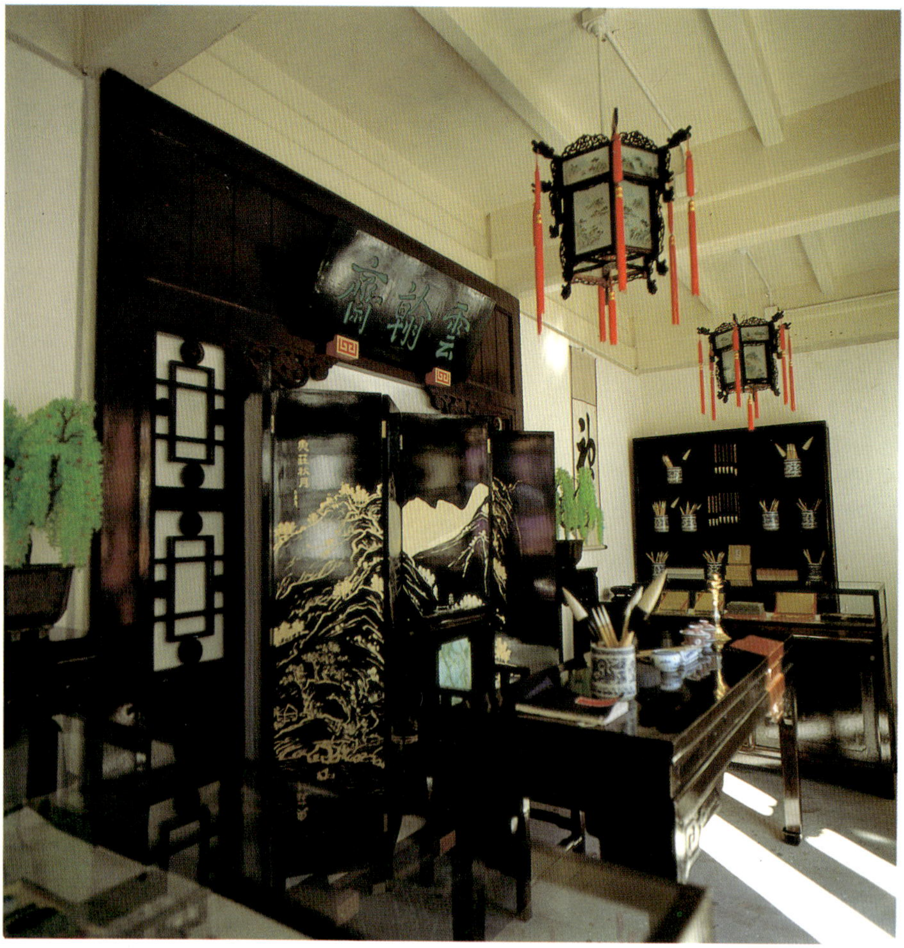

齋翰堂　文房四寶店鋪。　Yunhanzhai Stationary Shop.
圖爲内景。

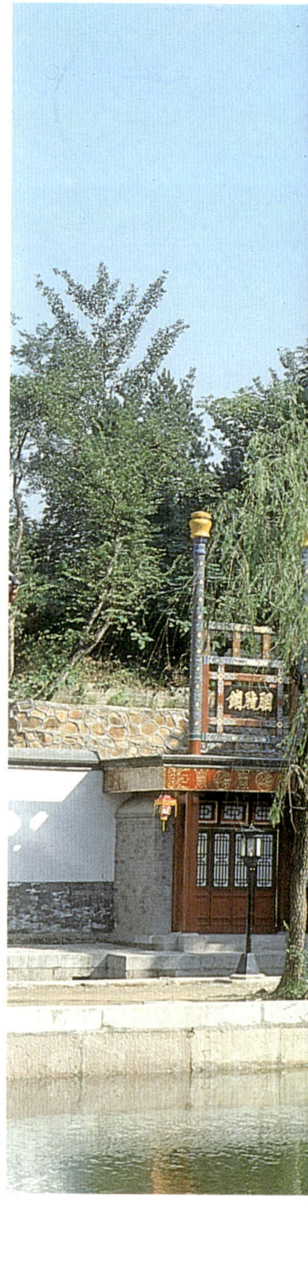

通源號奶茶館 位於蘇州街東街，遊人可登樓小吃，亦可品茗賞景。

Tongyuanhao Milk Tea House. The tea house stands on the eastern side of the Suzhou Street. The visitor can enjoy the beautiful scenery while drinking milk tea in the house.

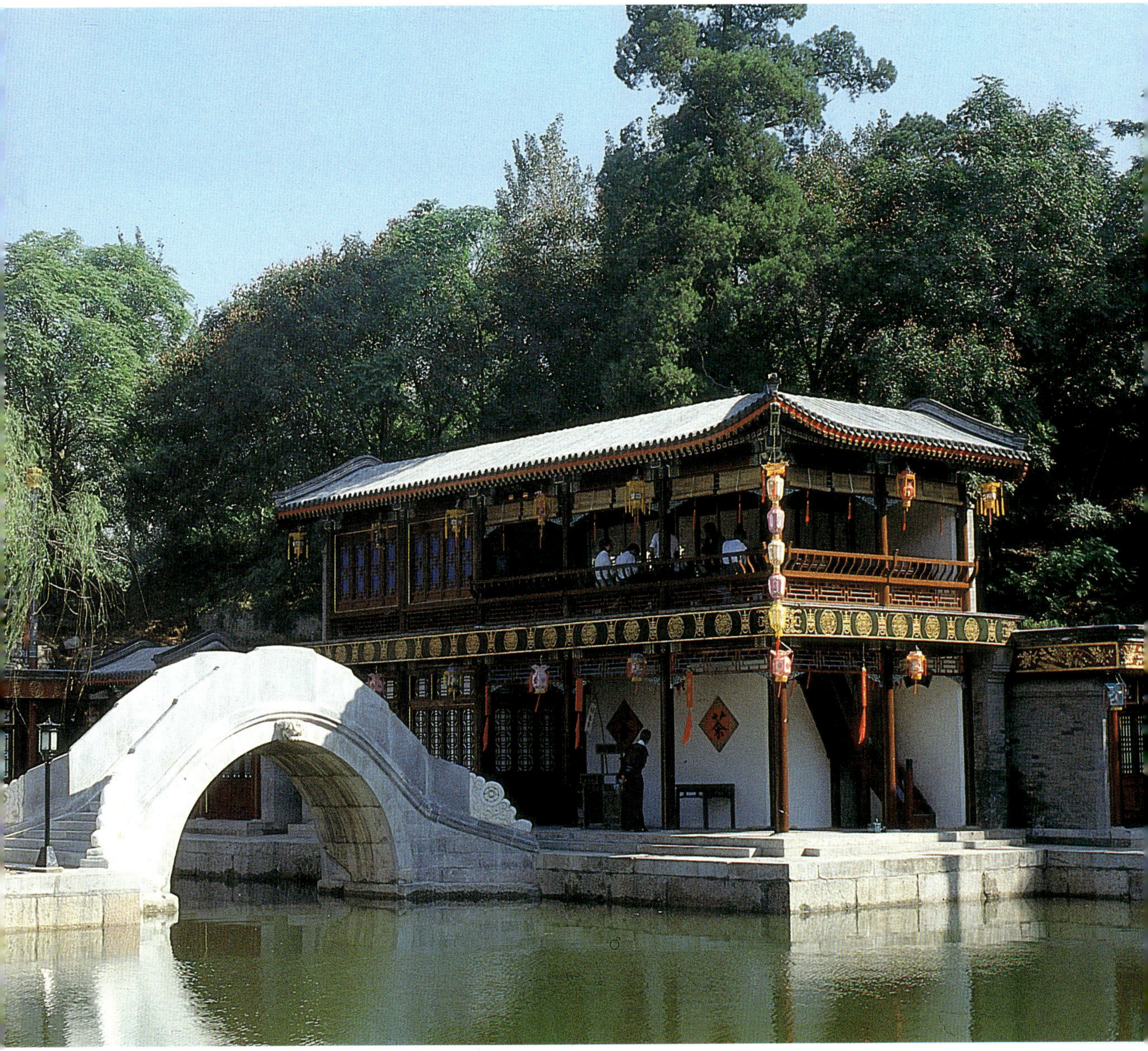

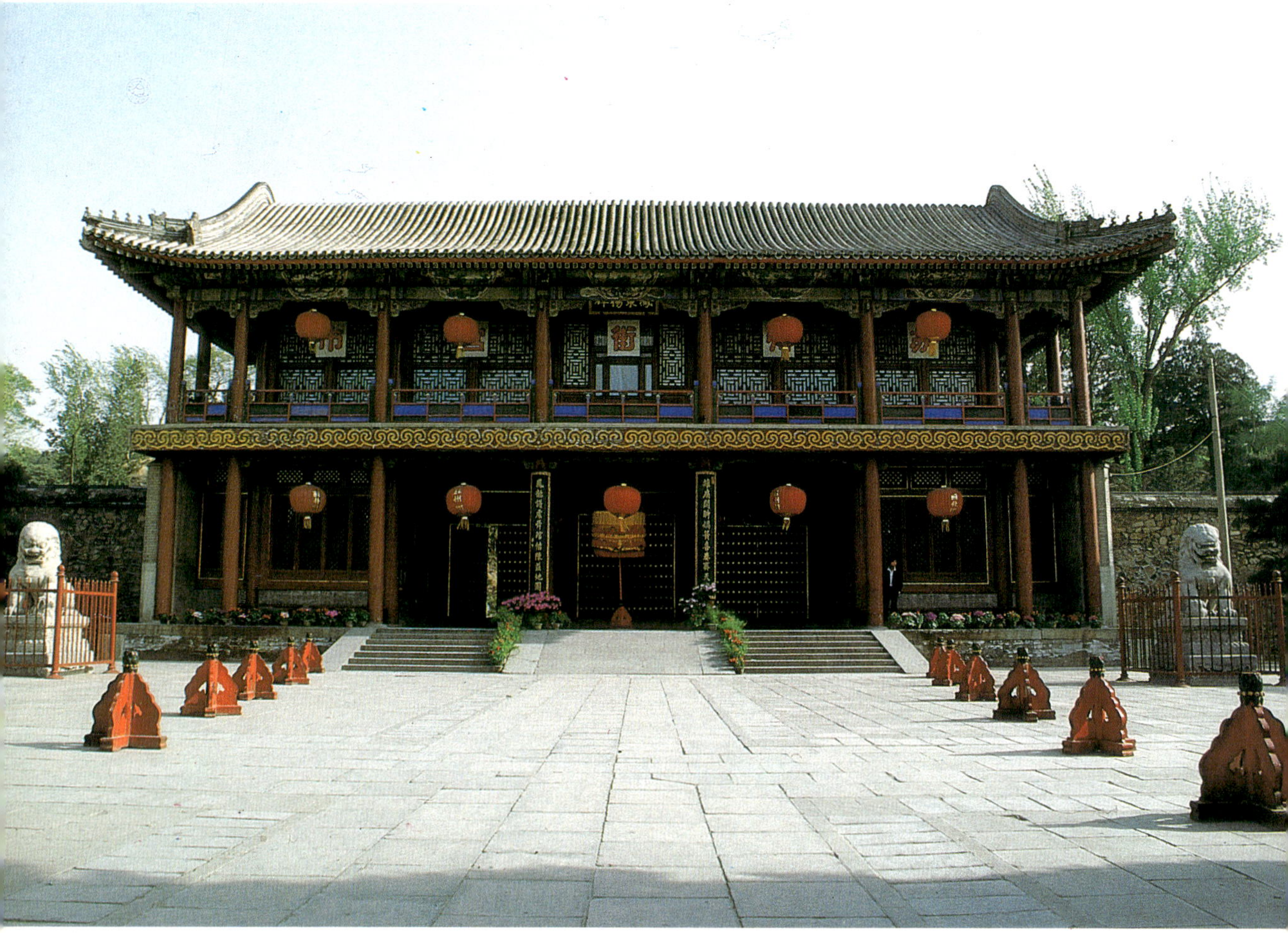

北宫門　爲二層樓宫門。乾隆皇帝的母親常登樓觀看門外前鋒營騎兵習武，故又稱“閲武門”。

North Palace Gate. This two-storeyed gate is where Emperor Qianlong's mother used to come to watch the cavalry exercises of the Vanguard Battalion stationed outside the gate. It is also known as the Military Review Tower.

衛星遥感頤和園全景圖

A picture of the summer palace from a satellite.

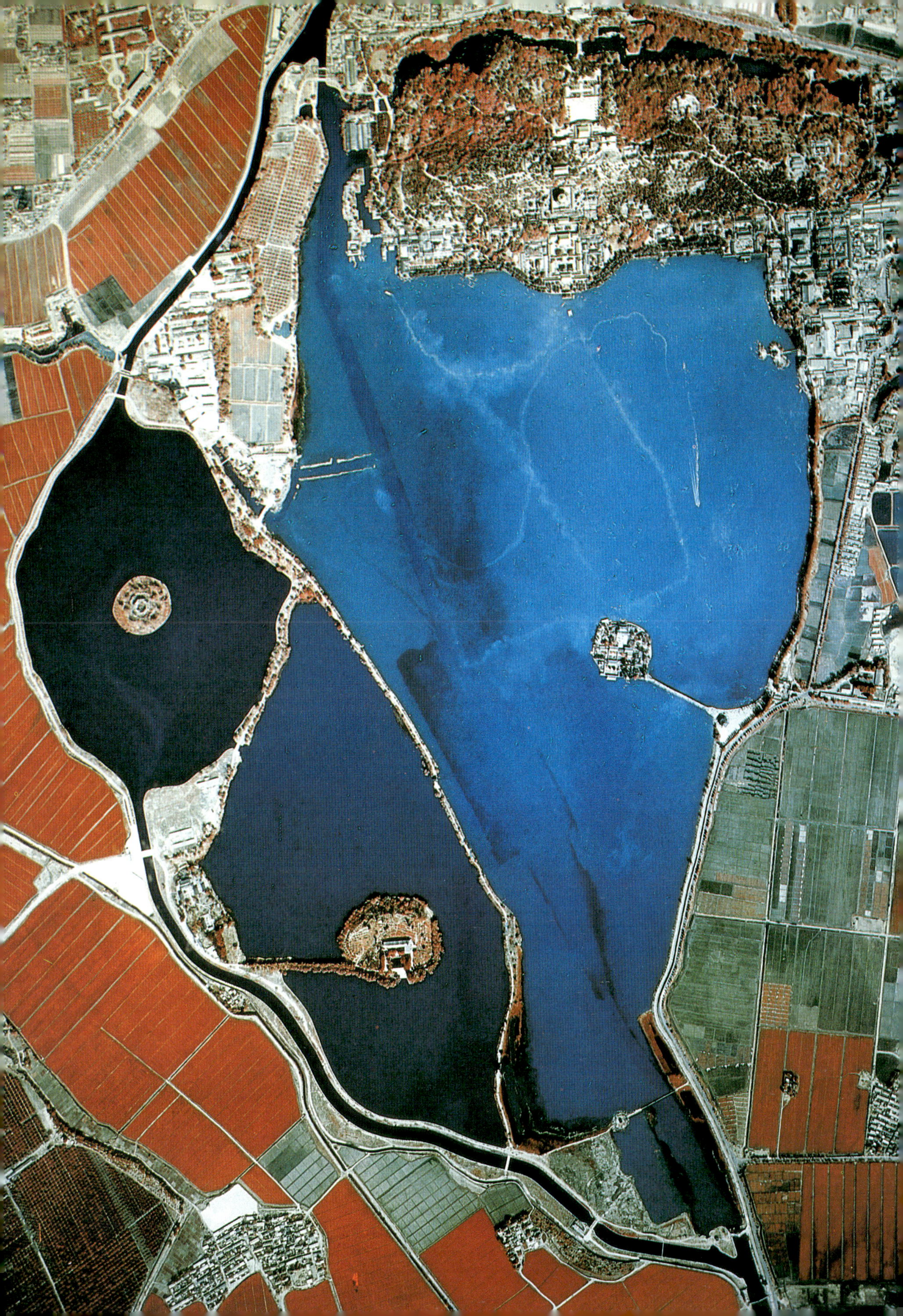

編後話

有關介紹頤和園的圖書和畫册，本書不是第一本。但在書中明確地把頤和園劃分爲三個景區，順序介紹，尚屬首次。我們這樣做，不僅是根據有關專家的見解，更主要的是這種劃分既符合頤和園佈景的實際情況，又便於遊客省時快捷地循區遊覽。我們在介紹時，凡涉及主要建築物和重要景點，一般都作了比較詳細的描述，並提供有關背景材料，講明它們的建築風格和藝術特色。此外，在《漫話頤和園》一文中，我們還概述了頤和園的建園史和造園藝術，以便讀者從整體上對該園有更深的了解。

在本書的編輯過程中，曾得到頤和園管理處劉永聚和徐鳳桐等先生的鼎力襄助，他們爲此做了許多工作；尤令我們感動的是，溥傑老先生在耄耋之年爲我們題寫書名，謹在此一併致謝。

編　者

一九九一年六月

AFTERWORD

THIS album is not the first book to introduce the famous Summer Palace, but it is the first book that divides it into three distinctive scenic areas and introduces it in proper order. Our reasons for presenting this book in this form is based not only on the opinions of specialists in this field, but also because for visitors who, after reading the album, find it easier to tour the imperial garden. When we wrote the captions, we made a fairly detailed introduction to major buildings and important scenic spots, providing some materials about their background, architectural style and artistic features. In the forefront article we gave a brief account to the history of the garden and the art of its layout, in order to enable the reader to form a general picture of the garden as a whole.

In the course of compiling this album, the experts and staff members of the Summer Palace Administration Office gave us a lot of help, and Mr Liu Yongju and Mr Xu Fengtong, in particular, did a great deal of work for us. What moved us most is that Mr Pu Jie (brother of the last emperor of the Qing Dynasty), in disregard of his advanced age, wrote the title of this album for us. Here we express our greatest gratitude to all of them.

The Editors
June, 1991

編　　輯　望天星
翻　　譯　熊振儒
攝　　影　曲維波　劉思功
姜景餘　高明義
力　强　董宗貴
茹遂初　羅文發
劉啓俊　胡維標
張肇基　牛嵩林
劉　臣　孫樹明
何炳富　姚天新
裝幀設計　李士伋

颐　和　园
望天星　编　熊振儒　译
*
中国世界语出版社出版
北京 1201 厂制版
民族印刷厂印刷
中国国际图书贸易总公司发行
(中国北京车公庄西路 35 号)
北京邮政信箱第 399 号　邮政编码 100044
1996 年(16 开)第一版第五次印刷
ISBN 7-5052-0072-0/K·14(外)
05000
85-CE-416P

颐和园位置图

THE LOCATION OF SUMMER PALACE

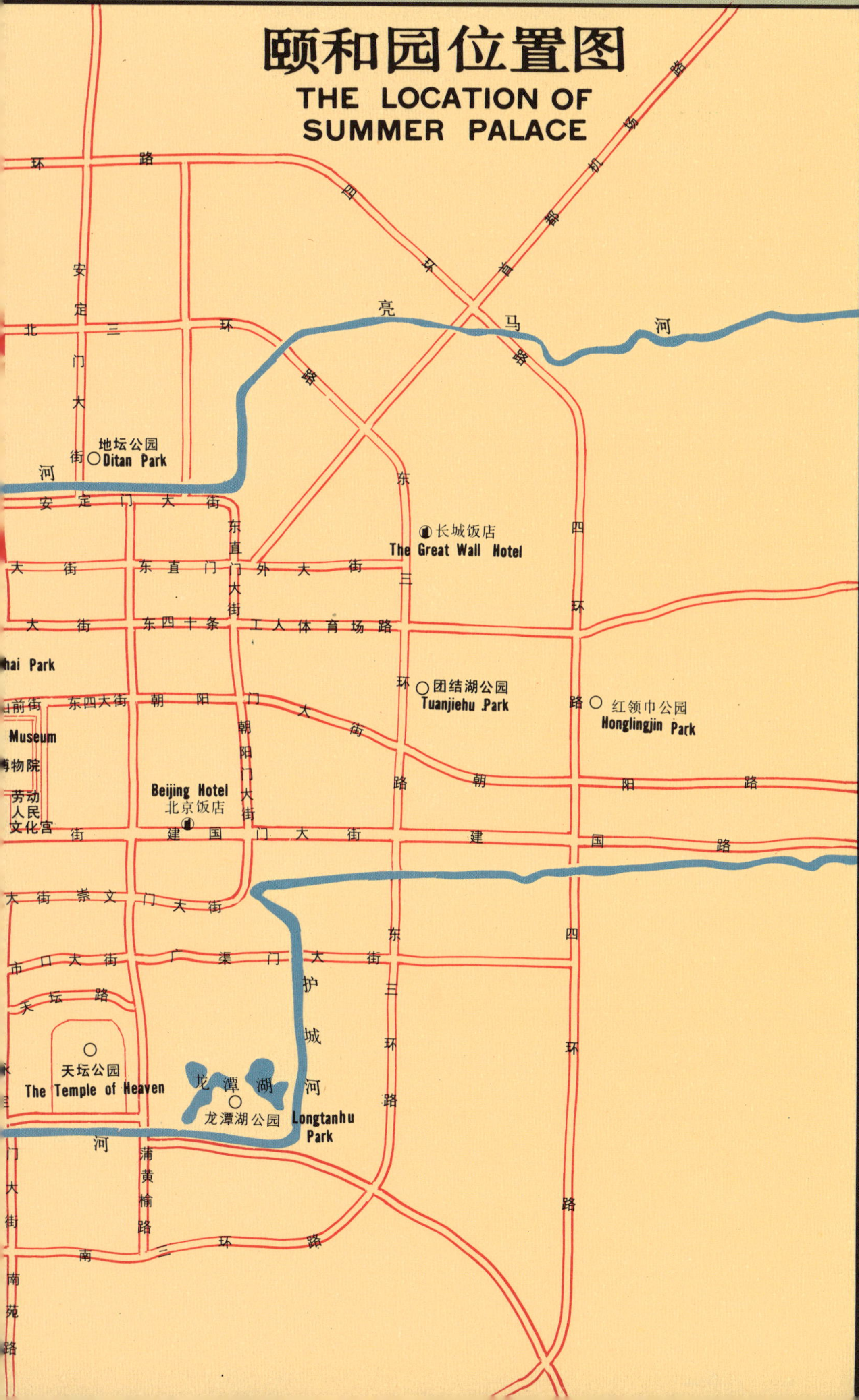

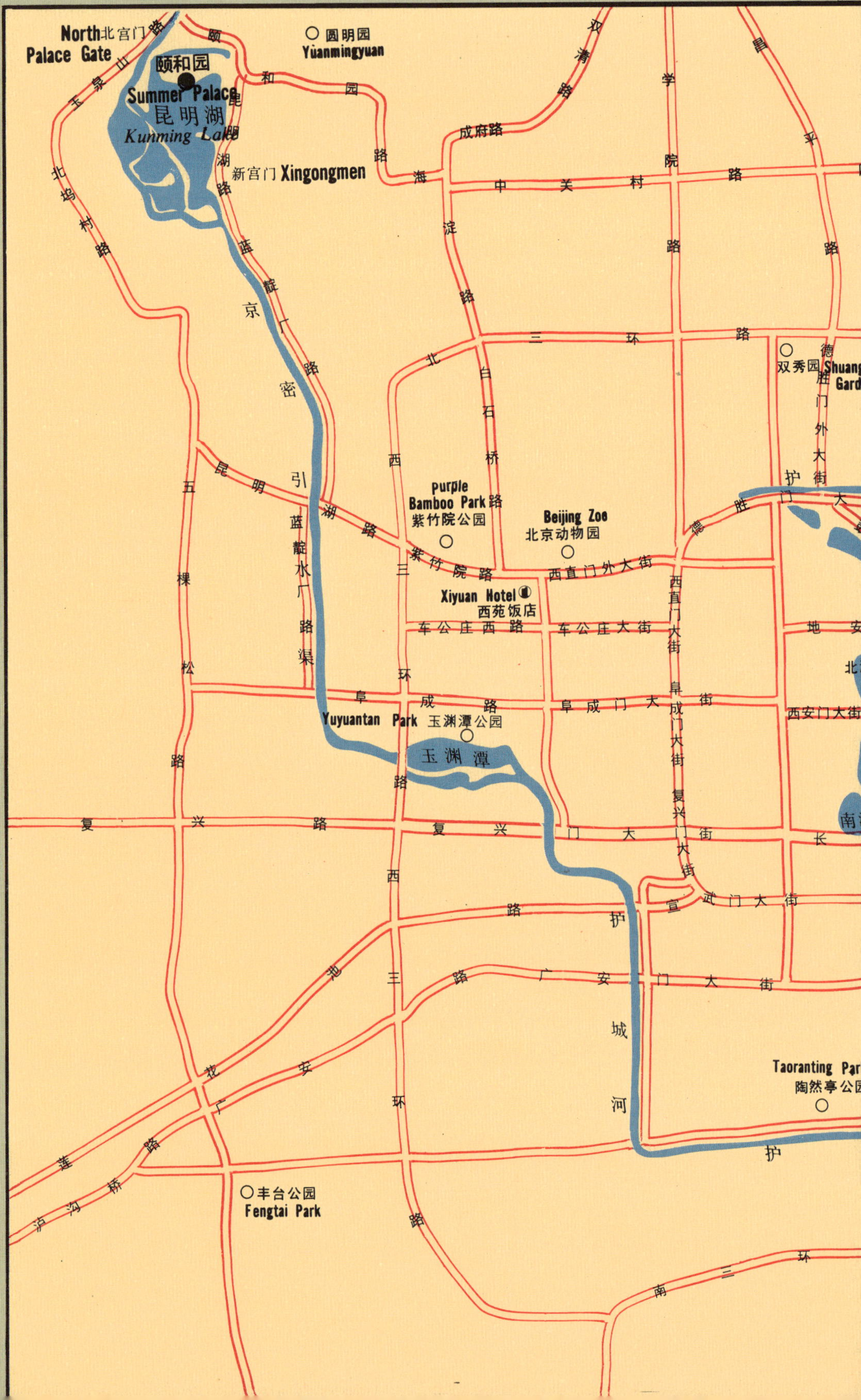
North 北宫门
Palace Gate
颐和园
Summer Palace
昆明湖
Kunming Lake
圆明园
Yuanmingyuan
新宫门 Xingongmen
颐和园路
海淀路
成府路
双清路
学院路
中关村路
北坞村路
玉泉山路
昆明湖路
蓝靛厂路
京密引水渠
北三环路
白石桥路
昆明湖路
五棵松路
西三环路
purple
Bamboo Park
紫竹院公园
紫竹院路
Beijing Zoo
北京动物园
西直门外大街
西直门大街
Xiyuan Hotel
西苑饭店
车公庄西路
车公庄大街
阜成路
阜成门大街
阜成门外大街
Yuyuantan Park 玉渊潭公园
玉渊潭
复兴路
复兴门大街
复兴门外大街
宣武门大街
广安门大街
护城河
莲花池路
广安路
Taoranting Park
陶然亭公园
丰台公园
Fengtai Park
泸沟桥路
南三环
双秀园 Shuangxiu Garden
德胜门外大街
西安门大街